P9-AZX-277

also by mimmetta lo monte

LA BELLA CUCINA

Mimmetta Lo Monte's

CLASSIC

SICILIAN

COOKBOOK

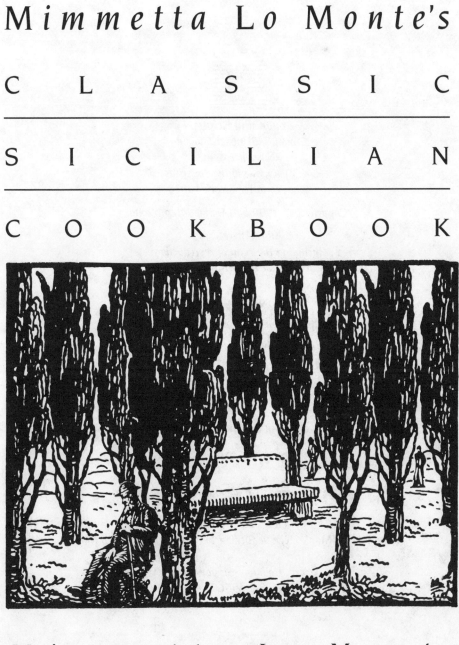

Mimmetta Lo Monte

SIMON AND SCHUSTER   New York London Toronto Sydney Tokyo Singapore

Simon and Schuster
Simon & Schuster Building
Rockefeller Center
1230 Avenue of the Americas
New York, New York 10020

Copyright © 1990 by Mimmetta Lo Monte

All rights reserved
including the right of reproduction
in whole or in part in any form.

SIMON AND SCHUSTER
and colophon are registered trademarks
of Simon & Schuster Inc.

Designed by Bonni Leon

Manufactured in the United States of America

1   3   5   7   9   10   8   6   4   2

Library of Congress Cataloging in Publication Data

Lo Monte, Mimmetta.
Mimmetta Lo Monte's classic Sicilian cookbook/Mimmetta Lo Monte.
p.   cm.
1. Cookery, Italian—Sicilian style.   I. Title.
TX723.2.S55L6   1990
641.59458—dc20   89-26339
CIP
ISBN 0-671-67757-8

To my mother

and my

daughter

Acknowledgments

Thanks to Meg Ruley. If it hadn't been for

her pushing me and believing in this book,

it would probably still be tucked away in boxes.

Thanks also to Carole Lalli and Laura Yorke

for seeing the beautiful swan in the

ugly duckling.

Contents

TWO

SECONDI PIATTI

second courses

99

CARNI
meats
106

PESCI
fish
157

UOVA
egg dishes
183

THREE

CONTORNI

side dishes

189

VERDURE
vegetables
193

PANE
bread
236

FOUR

DOLCI

desserts

243

Introduction

I arrived in the United States in March 1965. I arrived in New York by ship, in the best tradition of the mainstream of Sicilian immigrants at the beginning of the century.

On the surface, at least, one could find no other similarities between my arrival and the one of my predecessors. The boat was a luxury liner. There was no more Ellis Island to be herded through—in fact, I only learned about its existence a few years ago. I was equipped with Gucci leather cases rather than cardboard luggage tied with strings. While the United States didn't hold the appeal of the promised land for me, it happened to be the country of origin of my newly wedded husband.

Thank God it was New York and not the suburbs I had to deal with for my first couple of months in the States. As rough as New York can be, and as shy, inexperienced and pregnant as I was, I still was a city girl, and no city is as exciting as New York. There were friends to make the transition easier, and I can say that friends I have found here have become one of the best aspects of my life.

One thing that warmed my heart was that as soon as people found out that I was from Sicily, they immediately started talking about food. Everyone seemed to have had a friend whose "Italian" mother cooked huge meals. But this also puzzled me, because in the majority of cases, these people knew very little about Sicily.

To all too many Americans, including some of Sicilian extraction, until recently Sicily has meant a barren land: no comforts, sullen people, unimaginative and heavy food, and aside from very predictable and regimented Mafia activities, a crimeless place.

In everybody's mind Sicily seemed to be not much more than a starting point for some people who were tired of being hungry and poor, who packed up their belongings and came here to begin a new life.

So I struggled for identity. For quite a few years, meeting Italian-Americans only made the struggle harder. What they considered to be "Italian"—food, tradition, culture, looks—was alien to me, and, for my taste, rather undesirable. To think out the reasons behind these different views became a point of great interest.

I discovered that most Sicilian-Americans themselves did not know very much about Sicily, but still loved it and were proud (although at times defensively so) of even that little they knew. Sadly, though, I found that some parents had chosen not to teach their dialect to their children, as they considered it a source of embarrassment, conscious that it was not correct Italian. Today people know much more about Sicily, but the cuisine created by the immigrants has remained, and it is quite different from the cuisine in Sicily—both from what it was in the past and from what it is now.

The Sicilian cuisine on the island today combines ingredients seeking lightness, simplicity, sparseness, and relies very heavily on vegetables, nuts, and fish. It is a cuisine that uses rice extensively and has a variety of sweet and sour dishes, with either meat, fish, or vegetable bases, that are eaten cold.

I should add that I do not consider Sicilian food as "southern Italian" food. Sicily may be, geographically speaking, to the south of Italy, but it is not southern Italy. Sicily is an island. It has its own identity geographically and gastronomically. Similarities and absorption of dishes from Italy have occurred. They range from the adoption of polenta, to Pesto Genovese, Gnocchi Alla Romana, and so on. People have mistakenly attributed red and heavy meat sauces to Sicilian cuisine, when in fact such sauces take a backseat to a wide variety of nontomato and nonmeat dishes.

The nature of cuisine is not static; it is conditioned by changes in availability of ingredients, by elements absorbed from outside, by personal additions, by changes in the economy of a place. Change in cuisine is valid when it remains within boundaries that respect the soul of that particular kind of cuisine, and as long as quality doesn't suffer. Furthermore, cuisine representative of a country should not be its restaurant cuisine, but the ensemble of dishes that have entered into daily use within families of that country.

The cuisine that Sicilian immigrants have established today here in the States I call "Sicilian-Immigrant" cuisine as opposed to Sicilian cuisine because it lacks certain elements and has picked up other elements not in tune with Sicilian cuisine.

The increasing prosperity of the Sicilian immigrants contributed to the development of the current hybrid cuisine in the States. Meats and sauces, which had been used very sparingly and seldom, since they were a luxury in Sicilian villages, were now emphasized to signify the immigrants' new financial status. The immigrants set aside vegetable, cheese and egg dishes, the everyday meals of the poor past, since they were reminders of long days spent in the fields. They were to be used only in the intimacy of the family, who became almost as secretive with them as with the memories they brought—the fatigue, the constant fight with dry weather, torrential rains, uncertain crops, and unsympathetic landowners.

Among the first Sicilian immigrants to the United States were some women who cooked in the best and the purest tradition, and who were good cooks. Unfortunately, they did not keep notes on their recipes, and their children and grandchildren realized too late, once these dishes were gone, that all they had left were elusive memories of smells, flavors, and looks. Perhaps they had been too busy to watch their mothers and grandmothers cook, or maybe they had never realized how big a part of their life such cooking was, and how much they would come to miss it.

Many people in my cooking classes have come to me to try to recapture those memories of the old authentic cuisine. Where did those smells come from, those flavors, those looks? They came from Sicily, like their ancestors. But, in fact, the trip to this country was only the most recent step in the migration of people who came to Sicily from North Africa, Italy, Greece, Arabia, northern Europe, France, Spain, Austria, Germany, and Albania.

Some of the dishes in this book bring back to life that true cuisine. They are the dishes passed on orally to me by very old people living in farms and villages in Sicily, who are not very different from the Italian immigrants who came to this country in the first part of this century.

Every visit I make to Sicily, I have to acquaint myself with subtle changes that time and progress bring in the way of living and in the nature of the place. Some changes that I regret, but have been able to remedy somewhat, are changes in traditional dishes. Other changes, in the way of eating and in the ways of thinking about food, occurred before I was born.

I would have never found out about these older traditions had my mother not kept for me a little, old cookbook that belonged to my Grandfather Alfredo. This old cookbook has been the inspiration for *Classic Sicilian Cooking*. Since my mother gave me the book a couple of years ago, I have become aware of the much wider range of ingredients used in the past compared to those used today, and how differently they were combined.

My curiosity piqued as I started hunting for old, forgotten recipes and found many in handwritten cookbooks that families in Sicily seem to have held on to and still treasure. These recipes have been passed on from generation to generation, but without really ever being put into use, except once a year, for some very special event. I also started to inquire about "unwritten" recipes, those of humble people, who couldn't or wouldn't write them, and which would certainly get lost in a matter of years if unrecorded.

LA CUCINA DI FAMI

Istruzioni genera

Obblighi del padrone di casa.

Quando si vuol dare un pranzo, si deve evitare di riunire persone che fra loro non si veggano di buon occhio, o che siano troppo disparate per condizione sociale, e per educazione: e nem- invitarsi alla stessa mensa uomini di vedute op-

Recipe-giving involves a very long ceremonial. Initially I had to be introduced to villagers by someone who held a very respected status in the community. Then I would spend hours conversing with the villagers about different matters of life, weighing each word carefully (and being very subtle and cunning) before I could ask these people to divulge their recipes to me. Finally, when it was obvious from the conversation that I was "part of the clan"—one of them, a real Sicilian—the recipes were given to me.

There were instances in which I failed to get a recipe because I did not have the chance to spend time talking with the people to build up some trust. Consequently I was still considered an outsider. Other times, I would be handed crazy recipes clearly derived from current TV shows because the villagers wanted to let me know that, after all, they were not ignorant peasants. Yet, as they warmed up, traditional recipes would be revealed.

The study of these old recipes—both written down and handed down by word of mouth—made me come to the conclusion that the food being eaten today in Sicily is the food the middle class ate in the past. In addition, Sicilian "fast food"—the staple of the poor but certainly not disdained by the rich—has also held its place, and it is cooked, served, and enjoyed today as it was sixty years ago.

What seems to have gotten lost are the grand dishes of the upper class—the aristocracy, the bourgeoisie, both of towns and villages—and the humblest food of the poor villagers, the farmers. The main reason for all this, I am sure, has been economic: for the upper classes, it has become necessary to cut down the time and expense of preparing the grand dishes; for the lower classes, whose economic status has improved, it has become possible to elevate their quality of life.

Society in Sicily during the last century was highly stratified—things are changing slowly. The upper classes—the aristocracy and the rich bourgeoisie—were absolutely impenetrable; well off culturally and economically, they were quite unwilling to share their well being. They had the luxury of enjoying various cuisines.

The lower classes were poor, culturally and of course economically. Sicilian farmers lived together in small communities, whose origins sometimes went back centuries. Their experience did not go any farther than the perimeter of land they could reach every day at dawn, on foot or by mule or donkey-back, to go to work in the fields. The men gathered in their village square to socialize on holidays and warm summer nights, while the women stayed home, only leaving their houses to go to church and to fetch water.

If the church that dominated the village square had artistic or historic significance, that fact was unknown to the villagers, or at least had no relevance to their lives. They found the strength to cope with hard days of labor not in the contemplation of some cathedral of unmatched beauty, symbolizing power and riches and the glory of the past; but rather, through their strength in clinging to their present, their family, their community, with the same stubbornness the small houses they lived in clung to the hill slopes. Many couldn't read, and if they ever came in touch with glimpses of history by listening to old people's tales, such glimpses were well buried by layers of superstition and embellishments.

Each social level held a monopoly on a certain kind of cuisine. In cities, there was the cuisine of the aristocracy, the rich bourgeoisie, the middle class, the lower middle class and the common workers. In small towns and villages of the interior there was the cuisine of the well-off bourgeoisie and the common workers. There was also the cooking of the villages of the coast, the cooking on the farms, and the cooking of convents (mainly desserts) that catered to the rich.

All these different cuisines are represented in *Classic Sicilian Cooking*. You will experience the food of the humble, often rather laborious to make and characterized by the heavy use of vegetables. There are also samples of the so-called Sicilian "fast food"—"fast" pertaining only to the way it is eaten, and certainly not to the preparation! You will enjoy dishes which are habitually eaten today by rich and poor, and which are relatively simple to make.

Of course there will be recipes by the epicurean author of the old cookbook belonging to Grandfather Alfredo. I have included a select number of its recipes here—those that can be realistically duplicated, considering the ingredients called for and the time involved. Most importantly, I have tried to include the mood of the old cookbook and its vision of food. These recipes, because of the quality of ingredients and their preparation, or because of their simple sophistication, reveal the status of the people who ate them. Some of these recipes will be almost . . . holy, as they come from convents and are certainly heavenly in taste (for a Sicilian).

There is yet another kind of cuisine included in this book: my own personal cuisine, born of my taste for the food I grew up with, and the acquired taste for the very unusual combinations revealed by the old forgotten recipes. My belief in good eating habits and in reducing culinary labor to a minimum has influenced the shaping of the recipes. My goal has been to preserve the originality of the old flavors while using as little preparation and cooking time as possible, as well as avoiding unhealthy ingredients.

How can you determine which cuisine each recipe is from? Portion size is a key. In general, the large, complicated recipes (lots of servings, long preparations) are from the old, nearly forgotten style of cooking. These were dishes for special occasions, and therefore for large numbers of people. Remember, too, that the average family of the time could easily have included twelve or more people. I have been able to reduce the yield for some of these recipes but some would lose part of their charm and flavor if presented in smaller versions.

Recipes reflecting Sicilian cuisine of today, such as "fast food" or old staples, are generally recipes that cater to fewer people. Many recipes in this book which serve four to eight people can be included in this cuisine.

As for my personal recipes, many are designed for just one serving (very handy if you are a cook in a good restaurant or entertaining a loved one, according to my experience). These recipes can be doubled very easily, or increased to yield four servings. There is no specific advice I can give for increasing portions: personal experience and common sense should guide chefs who want to do so (or who want to decrease portions). But as a general word of advice, remember that if a recipe has to be doubled, the containers in which the food is being cooked should be doubled as well.

How are these recipes served? Today, a normal, middle-of-the-day dinner in the average Sicilian family is a three-course meal. But this custom is slowly changing. Because of lack of time and too much work, meals today are slowly changing to be just one course, such as a pasta, or fish, or meat, with a vegetable as a side dish and fruit to end the meal. But given the chance, any Sicilian would prefer the old three-course meal.

While the rhythm of modern life is reducing the middle-class meal to just one course, poverty has always shaped this eating pattern for the lower class. In the past it was very common for the poor working class to have a one-dish meal: Many of the peasant dishes in the book are examples of such meals. On the other hand, the privileged, the rich, ate as many courses as their stomachs could take, and more. Of course they also had gout, bad digestion, fainting spells and fat to hide—all problems that the lean diet of their poor contemporaries did not cause. In this book, while I've perhaps altered certain old recipes to make them healthier, I've made sure to keep their excessive, rich flavors intact.

A Few Words About Grandfather Alfredo's Cookbook

Grandfather Alfredo's cookbook has obviously been written by an upper-class gourmet with a good sense of humor and a very keen knowledge of food—whose name will probably remain forever unknown. The front page of the book, with the name of the author, was torn off and lost long ago. The book is dedicated to a duke named Morbilli, and it opens with an introductory poem that sings the merits of cooking. It gives some very condensed but efficient advice on how to approach cooking (it must be fun, can be taken up by both men and women, and, if done as he advises, can combine good taste and economy); some key to how many people his recipes are intended to serve (his ideal number is twelve); and a list of utensils needed to have a well-equipped kitchen.

The unknown author—to make the reader aware that words are not being used casually or out of ignorance of the "proper" words—also points out that dialectal terms used will be written in cursive. He finds that dialect may be more appropriate in naming certain ingredients and techniques.

For quite a while I had trouble understanding the author's obsolete vocabulary, let alone the dialect! I had to read the book many times over before I could really grasp its meaning. When I did, I felt that a world of supreme gluttony had opened before my eyes.

In addition to the herbs and flavorings that still to this day are used in Sicilian cooking, such as rosemary, oregano, sage, mint, lemon, parsley, etc., these recipes call for ground coriander, tarragon, sorrel, chervil, juniper berries, and wild thyme—herbs and flavorings that are either excluded or very seldom included in today's Sicilian cuisine.

Some of the vegetables the author includes in his dishes, such as parsnips and leeks, if asked for today in a Sicilian market would only get one a blank stare. Truffles and

A friend of grandfather Giovanni Lo Monte.

"unborn eggs" are very common ingredients in his fillings. Cinnamon, cloves, candied squash, fruit such as pomegranates, and cheese combined with sugar are often used to flavor and dress meat and fish. Pistachios, pine nuts, almonds, walnuts, and chestnuts are used lavishly to enrich first courses, second courses, side dishes, and desserts.

Fruit is used as a side dish much the way vegetables are used. Often, a touch of sweet-and-sour taste is added to a recipe by adding lemon, vinegar, and sugar. Caviar, botargue (salted tuna-fish roe), anchovies, oysters, and capers add zest to food.

Interestingly enough, tomatoes are one of the least-recurring ingredients in these recipes, outweighed by truffles, parsnips (considered exotic in Sicilian cooking), unborn eggs, artichoke hearts, plums, apricots, and many other vegetables.

Advice is given on preserving fresh fruit, as well as on making preserves, ice cream, and liqueurs. The reader is also given tips on wine: how to keep it from turning into vinegar, how to find out if it has been *adulterato* with chemicals, if it has been diluted with water, and even how to keep it undamaged by . . . thunder and lightning! We are also given a remedy for hangovers and drunkenness, and advice on how to prevent getting drunk (eat almonds, raw cabbage, and drink half a glass of raw olive oil)—try these next time you are planning to do heavy drinking. At the end of the book, the author instructs us on how to cut or dismember a variety of animals, both quadrupeds and finned ones.

The most amazing thing about this cookbook is that the author manages to pack all of this information into a 76-page, 4½- by 8-inch book.

Of course, there are many details the author deems unnecessary. For instance, at the beginning of the book, he states that the recipes are intended for twelve people. That information is meant to take care of telling us the amounts of ingredients to use. With pastry, though, he gives very accurate measurements in every recipe, and he describes procedures accurately, if sparsely.

We must bear in mind that until very recently instructions for Sicilian cooking consisted of "a little bit of this and a little bit of that," and if you asked for more detail, you were looked at with compassion—"The poor thing doesn't have an idea of how to cook, what is wrong with her?"

The hand-written recipe notebooks of my ancestors that I have collected over time, and the recipes I have collected orally after much prodding, have a lot in common with the little, old cookbook: they disregard measurements of any kind, including ingredients, temperature, and time—(except for dessert recipes), and they often include a touch of poetry and magic.

This approach to cooking shows that it was really considered an art. Would a painter establish in detail quantities and flow of colors to use, or would a sculptor establish to compass precision the angle at which a hip would curve? Certainly not. In the same manner, a cook wouldn't plan measurements ahead, but let his feeling for food guide his hand.

Today we are all ready to admit that, for the most part, we lack certain qualities that people in the past seem to have had (of course, we have others) and that, given our shortcomings, well-spelled-out recipes save us a lot of trouble. Consequently I have added accurate measurements and instructions to the old recipes I've included here.

Since the time of my arrival in this country, many people have gone out of their way to offer me food they hope will make me exclaim, "Ah, that's Italian."

Up until now, I have said that very seldom. At friends' homes, in front of cannoli with shells like cardboard and filling like plaster, frittate baked in the oven, and pasta drowned in undefinable sauces, I have found it very hard to be both honest and polite.

As for the food offered in some so-called "Italian" restaurants—three little mounds on an oval plate, one certainly hiding pasta, one some deadly combination of peppers and sausage or chicken, and one never to be understood—it's difficult to respond without giving offense.

The most harmless comment I have been able to give to food on oval plates has been "glorified cafeteria food"; meanwhile I cross my fingers and hope that the taste won't stay with me through the night.

Food is my anchor to the past and my strength of the present. Seeing Italian food butchered, misspelled, and improperly served inspired me to start writing recipes and to give cooking classes. My ultimate hope is that others can see more in food than just . . . calories!

I write about food not only because I love it, but also because I love Sicily, and I wish to preserve and treasure this essential part of Sicilian culture, which expresses the taste, the creativity, and the background of a people.

Though I believe that cuisine is in constant evolution, I also believe that some things in a cuisine should be kept unchanged as a legacy of the past, just as other worthy forms of art representative of the past are preserved. For this belief, I am very grateful to the unknown author of the "little, old book," to the friends and relatives who saved the family recipes, to the people who let me search in their memory—memories of food forgotten.

A
Brief
History
of
Sicily

To retrace the origins that make up the Sicilian culinary tradition is like attempting to make your way through a labyrinth with the help of several maps, none matching, all eroded by time. You think you have gotten somewhere, and instead you find yourself back where the itinerary started.

Grandfather Alfredo's little, old cookbook gave me a first glimpse of the path to follow, and the many notebooks from family and friends—along with a good deal of oral information—have made the path ever more clear. Once the type of food eaten has been established, as well as the fashion in which it was eaten—in the recent past and in the more remote past—the task of giving it an ethnic identity is possible, but remains open to controversy. Information is sometimes contradictory and sometimes lacking; a lot is left to personal instinct and to individual judgment.

The first people we have record of as inhabitants of Sicily are the "Sicani," established on the island in neolithic times, coming from North Africa, and the Siculi, of Indo-European origin. They occupied the west and the east of Sicily respectively, and defined characteristics in those areas that can still be seen today.

Looking at a map of the Mediterranean Sea, it's easy to see why the west of Sicily would be so susceptible to African influence, and the east to the Greek. The Greeks established colonies along the east coast of Sicily around the middle of the eighth century B.C.; Naxos was the first. Sometime later, the Phoenicians established colonies along the west coast (Mozia, Marsala), and the northwest coast (Palermo and Solunto), in accordance with their expansionist commercial policies.

The Greeks, establishing Selinunte, had slowly pushed themselves as far west as they would ever get. Their attempt to go any farther clashed with the sphere of interest of the Phoenicians. Consequently, Sicily went through centuries of struggle; Greek colonies fighting the Phoenicians, then fighting one another, ultimately allied with Rome in the Punic Wars against Carthage. One wonders how, with all this fighting, people had the time to build the splendid towns they did. It is in the latter part of the third century B.C. that Sicily was totally taken over by the Roman Empire.

Whereas during Greek times the population had been concentrated in large cities (since the Greeks were traders), during the Roman rule people were scattered through small towns, responding to a need dictated by their economy, which was based on agriculture.

Through antiquity, Sicily was renowned for its fertile land, its mild climate, and its art treasures. The Romans enjoyed all of the great qualities of Sicily without adding any substantial contributions (if compared to what the Greeks had done), aside from some theaters and some villas. The Roman rule lasted for approximately a thousand years—they lost Sicily for brief periods to the Goths and the Vandals. During the end of their rule, Sicily felt the influence of the Byzantines. These thousand years were the longest period Sicily ever spent under one influence, and that is when Sicilians established their ethnic identity.

In the ninth century, the Arabs, taking advantage of the weakness of the Byzantine Empire, conquered Sicily, whose coasts they had raided for a while.

The Arabs introduced the culture of the lemon, the mulberry, and the bitter orange, and, among other things, cotton and sugar cane. Saffron, coriander, and cumin seeds were the closest things to spices people of the island had. Their food was enlivened by herbs such as rosemary, oregano, fennel, sage, parsley, marjoram, bay leaf, and onions. Wheat was a staple, probably in the form of flat breads. Legumes such as fava beans, lentils, and chick-peas were also very common. Though I have always been reluctant to give Sicilian dishes a label of origin, a few things are of unmistakable Arabic origin: *couscous, cubbaita, gelato, mandorlato,* and *gelato di campagna* (fondantlike, multicolored, with nuts and candied fruits).

The Arabs were masters in salting and preserving fish, and in fishing. The Sicilian *uovo di tonno,* tuna roe—pressed, salted, and dried—goes back to Arab times, as does the manner of fishing swordfish, a real ritual, where the fishermen still observe the old assignment of tasks and use Arabic words to communicate up to this day.

By the end of the eleventh century, Sicily was conquered by yet another people— the Normans, under Roger d'Auteville. The Arabs had brought to Sicily a sophistication and a refinement unknown to the occident. The Normans appreciated this refinement, along with any other qualities displayed by the different groups that made up the Sicilian population. Showing remarkable mental openness, they allowed freedom of religion, acknowledged the various skills of the people (regardless of their religion) and put these skills to good use.

Up until this point in history, we can mainly guess at what people ate by studying the flora and fauna of the time. For instance, though their cultivation wasn't widespread, olive trees and grapes were already in Sicily during Greek and Roman times, and so were almonds, pomegranates, and very likely, pistachios. The Normans enjoyed these foods, along with the many others introduced by their predecessors, although they did not bring many food novelties to the island themselves.

After the Normans, Sicily was ruled by a Germanic people known as the Suebi, the French with Charles d'Anjou for a very brief period, the Spanish with the Aragons and the Castilians, and the House of Savoy very briefly. The Savoys found it more advantageous to make an island swap and took Sardinia, closer to their homeland, giving Sicily to the Austrians. In the first half of the eighteenth century, Sicily passed to the Bourbons, kings of Naples, until in 1860 Sicily came into Italian hands—and that is where Sicilians are today!

The French had been very insensitive to the traditions of the local people. It was this insensitivity that sparked a ferocious rebellion. The evening of March 31, 1282, while Sicilians were gathering in front of the church of Santo Spirito on the outskirts of Palermo to attend a traditional post-Easter ceremony, a French soldier approached a young married woman in an offensive manner. The reaction was what anyone who knows Sicilians would have expected. The woman's husband avenged the insult immediately by mercilessly knifing the soldier. The other soldiers were killed likewise by the crowd of Sicilians as the bells started ringing the Vespers. By the following morning approximately two thousand French had been slaughtered in Palermo. The rebels showed no mercy toward children and women: Sicilian women who had married Frenchmen were killed as well.

Food, curiously, gets into this tragic event. To identify the French, suspects were made to repeat the word *"ciciri"* (chick-peas in Sicilian dialect). The inability of sounding *c* and *r* was a giveaway that one was French and resulted in a death sentence. The French were driven out and, despite a twenty-year war, could not regain control of the island, which because of the marriage of Manfredi's daughter to an Aragon, passed to the Aragons. (Manfredi was the bastard son of the famous Suebi king, Frederick II. He succeeded Frederick II, and was fought by the Papal authority, who tried to replace him and the Suebi dynasty with Charles d'Anjou.)

Such a brief and unwelcome stay by the French was unlikely to have determined their influence on Sicilian cuisine. Rather, that influence came from the taste for decadent indulgence developed by the Sicilian aristocracy in the following centuries. The Spanish introduced familiar foods, their own elaboration of the dishes of the common Arab past. They also introduced food novelties of the newly discovered world, the Americas.

One can also recognize the Middle East, Greek, and Spanish influence in some ways of preparing food: cabbage leaves stuffed with rice, flavored with lemon; stews thickened with egg yolks mixed with lemon juice; the thinnest layers of dough, hand stretched, stacked with vegetable layers; eggplant dishes; *"panelle"* (chick-pea flour cakes).

After the Aragons (about 1300 A.D.), feudalism put down deep roots in Sicily. The land was divided among a few; the old aristocracy and a new aristocracy created by the Spanish, who awarded titles and land to people who had helped them seize power. The aristocracy enjoyed all the privileges wealth gives—palatial residences in the cities, filled with incredible art treasures; villas in the country; castles on the coast and servants who catered to every necessity.

Of the luxuries the aristocracy enjoyed, one more than any other was considered a measure of their status: the quality of the food at their table. Politically, Sicilians entered a very difficult period from 1700 to 1800, when the rule of Sicily passed from the House of Savoy to the Austrians and then the Bourbons. The preoccupation with food reflects in part the desire to escape problems which—given the historical moment—were unsolvable. The old traditional food habits were kept alive among the lower classes, while chefs imported from France, called *"monsu"*—a deformation of the word *monsieur*—ruled the cavernous kitchens of the rich. Upon impact with the local tradition, the French cuisine underwent as much change as the word *monsieur*.

It was as impossible to keep elements from past cultures, which had been very much loved, from creeping in, as it was to disregard the Spanish influence. So the *monsu* created a glorious cuisine which stunned any foreign visitor who tried it. This cooking is known as the *cucina baronale:* the baronial cuisine. Thus French terms, duly altered, became part of the local culinary terminology: *fricandò, fricassea, ragù, "gattò," "colì," "matalotta."*

The food habits acquired by the aristocracy over a period of almost half a millenium—from the times of the Spanish to the Bourbons—were kept through the first few decades of Italian independence. At the beginning of this century they started being set aside, maybe because they were only of a selected elite, certainly because of social changes. Some obviously Spanish-accented cuisine, such as *" 'mpanate,"* which had taken hold in the cooking of small towns and in the country began to disappear as well. Fortunately love for food was never set aside and, passed on to others, has made it possible to reconstruct so much of a period that, at least with regard to the culinary accomplishments, can be looked at with pride.

In retrospect, then, the impression of Sicily as a barren and sullen land was built on the very limited and often hazy image Sicilian immigrants had of their own country and that they had passed on. But as we have seen, a different perception of Sicily, one as an island which has played a key role in the development of Mediterranean cultures, emerges from deeper knowledge. I hope that Sicilian-Americans will be the ones who will enjoy this new perception the most because they will be able to regain sight of a past they have never fully known.

O N E

PRIMI PIATTI

first courses

PASTA

RISO

rice

MINESTRE

soups

GNOCCHI, ET CETERA

gnocchi and other first courses

1985

It is the winter, and I am back in Sicily for a long visit. The name Sicily, to me, brings images of loveliness, a sparkling sea, sometimes so still and smooth as to have the gloss of oil, a countryside carefully cultivated, where fields with different crops are neatly defined, patches of different colors—all fitting together like a gigantic puzzle that follows the movement of the hills and of the plains.

I love the trees of Sicily that stand alone in the landscape, imprinting on it the aspect most peculiar to their beauty. Palms adorn it with grace, maritime pines give it majesty, the carob tree lends a natural flat roof that offers relief from the sun, and reassurance.

At the horizon, the sky rises sharply from the fields to arch, cloudless, reaching toward the sea, in an undetectable line. It is easy to forget how green the countryside can be in Sicily in the winter. It has come as a surprise to me, after yearly summer visits—visions of golds, yellows, with occasional dark spots of greenery, interrupted by a bright feast of flowers—to see Sicily blanketed in green and gentleness. It makes me want to fall into the past and recall things as far back as I can remember.

Palermo

1943

At least for us in Sicily, the war nightmare is over. Families are still waiting for news of the men who have fought and are still unaccounted for. Uncle Saverio is one of them. There is talk of separating from Italy and becoming an American satellite state. There is the beginning of an internal war waged against Giuliano—the legendary bandit—with a very equivocal alliance of Mafia and government.

There is uncertainty in the air, but in spite of it people are hopeful. There is a carefree joy in the way they walk in the streets. The bombed buildings, sometimes huge heaps of debris, sometimes giant empty shells, already belong to the past.

We have come back to town from our country hideout. Not many goods are available, but nobody seems to mind too much. The only thing I did hear complaints about is the lack of decent bread and decent pasta. Proper ladies of that time did not make bread and pasta, but Mother has decided to do so rather than hear Father complaining. After all, the maid has "robust wrists" and she does all the kneading.

Broomsticks are propped across the backs of kitchen chairs, and pasta hangs there to dry. The gas company has not restored the service yet, and the stove sits unused. Fortunately, the kitchen has coal burners. They are built into a masonry counter, covered with glossy pale-gray tiles, patterned in a traditional indigo design. The baking is done in a "top-of-the-stove oven," a funny little dome-shaped contraption.

War has come to an end, just at the right time, now that the city is safe again, the schools reopen and we can go. My brother attends first grade at the Jesuits' school. I should go to kindergarten, but Mother and Father decide I am not yet ready to leave the house.

One way to feel that things are back to normal is to have good food. Coffee and sugar have been long missed, but now they are occasionally available again. The maid,

Paolina, dates an American soldier. The family calls him "il Filippino"; his real name is Montero.

She brings home cans of salted butter, and some strange-looking meat nobody likes (Spam). Mother loves peanut butter; Paolina has brought home a can as big as a bucket. Mother eats so much of it that she gets very ill, and we cannot even say the word "peanut" anymore.

Grandfather Alfredo talks with regret of the years before the war when Uncle Peppino who had a high post with the fascist government, brought fresh truffles from Rome, and they all got together for culinary feasts at the "Palazzina Cinese," a lovely hunting cottage of the Bourbon kings, in the park "La Favorita," where Uncle Peppino had lodgings while on official business. Grandfather Alfredo writes two long pages in his notebook on how to clean truffles and how to make truffle sauces.

Uncle Gianni, drafted at the beginning of the war, just out of medical school, has spent most of the war in a prison camp in Greece. Now back in Italy, he has worked in a military hospital in northern Italy. When he comes back home he tells us that one day, without his knowledge, the nurses fed him "cat." When he found out, he was very upset and called them very bad names.

We still have no news of Uncle Saverio. He is a partisan. I have heard Mother and her sister whispering it—it is something you cannot say loudly and it is something children shouldn't overhear.

We run twenty blocks, Mother and I, the night Mother has the news that he is back home, at my grandparents'. He is sitting in front of a huge plate of pasta, and everyone lovingly watches him eat, every mouthful progressively restoring his strength, putting distance away from the ugliness of war and bringing him back to the reality of family life.

Great-grandfather Saverio is with us, too. He is over ninety; a huge snow-white moustache sticks out from the sides of his face. I can never understand how he can eat without getting it dirty. I know I have a very hard time not getting my face dirty with tomato sauce. When I am eating at home, it doesn't matter, because Father takes me to the bathroom and very gently washes my mouth off. But when I have lunch at school, the nuns don't do that, and I get a rash.

To Uncle Gianni, Great-grandfather Saverio says very often, "Let me die full." Uncle wants him to eat only certain things, otherwise he really may get sick and die. Great-grandfather doesn't worry about dying, though, as long as it happens after a good meal.

Great grandfather Saverio (white moustache), Great-uncle Poalo, Great uncle Peppino, Mother and other children.

Great-grandfather Saverio with Uncle Saverio.

Insert: Uncle Saverio.

A Word About First Courses

Eating a meal consisting of several courses does not signify over-eating, but stresses the importance of balancing different foods that well-planned meals should have. Furthermore, courses allow you to enjoy each dish in an uncrowded manner: the table becomes a stage where each course plays its part. Among the first and second courses, and among the side dishes used to complement second courses, there are some which may function—if one so wishes—as a one-dish meal. These include a combination of ingredients which can satisfy all that the body needs. Allow a larger quantity per serving, and, especially if they are short in starch, serve bread on the side.

First courses are heavy in starch. They include pasta and other flour-based dishes, as well as rice, potatoes, and dishes based on cornmeal. Starches—rather bland per se—take on character with the addition of vegetables, meat, fish, cheese, herbs, and other flavorings.

In Sicily, vegetables are the most common ingredient one finds mixed with pasta or rice. In fact, pasta dishes including vegetables are the most common first courses, followed by pasta or rice with fish or meat. Substantial soups are also very popular as first courses.

Generally, the most popular dishes today are those that are easiest to make and healthiest to eat. But if we distance ourselves from what is average today, then we can discover first courses that have been cast aside by time, and which are very seldom or never made. These are often richer and more time-consuming recipes; to prepare them and to savor them, however, is a bridge with the past.

PASTA

Cooking Pasta

To cook pasta to the proper point of doneness—pleasantly firm—is a simple but rather elusive matter. Some of the factors which determine the cooking time include: the ingredients used, the diversity of shapes, the thickness, the degree of moisture contained, the amount of pasta cooked, the heat supplied, and whether the pasta is dry or fresh, commercially made or homemade. Consequently, there cannot be a "recipe" for cooking pasta, but just a description of steps to take.

Begin by weighing the amount of pasta to be used. Break long-strand, dry commercial pasta in half. Fresh pasta may need loosening. Fill a large vessel with water, enough for the pasta to float freely. Add salt—about a teaspoon per quart of water. Heat until the water boils, add the pasta, and stir until the pasta is well separated. Let the water boil without a lid until the pasta has reached the right point of doneness, which is determined by frequently tasting the pasta after it has lost stiffness. When your teeth bite into the pasta and find it pleasantly firm—the well-known "al dente" stage—you will know it's properly cooked.

As soon as pasta is done, immediately lower the temperature of the pasta by adding some cold tap water to it. Drain and immediately mix the pasta with the sauce/topping, reserving some of the drained water.

Plain pasta allowed to sit even for the shortest time always clumps, making it very awkward to work in the sauce/topping. Mixing the pasta with the sauce/topping right after draining it gives you better control. If, after combining, the pasta does not "flow" right, add some of the reserved water to loosen it.

If the sauce/topping to be used is at room temperature or cold, don't add cold water to the pasta before draining it. The sauce/topping will cool off the pasta while getting warm in turn. In some recipes, the pasta must be set aside before being used. In such cases, thoroughly cool the pasta and then treat as the recipe instructs.

SALSA DELLA ROCCA

sauce from rocca

serves 6

This sauce is the way a noble family from Rocca di Caprileone, a charming, small coastal town, celebrates the freshly pressed oil from the new crop of olives grown on their land.

3 LARGE ONIONS	SLICED VERY THIN, LENGTHWISE
¾ CUP EXTRA-VIRGIN OLIVE OIL*	PREFERABLY NEW OIL
2 CUPS FRESH BASIL	GENTLY PACKED LEAVES; CUT INTO THIN STRIPS
½ TEASPOON SALT	
½ TEASPOON BLACK PEPPER	FINELY GROUND
¾ POUND SPAGHETTI	COMMERCIAL

Cover the sliced onions with water and set aside for a couple of hours. Drain very well.

In a covered skillet, cook the onions in the oil on low heat until soft, stirring occasionally. Uncover, increase the heat to medium, and cook, stirring often, until the onions are thoroughly wilted and translucent. Turn off the heat. Add the basil, salt, and pepper.

Cook the pasta (see page 31). Reserve some of the drained water.

Toss the pasta with the sauce. If the pasta does not have a "slippery" look, add a small quantity of the reserved water. Serve immediately.

* FRESHLY RENDERED LARD CAN BE USED INSTEAD OF THE OIL. IF YOUR ARTERIES CAN AFFORD IT, IT IS WORTH TRYING.

CONDIMENTO AI PEPERONI

bell pepper sauce

serves 4 to 6

8 LARGE PEPPERS	FLESHY; RED, GREEN, AND YELLOW
5 CLOVES GARLIC	SLIGHTLY CRUSHED; UNPEELED
⅓ CUP OLIVE OIL	
½ TEASPOON SALT	
½ CUP FRESH BASIL	LOOSELY PACKED LEAVES; CUT INTO THIN STRIPS
I HEAPING TABLESPOON PINE NUTS	
¾ POUND SPAGHETTI, LINGUINE, OR ROTINI*	COMMERCIAL

Preheat the oven to 400° F.

Roast the peppers in the oven for 1 hour and 10 minutes, turning them at least once. Cool, peel, and seed the peppers, reserving the juice if any. Cut into ⅓-inch strips.

In a large skillet, cook the garlic in the oil until aromatic and barely golden. Add the peppers and stir over high heat for a few minutes. Add the salt.

Meanwhile, cook the pasta (see page 31).

Toss the pasta with the garlic-pepper mixture, the basil, pine nuts, and the juice, if any, collected while peeling the peppers. Serve immediately.

* IF ROTINI PASTA IS USED, THIS DISH CAN BE EATEN AT ROOM TEMPERATURE BECAUSE SHORT PASTA OF IRREGULAR SHAPE DOES NOT STICK TOGETHER BUT STAYS FIRM WHEN ALLOWED TO GET COLD. LONG STRAND PASTA AND SHORT PASTA OF SMOOTH SHAPE STICK TOGETHER WHEN ALLOWED TO GET COLD.

CONDIMENTO HOTEL PATRIA

sauce hotel patria

serves 6 to 8

This topping is served at the Hotel Patria restaurant. The hotel, placed in the heart of the baroque part of Palermo, was one of the oldest hotels in the city. Bombed and destroyed during World War II, part of the ruins were restored recently to house a restaurant of the same name. The restaurant opens onto the hotel's beautiful courtyard, where people dine in the summer.

4 POUNDS EGGPLANT	(NO LESS THAN 4) SMALL, SKINNY ONES
I TABLESPOON SALT	
OLIVE OIL	ENOUGH FOR A ¾-INCH DEPTH IN AN 8-INCH SKILLET
4 SMALL RED CHILI PEPPERS	WHOLE, DRY
4 OUNCES SALTED RICOTTA	SHREDDED IF HARD, OTHERWISE, CUT INTO VERY SMALL PIECES
¾ CUP GRATED ITALIAN CHEESE	PECORINO ROMANO OR CACIOCAVALLO
¾ POUND SPAGHETTI OR ROTINI	COMMERCIAL

Cut off the ends of the eggplant but do not peel them. Cut the eggplant into 2-inch long sticks, about ½ inch thick. Place the sticks in a large bowl filled with water and add 1 tablespoon salt. Weigh the eggplants down in the water by placing a plate on top of them. Drain after 30 minutes, pressing lightly against the colander to remove excess water.

In a skillet, heat the oil until it is smoking. Over high heat, fry the eggplant sticks without crowding them in the skillet. Turn them as necessary, to brown evenly. Remove the eggplant with a slotted spoon, letting as much oil as possible drain back into the skillet.

Place the eggplant in a dish (no paper to line dish). Repeat until all eggplant is fried.

Transfer ¾ cup of the oil used for frying the eggplant to another very large skillet. Cook the chilies for about 10 minutes over very low heat. Turn off heat. Press the chilies down with a spoon, then add the eggplant.

Meanwhile, cook the pasta (see page 31).

Remove and discard the chilies from the eggplant. Add the cheeses and toss with the pasta. Serve immediately.

CAPELLINI CON FIORI DI ZUCCA

angel-hair pasta with squash blossoms

serves 6

The cost of squash blossoms is incredibly high, and unjustifiably so, because the flowers picked are the ones that won't bear squash, and are therefore useless to most people. The blossoms, however, have such a unique flavor that occasionally it is very well worth your while to enjoy them.

IO OUNCES SMALL TO MEDIUM SQUASH BLOSSOMS	70 TO 80
¾ CUP OLIVE OIL	
¾ TEASPOON SALT	
1¼ POUNDS ZUCCHINI	4 SLENDER ONES
2 MEDIUM LEEKS*	
2 TEASPOONS TOMATO PASTE	
½ TEASPOON BLACK PEPPER	FINELY GROUND
½ POUND ANGEL-HAIR PASTA (CAPELLINI)	COMMERCIAL

Inspect the blossoms carefully, open up the petals to check the pistils and if they are rotting remove them. Small and medium flowers generally do not have this problem. Furthermore they have tender sepals (the little green spikes at the end of the stem, that surround the corolla), while large flowers' sepals are tough and must be picked off. Wash the blossoms carefully.

Heat half the oil in a skillet. Add the blossoms and stir, over high heat, for about 4 minutes. Any water trapped in the flowers while they were being rinsed should boil out in that span of time, and blossoms should be at the right point of doneness. Stir in ¼ teaspoon salt, and set blossoms aside.

Cut each of the zucchini in three sections, then julienne into ⅓-inch thin sticks. (Use the French fry cutter in your food processor, if you have one.)

Heat the remaining oil in a very large skillet. Add the zucchini and leeks, stirring over high heat for about 3 minutes. Push the vegetables to one side of the pan and add the tomato paste apart from them. Stir the paste briefly with drippings. Add ½ teaspoon salt and combine the contents of the skillet together. Turn off the heat. Mix in the squash flowers and the pepper.

Cook the capellini in plenty of salted water. Remove it from heat when still underdone and run cold water in the pot. Drain the pasta, reserving some of the drained water.

Toss the pasta with vegetables. If too dry, add a small amount of the reserved water. Serve immediately.

* DISCARD ANY GREEN PART OF THE LEEKS AND TOUGH OUTER LEAVES. QUARTER THEM LENGTHWISE, LEAVING THE ROOT END ATTACHED. SWISH THEM IN WATER TO WASH OFF ANY DIRT, THEN CUT OFF THE ROOT END.

CONDIMENTO ALLE ZUCCHINE

green squash sauce

serves 4

2 POUNDS SLENDER ZUCCHINI	CUT INTO STICKS 2½ INCHES LONG, A LITTLE LESS THAN ½ INCH THICK
4 TABLESPOONS (2 OUNCES) BUTTER	UNSALTED
2 TABLESPOONS OLIVE OIL	
½ TEASPOON SALT	
½ TEASPOON BLACK PEPPER	FINELY GROUND
3 EGG YOLKS	EXTRA-LARGE; LIGHTLY BEATEN IN A LARGE BOWL
½ CUP GRATED PARMESAN	
¾ CUP PARSLEY	LOOSELY PACKED LEAVES; FINELY CUT
½ POUND SPAGHETTI OR LINGUINE	COMMERCIAL

In a large skillet, cook the zucchini with the butter and the oil over low heat, covered, for about 20 minutes, stirring occasionally.

Turn the heat to high and cook, uncovered, for 3 minutes, while stirring. Add the salt and pepper.

Cook the pasta (see page 31). Do not add cold water before draining. Reserve some of the drained water.

Toss the hot pasta with the egg yolks in the bowl. Mix in the zucchini, Parmesan, and parsley. If the pasta clumps, add small amounts of the reserved water to loosen. Serve immediately.

SUGO "MILINCHIO"

sauce "milinchio"

serves 6

1 LARGE ONION	CUT INTO VERY SMALL PIECES
6 CLOVES GARLIC	CUT INTO A FEW PIECES
⅔ CUP OLIVE OIL	
4 TABLESPOONS TOMATO PASTE	
BLACK PEPPER, TO TASTE	FINELY GROUND
½ TEASPOON SALT	
CAYENNE PEPPER, TO TASTE	OPTIONAL
1 POUND SPAGHETTI OR LINGUINE	COMMERCIAL
GRATED PARMESAN OR PECORINO ROMANO	

In a large pan, cook the onion and the garlic in the oil over low heat until very aromatic.

Stir in the tomato paste, pepper, salt, and cayenne, if desired. Cook over medium heat for a couple of minutes, stirring well to prevent scorching and sticking to the bottom of the pan.

Cook the pasta (see page 31). Drain and reserve some of the drained water. Toss the pasta with the sauce. If the pasta clumps together, add small amounts of the reserved water to loosen it. Serve immediately.

Have the grated cheese available at the table.

Sugo "Milinchio" For Lovely Rosa

Rosa was one of daughters of Nonno Angelica. My mother the most beautiful and three.

During the war, and no treatment was could barely eat. appeal to her, Greather into eating pasta a sauce she made in a oil, onion, garlic, and

Although an the only family casualty marked the end of her Remembering that time the cities, the hardship by my family in very words loaded with

the three beautiful Alfredo's sister, Maria would say that she was the most gifted of the

Rosa became very ill, available to her. She When nothing would aunt Maria could coax with *sugo "milinchio,"* few minutes with olive tomato paste. indirect one, Rosa was of the war, which youth and beauty. and the exodus from would be summed up few words, but anxiety and fear—

lo sfollamento, i bombardamenti, il mercato nero—.

But when I prepare *sugo "milinchio,"* I think about Rosa and not about the horrible period of history we lived through.

PESTO ALL' AVOCADO

avocado pesto

serves 10 or 12

This is a versatile sauce that can be used on gnocchi, or as a dip for vegetables.

½ CUP ALMONDS	BLANCHED
½ CUP WALNUTS	
1 LARGE AVOCADO	PREFERABLY FROM CALIFORNIA
⅓ CUP GRATED PARMESAN	
5 TO 10 CLOVES GARLIC	
2 CUPS FRESH BASIL	LOOSELY PACKED LEAVES
½ TEASPOON THYME	DRY LEAVES
½ TEASPOON MARJORAM	DRY LEAVES
⅔ CUP OLIVE OIL	
½ TEASPOON SALT	
⅔ CUP WARM WATER	
1¾ POUNDS SPAGHETTI OR LINGUINE	COMMERCIAL; OR FRESH TAGLIATELLE

Soak the almonds and walnuts in hot water for 1 hour, then drain.

Blend all the ingredients except the water in a food processor. Add water in small quantities until the pesto is light and creamy.

Cook the pasta (see page 31). Do not add cold tap water before draining. Reserve some of the drained water.

If the pasta clumps together, add small amounts of the reserved water to loosen it. Toss the pasta with the sauce. Serve immediately.

SALSA DI POMODORO PASSATA

strained tomato sauce

serves 4

½ CUP OLIVE OIL	QUANTITY CAN BE INCREASED OR DECREASED TO TASTE
½ SMALL ONION	CUT INTO VERY SMALL PIECES
2 CLOVES GARLIC	UNPEELED; SLIGHTLY CRUSHED
3 CUPS TOMATOES	CANNED AND PEELED, DRAINED WELL (JUICES RESERVED); SEEDED, CUT INTO VERY SMALL PIECES
I TO 2 TEASPOONS HONEY	
I TEASPOON SALT	
HERBS*	A FEW LEAVES EACH OF PARSLEY, BASIL, ROSEMARY, SAGE, OREGANO, AND SORREL (PREFERABLY FRESH)
⅔ POUND SPAGHETTI, RIGATONI, OR SIMILAR PASTA	COMMERCIAL; OR FRESH FETTUCCINE
GRATED PARMESAN OR PECORINO ROMANO	

Place the oil, onion, and garlic in a medium-sized pot. Cook until aromatic. Press the garlic down, then remove and discard it.

With the heat on high, add the tomatoes, 1 teaspoon honey, and salt. Cook, uncovered, until the tomatoes sizzle, stirring occasionally.

Add the packing juice and the herbs. Bring to a boil, reduce the heat to medium or low, place a lid on the pan slightly ajar and cook about 15 minutes, stirring occasionally. Taste the sauce. If it is unpleasantly tart, add the remaining teaspoon of honey and/or a little more salt.

Pass the sauce through a strainer, with large holes. The sauce can be used unstrained as well.

Cook the pasta (see page 31).

Toss the pasta with the sauce. Serve immediately. Have grated cheese available at the table.

* YOU CAN USE ONLY ONE OF THESE HERBS OR AS MANY AS YOU WANT; INCREASE THE QUANTITY OF LEAVES AS YOU DECREASE QUANTITY OF HERBS USED.

SALSA ALLE ERBE FRESCHE

sauce with fresh herbs

serves 6 to 8

1 SMALL ONION	CUT INTO VERY SMALL PIECES
3 CLOVES GARLIC	UNPEELED; SLIGHTLY CRUSHED
½ TO ⅔ CUP OLIVE OIL	
1 CUP HERBS	A COMBINATION OF THYME, ROSEMARY, AND OREGANO LEAVES (STRIPPED FROM THE HARD STEMS) AND A FEW LEAVES OF MINT, BASIL, AND SAGE
2 TEASPOONS SALT	
6 CUPS TOMATOES	CANNED AND PEELED, DRAINED WELL (JUICES RESERVED); SEEDED, CUT INTO VERY SMALL PIECES
1¼ POUNDS SPAGHETTI, RIGATONI, OR SIMILAR PASTA	COMMERCIAL
GRATED PARMESAN	

In a large pot, cook the onion and the garlic in the oil. As soon as the onion and garlic become aromatic, turn the heat to high and add the tomato pieces. Cook, uncovered, without stirring until the tomatoes sizzle.

Add herbs and salt, stir. If the sauce looks very dry, add just enough juice collected while seeding the tomatoes to moisten it. Turn the heat to medium, cook, covered, for 20 minutes, stirring occasionally. Keep adding juice in small amounts as the sauce dries out. If necessary, add some of the packing juice as well.

Cook the pasta (see page 31).

Toss the pasta with the sauce. Serve immediately.

Have some grated cheese available at the table.

SALSA DEL DUCA

the duke's sauce

serves 6 to 8

The ingredients in this recipe reflect the style of sauces found in the Duke's cookbook. Prepare this sauce in a very large skillet, or divide the ingredients between two large ones.

¼ POUND CHICKEN LIVERS	
½ TO ⅔ CUP OLIVE OIL	
5 TO 6 SPRING ONIONS	WHITE PART AND ONLY FIRST INCH OF THE GREEN PART; SLICED INTO THIN ROUNDS
4 TO 6 SMALL RED CHILI PEPPERS	WHOLE, DRY
¼ POUND DANISH HAM	CUT INTO 1 THICK SLICE; DICED VERY SMALL
6 CUPS FIRM TOMATOES	CANNED AND PEELED, DRAINED WELL; SEEDED, CUT INTO VERY SMALL PIECES; RESERVE JUICE
1½ TEASPOONS SALT	REDUCE IF HAM IS VERY SALTY
½ TEASPOON SAGE	10 LEAVES, IF FRESH
1¼ POUNDS SPAGHETTI, RIGATONI, OR SIMILAR PASTA	COMMERCIAL
GRATED PARMESAN	

In a saucepan, cover chicken livers with water and boil for 8 minutes. Drain, then dip them into cold water and dice very small.

Cover the bottom of a skillet with the oil. Add the onion and chilies. Heat until aromatic. Add the chicken livers and the ham. Stir for a minute over high heat, then add the tomatoes. If you do not like your food too hot, remove all or some of the chilies at this point.

Cook the sauce over high heat until it sizzles. Add the juice collected while seeding the tomatoes and the salt, and cook for 10 to 15 more minutes, stirring occasionally. In the last few minutes of cooking, add the sage. While cooking, do not stir the sauce often. Check the heat and adjust as necessary: tomatoes are supposed to stick slightly to the pan so that they can be easily loosened when stirring.

Cook the pasta (see page 31).

Toss the pasta with the sauce. Serve immediately.

Have some grated cheese available at the table.

PASTA "ACCIURATA"

pasta "in bloom"

serves 8

"*Acciurate*" is the Sicilian dialect word for the black shriveled-up olives used in Sicily in this kind of dish. Such olives have dried out, producing in the process a light mold.

¼ POUND BLACK OLIVES	OIL CURED, REMOVE PITS; EACH CUT UP INTO A FEW PIECES
8 CLOVES GARLIC	CUT INTO A FEW PIECES
I TABLESPOON WHOLE FRESH ROSEMARY LEAVES	CUT SMALL
¾ CUP OLIVE OIL	PLUS 2 TABLESPOONS TO TOAST BREAD CRUMBS
16 SMALL ANCHOVY FILLETS	PACKED IN OLIVE OIL; MASHED
I TEASPOON BLACK PEPPER	FINELY GROUND
½ CUP BREAD CRUMBS	UNFLAVORED
I¼ POUNDS SPAGHETTI	COMMERCIAL

Cook the black olives, garlic, and rosemary in the oil over low heat, until aromatic. Turn off the heat, and stir in the anchovies and the pepper.

In a cast-iron skillet, over medium-high heat, toast bread crumbs lightly with 2 tablespoons of olive oil.

Cook the pasta (see page 31). Reserve some of the drained water.

Toss the pasta with the sauce. If the pasta does not have the "slippery" look, add some of the reserved water to loosen it. Serve immediately topped with the bread crumbs.

FETTUCCINE AL SALMONE

fettuccine with salmon

serves I

2 TABLESPOONS BUTTER	UNSALTED
I TABLESPOON OLIVE OIL	
2 TO 3 SPRING ONIONS	CUT LENGTHWISE INTO THIN STRANDS; LEAVE TENDER GREEN PART ON
I½ TO 2 OUNCES SMOKED SALMON	CUT INTO SMALL PIECES
BLACK PEPPER, TO TASTE	
3 OUNCES FETTUCCINE, LINGUINE, OR SPAGHETTI	COMMERCIAL

In a skillet over low heat, heat butter, oil, and spring onions until the onions are wilted, but the green parts are still bright. Turn off the heat, add the salmon, and sprinkle with pepper.

Cook the pasta (see page 31). Reserve some of the drained water.

Toss the sauce with the pasta. If necessary, loosen up the pasta with a small amount of reserved water. Serve immediately.

RAGÙ DI ANATRA

duck ragout

serves 6

Besides serving this ragù on pasta, you can serve it on rice, gnocchi, or polenta.

I OUNCE DRIED PORCINI MUSHROOMS	
½ CUP OLIVE OIL	
I MEDIUM ONION	CUT INTO VERY SMALL PIECES
2 CLOVES GARLIC	
3 POUNDS DUCK LEGS	(THREE 5-POUND BIRDS YIELD APPROXIMATELY 3 POUNDS LEGS) FAT AND SKIN REMOVED
½ CUP RED WINE	DRY
I (6 OUNCE) CAN TOMATO PASTE	
¼ CUP FRESH SAGE	LOOSELY PACKED LEAVES
I½ TEASPOONS SALT	
I TEASPOON BLACK PEPPER	FINELY GROUND
I POUND FETTUCCINE	FRESH OR COMMERCIAL

Soak the mushrooms in cold water until plump but not mushy. Wash very well, removing any sand and dirt. Drain and cut into small pieces.

To a large pot, add the oil. Add the onion and garlic, cooking over medium heat until aromatic. With the heat on high, add the duck and sear it. Add the wine, let it evaporate. Add the tomato paste, enough water to barely cover the duck, mushrooms, sage, salt, and pepper. Stir well. Cover and simmer until tender, about 2 hours.

Remove the duck from the sauce, remove and discard the bones, then cut the meat in small pieces. Return the meat to the sauce.

Cook the pasta (see page 31).

Toss the pasta with the sauce. Serve immediately.

CONDIMENTO AL PESCESPADA

swordfish sauce

serves 8

2 POUNDS SWORDFISH	PREFERABLY CUT INTO 1 THICK SLICE
1¼ CUPS OLIVE OIL	
10 SMALL ANCHOVY FILLETS	PACKED IN OLIVE OIL, DRAINED WELL
6 CLOVES GARLIC	CUT INTO VERY THIN SLICES
1 TABLESPOON PINE NUTS	
1 TABLESPOON CURRANTS	
¼ TEASPOON BLACK PEPPER	FINELY GROUND
½ TEASPOON SALT	SCANT
1½ POUNDS SPAGHETTI OR LINGUINE	COMMERCIAL
1 CUP FRESH PARSLEY	LOOSELY PACKED LEAVES; CUT FINELY

In a covered skillet over very low heat, cook the swordfish in ¼ cup oil for about 10 minutes, turning once. The fish is done when you can flake it easily. The cooking time will vary depending on the thickness of the slice. Remove the fish from the pan.

Mash the anchovies in the liquid left in the pan. Flake the fish, and remove bones, skin, and any dark brown meat. Return the flaked fish to the pan.

In a small saucepan over medium heat, cook the garlic in the remaining oil until it is lightly browned. Add the garlic to the fish sauce, along with the pine nuts, currants, pepper, and salt. Mix well.

Cook the pasta (see page 31).

Toss the pasta with the sauce and the parsley. Serve immediately.

CONDIMENTO AL TONNO E POMODORO CRUDO

raw tomato and tuna sauce

serves 4 to 6

1¼ POUNDS FRESH TOMATOES	PEAR SHAPED, RIPE, BUT FIRM, UNPEELED; CUT INTO VERY SMALL CUBES
6½ OUNCES TUNA	PACKED IN OIL; DRAINED WELL, MASHED
2 CLOVES GARLIC	CUT INTO VERY SMALL PIECES
1 CUP FRESH BASIL	LOOSELY PACKED LEAVES; CUT INTO VERY THIN STRIPS
2 SMALL ANCHOVY FILLETS	PACKED IN OLIVE OIL; DRAINED WELL, MASHED
⅓ CUP OLIVE OIL	
½ TEASPOON SALT	
¼ TEASPOON CAYENNE PEPPER	OR TO TASTE
¾ POUND SPAGHETTI OR ROTINI	COMMERCIAL

In a large bowl, mix all of the ingredients except the pasta and let them stand for 1 hour.

Cook the pasta (see page 31). Do not add cold tap water before draining.

Toss the pasta with the sauce. Serve immediately.

PASTA DEL COLONNELLO

"the colonel's" pasta

serves 1

"Il colonnello" was the code name of my uncle Saverio when he was a partisan. This is a pasta he cooked for me during one of my visits to Palermo.

1 CUP EGGPLANT*	¾-INCH CUBES
1 TABLESPOON SALT	PLUS ⅛ TO ¼ TEASPOON
OLIVE OIL	ENOUGH FOR A ¾-INCH DEPTH IN AN 8-INCH SKILLET PLUS 3 TABLESPOONS
1 CUP ZUCCHINI	¾-INCH CUBES
4 OUNCES SWORDFISH	CUT INTO ¾-INCH CUBES, ABOUT ½ CUP
FLOUR	UNBLEACHED, ALL-PURPOSE; FOR COATING
1 CLOVE GARLIC	THINLY SLICED
LEMON ZEST	A GRATING
1 TEASPOON FRESH PARSLEY	CUT FINELY
BLACK PEPPER, TO TASTE	FINELY GROUND
2½ TO 3 OUNCES SPAGHETTI OR LINGUINE	COMMERCIAL

Deep fry the eggplant (see page 34). Set aside and keep warm.

In a large skillet, over medium-high heat, cook the zucchini (and the mushrooms if using) in 3 tablespoons oil, until pleasantly crisp. Lightly coat the swordfish with the flour, add it to the skillet, and lightly brown it, over high heat. Add the garlic and the lemon zest, stir briefly, then remove from the heat.

Add the parsley, salt, and pepper to the contents of the skillet. Cook the pasta (see page 31). Reserve some of the drained water. Toss the contents of the skillet with the pasta. If necessary, add a small amount of reserved water to loosen up pasta. Gently mix in the eggplant. Serve immediately.

* INSTEAD OF EGGPLANT, YOU CAN USE 1 OR 2 SHIITAKE MUSHROOMS, THINLY SLICED.

A Recollection on the Origin of Pasta in Sicily

Although the Normans and the Suebi did not bring many food novelties to Sicily, they were essential to the preservation of the already advanced and sophisticated Sicilian cuisine. The scholars and artists the court protected recorded the marvels of their times, and it is thanks to one of these protégés, the Arab geographer Edrisi, that we have the first descriptions of a type of pasta. In his book, called *Kitab-Rugiar* (The Book of Roger), from the year 1154, not only does he describe the fine strands produced by the mills, but he also mentions Trabia, the town where the pasta was made. Very close to Palermo and set in lovely countryside, Trabia is also a place where my family took refuge from the war in 1943. Edrisi calls the food he describes *itriyah*. Tria, in fact, is the dialect word used today for angel-hair pasta as well as for a piece of equipment used in making pasta.

Pasta making is still one of the main activities of Trabia, but not in quite so large a scale as it was during the time of Edrisi's tale. According to him, pasta was a very exclusive product, much sought after, which was exported from Trabia in large quantities to Christian and Muslim countries.

PASTA AL CAVIALE E POMODORO

pasta with caviar sauce

serves 12

5 CLOVES GARLIC	VERY THINLY SLICED
2 TABLESPOONS CAPERS	PACKED IN VINEGAR; MEASURE AFTER WELL SQUEEZED
5 SMALL RED CHILI PEPPERS	WHOLE, DRY
1 CUP OLIVE OIL	
7 OUNCES LUMPFISH CAVIAR	
12 ANCHOVY FILLETS	PACKED IN OLIVE OIL; DRAINED, MASHED
4 POUNDS FRESH TOMATOES	PEAR SHAPED, RIPE, BUT FIRM, UNPEELED; CUT INTO ⅓-INCH CUBES
1 ¼ POUNDS SHELLS	COMMERCIAL

In a large skillet over medium heat, cook the garlic, capers, and chilies in the oil until aromatic. Press the chilies down in the pan, then remove and discard them. Turn the heat off. Add the caviar and the anchovies.

Cook the pasta (see page 31). Do not add cold water before draining. Shake the colander very well, to eliminate any water trapped into the shells. It is very important that the pasta is well drained because in combination with the tomatoes, any excess water will result in a soupy dish.

Toss with the tomatoes and the caviar sauce. Serve immediately.

TIMBALLO DI CAPELLINI

capellini timbale

serves 8

½ CUP OLIVE OIL	
1 MEDIUM ONION	CUT INTO VERY SMALL PIECES
1¼ POUNDS GROUND BEEF	VERY LEAN ROUND
1 POUND GROUND PORK	VERY LEAN BONELESS LOIN
½ CUP WHITE WINE	DRY
2 TABLESPOONS TOMATO PASTE	
1 TEASPOON SALT	
10 OUNCES FROZEN PEAS	PARBOILED
BECHAMEL	RECIPE FOLLOWS (ALTER INGREDIENTS TO 4 CUPS MILK, 6 TABLESPOONS FLOUR, 1 TEASPOON SALT, AND OMIT THE BUTTER)
1 TEASPOON BLACK PEPPER	FINELY GROUND
¾ CUP GRATED PARMESAN	
9 TABLESPOONS (4½ OUNCES) BUTTER	UNSALTED
BREAD CRUMBS	UNFLAVORED, FOR COATING
1 EGG	EXTRA-LARGE
2 EGG YOLKS	EXTRA-LARGE
1 POUND ANGEL-HAIR PASTA (CAPELLINI)	COMMERCIAL

Preheat the oven to 325° F.

Cover the bottom of a very large skillet with the oil. Add the onion and cook over medium-low heat until aromatic. Turn the heat to high, add and brown the meats. Do not stir. Turn with a spatula only when the meats start sizzling. After they sizzle again, break up the meats and stir. Ground meat releases a lot of liquid, and stirring prevents the heat from building up and drying out the liquid, which prevents the meat from getting seared and from browning.

Add the wine and deglaze the pan, scraping up any browned bits from the skillet. Add the tomato paste, 2 tablespoons of water, and the salt. Stir well, cover, and cook over low heat for about 15 minutes. Turn off heat.

Add the peas, bechamel, and pepper. Let the mixture cool some, then stir in the Parmesan.

Coat a baking dish, approximately 10 by 12 by 3 inches with a tablespoon of the butter, then with bread crumbs. Set aside.

Cut the remaining butter in very thin patties and spread them on another very shallow, wide dish.

Beat egg and yolks until well mixed.

Cook the pasta (see page 31). Add plenty of cold tap water before draining it. Capellini should be very much al dente. Reserve some of the drained water. Pour the capellini in the dish with the butter, toss very quickly, then toss in eggs. Mix with the meat mixture. If the pasta clumps together, add small amounts of the reserved water to loosen it. Transfer to the baking dish. Bake in the oven for 1 hour.

Serve immediately or, if you wish to unmold the timbale, let it cool at least 15 minutes first.

BESCIAMELLA

bechamel sauce

makes 3 cups

4½ TABLESPOONS FLOUR   UNBLEACHED, ALL-PURPOSE
3 CUPS MILK
1 TEASPOON SALT
2 TABLESPOONS BUTTER   UNSALTED

In a good saucepan, dissolve the flour in a small amount of milk. Add the rest of the milk gradually, thinning out the initial flour-milk mixture so that no lumps are left.

Add the salt and the butter. Cook over medium heat, stirring constantly. Stir well, through and around—reaching the bottom and the sides of the sauce pan—always in the same direction.

To make a larger amount of sauce, dissolve the flour as directed. Add ⅓ to ½ of the remaining milk. Scald the rest and stir it in with the salt and the butter. Cook as per directions.

PASTA DI CARNEVALE

mardi gras pasta

serves 10

2 LARGE CARROTS	DICED VERY SMALL
I MEDIUM ONION	CUT INTO VERY SMALL PIECES
2 CLOVES GARLIC	
⅔ CUP OLIVE OIL	PLUS 4 TABLESPOONS FOR TOASTING ALMONDS
I½ POUNDS PORK LOIN	BONELESS, NO FAT; CUT INTO 7 OR 8 SLICES
¼ CUP WHITE WINE	DRY
I2 OUNCES TOMATO PASTE	
I TEASPOON SALT	
I½ POUNDS RIGATONI	COMMERCIAL
I CUP WHOLE ALMONDS	SKINS ON, TOASTED*, CRUSHED COARSELY
I TEASPOON GROUND CINNAMON	
I TEASPOON BLACK PEPPER	FINELY GROUND
I CUP GRATED PECORINO ROMANO	OR OTHER PECORINO SUCH AS SARDO OR SICILIAN, OR OTHER SHARP CHEESE

In a large skillet over medium-low heat, cook the carrots, onion, and garlic in the oil until aromatic. Increase the heat to high. Add the pork and sear it. Add the wine, let it evaporate for about 30 seconds, then add tomato paste, 1½ cups water, and salt. Stir well. Bring to a boil, lower the heat, cover, and simmer until the pork can be shredded by pulling it apart with a fork, about 1½ to 2 hours.

Shred the pork, return to the sauce, and set it aside.

Coat a baking dish, approximately 9 by 12 by 3 inches, with oil.

Preheat the oven to 375° F.

Cook the pasta (see page 31). Toss the pasta with the almonds, cinnamon, pepper, meat sauce, and all but ¾ cup of the cheese. Pack in the baking dish, top with the remaining cheese.

Bake in the oven for 15 minutes. Turn off the oven and let the pasta rest in it for an additional 15 minutes before serving.

* TO TOAST THE ALMONDS: IN A HEAVY CAST-IRON SKILLET OVER MEDIUM HEAT, VERY QUICKLY STIR THE ALMONDS WITH 4 TABLESPOONS OF OLIVE OIL UNTIL THEY CRACKLE. REMOVE FROM SKILLET AND BLOT WITH PAPER TOWEL. ALLOW THE ALMONDS TO COOL.

SALSA DI POMODORO INFORNATA CON PASTA

baked tomato sauce with pasta

serves 4

The tomato halves used in this recipe can also be served, without pasta, as a side dish.

⅔ CUP OLIVE OIL

1½ POUNDS FRESH TOMATOES — PEAR SHAPED, MEDIUM, RIPE, UNPEELED; CUT IN HALF, LENGTHWISE

¼ CUP GRATED PECORINO ROMANO — OR OTHER PECORINO SUCH AS SARDO OR SICILIAN, OR OTHER SHARP CHEESE

¼ CUP BREAD CRUMBS — UNFLAVORED

2 CLOVES GARLIC — CUT INTO VERY SMALL PIECES

1 TEASPOON OREGANO — DRY LEAVES

¼ TEASPOON BLACK PEPPER — FINELY GROUND

¼ TEASPOON SALT

½ POUND PENNE OR SIMILAR PASTA — COMMERCIAL

Preheat the oven to 425° F.

Cover the bottom of a baking dish with the oil. Dip the cut surface of each tomato half in the oil, then place in the pan cut-side up. The tomatoes should fit closely together in one layer.

Combine the cheese, bread crumbs, garlic, oregano, pepper, and salt, then top each tomato half with it.

Bake for 40 minutes in the oven. If the drippings start burning, decrease the heat to 375° to 400° F.

Cook the pasta (see page 31). Drain.

Add the pasta to the dish with the tomatoes, toss, and serve immediately.

"TIMPALLO" DI MACCHERONI

maccheroni timbale

serves 10

This recipe is a good example of the pasta dishes made during the times of the Duke's Cookbook. It is certainly very far from a quick, everyday meal.

Crust

2⅔ CUPS FLOUR	UNBLEACHED, ALL-PURPOSE
⅓ CUP SUGAR	
½ TEASPOON SALT	
7 TABLESPOONS (3½ OUNCES) BUTTER	(OR USE MARGARINE) UNSALTED
½ CUP COLD WATER	
I EGG	EXTRA-LARGE

Filling

4 EGGS	EXTRA-LARGE
I OUNCE DRY MUSHROOMS	PREFERABLY PORCINI
I½ POUNDS GROUND BEEF	VERY LEAN ROUND
2 TABLESPOONS BREAD CRUMBS	UNFLAVORED
FLOUR	UNBLEACHED, ALL-PURPOSE, FOR COATING
I¼ CUPS OLIVE OIL	
5 QUAIL	SPLIT IN HALF
½ POUND SAUSAGE	FRESH, MILD
I MEDIUM ONION	CUT INTO VERY SMALL PIECES
2 CELERY RIBS	CUT INTO VERY SMALL PIECES
I LARGE CARROT	CUT INTO VERY SMALL PIECES
I TABLESPOON BUTTER	UNSALTED
½ CUP WHITE WINE	DRY
12 CUPS LIGHT CHICKEN OR BEEF STOCK	SEE PAGE 72
I CLOVE GARLIC	CUT INTO VERY SMALL PIECES
½ TEASPOON SALT	
½ TEASPOON BLACK PEPPER	FINELY GROUND
10 OUNCES PROVOLA	MILD; THINLY SLICED
⅔ CUP GRATED PECORINO ROMANO	OR OTHER PECORINO SUCH AS SARDO OR OTHER SHARP CHEESE
¾ POUND PENNE OR SMALL RIGATONI	COMMERCIAL

To make the crust: Mix together the dry ingredients, then cut in the butter until the mixture looks like coarse crumbs. Sprinkle in the water. Add the egg. Knead until the dough is very smooth and elastic. The dough must be very firm; if too difficult to knead, add a small amount of water.

Wrap the dough in wax paper and let it rest in a cool place for a couple of hours. The dough can be prepared a few days in advance and refrigerated; bring to room temperature before using.

To make the filling: Hard-boil 2 eggs and set aside. Soak mushrooms in water until they soften. Remove from water, rinse carefully to remove all sand and dirt, and cut into large pieces.

Separate 2 eggs. Set aside the egg whites in one bowl and 1 egg yolk in another bowl. In a bowl, mix the beef with the other yolk and bread crumbs. Shape into balls the size of a large cherry, lightly coat with flour.

In a very large skillet, over medium-high heat, heat ⅔ cup oil. Sauté the meatballs until light brown. Set aside.

In the same pan where you cooked the meatballs—adding more oil if necessary—sauté the quail halves, over high heat, until seared. Set aside.

Using a fork, pierce the sausage and place into a saucepan. Cover with water, bring to a boil over low heat, and cook for 20 minutes. Drain, remove casing, and slice in approximately ¼-inch rounds. Set aside.

In a large skillet, cook over medium-low heat the onion, celery, and carrot in the butter and ½ cup of oil until aromatic. With heat on medium high, add the sausage and lightly brown. With heat on high, add the meatballs, quail and their drippings. When sizzling, add the wine and let it evaporate about 30 seconds. It may be necessary to divide the ingredients between two pans for this quantity of ingredients to sizzle.

Add ¾ cup stock to the pan, then the mushrooms, garlic, salt, and pepper. Cover and simmer 30 minutes. Turn off heat. Remove the quail, remove meat from the bones, and return the meat to the pot. Add the hard-cooked eggs, cut into small pieces.

Line a baking dish, approximately 10 by 14 by 3 inches (not any smaller) with two-thirds of the rolled-out crust. Brush some of the reserved egg whites over the crust.

Preheat the oven to 375° F.

Cook the pasta in the remaining stock, drain before it reaches the al dente stage, that is, it should be slightly underdone (see page 31).

Mix the pasta with the meat filling. Pack half of the pasta-meat combination into the crust, sprinkle with half the grated cheese, and cover with half the provola slices. Repeat the process with the remaining filling and cheese. Cover with the remaining crust, pressing the excess edge of the top crust against excess edge of lining crust. Trim the ragged top part of crust joint with a ravioli cutter, pressing it against the pan edge. Pull the crust edge slightly from the side of pan. Moisten the joint with egg white, keeping the egg white away from pan sides or it will cause the crust to stick to it.

With a small knife, cut an even pattern into the top crust. Slots should be every 2 inches. Bake in oven for 1 hour. During the last 10 minutes of baking, brush the reserved egg yolk on the crust.

Let the timbale rest on counter 15 minutes before serving.

TIMBALLO DI COLLESANO

timbale from collesano

serves 10 to 12

My parents were very hospitable. Their summer house on the coast of Sicily was always filled with guests and Mother always had some help with the cooking. This is a recipe a woman from Collesano added to the family repertoire.

1½ CUPS OLIVE OIL	PLUS SOME OIL FOR COATING
1 VERY LARGE ONION	CUT INTO VERY SMALL PIECES
1½ CANS (9 OUNCES) TOMATO PASTE	
2 POUNDS BROCCOLI	FLORETS AND TENDER STEMS ONLY; SLICED INTO THIN ROUNDS
2 POUNDS FENNEL	TENDER, GREEN FEATHERY LEAVES OF THE HEART ONLY, NO TOUGH OUTER LEAVES NOR GREEN LEAF STALKS (SEE PAGE 204); QUARTERED AND SLICED INTO THIN WEDGES
1½ TO 2 TEASPOONS SALT	
20 SMALL ANCHOVY FILLETS	PACKED IN OLIVE OIL; DRAINED, MASHED
1 CUP GRATED PECORINO ROMANO	OR OTHER PECORINO SUCH AS SARDO OR OTHER SHARP CHEESE
1 TEASPOON BLACK PEPPER	FINELY GROUND
2 CUPS BREAD CRUMBS	UNFLAVORED
18 OUNCES PENNE OR SIMILAR PASTA	COMMERCIAL
GRATED CHEESE	

Pour ⅔ cup oil in each of two large pans, divide the onion between them, and cook it over medium-low heat until aromatic. Increase the heat to medium-high, divide the tomato paste between the pans, stirring it for a couple of minutes. Add 1 cup of water to each pan. Stir well. Add the broccoli to one pan, the fennel to the other, and enough additional water to cover the vegetables two-thirds of the way up. Stir a scant teaspoon of salt into each pan. Cover and simmer until the vegetables are tender, but not too soft.

Uncover the pans and reduce the liquid over low heat, stirring often, until about half of the initial quantity remains. The liquid should look thick.

Remove a tablespoon of liquid from either pan and, in a separate bowl, mix well with the anchovies. Add the vegetables, cheese, and the pepper.

In a cast-iron skillet, heat 2 tablespoons of olive oil. Add 1⅓ cup bread crumbs, stirring constantly over medium heat until golden brown. Add to the vegetable mixture. Taste, add remaining salt if necessary.

Coat a baking dish, approximately 10 by 14 by 3 inches, with oil, then with the remaining ⅔ cup bread crumbs.

Preheat the oven to 325° F.

Cook the pasta (see page 31).

Mix the pasta with the vegetable mixture, then pack it into the baking dish. Bake in the oven for 45 minutes. Serve immediately, if you wish to unmold the timbale, let it cool at least 15 minutes first.

Have grated cheese available at the table.

LASAGNE DI CASA

homemade lasagne

yields about 1¼ pounds

I POUND FLOUR	UNBLEACHED, ALL-PURPOSE
3 EGGS	EXTRA-LARGE

On a counter, make a well in the flour, add the eggs to the well, beat them with a fork until roughly mixed. Start mixing some of the flour into the eggs, mixing as much as the eggs will absorb. Then add in the rest of the flour. The mixture will be very dry and crumbly. Knead, while adding water by the tablespoon, until you obtain a very stiff dough. The dough should have quite a bit of resistance when poked with a finger.

After the initial kneading, if you let the dough rest covered with an inverted bowl for 5 to 10 minutes, you'll find it more manageable and easier to knead. The dough is ready to roll when it is very smooth and, if cut with a sharp knife, compact.

Cut the dough into 4 to 5 sections to make rolling easier and roll it a little thinner than commercial lasagne. Keep the dough you are rolling dusted with flour, and keep the dough you are not working with covered with an inverted bowl to prevent drying.

Cut the rolled dough into strips approximately 8 inches long by 1½ inches wide, or 4-inch squares.

The pasta should be cooked shortly after it is rolled out: it will crack if it dries.

NOTE: I ADVISE THE USE OF A MANUAL PASTA MACHINE, SUCH AS AN ATLAS, SINCE ROLLING OUT THE DOUGH BY HAND CAN BE QUITE ARDUOUS.

PASTICCIO DI RADICCHIO E LASAGNE

baked radicchio and lasagne

serves 8 to 10

6 CUPS BECHAMEL	(SEE PAGE 48) DOUBLE THE RECIPE
½ TEASPOON NUTMEG	GROUND
6 OUNCES VERY LEAN BACON	CUT INTO VERY SMALL PIECES
½ CUP OLIVE OIL	
1 LARGE ONION	CUT INTO VERY SMALL PIECES
3 POUNDS RADICCHIO	OR 2 POUNDS ESCAROLE AND 1 POUND BELGIAN ENDIVE
4 LARGE LEEKS*	CUT INTO SMALL PIECES
8 TABLESPOONS (4 OUNCES) BUTTER	UNSALTED
1 TEASPOON SALT	
BLACK PEPPER, TO TASTE	FINELY GROUND
1 CUP GRATED PARMESAN	
¾ POUND LASAGNE	COMMERCIAL OR HOMEMADE (SEE PAGE 54)

Prepare the bechamel, mix in the nutmeg, and set aside.

In a large, heavy pot, cook the bacon and oil over very low heat, until the bacon fat is transparent. Add the onion and cook over medium heat until aromatic. Add the radicchio (or escarole and endive), the leeks, and the butter. Cook, covered, over very low heat, stirring occasionally, until the vegetables are soft, about 30 minutes. Add the salt and pepper to taste. Turn off the heat. If radicchio leaves are still holding together, cut off ends.

Preheat the oven to 350° F.

Cook the pasta (see page 31). After draining, dip the pasta in plenty of icy cold water. Drain again and spread on oiled cookie sheets.

Generously coat the bottom of a baking dish, approximately 10 by 14 by 3 inches, with butter. Layer one quarter of bechamel in the dish, then sprinkle well with one quarter of the cheese. Divide the lasagne into three portions. Arrange layers of ingredients in the pan as follows: lasagne, vegetables, bechamel, cheese; repeat; then lasagne, bechamel, cheese.

Bake in the oven for 45 minutes. Serve hot.

* TO CLEAN LEEKS, CUT DOWN TO ROOT—NOT THROUGH IT—LENGTHWISE. SWISH IN WATER UNTIL DIRT IS WASHED OFF.

PASTA CON "BROCCOLE" AL FORNO

baked pasta and cauliflower

serves 8

3 POUNDS CAULIFLOWER	WITHOUT OUTER LEAVES OR TOUGH STEMS
1 MEDIUM ONION	CUT INTO VERY SMALL PIECES
¾ CUP OLIVE OIL	
4 OUNCES TOMATO PASTE	
½ TEASPOON SALT	
6 SMALL ANCHOVY FILLETS	PACKED IN OLIVE OIL; DRAINED WELL, MASHED
½ CUP WHOLE ALMONDS	SKINS ON, TOASTED (SEE PAGE 49);
	CRUSHED COARSELY
2 TABLESPOONS PINE NUTS	
2 TABLESPOONS CURRANTS	
BLACK PEPPER, TO TASTE	FINELY GROUND
¾ POUND PENNE, SMALL RIGATONI,	
OR SIMILAR SHORT PASTA	COMMERCIAL

Parboil cauliflower divided in large sections. Drain and cut off floret ends. Slice stems into thin rounds.

In a large skillet, cook the onion in the oil until aromatic. Add the tomato paste and cook over high heat, while stirring, for a couple of minutes. Add 1 cup water, salt, and the anchovies. Stir well and cook, uncovered, over medium heat for 5 minutes. Add the cauliflower, stir well, cover, and cook over medium heat about 10 more minutes. Add the nuts, currants, and pepper. Turn off heat.

Preheat the oven to 350° F.

Cook the pasta (see page 31).

Toss the pasta with the sauce. Coat a baking dish, approximately 8 by 12 by 2 inches, with olive oil. In the dish, alternate three layers each of the cheese and the pasta-cauliflower mixture, starting with pasta and ending with the cheese. Pack it down. Bake in the oven for 40 minutes. Serve immediately.

Pasta con broccole al forno

Dopo aver fatto soffriggere della
cipolla, vi si mettono delle
rape, nella proporzione di
tre per mezzo chilo di pasta;
poi vi si aggiunge dell'estratto
di pomidoro e si allunga con
l'acqua e si lascia cuocere.
In questo sugo già pronto vi
si mettono i cavolfiori quasi
completamente cotti nell'acqua,
e si finiscono di cuocere.
Aggiungete al sugo pinoli, pomolia
e mandorle brustolite.
Con una parte di questa
salsa condite la pasta e con
l'altra intramezzatela nel
metterla in tegame.
Spolveretevi in ogni strato
formaggio e lasciate cuocere
nel forno a tra due fuochi

PASTICCIO DI LASAGNE, CARNE E SPINACI

baked lasagne with meat and spinach

serves 10 to 12

1 SMALL ONION	CUT INTO VERY SMALL PIECES
½ CUP OLIVE OIL	
1¾ POUNDS GROUND BEEF	VERY LEAN ROUND
12 TABLESPOONS (6 OUNCES) BUTTER	UNSALTED
1¼ POUNDS SPINACH	(FRESH OR FROZEN) CUT LEAF
2 CUPS GRATED PARMESAN	
1 TEASPOON SALT	
6 CUPS BECHAMEL	(SEE PAGE 48) DOUBLE THE RECIPE, BUT DON'T USE BUTTER OR SALT
1¼ POUNDS LASAGNE	COMMERCIAL OR HOMEMADE (SEE PAGE 54)

In a very large skillet over low heat, cook the onion in the oil. As soon as onion becomes aromatic, turn the heat to high, add and brown the meat, without stirring. Turn the meat with a spatula only when it starts sizzling; after the meat is turned and starts sizzling again, break it up and stir. Beef releases a lot of liquid, and stirring prevents the heat from building up and drying out the liquid, which keeps the meat from getting seared. Once the beef is browned, turn off heat.

Generously coat a large baking dish, 10 by 14 by 3 inches, with butter.

Parboil the spinach and squeeze until it can be packed in 1 cup.

In the skillet, mix the beef with the Parmesan, salt, bechamel, spinach, remaining butter (except for 2 tablespoons).

Preheat the oven to 325° F.

Cook the pasta (see page 31). After draining, dip the pasta in plenty of icy cold water. Drain again and spread on oiled cookie sheets.

Alternate layers of lasagne and beef-spinach mixture in the buttered dish, ending with a layer of lasagne topped by a very thin layer of beef-spinach mixture, and dotted with the remaining 2 tablespoons of butter.

Bake in the oven for 1 hour and 10 minutes. Wait 10 to 15 minutes before serving.

RISO
rice

RISOTTO RAPIDO *

quick risotto

serves 8 as a first course

10 CUPS CHICKEN STOCK	VERY STRONG (SEE PAGE 72), MORE, IF NEEDED
½ POUND SMALL MUSHROOMS	CAPS ONLY, WELL WASHED
8 TABLESPOONS (4 OUNCES) BUTTER	UNSALTED
1 SMALL ONION	CUT INTO VERY SMALL PIECES
4 CUPS ITALIAN *ARBORIO* RICE	OR A GOOD-QUALITY JAPANESE RICE
SALT, TO TASTE	
BLACK PEPPER, TO TASTE	FINELY GROUND
GRATED PARMESAN	

Heat the stock until boiling. Turn off heat.

Clean the mushrooms under running water, stem-side down, running your finger over the caps very well. Cut off the stem ends.

In a very large heavy pot, melt the butter over low heat. Add the onion and let it cook until aromatic. Add the rice and stir until it is well coated with the butter.

Add 4 cups of the stock to the rice. Stir, cover, and simmer until all the liquid is absorbed. Uncover and stir several times while cooking, making sure the heat is very

* NOTE ON CLASSIC RISOTTO COOKING: ADDING THE STOCK IN A LARGE AMOUNT AND ALLOWING THE RICE TO ABSORB IT IN A COVERED VESSEL, OVER LOW HEAT, CUTS DOWN THE LABOR INVOLVED IN MAKING RISOTTO THE CLASSIC WAY. HOWEVER, IF YOU WANT TO MAKE RISOTTO THE CLASSIC WAY AFTER HAVING COATED THE RICE WITH THE BUTTER, HEAT ON HIGH AND START ADDING WARM STOCK—USE A STRONG CLEAR STOCK—BY THE ½ CUP, STIRRING UNTIL ABSORBED/EVAPORATED. REPEAT UNTIL RISOTTO IS DONE. ADD THE MUSHROOMS WHEN RISOTTO IS BARELY DONE—STILL CRUNCHY. YOU MAY NEED AS MUCH AS 16 UPS OF STOCK. IF YOU RUN OUT OF STOCK BEFORE RISOTTO IS DONE, ADD WARM WATER.

low and the rice is not getting scorched. Add the mushrooms and 4 more cups of stock. Stir, cover, and simmer until the liquid is absorbed.

Taste to see if the rice still has a distinct hard core. If so, add 1 more cup of stock, cover, and cook until the liquid is absorbed but the rice still looks moist. Taste again; if the rice still has a crunch to it, add 1 more cup of stock, cover, and again cook a few minutes longer. Taste. If the rice is pleasantly firm and creamy, the risotto is ready. If there is excess liquid, let it boil for a few minutes, stirring very well over medium-high heat until rice looks creamy. It is very important that you scrape the bottom of the pan all around while stirring, or the rice will get scorched.

If after adding the last cup of stock, the rice is still a little too "al dente," add more stock or plain water, in small quantities, until the rice is firm, but not crunchy. Add salt and pepper to taste toward the end of the cooking. Serve immediately.

Serve grated Parmesan at the table.

Cooking Rice

Rice is a food staple used across the world and is cooked using many different methods. This depends, among a variety of things, on the quality of the rice, the cultural and individual tastes, and the results one wants to achieve.

Northern Italians are known to be rice growers and consumers, but it comes as a surprise to most that rice has been part of Sicilian cuisine since the Arab conquest. The finest kind of rice used in Italy—sopraffino (very fine)—has a large grain and it is a must to use for a good risotto. It is commercially known as arborio. Under the proper cooking conditions, while keeping a firm consistency, it releases just the right amount of starch to create the desirable creaminess typical of risotto. I prefer to always use arborio, not only for risotti, but also for timbales and similar dishes, such as soups and puddings. There is also very good quality Japanese rice, similar in grade to the rice used by Italians for timbales, which can be substituted for arborio even to make risotto, when arborio is not available.

A lower grade of rice, smaller in size than arborio, while generally not found in the States, can be used for timbales and similar dishes. The lowest grade of rice (which I've never found in the States) has a very small grain which does not hold the cooking and is barely acceptable for soups and puddings. Its only redeeming quality is that it is very inexpensive.

There is yet another kind of rice Italians consume, comparable to American "converted" rice. It does not release starch, and the grains—properly cooked—stay firm and loose.

The techniques for cooking rice vary due to many factors. Consequently, as a general rule, the cooking time or the quantity of cooking liquid for the rice cannot be given. Keep in mind the following relevant factors: The recipe ingredients used along with the rice can affect its cooking; the time one has available (there are tricks to make the preparation of risotto less time-consuming; see risotto rapido); the quantity cooked (a large quantity of rice will cook differently than a small one); the kind of cooking vessel used (high side, low side, large, small, aluminum, stainless steel, thin, thick, etc.); the type of burner (electric, gas, large, small); even the way a person stirs can accelerate or slow down the cooking process and also the evaporation/absorption of the liquid. The age of rice will also affect the absorption of liquid. These are factors which somewhat influence the cooking of any dish, not just rice. In the case of rice, they become extremely important because of the nature of the ingredient, a tiny little grain which, once overcooked, is almost unretrievable. However, there is a rather simple way to make palatable a rice dish which has been overcooked or which is left over and stuck together: Use it to make a timbale! Keep this resourceful tip in mind before you throw your hands up in the air and your mushy rice in the garbage.

RISOTTO CON ZUCCA GIALLA

butternut squash risotto

serves 6

⅓ CUP OLIVE OIL

3 TO 4 TABLESPOONS (1½ TO 2 OUNCES) BUTTER — UNSALTED

3 POUNDS BUTTERNUT SQUASH — PEELED, SEEDS AND STRINGY PARTS REMOVED; DICED

1½ CUPS ITALIAN *ARBORIO* RICE — OR GOOD-QUALITY JAPANESE RICE

1½ TEASPOONS SALT

GRATED PARMESAN

Add the oil, the butter, and the squash to a heavy pot over medium heat, and stir for a few minutes.

Add enough water (hot) to barely cover the squash, bring to a boil, and simmer, covered, until soft, about 15 minutes.

Add the rice and salt. Stir, adding enough tap water to cover the rice well, and simmer, covered, adding more water as it gets absorbed by the rice. Continue to stir frequently until the rice is done—firm but not crunchy.

Serve immediately topped with Parmesan.

RISO AL VINO

rice in wine

serves 12

Once in a while a guest who does not know me very well brings me a bottle of white wine or champagne both very far from being dry. Even so, I don't let them go to waste. They are quickly used to make a wonderful first course, presented here. When serving, very little cheese should be added at the table, to savor the original taste of the dish.

I VERY LARGE ONION	CUT INTO VERY SMALL PIECES
2 STICKS (½ POUND) BUTTER	UNSALTED
2 TABLESPOONS OLIVE OIL	
5 CUPS CONVERTED RICE	
I½ TEASPOONS SALT	
8 CUPS WHITE WINE	DRY
½ CUP SHERRY	MEDIUM DRY
I CUP HEAVY CREAM	
½ CUP GRATED PARMESAN	

In a large heavy pot, over medium heat, cook the onion in the butter and the oil until aromatic. Stir in the rice unti it is well coated with the butter. Over high heat, add the salt and start adding the wine a cup at a time, stirring thoroughly and continuously, and cook until the liquid is absorbed. As the wine is absorbed, add more. Add the sherry last. Remove from the heat when the sherry is absorbed and stir in the cream and the cheese.

Serve immediately, making extra cheese available at the table.

NOTE: 8½ CUPS CHAMPAGNE (NOT TOO DRY) OR 8½ CUPS FRUITY (NOT DRY) WHITE WINE CAN BE SUBSTITUTED FOR THE WINE AND SHERRY COMBINATION.

RISOTTO DI VERDURE

vegetable risotto

serves 6 to 8

2 LARGE CARROTS	CUT INTO ⅓-INCH CUBES
1 HEART CELERY	USE ONLY THE WHITE CORE WITH LEAVES, CUT INTO ⅓-INCH CUBES
1 SMALL ONION	CUT INTO VERY SMALL PIECES
6 TABLESPOONS (3 OUNCES) BUTTER	(OR USE OLIVE OIL) UNSALTED
5 TABLESPOONS OLIVE OIL	
1½ CUPS ITALIAN *ARBORIO* RICE	OR GOOD-QUALITY JAPANESE RICE
20 ASPARAGUS TIPS	TENDER; CUT INTO ½-INCH SECTIONS
2 LARGE ARTICHOKES	TENDER; QUARTERED AND SLICED INTO WEDGES, A LITTLE THINNER THAN ¼ INCH THICK (SEE PAGE 212)
3 TO 4 CUPS BEEF STOCK	STRONG, CLEAR (SEE PAGE 72)
1½ TEASPOONS SALT	
½ CUP GRATED PARMESAN	
1 TEASPOON BLACK PEPPER	FINELY GROUND

In a very large heavy skillet over medium heat, cook the carrots, celery, and onion in the butter and oil, stirring until aromatic. Stir in the rice until it is well coated with the butter and oil. Add the asparagus, artichokes, 3 cups hot stock, and the salt. Stir, bring to a boil, cover, and simmer until rice is firm but not crunchy. Check the level of liquid often and stir well, scraping the bottom of the pan frequently. If the liquid dries out before rice is done, add small quantities of hot stock (¼ to ½ cup) or hot water and stir.

Mix in the cheese and the pepper. Serve immediately.

NOTE: STRING BEANS AND PEAS CAN BE SUBSTITUTED FOR THE ASPARAGUS AND ARTI-CHOKES. IF USING STRING BEANS, CUT THEM INTO ½-INCH SECTIONS.

RISO VERDE

green rice

serves 6 to 8

This dish can be served hot or at room temperature. For a stronger garlic taste, stir in an extra garlic clove, cut into very small pieces, before serving.

5 CLOVES GARLIC	CUT INTO THIN SLICES
½ CUP OLIVE OIL	
1⅔ CUPS CONVERTED RICE	
2½ POUNDS FRESH SPINACH	CUT INTO THIN STRIPS
½ TO 1 TEASPOON SALT	ADJUST TO ANCHOVIES' SALTINESS
3 TABLESPOONS CURRANTS	
¼ CUP PINE NUTS	
2 2-OUNCE CANS ANCHOVIES	FLAT FILLETS, PACKED IN OLIVE OIL; DRAINED WELL, MASHED

In a heavy large pot, cook the garlic in the oil over low heat until slightly aromatic. Stir in the rice until it is well coated with the oil. Add 1¼ cups hot water, the spinach, and salt. Stir over medium heat until the spinach is wilted.

Reduce the heat to low, cover, and cook until the rice is al dente, firm but not crunchy, about 10 minutes. While cooking, check the level of liquid every now and then. After the first 5 minutes, the spinach should have released enough moisture to cover itself and the rice. If not, it means that the heat needs adjusting—either it is too low to allow the spinach to release moisture, or it is too high, drying out too fast.

When the rice is al dente, add the currants and the pine nuts. Cook, uncovered, over high heat to dry out any excess liquid. Add the anchovies, adjust salt, mix well, and turn off heat.

Serve either hot or at room temperature.

ANELLO DI RISO

rice ring

serves 8 to 10

A few summers ago I ate the best *anello di riso* I've ever had at the summer home of some friends who live in the middle of a vineyard close to the coast of Sicily facing Africa. Tomatoes, eggplant, and basil were freshly picked from the vegetable garden behind the house. Their tastes were alive with the sun and with the richness of the soil. Without the rice, the tastes would have been overpowering.

1½ TO 1⅔ CUPS OLIVE OIL	PLUS ENOUGH FOR DEEP FRYING EGGPLANT
4 POUNDS FRESH TOMATOES	PEAR SHAPED, RIPE BUT FIRM; CUT INTO HALVES LENGTHWISE
4 POUNDS EGGPLANT	DO NOT PEEL; CUT INTO 1-INCH CUBES (TO PREPARE FOR FRYING, SEE PAGE 223)
2 TABLESPOONS BUTTER	UNSALTED
1 LARGE ONION	CUT INTO VERY SMALL PIECES
2¾ CUPS ITALIAN *ARBORIO* RICE	OR GOOD-QUALITY JAPANESE RICE
2 TEASPOONS SALT	
2 CUPS FRESH BASIL	LOOSELY PACKED LEAVES
3 CLOVES GARLIC	CUT INTO VERY SMALL PIECES
1 TEASPOON BLACK PEPPER	FINELY GROUND

Preheat the oven to 425° F.

Pour ¾ cup of oil in each of two baking dishes in which the tomatoes will fit in one layer, close together. Coat the tomatoes with the oil in the pans and arrange them cut-side up. Bake in the oven for 40 minutes. Check and lower heat if they start getting scorched. Set aside, keep warm.

Heat ¾-inch layer of oil in a skillet. Fry the eggplant in the oil over very high heat. Do not crowd the eggplant while frying, and do not stir. Turn the eggplant as necessary for even browning. When the cubes turn brown, remove with a slotted spoon and set aside. Do not blot out excess oil. Keep the oil level as close to ¾ inch as possible throughout frying. Once removed, keep the eggplant warm.

Bring 7½ cups water to a boil. Remove the tomatoes from the baking dishes, and add them to the eggplant. Set them aside.

Drain the oil from the baking dishes into a medium-sized pot, add the butter and onion, and cook over medium-low heat until aromatic. Add the rice and stir for about a minute, then stir in the boiling water and 1 teaspoon salt. Turn the heat to very low, cover, and cook until the rice is firm but creamy.

While cooking the rice, check several times, stirring well down to the bottom of the pot, as rice tends to stick to it. Add a little water if the rice gets too dry before it is done.

While the rice is cooking, blend in a food processor 1¾ cups basil leaves with very little olive oil (enough to make a thick paste), and mix it with the rice when it is done. Pack the mixture in a ring mold, and let it stand for about 10 minutes. Unmold onto a large serving plate (if rice unmolds unsuccessfully, shape it into a ring with slightly oiled hands).

Mix the eggplant and tomatoes with the garlic, pepper, and the remaining salt—or as much of it as suits your taste—and arrange around the rice ring. Top with the leftover basil leaves.

Serve immediately or at room temperature.

"GATTÒ" DI RISO

rice gâteaux

serves 6 to 8

The name *gattò*, Italian at first sight, is in fact a phonetical and semantical deformation of the French word *gâteaux*, used in Sicily to define a baked dish, in most cases, savory. Nevertheless, this dish is very Arabic in spirit and was incorporated into Sicilian cuisine during the Arab rule of the island.

5 CUPS STRONG CHICKEN STOCK	SEE PAGE 72
2½ CUPS CONVERTED RICE	
1 LARGE ONION	CUT INTO VERY SMALL PIECES
¾ CUP OLIVE OIL	
1½ POUNDS GROUND BEEF	VERY LEAN ROUND
¼ TEASPOON FENNEL SEED	
¼ TEASPOON GROUND CINNAMON	
1 TEASPOON BLACK PEPPER	
4 TABLESPOONS (¼ CUP) CURRANTS	
4 TABLESPOONS (¼ CUP) PINE NUTS	
8 OUNCES FROZEN PEAS	PARBOILED
1 TEASPOON SALT	
4 TABLESPOONS FLOUR	UNBLEACHED, ALL-PURPOSE
2 CUPS MILK	
5 EGG YOLKS	EXTRA-LARGE
BUTTER	UNSALTED, FOR COATING
BREAD CRUMBS	UNFLAVORED

In a large pot, bring the stock to a rolling boil. Add the rice, and cook, covered, on very low heat, until the stock is absorbed. Cool some.

Preheat oven to 375° F.

In a very large skillet, over medium heat, cook the onion in the oil, until aromatic. Turn the heat to high. Add the beef and brown it. To brown beef properly, do not stir. Turn the meat with a spatula only when it starts sizzling, after the meat is turned and starts sizzling again, break it up and stir.

Add the spices, the currants, the pine nuts, peas, and salt. Turn off heat.

In a bowl, dissolve the flour in a little milk. Add in the rest of the milk, stirring constantly, then add to the meat mixture. Cook over medium-low heat, stirring constantly, until thick. Cool some. Stir in the rice and the egg yolks.

Coat a 12-inch round pan, close to 3 inches deep, with butter. Dust with bread crumbs. Pack in the rice mixture, sprinkle the top with bread crumbs.

Bake in the oven for 40 minutes.

NOTE: VERY LEAN GROUND PORK CAN BE SUBSTITUTED FOR PART OF THE GROUND BEEF.

"SORTÙ" DI RISO

rice timbale

serves 10 to 12

Although the name of this dish is Neapolitan, the origin of the dish is Arabic, at least in this Sicilian version. You will need to prepare the *Risotto rapido* and the bechamel sauce in advance.

2½ POUNDS CHICKEN	(BREAST AND LEGS OF A FRYER) CUT BREAST IN HALF, SEPARATE DRUMSTICKS FROM THIGHS
1 TEASPOON SAFFRON	
1 RECIPE *RISOTTO RAPIDO*	(SEE PAGE 59) ALLOW TO COOL BEFORE USING
½ CUP GRATED PARMESAN	
1 EGG	EXTRA-LARGE
4 EGG YOLKS	EXTRA-LARGE
¼ POUND CHICKEN LIVERS	
1¼ CUPS OLIVE OIL	
½ POUND CARROTS	SLICED INTO VERY THIN ROUNDS
1 MEDIUM ONION	CUT INTO VERY SMALL PIECES
4 TABLESPOONS (2 OUNCES) BUTTER	UNSALTED
¾ POUND ASPARAGUS TIPS	CUT INTO ½-INCH SECTIONS
½ POUND DANISH HAM	CUT INTO VERY SMALL PIECES
½ POUND PROVOLONE	CUT INTO VERY SMALL CUBES
1 CUP BECHAMEL	SEE PAGE 48
½ CUP FRESH PARSLEY	LOOSELY PACKED LEAVES; CUT VERY SMALL
¼ CUP FRESH THYME	LOOSELY PACKED FRESH LEAVES, OR ½ TEASPOON DRY, GROUND LEAVES
2 TABLESPOONS FRESH ROSEMARY	LOOSELY PACKED LEAVES, OR ½ TEASPOON DRY LEAVES
¾ TEASPOON SALT	
1 TEASPOON BLACK PEPPER	FINELY GROUND
BREAD CRUMBS	UNFLAVORED, FOR COATING

Preheat the oven to 350° F.

Bake the chicken in the oven for 40 minutes. Leave oven on. Remove and discard skin, fat, and bones. Cut meat into small pieces and set aside.

With a rolling pin, crush the saffron to a powder between wax paper.

In a large bowl, mix the risotto with the saffron, Parmesan, 1 whole egg, and 1 egg yolk. Set aside.

In a large skillet over high heat, sear the chicken livers in ½ cup of oil. Cut into small pieces, set aside. Reserve the drippings.

In a different skillet, over low heat, cook the carrots and onion in ¾ cup of oil and 2 tablespoons butter until aromatic. Adjust heat to medium-low. Add the asparagus and cook until pleasantly crisp.

In a large bowl, mix the vegetables with the chicken, chicken livers, and their drippings, ham, the provolone, the remaining 3 egg yolks, the bechamel and the herbs, salt and pepper. Set aside.

Coat a round baking dish, approximately 10 inches in diameter, 4 inches deep, with butter and dust with bread crumbs. Coat the bottom and the sides of the dish with a little over two-thirds of the risotto, add the meat-vegetable mixture, and cover with the remaining risotto, sealing the edges well.

Dot the risotto top with the remaining 2 tablespoons butter. Bake in the oven for 1½ hours. Let it cool at least 20 minutes, before unmolding.

ARANCINE

little oranges

serves 12

Sicily is famous for its citrus fruit. The area around Palermo is still known as "*la conca d'oro*," the golden bowl, because it is intensely cultivated with orange trees. In recent years urban development has destroyed most of the groves. *Arancine*, little oranges, is a name which fits very well these stuffed rice balls, rounded like an orange and covered with a golden crust.

The flavor of the dish, the rice combined with the currants and the pine nuts, betrays its Arabic origin. It is a typical dish of Palermo, where it is one of the items served in the "*friggitorie,*" the "fast food" places of that city.

1 RECIPE *RISOTTO RAPIDO*	(SEE PAGE 59) OMIT MUSHROOMS
5 EGGS	EXTRA-LARGE, SEPARATE YOLKS FROM WHITES

½ POUND GRATED PARMESAN	
I LARGE ONION	CUT INTO VERY SMALL PIECES
3 CLOVES GARLIC	CUT INTO LARGE PIECES
2 RIBS CELERY	VERY TENDER; CUT INTO VERY SMALL PIECES
¾ CUP OLIVE OIL	
2 POUNDS BEEF ROUND	VERY LEAN; CUT INTO I-INCH SLICES
½ CUP WHITE WINE	DRY
I½ CANS (9 OUNCES) TOMATO PASTE	
I½ TEASPOONS SALT	
I TEASPOON BLACK PEPPER	FINELY GROUND
¼ POUND PEAS	FROZEN OR FRESH, PARBOILED
⅓ CUP CURRANTS	
⅓ CUP PINE NUTS	
BREAD CRUMBS	UNFLAVORED, FOR COATING
PEANUT OIL	(OR CORN OIL OR SIMILAR OIL) AS NEEDED FOR DEEP FRYING

Prepare *Risotto rapido.*

As soon as the *risotto* has cooled off some, mix in the egg yolks and the Parmesan. Spread on a wide dish and set aside.

In a very large skillet, over medium heat, cook the onion, garlic, and celery in the olive oil, until aromatic. Over very high heat, add and sear the beef. Add wine, let it evaporate about 30 seconds, then stir in the tomato paste and enough water to barely cover the meat. Add salt and pepper, cover, and simmer until the beef can be shredded with a fork—about 2½ hours, depending on the quality of the beef.

Shred the slices in the skillet, mix in the peas, currants, and pine nuts. The sauce should be very dry.

Shape the rice into 24 balls. Poke a large hollow space in each ball and fill it with the meat sauce. Pull some of the rice over the filling to seal it in.

Coat the stuffed rice balls with the reserved egg whites, smoothing them over their surface. Roll the balls in the bread crumbs, set aside without crowding. With your hands completely clean of egg white, pack each rice ball well, keeping your hands cupped.

Deep fry the rice balls in the peanut oil until golden, keeping the temperature between 300° and 350° F. Do not crowd and do not pierce the balls when turning. Turn only as necessary for even browning.

Set on paper towel to absorb the excess oil, keep warm.

Serve immediately.

MINESTRE
soups

CROSTINI

croutons

These croutons add character to many soups. Try serving them with *Brodo di Pesce* (see page 71), *Brodo di pollo o di Manzo* (see page 72), and *Minestra di Zucchine* (see page 72).

BREAD	AS NEEDED; USE VERY DENSE ITALIAN BREAD OR SEEDLESS RYE IN ½-INCH SLICES
BUTTER	(OR OLIVE OIL) AS NEEDED
BLACK PEPPER	FINELY GROUND; OPTIONAL

Preheat the oven to 350° F.

Coat both sides of bread with butter or oil. Cut into 1-inch squares. Bake on a cookie sheet in the oven until crunchy, about 10 to 15 minutes or longer. If desired, sprinkle black pepper on the bread.

A Word About My Soups

Please don't expect these soups to be delicate. They are hearty, substantial soups that, with a piece of good, thick bread, can be satisfying in themselves for simple lunches or suppers.

BRODO DI PESCE

fish stock

yields about 6 cups stock

¾ CUP OLIVE OIL	
I LARGE ONION	CUT INTO SMALL PIECES
4 LARGE RED SNAPPER CARCASSES	(ABOUT 5 POUNDS) HEAD INCLUDED
2 POUNDS BLACK SEA BASS	CLEANED AND SCALED, LEAVE WHOLE WITH HEAD AND TAIL ON
I POUND EEL*	CLEANED, LEAVE HEAD AND TAIL ON; CUT INTO THREE SECTIONS
I POUND SQUID	CLEANED (SEE PAGE 177), LEAVE HOOD AND TENTACLES WHOLE
2 POUNDS PARSNIPS	PEELED
8 LARGE TOMATOES	CANNED AND PEELED; SEEDED, CUT INTO SMALL PIECES
I CUP PARSLEY	LOOSELY PACKED LEAVES
3 LARGE CLOVES GARLIC	CUT INTO SMALL PIECES
2 TEASPOONS SALT	
I TO 2 TEASPOONS BLACK PEPPER	FINELY GROUND

Cover the bottom of a stock pot with the oil. Add the onion and cook until aromatic. Add remaining ingredients—with the exception of the pepper—and enough water to barely cover.

Bring to a boil, cover, and simmer for 1½ hours. Add pepper to taste. Strain the stock, reserving the edible parts of the fish as well as the squid and the parsnips. Do not overlook the cheeks and nape of the red snappers' heads; it's the finest flesh.

Cut squid body into ½-inch rings, separate the tentacles, but do not take apart one by one. Leave in groups of a few tentacles each.

Cut the parsnips into small pieces.

Serve the stock with the solid ingredients along with *Crostini* (see page 70).

The stock can also be used to moisten *Cuscus alla mandorla* (see page 97); and the solid ingredients can also be added to enrich the *cuscus*.

To use as a pasta sauce, reduce the stock to 3 cups—with or without the addition of the solid ingredients (with the exception of the parsnips). It will make enough to dress 1 pound of spaghetti, and to serve 6 to 8 people.

---

* EEL MAY BE REPLACED BY ONE MORE POUND OF THE FISH CALLED FOR OR ONE EXTRA POUND OF SQUID.

BRODO DI POLLO O DI MANZO

chicken or beef stock

yields 8 to 10 cups

4 POUNDS CHICKEN *OR* 3 POUNDS BEEF BRISKET	CUT INTO LARGE PIECES
2 VERY LARGE PARSNIPS	
2 VERY LARGE CARROTS	
1 LARGE YELLOW ONION	CUT INTO LARGE PIECES
6 SPRIGS FRESH PARSLEY	

Place all the ingredients in large pot, add 12 cups of water or more to cover the ingredients.

Bring to a boil, skim sediment from surface, cover and simmer at least 1 hour if using chicken, 2 if using brisket.

Strain, chill, and remove and discard the hardened fat. If you are in a hurry and have no time to chill the stock, you can remove the fat by placing a paper towel flat on the surface of the stock. The fat, which floats to the surface, will be absorbed by the paper towels.

This process will yield a light stock. The meat and vegetables can also be used. Try eating them with *Salsa alla menta di Maria Angelica* (see page 108), *Salsa alle noci* (see page 108), and *Salsa al dragoncello* (see page 107).

If you want a strong, clear stock, once the meat and vegetables are removed, allow the liquid to simmer, uncovered, until reduced to 5 to 6 cups. If you want a strong, heavy stock, cook the stock (with meat and vegetables in it) longer: 2 to 3 hours for chicken, up to 4 hours for beef. Reduce stock to 6 to 8 cups, letting it simmer, uncovered, in the last hour of cooking.

MINESTRA DI ZUCCHINE

squash soup

serves 6

2 POUNDS SUMMER SQUASH	DO NOT PEEL OR REMOVE ENDS
1 CUP ALMONDS	BLANCHED; FINELY GROUND
3 TABLESPOONS GRATED	
PARMESAN	
1 TEASPOON GROUND CINNAMON	
1½ TABLESPOONS SUGAR	
½ TEASPOON SALT	
3 CUPS MILK	OR HALF-AND-HALF

Bring a large pot of water to a rolling boil, add the squash, then bring the water back to boil as fast as possible. Boil the squash, uncovered, for 10 minutes. Drain, remove the ends, cut the squash into chunks, and cool.

Puree all the ingredients except the milk in a food processor, using the steel blade. Chill. Before serving, stir in the milk.

Serve with *Crostini* (see page 70).

JOTHA

cabbage and potato soup

serves 8

Traditionally this recipe is made with *crauti* (Italian for sauerkraut). I prefer to use fresh cabbage and add a little vinegar for tartness.

2 STRIPS BACON	CUT INTO VERY SMALL PIECES
5 TABLESPOONS (2½ OUNCES) BUTTER	UNSALTED
1 LARGE ONION	CUT INTO VERY SMALL PIECES
1 TABLESPOON FLOUR	UNBLEACHED, ALL-PURPOSE
2 TO 3 CUPS CHICKEN OR BEEF STOCK	(SEE PAGE 72) OR USE GOOD-QUALITY BOUILLON CUBES
1 POUND CABBAGE	CUT INTO THIN STRIPS
1½ POUNDS POTATOES	PEELED; CUT INTO ⅓-INCH CUBES
2 LARGE CARROTS	CUT INTO ⅓-INCH CUBES
⅓ CUP APPLE CIDER VINEGAR	
1½ TEASPOONS SALT	
½ POUND DITALINI	OR 1½ CUPS ITALIAN *ARBORIO* RICE (OR GOOD-QUALITY JAPANESE RICE)

In a large pot, cook the bacon and butter over low heat until the bacon looks transparent. Add the onion and cook until aromatic. Stir in the flour until it darkens a little. Slowly stir in 2 cups stock. Add the cabbage, potatoes, carrots, vinegar, salt, and enough of the remaining stock to barely cover.

Cover and cook over very low heat for 2½ hours. During the last hour of cooking check the soup often, and stir down to the bottom of the pot to prevent scorching. Add small amounts of stock—or water if there is no stock left—to keep the ingredients barely covered with liquid.

Cook the pasta (see page 31). Add to the vegetables and serve immediately. If using rice, cook it in 6 cups of well salted water until al dente, drain, and mix with the vegetables.

Always reserve some of the water drained from the pasta or the rice: if the soup is too thick, add some of the water to loosen it. However, this soup is supposed to be thick enough to be able to eat it with a fork.

MINESTRA DI PATATE DI MARIA
maria's potato soup

serves 8 to 10

¾ CUP OLIVE OIL	
1 VERY LARGE ONION	CUT INTO VERY SMALL PIECES
4 POUNDS POTATOES	PEELED; CUT INTO SMALL CUBES
10 OUNCES MORTADELLA	THICKLY SLICED, CUT INTO VERY SMALL CUBES
6 SMALL RED CHILI PEPPERS	WHOLE, DRY
1 TEASPOON SALT	
2 CUPS CHICKEN STOCK	(SEE PAGE 72) OR USE GOOD-QUALITY BOUILLON CUBES (OPTIONAL)
½ POUND DITALINI OR SPAGHETTI	COMMERCIAL; IF USING SPAGHETTI, CRUSH INTO SMALL SECTIONS
DENSE ITALIAN BREAD	OPTIONAL
GRATED PARMESAN	

Cover the bottom of a large pot with the oil, add the onion, and cook until aromatic.

Add all the other ingredients and enough hot water or stock to cover. Simmer until the potatoes are done.

Cook the pasta (see page 31).

Combine the pasta and soup and let stand 10 minutes before serving.

Soup may be served without pasta, with slices of dense bread on the side.

Serve grated cheese on the side.

MINESTRA DI ERBE E PATATE
herb and potato soup

serves 8 to 10

3 POUNDS POTATOES	(ALLOW EXTRA FOR WASTE) PEELED; CUT INTO ½-INCH CUBES
1 LARGE ONION	MINUTELY CUT
2 CLOVES GARLIC	CUT INTO VERY SMALL PIECES
A HANDFUL FRESH MINT	FINELY CUT
A HANDFUL FRESH BASIL	FINELY CUT
A SMALL SPRIG FRESH ROSEMARY	FINELY CUT
10 LEAVES FRESH SAGE	FINELY CUT
2 TO 3 TEASPOONS SALT	
3 TABLESPOONS (1½ OUNCES) BUTTER	UNSALTED

¾ POUND DITALINI OR SHELLS	COMMERCIAL
½ POUND SHARP PROVOLA	WELL AGED, IMPORTED; CUT INTO VERY
	SMALL CUBES
BLACK PEPPER, TO TASTE	FINELY GROUND

In a large pot, place the potatoes, onion, garlic, and herbs. Cover with plenty of water. Add the salt and butter, bring to a boil, reduce heat to medium low, cover, and cook until the potatoes are al dente, stirring periodically.

Uncover, increase the heat to high, and add the pasta. Stir well, adjust the heat so that soup cooks just under a rolling boil. Remove from the heat as soon as the pasta is al dente, and dip the pot in a container with water and ice. Stir in the cheese, and add pepper to taste. Serve immediately.

NOTE: IF THERE IS VERY LITTLE LIQUID AFTER YOU ADD THE PASTA, ADD ENOUGH HOT WATER TO BARELY COVER THE PASTA AND POTATOES.

FAVE A "CUNIGGHIO"

rabbit fava beans

serves 6

"*Cunigghio*" is the Sicilian dialect word for rabbit. When you eat the fava beans in this recipe, they pop out of their skins as fast as a rabbit darts to and from his burrow, hence the recipe name.

Favas are supposed to be eaten one by one, and the skins discarded. Sicilians manage to do so without the help of their fingers. The soup is served with a dense Italian bread, which gets broken into little morsels and is used to soak up the liquids.

4½ CUPS VERY LARGE FAVA BEANS	STILL GREEN, SHELLED (4 TO 5 POUNDS
	UNSHELLED), SEE PAGE 230
3 CLOVES GARLIC	LARGE
¼ CUP OLIVE OIL	
¾ TEASPOON SALT	
½ TEASPOON BLACK PEPPER	FINELY GROUND
DENSE ITALIAN BREAD	

Remove the eyes from the fava beans, by removing the skin from the very top part of the bean, where there is an indentation.

In a large pot, cover the beans with water. Add garlic, oil, salt, and pepper, bring to a boil, and simmer, covered, for about 40 minutes or until the beans inside the skins are very tender. Remove from the heat. Serve in bowls with some dense Italian bread (like a sour dough bread) on the side.

This dish can also be served with *Fette dorate* (see page 76).

MINESTRA DI CECI ED AGLIO

chick-pea and garlic soup

serves 8

1 POUND CHICK-PEAS	SORTED AND RINSED
2½ TEASPOONS SALT	
20 CLOVES GARLIC	THINLY SLICED
2 LARGE CELERY HEARTS	LARGE LEAVES INCLUDED; RIBS CUT INTO VERY SMALL CUBES
4 BAY LEAVES	
1 CUP OLIVE OIL	
½ TEASPOON BLACK PEPPER	
1 TEASPOON CELERY SEED	
GRATED CHEESE	
FETTE DORATE	RECIPE FOLLOWS

Soak the chick-peas in plenty of water for 24 hours, changing the water and rinsing well at least twice, while soaking.

In a large pot, cook the chick-peas in 14 cups of water and 2 teaspoons salt for 2½ hours at a low boil, covered, leaving the lid slightly ajar.

Add the garlic, celery, bay leaves, oil, and pepper, bring to a boil, cover, and simmer for 30 more minutes. Add the celery seed.

The soup is supposed to be very thick. If there is still a lot of liquid, cook the soup, uncovered, at a medium boil until the liquid is reduced and the soup thickened. Taste, adjust salt, and serve hot.

Grated sharp cheese can be served on the side, along with *Fette dorate*.

FETTE DORATE

golden bread slices

serves 1

OLIVE OIL	
4 SLICES BREAD	SOUR DOUGH BAGUETTE, OR BAGUETTE OF VERY DENSE CONSISTENCY; ½ INCH THICK

Optional

SALT	
BLACK PEPPER	FINELY GROUND

Preheat the oven to 350° F.

Pour a very thin layer of oil on a flat plate and rub both sides of the bread slices in it. Sprinkle with salt and pepper, if desired.

Place the slices on an oil-coated cookie sheet and bake, 5 minutes per side or until light brown.

MINESTRA DI FAVE E ZUCCA

fava beans and squash soup

serves 10

To remove the skin from each individual fava bean is a very tedious task—maybe this is why nobody seems to cook this *minestra* anymore. But the texture and the taste of this soup are so wonderful, that I find it well worth the time.

¾ TO 1 CUP OLIVE OIL	
1 MEDIUM YELLOW ONION	CUT INTO SMALL PIECES
¾ POUND FENNEL	
3 CUPS FAVA BEANS	(3 TO 4 POUNDS UNSHELLED) SHELLED; SKINS REMOVED (SEE PAGE 230)
1¾ POUNDS BUTTERNUT SQUASH	PEELED, SEEDS AND STRINGY PART REMOVED; CUT INTO ½-INCH CUBES (SEE PAGE 225)
¾ TO 1 TEASPOON SALT	
½ TEASPOON BLACK PEPPER	FINELY GROUND
6 OUNCES DITALINI OR SHELLS	COMMERCIAL
GRATED CHEESE	

In a medium pan, heat the oil, add the fennel and the onion, stirring over medium-high heat, until aromatic. Add the fava beans, squash, salt, and pepper. Barely cover with water, bring to a boil, cover, and simmer until tender, about 1 hour. The fava beans will become very mushy and some will disintegrate, thickening the liquid.

Cook the pasta (see page 31), drain, and mix with the vegetables.

Serve the soup with some grated caciocavallo or Parmesan on the side.

MINESTRA DI CECI E CARDONI

chick-pea and cardoon soup

serves 8 to 10

1 POUND CHICK-PEAS	SORTED AND RINSED
2½ TEASPOONS SALT	OR TO TASTE
2 LARGE ONIONS	CUT INTO VERY SMALL PIECES
1 CUP OLIVE OIL	
2 LARGE HEADS CARDOONS*	TENDER (OR 6 FRESH ARTICHOKES; SEE PAGE 212)
1½ POUNDS BEET GREENS	CUT INTO SMALL PIECES
15 LARGE TOMATOES	CANNED AND PEELED; SEEDED, CUT INTO SMALL PIECES
6 SMALL RED CHILI PEPPERS	WHOLE, DRY

Soak the chick-peas in plenty of water for 24 hours, changing the water and rinsing well at least twice, while soaking.

In a large pot, cook the chick-peas in 14 cups of water and 2 tablespoons of salt for 2½ hours at a low boil, covered, leaving the lid slightly ajar. The chick-peas should be soft, but not mushy.

In a skillet, sauté the onion in ½ cup of the oil until aromatic, and add it to the chick-peas with the remaining ingredients, except the remaining ½ cup oil.

Bring to a boil and simmer 30 more minutes. The soup should be fairly thick. If there is too much liquid, cook uncovered at high heat for the last 10 minutes.

Taste, adjust salt, if necessary, stir in the remaining oil. Serve hot.

If desired, serve with *Fette dorate* (see page 76).

* CARDOONS ARE VERY DIFFICULT TO FIND. YOU MAY SUBSTITUTE ARTICHOKES FOR THEM. IF YOU ARE LUCKY ENOUGH TO FIND CARDOONS, DISCARD THE OUTER TOUGH LEAF STALKS. PARBOIL, THEN CUT STALKS INTO ½-INCH SECTIONS. TO READ MORE ABOUT CARDOONS, SEE PAGE 197.

MINESTRA DI CECI E ASPARAGI

chick-pea and asparagus soup

serves 8 to 10

I POUND CHICK-PEAS	SORTED AND RINSED
I POUND PARSNIPS	CUT INTO VERY SMALL PIECES
¾ TO I CUP OLIVE OIL	
2½ TEASPOONS SALT	
2 POUNDS ASPARAGUS TIPS	CUT, EXCEPT FOR THE VERY TIP END, INTO THIN ROUNDS

Soak the chick-peas for 24 hours in plenty of water, changing the water and rinsing well at least twice, while soaking.

In a large pot, cook the parsnips very slowly in the oil, until they start browning. Add the drained chick-peas, the salt and 12 cups of water, bring to a boil, reduce heat, and simmer until tender, covered, about 2½ hours, leaving the lid slightly ajar.

Add the asparagus, increase the heat to high, and boil, uncovered, about 5 minutes, or just enough for the asparagus to be pleasantly crisp. If the level of liquid is too low to barely cover the vegetables, add some hot water. The soup should be very dense.

If desired, serve with *Fette dorate* (see page 76).

MINESTRA DI FINE INVERNO

end of the winter soup

serves 10

This soup is made at the end of the cold weather months, using the last of any dry beans and winter greens; with spring, soups will change character and will be made with fresh legumes and spring vegetables.

1½ POUNDS LEGUMES	ANY COMBINATION OF LENTILS, PINTO BEANS, WHITE BEANS, AND FAVA BEANS (BEANS MUST ALL BE DRY, NOT FRESH)
¾ CUP OLIVE OIL	
1 MEDIUM ONION	CUT INTO SMALL PIECES
4 SMALL BUNCHES KALE	(OR USE COLLARD GREENS OR A COMBINATION OF THE TWO) DISCARD THE TOUGH OUTER LEAVES; CUT INTO VERY SMALL PIECES
1 MEDIUM HEAD ESCAROLE	CUT INTO SMALL PIECES
1 SMALL BUTTERNUT SQUASH	PEELED, SEEDS AND STRINGY PART REMOVED; DICED VERY SMALL
1 TABLESPOON SALT	
BLACK PEPPER, TO TASTE	FINELY GROUND
TWO FISTFULS RICE	CONVERTED, ITALIAN *ARBORIO*, OR GOOD-QUALITY JAPANESE

Soak whatever combination of beans you have in water, overnight, changing the water and rinsing well at least twice, while soaking. Make sure the water level is way above the beans. Fava beans, available in Greek stores, should be without the skins: not all fava beans need soaking over night. To test, cook a few in plenty of water, and see if they get soft (the consistency of well-done potatoes), within 45 minutes. If they do not, soak them before using them. Lentils need no soaking.

Put the oil in a large heavy pot, add the onions, and cook over low to medium heat until aromatic. Add the remaining ingredients except the rice and enough water to rise no more than 2 inches above the vegetables. Bring to a boil, cover, and simmer. As soon as the water gets absorbed, add some more, in small amounts at a time—just enough to keep the level of the water slightly above the vegetables.

When the beans are tender, after about 1 to 2 hours, add the rice. Serve as soon as the rice is al dente.

GNOCCHI, ET CETERA

gnocchi and other first courses

GNOCCHETTI DI SPINACI E PISELLI

spinach and pea gnocchi

serves 6

10 OUNCES PEAS	FROZEN OR FRESH; PARBOILED, DRAINED
1 POUND SPINACH	FRESH OR FROZEN; CUT LEAF, PARBOILED, SQUEEZED UNTIL IT CAN BE PACKED INTO ¾ CUP
½ CUP GRATED Parmesan	
¼ TEASPOON GROUND NUTMEG	
¼ TEASPOON GROUND CORIANDER	
¼ TEASPOON SALT	
¼ TEASPOON BLACK PEPPER	FINELY GROUND
1 EGG	EXTRA-LARGE
2 EGG YOLKS	EXTRA-LARGE
1 POUND RICOTTA CHEESE	DRAINED WELL; PATTED WITH LAYERS OF PAPER TOWEL OR CLOTH UNTIL MOISTURE IS ABSORBED
2 CUPS BREAD CRUMBS	(OR MORE) UNFLAVORED
Flour	UNBLEACHED, ALL-PURPOSE; FOR COATING
10 CUPS LIGHT CHICKEN OR BEEF STOCK	SEE PAGE 72
Olive oil	

Serving Suggestions

6 TO 8 TABLESPOONS (3 TO 4 OUNCES) BUTTER	UNSALTED
1½ RECIPES *Salsa di pomodoro passata*	SEE PAGE 39
1 CUP GRATED Parmesan	OR TO TASTE

> ranno con parmeggiano, o butiro, essendo cotti in
> brodo di carne, o di polli, sarà meglio. Se poi fa-
> ranno cuocere in brodo di sostanza chiarificato, si
> appresteranno brodosi senza niente altro.
>
> *Gnocchetti, di spinaci, e piselli.*
>
> Bolliti gli spinaci, e i piselli freschi si pestano con
> pan grattato, ricotta, parmeggiano, ed aromi, e se
> ne fa una pasta ligata con uova. e formatine i gnoc-
> chi, si fanno cuocere in buon brodo, e si pongono
> con parmeggiano, e butiro o pure infarinati, e in-
> dorati si friggono involti prima in pan grattato.
>
> *Granata di animelle.*
>
> *Bardata* di lardo la *cassarola* vi si mette un so-
> lajo di carne di *annecchia* o di vitella, sottilmente
> tagliata, e battuta col coltello facendo che anzi un
> buon dito intorno al giro della *cassarola.* Poi vi si
> mettono in giro per lungo, braciolette della stessa
> carne con fette di pastenache tra l'una e l'altra bra-

In a pan, over medium-high heat, stir the peas very briefly until dry. Let them cool.

Puree the spinach, peas, the Parmesan, nutmeg, coriander, salt, and pepper in a food processor.

In a bowl, using a spoon or a whisk, blend the egg and yolks with the ricotta, then mix in 1½ cups bread crumbs.

Combine the ricotta mixture and the spinach mixture using a spoon or a whisk. Between the palms of your hands, lightly roll a small amount of the mixture into a cherry-sized ball. If the mixture is too sticky and soft to roll, add a small amount of bread crumbs, and test again. Stop adding the bread crumbs as soon as you are able to form a soft but not sticky ball, if handled lightly.

To form *gnocchetti,* roll all the mixture into cherry-sized balls, or olive-shape ones. Set balls aside on a lightly floured cookie sheet. Do not crowd.

In a large pot, bring the stock to a rolling boil, slide in ¼ of the *gnocchetti* and let the stock return to a boil. *Gnocchetti* will surface in about a minute from the time they are added to the stock. Once they surface, let them cook 2 minutes, remove with a slotted spoon, set aside in a dish lightly coated with olive oil or butter, and keep warm. Repeat until all the *gnocchetti* are cooked.

Gnocchetti can be served in one of the following ways:

Place the *gnocchetti* in a soup tureen, add the stock in which they were cooked, and serve, making grated Parmesan available at the table.

Melt the butter, toss with the *gnocchetti,* then sprinkle about 1 cup, to taste, of Parmesan on top. Serve or warm in a preheated 375° F. oven for about 10 minutes.

Place the *gnocchetti* in a dish coated with olive oil, add the *Salsa di pomodoro passata* and about 1 cup, to taste, of Parmesan. Serve or warm in a preheated 375° F. oven, for about 10 minutes.

GNOCCHI DI SPINACI E PISELLI FRITTI

fried spinach and pea gnocchi

serves 6

This gnocchi can also be served as a side dish, to accompany meats, with no toppings.

10 OUNCES PEAS	FROZEN OR FRESH; PARBOILED, DRAINED WELL
1 POUND SPINACH	FRESH OR FROZEN, CUT LEAF; PARBOILED, SQUEEZED UNTIL IT CAN BE PACKED INTO ¾ CUP
½ CUP GRATED PARMESAN	
¼ TEASPOON GROUND NUTMEG	
¼ TEASPOON GROUND CORIANDER	
¼ TEASPOON SALT	
¼ TEASPOON BLACK PEPPER	FINELY GROUND
5 EGGS	EXTRA-LARGE; SEPARATED
1 POUND RICOTTA	DRAINED WELL; PATTED WITH LAYERS OF PAPER TOWEL OR CLOTH UNTIL MOISTURE IS ABSORBED
4 CUPS BREAD CRUMBS	(YOU MAY NEED TO USE MORE) UNFLAVORED
FLOUR	UNBLEACHED, ALL-PURPOSE; FOR COATING
CORN OIL	AS NEEDED FOR DEEP FRYING (ABOUT 2 INCHES DEEP IN FRYER)
1½ RECIPES *SALSA DI POMODORO PASSATA*	SEE PAGE 39
GRATED PARMESAN	

In a pan, over medium-high heat, stir the peas briefly until dry. Let them cool.

Puree spinach, peas, Parmesan, nutmeg, coriander, salt, and pepper in a food processor.

In a large bowl, using a spoon or a whisk, blend 1 whole egg and 2 yolks with the ricotta, then mix in 1½ cups bread crumbs.

Combine the ricotta mixture and the spinach mixture using a spoon or a whisk. Between the palms of your hands, lightly roll a small amount of the mixture into a cherry-sized ball. If the mixture is too sticky and soft to roll, add a small amount of bread crumbs, and test again. Stop adding the bread crumbs as soon as you are able to form a soft but not sticky ball, if handled lightly.

To form the gnocchi, shape the mixture into walnut-sized balls, then flatten them, and coat them with flour. In a bowl, lightly beat together 2 whole eggs and 2 egg whites. Dip the gnocchi in the eggs, then coat them with bread crumbs. Set aside on a surface sprinkled with bread crumbs.

Heat as much oil as necessary to deep fry and fry gnocchi over high heat until they have a light brown crust. Set on paper towels or a rack to drain; keep warm.

Serve topped with tomato sauce. Make grated Parmesan available at the table.

PIZZARONI

semolina dumplings

serves 4

yields 16 2-inch dumplings

I found this recipe among Nonna Severina's recipes; since my mother did not recall this dish, we can assume it hasn't been made in a very long time.

½ POUND PROVOLA	MILD; CUT INTO VERY SMALL CUBES
¼ TEASPOON GROUND CORIANDER	
½ TEASPOON BLACK PEPPER	FINELY GROUND
1 POUND SEMOLINA FLOUR	
¾ TEASPOON SALT	
½ CUP GRATED PARMESAN	
OLIVE OIL	FOR COATING
8 SMALL ANCHOVY FILLETS	PACKED IN OLIVE OIL, DRAINED; CUT IN HALF
1 OUNCE PECORINO ROMANO	CUT INTO 16 SMALL CUBES
2 EGGS	EXTRA-LARGE; BEATEN BRIEFLY WITH A FORK
BREAD CRUMBS	UNFLAVORED; FOR COATING
CORN OIL	ENOUGH TO DEEP FRY

In a bowl, mix the provola, coriander, and pepper. Set aside.

In a large pot, bring 4 cups of water to a boil. With the heat on medium-low, pour in the semolina in an even stream, stirring constantly and energetically, until it is the consistency of a rough mash, about 5 minutes. Remove from the heat, add the salt and Parmesan, and work with a potato masher for a few minutes. As soon as it is cool enough to handle, knead it until fairly smooth.

Coat a smooth surface (preferably marble) with olive oil, and pat the mixture down in a thick square. Keep your hands coated with olive oil, or they will stick to the mash.

With a rolling pin coated with olive oil, roll into a larger square, approximately 16 by 16 inches. Cut it into four equal squares, and further cut each section in four squares, resulting in sixteen semolina dough squares.

Place half an anchovy and a cube of pecorino Romano in the middle of each square. Divide the provola mixture among the squares, placed in the middle. Bring the corners of the squares up and over the filling, to meet in a point. Press the edges together to seal, press—keeping the pointy shape—the corners, smoothing the dough.

Coat the dumplings with the beaten eggs and smooth the surface further, packing the dumplings with cupped hands. Coat with bread crumbs.

In a deep fryer heat enough corn oil to submerge the dumplings. When the oil reaches the smoking point reduce the heat to medium-high, and add some of the *Pizzaroni*. Do not crowd. Fry them in small batches for about 1½ minutes or until golden. Faster or slower cooking will affect the dumplings; adjust the heat as needed.

Serve hot.

A Lunch of Gattò in the Sicilian Countryside

In a past summer, I visited a family of Sicilian farmers who still consider eating meat a luxury but who have plenty of cheese and vegetables available. For our meal, they suggested the *Gattò di patate e spinaci* as a filling, nourishing dish. It is a one-dish meal that they serve along with a tomato-onion-and-olive salad doused with plenty of olive oil, oregano, salt, and pepper.

In their country home, air-conditioned rooms, screened-in porches, and manicured lawns couldn't seem more remote: We ate lunch sitting on benches placed along the side of a long, unfinished wood table. A clay tile-covered shelter—an extension of the house roof—gave an illusion of coolness. One was lulled by the mixture of sounds and smells. Some sounds were very distant—trucks on the highway, loudspeakers of an itinerant vendor. Some were closer—the buzzing of a cloud of insects flying in a circle, the hooves of mules unevenly hitting the stone paving of the back road. Meanwhile the far-reaching smell of the stable mingled with the smell of the wood-burning oven.

While we were eating, I looked at the faces around the table. I could see in the eyes of the older people the resigned consciousness of being the last of a breed, and an impossible wish to exist without the influence of the outside world. They saw my sadness, and I saw their embarrassment at my having sensed their feelings. Pulling out my notebook and jotting down the *gattò* recipe helped everybody to relax and get accustomed to the idea that we had all become intimate in just a few hours. Some people pushed a bench to the wall, and with our backs leaning against it, we started an unharried conversation. I was questioned about the United States: Did I like living there, did we have fresh vegetables, did people eat pasta, did people eat only canned food? I tried to describe what the everyday life and diet of an average family is. I knew I wasn't believed when I told them about the abundance of fresh produce, and I knew they were skeptical about my assurance that pasta was very popular.

An old man noticed I was staring outside the shelter: He lifted his arm and made a large circular gesture that seemed to cover the entire horizon. "Do you have *this?*" he asked. "No, we do not, this is why I come back," I answered. He nodded, satisfied, and retired, followed by most of the people. I stayed on the bench: Some dogs lay around, stretched out on the tile pavement. The sun poured heat over the fields, over the patient stillness of the Sicilian countryside. The only noises now to be heard were the screech of the cicadas and the rustle of the dried grass as lizards scurried through it.

I parted from them at sundown. Before going away I felt I owed these people something. "Americans eat pasta . . . out of cans," I whispered to the woman who had given me the *gattò* recipe. Her laugh was immediate and high: "Pasta out of cans, pasta out of cans!" As she repeated what I had told her to the others, more laughs rang out. That was what they wanted to hear and what they wanted to remember—not that Americans had fresh vegetables, various kinds of pasta, and big cars. They wanted to know something that put Americans in perspective—that made them human, a little crazy, and much worse off than Sicilian farmers when it came to food. Canned pasta did it. With the promise I'd bring them a sample of canned pasta on my next trip, I left.

Hurray for *gattòs* and down with Spaghetti Os!

GATTÒ DI PATATE E SPINACI

potato and spinach gâteaux

serves 6 to 8

4 POUNDS SMALL BAKING POTATOES	ALLOW EXTRA FOR WASTE
3 EGGS	EXTRA-LARGE
10 TABLESPOONS GRATED PARMESAN	
2 TABLESPOONS BUTTER	UNSALTED; MELTED (PLUS MORE FOR COATING)
2 TEASPOONS SALT	
3 POUNDS SPINACH	FRESH OR FROZEN, CUT LEAF; PARBOILED
1 RECIPE BECHAMEL	SEE PAGE 48
4 OUNCES MOZZARELLA	DICED VERY SMALL
¼ POUND SALAMI	OR USE DANISH HAM; CUT INTO VERY SMALL PIECES
6 OUNCES EMMENTALER	DICED VERY SMALL
1 TEASPOON BLACK PEPPER	FINELY GROUND
BREAD CRUMBS	UNFLAVORED; FOR DUSTING
OLIVE OIL	FOR COATING

Preheat the oven to 375° F.

Boil, peel, and mash the potatoes.

In a bowl, mix the mashed potatoes with the eggs, 8 tablespoons of Parmesan, 2 tablespoons melted butter, and the salt. Set aside.

Cut the spinach into small pieces and mix it with the bechamel, 2 tablespoons Parmesan, the mozzarella, the emmentaler, the salami, and the pepper.

Coat a baking dish, approximately 7 by 12 by 2½ inches deep, with butter. Dust with bread crumbs.

Coat your hands with oil and line the pan with the potato mixture, shaping it into flat patties between your hands. Reserve about one third of the mixture.

Fill the pan with the spinach mixture. Cover with the reserved potato mixture, sealing the edges well with your fingers, then smooth the top. Bake in the oven for 45 minutes. Serve hot.

Signora Laura's Strudels

Some potato recipes, such as *Strudel di patate* (below) come from Trieste, following the love trail from Trieste to Palermo of "Signora Laura," a "triestina," who found the charm of a Sicilian railroad worker irresistible, followed him to Sicily and married him. "Signora Laura" does the cooking for a friend's family; she is the prototype of the cook, her rotund shape exuding tranquillity and competence. She gave me her recipes modestly, puzzled and flattered at the same time that I'd be interested in them. Her strudel recipe betrays the closeness of her town to Austria.

STRUDEL DI PATATE

potato strudel

serves 12

1½ POUNDS SMALL BAKING POTATOES	ALLOW EXTRA FOR WASTE
5 TABLESPOONS BUTTER	UNSALTED
1 CUP PARSLEY	LOOSELY PACKED LEAVES
½ CUP GRATED PECORINO ROMANO	OR OTHER PECORINO SUCH AS SARDO, OR OTHER SHARP CHEESE
¾ CUP GRATED PARMESAN	
2 EGGS	EXTRA-LARGE
3 EGG YOLKS	EXTRA-LARGE
¾ TEASPOON SALT	
½ TEASPOON BLACK PEPPER	FINELY GROUND
PASTA SFOGLIA DEL DUCA	SEE PAGE 318

Preheat the oven to 350° F.

Boil, peel, and mash potatoes.

Blend together the butter and parsley in a food processor, using the steel blade. Combine in a large bowl, with the mashed potatoes, the cheeses, the whole eggs, 2 egg yolks, salt, and pepper. Refrigerate, until cool.

Roll out the puff pastry on heavy duty foil into two approximately 14 inch squares.

In a large bowl, beat the potato mixture with a hand mixer or whisk, until soft. Spread it on each puff pastry square, leaving ½-inch margin on all edges. Pick up one side of the foil, lift, and move it forward forming the strudel roll. Repeat.

Lay the two rolls on a cookie sheet. Pierce them all the way through with a thin skewer at frequent intervals. Brush top with the remaining egg yolk. Bake in the oven for 20 minutes. Reduce the heat to 325° F. and bake 1 hour longer.

Serve immediately or at room temperature.

SFOGLIATA DI ZUCCHINE

zucchini in layers of pastry

serves 12

Pastry
¾ POUND FLOUR   (ABOUT 3 CUPS) UNBLEACHED, ALL-PURPOSE
5 TABLESPOONS OLIVE OIL
¾ CUP WARM WATER

Filling
2½ POUNDS ZUCCHINI   (ABOUT 6 TO 7 SLENDER AND DARK GREEN)
                        UNPEELED, SLICED ⅓ INCH THICK
OLIVE OIL   AS NEEDED
2 POUNDS RICOTTA   REMOVE MOISTURE BY PATTING WITH PAPER TOWEL
1 CUP GRATED PARMESAN
1 TEASPOON SALT
½ TEASPOON BLACK PEPPER   FINELY GROUND
3 EGGS   EXTRA-LARGE

To make the pastry: Beat the flour and the oil with wire beater in a Kitchen Aid or similar countertop mixer. When roughly mixed, change to hook beater. Add the water, except for 2 tablespoons and knead. The dough is ready when it is soft, but not sticky. If not soft, add the remaining water and beat until absorbed.

Set the dough, gathered into a ball, on a floured surface, preferably wood. Cover it with a thick bowl heated up, and then several layers of cloth (to preserve heat). Let it rest 30 minutes.

To make the filling: In a skillet, heat a 1-inch layer of oil until smoke is barely visible. Over high heat fry the zucchini, uncovered, in several batches, until light brown. Set the fried zucchini on wire rack, or on a tilted pan to drain excess oil.

In a large bowl, beat the ricotta, Parmesan, salt, and pepper until well mixed. Blend in the eggs without overbeating. Gently mix in the zucchini by hand.

To assemble the sfogliata: Divide the pastry in eight equal pieces. Roll each one on lightly floured cheesecloth into a 10- by 14-inch rectangle, to fit a deep baking dish the same size (it could be a different shape, but the same area and volume). After you roll the dough, lay each piece on a floured surface and cover it to prevent it from drying.

Preheat the oven to 375° F. Coat the baking dish with olive oil. Roll one layer of dough around a rolling pin, keeping it loose. Unroll it over the baking dish, from one end to the other. Sprinkle 1 tablespoon of oil over the dough layer and spread the oil by gently patting your open hands over the dough. Repeat process with two more layers of dough.

On top of the three stacked layers, distribute half the filling. Cover with two layers of dough, spreading oil on each, then place the remaining half of the filling and the remaining three layers of dough on top, spreading oil on each as before.

Bake in the oven for 40 minutes. Reduce heat to 350° F. and bake for 20 more minutes. Serve hot.

This dish can be made a couple of days in advance and reheated in a 250° F. oven, until the top dough layer is crisp.

TORTA PROVENZALE

provençale pie

serves 6 to 8

This is a recipe from a family notebook passed on to me by a lady from Sciacca.

PRIMI
PIATTI

•

91

Crust

12 TABLESPOONS (6 OUNCES) BUTTER	UNSALTED, CHILLED
¾ POUND FLOUR	(ABOUT 3 CUPS) UNBLEACHED, ALL-PURPOSE
3 OUNCES COLD WATER	

Filling

1 CUP MILK	
3 EGGS	EXTRA-LARGE
2 TABLESPOONS (1 OUNCE) BUTTER	UNSALTED; MELTED
1 TEASPOON SALT	
1 TEASPOON BLACK PEPPER	FINELY GROUND
5 FRESH ARTICHOKES	LARGE AND TENDER (SEE PAGE 212)

Preheat oven to 325° F.

To make the crust: In a bowl, cut the butter into the flour, until the mixture resembles fine grains. Toss in the water. Handle mixture lightly, just enough to gather it into a ball. Set aside, keep cool, and covered until ready to use it.

To make filling: In a bowl, blend the milk, eggs, butter, salt, and pepper with a fork, a whisk, or a hand beater. Do not overbeat.

Parboil artichokes, then quarter them and cut into ¼-inch thin wedges.

Mix the artichokes with the milk, egg, and butter mixture.

Roll out a little less than two-thirds of the crust and line a baking dish, approximately 7 by 11 by 2 inches deep. Put in filling and cover with the remaining crust, sealing the edges well. Flute the edges and punch holes on the top crust in a pattern.

Bake in the oven for 1 hour and 15 minutes. Let the pie rest 15 minutes before serving.

IMPANATA DI VERDURE

vegetable-filled pizza

serves 16

Dough

1 POUND SMALL BAKING POTATOES	ALLOW EXTRA FOR WASTE
2 POUNDS FLOUR	(ABOUT 6⅔ CUPS) UNBLEACHED, ALL-PURPOSE
1 TABLESPOON SUGAR	
1½ TEASPOON SALT	
2½ TABLESPOONS GRANULAR YEAST	
5 TABLESPOONS OLIVE OIL	

Filling

1¼ CUPS OLIVE OIL	
1 LARGE ONION	CUT INTO VERY SMALL PIECES
½ POUND BLACK OLIVES	SICILIAN OR GREEK; PITS REMOVED, CUT COARSELY
1¼ POUNDS BROCCOLI	(NET WEIGHT) NO HARD STEMS; PARBOIL; STEMS SLICED INTO THIN ROUNDS
1 POUND ASPARAGUS TIPS	PARBOIL; CUT INTO ½-INCH SECTIONS
1¾ POUNDS GREEN AND RED BELL PEPPERS	STEMS AND SEEDS REMOVED; CUT INTO ⅓-INCH WIDE STRIPS
2 POUNDS ZUCCHINI	CUT INTO ⅓-INCH ROUNDS
4 LARGE LEEKS*	
1 CELERY	USE THE TENDER CORE; CUT INTO VERY SMALL PIECES
2 TABLESPOONS TOMATO PASTE	
2 TEASPOONS SALT	OR LESS
½ TEASPOON BLACK PEPPER	FINELY GROUND
1 CUP RAISINS	

Preheat the oven to 375° F.

To make dough: Boil, peel, and mash the potatoes.

In a bowl, combine the flour, sugar, and salt. Dissolve the yeast in ½ cup warm water, then add to the dry ingredients along with the mashed potatoes, and the 5 tablespoons oil. Add enough tap water, about 1⅛ cups, to make a soft but not sticky dough. Knead until very smooth. Place in a ceramic bowl, cover, and set the bowl aside in a warm place. The dough will be ready to use when it has doubled in size. To

---

* TO CLEAN LEEKS, CUT OFF GREEN PART. CUT DOWN TO THE ROOT, NOT THROUGH IT, CROSSWISE. SWISH IN WATER UNTIL DIRT IS WASHED OFF. CUT THROUGH ROOT END.

handle the dough, coat your hands with oil.

To make filling: Divide 1¼ cups olive oil between two large skillets. Divide the onion between them and cook until aromatic. Add equal amounts of olives and vegetables to each skillet. Stir over high heat until pleasantly crisp. Stir 1 tablespoon tomato paste into each skillet. Divide the salt, pepper, and raisins between the skillets, cook a couple of minutes. The vegetable mixture should be fairly dry. Turn off heat.

Coat two baking dishes, approximately 10 inches in diameter, 3 inches deep, with oil. Divide the dough between the two dishes, stretching it so that enough will overhang the sides to cover, once filled. Coat the dough on the bottom of the pan with oil. Fill each with the vegetable mixture. Bring the overhanging dough over the filling and press it together to seal it where it joins. Brush the top with oil.

Bake in the oven for 45 minutes or longer, until the top is light golden. Serve hot. This dish is also pleasant at room temperature.

SFORMATO DI PANE

bread pudding

serves 6

This recipe makes good use of stale bread and is an effortless first course.

BUTTER	UNSALTED; FOR COATING
4 EGGS	EXTRA-LARGE
⅓ CUP MILK	
⅛ TEASPOON BLACK PEPPER	FINELY GROUND
12 TO 14 SLICES FRENCH BREAD	OR USE ITALIAN BREAD, OR VERY DENSE, GOOD-QUALITY, SANDWICH BREAD SLICED A LITTLE OVER ½ INCH THICK (ENOUGH SLICES OF IT TO TIGHTLY FIT TWO LAYERS IN AN 8-INCH DIAMETER BAKING DISH)
¾ POUND MOZZARELLA	CUT INTO THIN SLICES
¼ POUND EMMENTALER	CUT INTO THIN SLICES
⅛ TO ½ POUND DANISH HAM	SLICED VERY THIN

Preheat the oven to 350° F.

Coat an 8-inch diameter baking dish well with butter.

In a large bowl, combine the eggs, milk, and pepper. Briefly beat with a fork. Dip the bread slices in the egg mixture until well soaked. Arrange half of the slices in a layer on the bottom of the pan.

Cover the bread with half of the mozzarella and half of the emmentaler, all the ham, then the remaining cheese. Arrange the remaining bread on top in a layer; if any egg is left, pour it on top of the bread.

Bake in the oven for 40 minutes. Serve hot.

MIGLIACCIO DOLCE

sweet migliaccio

serves 6

This is a recipe from the Duke's cookbook as is the one that follows. It surprised me to discover that cornmeal (polenta) was used (and in a sophisticated way) by the Sicilian lovers of good food of the past. I had thought polenta had been introduced to the cuisine much more recently.

Besides being served as a first course, serve this dish as a side dish with meat dishes such as roast beef, pork, fowl, sausage, or game.

½ POUND POLENTA	(ABOUT 1⅔ CUPS) ITALIAN-STYLE CORNMEAL; REGULAR OR INSTANT
1½ TEASPOONS SALT	
3 TABLESPOONS (1½ OUNCES) BUTTER	UNSALTED
2 TABLESPOONS SUGAR	
1 POUND RICOTTA	DRAINED OF ANY LIQUID; DO *NOT* PAT DRY WITH PAPER TOWELS
⅓ CUP GRATED PECORINO ROMANO	OR SARDO OR A SIMILAR SHARP CHEESE
3 EGGS	EXTRA-LARGE

If you use instant polenta, follow the instructions on the box, and add the salt.

If you use regular polenta, bring 3½ cups of water and the salt in a large saucepan over low heat to a boil. Add the polenta in a thin, steady stream, stirring constantly with a whisk. Cook the polenta for 40 minutes, uncovered, while stirring. However, such a small amount of polenta, if cooked in a very heavy pot, can be cooked on low heat, covered by a lid (slightly ajar) and stirring well only occasionally.

As soon as the polenta is done, stir into it 2 tablespoons of the butter and the sugar. Mix in the ricotta and the pecorino. Add the eggs last, blending without overbeating, with a wooden spoon or using a mixer.

Preheat the oven to 375° F.

Coat an 8-inch soufflé dish with some of the leftover butter. Spoon the polenta mixture in, shaping the top in a low mound. Dot the top with whatever butter is left.

Bake in oven for 35 to 40 minutes, or until the top is slightly hard and specked with dark brown spots.

Serve hot.

MIGLIACCIO BRUSCO

savory migliaccio

serves 6

½ POUND POLENTA	(ABOUT 1⅔ CUPS) ITALIAN-STYLE CORNMEAL; REGULAR OR INSTANT
1½ TEASPOONS SALT	
3 TABLESPOONS BUTTER	UNSALTED
1 POUND RICOTTA	DRAINED OF ANY LIQUID, DO NOT PAT DRY WITH PAPER TOWELS
⅓ CUP GRATED PECORINO ROMANO	OR SARDO OR A SIMILAR SHARP CHEESE
3 EGGS	EXTRA-LARGE
½ POUND SAUSAGE	FRESH, MILD
1 TEASPOON BLACK PEPPER	FINELY GROUND
¼ TEASPOON FENNEL SEED	OMIT IF USING SAUSAGE CONTAINING FENNEL SEED

Cook the polenta as above. Add the butter, cheeses, and eggs.

Pierce the sausage in many spots. Place in a large pot, cover with water, and bring to a boil. Simmer, covered, for 20 minutes. Discard the water, remove the casing, and break the sausage into very small pieces.

Preheat the oven to 375° F.

In a skillet, cook sausage, covered, over very low heat, until lightly brown. Stir to prevent it from getting scorched.

Mix the sausage, pepper, and fennel seed with the polenta mixture. Bake in the oven for 35 to 40 minutes or until the top is slightly hard and speckled with dark spots.

Serve hot.

Preparing Cuscus in Erice

As I've said, much of Sicilian food and many eating habits bear the mark of the Arabs, helping to differentiate Sicilian cuisine from cuisines of the other regions of Italy. *Cuscus* (couscous), with fish stock or with vegetables, is the most obvious Arabic inheritance we have, and is a typical dish of the extreme west point of Sicily, which includes the town of Erice.

From my childhood, I remember that one form of entertainment Erice offered was to stroll through its narrow streets and to glance through the arched doors—at times left open—which led into the inner courtyards shared by groups of houses. They were all fastidiously kept. White polished stone made up the paving and the outdoor stairs that led to the dwellings. Some of the courtyards were architecturally more intriguing than others, luxuriant with fuchsias, begonias, and maiden hair fern.

In the summer the courtyard was the workplace for the women, the play space for the children, and it also served as an outdoor living room. In each one there was a well. One would see women plunging buckets in it and pulling out water, which often, bucket after bucket, was used to fill the *"pila"*: the outdoor tub for washing clothes, carved from one huge piece of stone. Once in a while one could see the women preparing *cuscus* on a makeshift table where several vessels were lined up. Small quantities of semolina were taken from one, then placed in a peculiarly shaped rustic ceramic container called a *"mafaradda,"* where the lightly dampened flour was transformed by rotating motions of the women's fingers into the *cuscus* grains. The grains were spread on a cloth, more flour was added to the *"mafaradda,"* and the process was repeated, industriously and mindfully. The *cuscus* was then sifted to select the right size grains—those barely larger than a pinhead. The larger grains were used as "pastina" (that is, small pasta), cooked in stock or simply topped with a trickle of olive oil and a sprinkle of grated cheese.

The *cuscus,* placed in a rustic ceramic colander-like container called a *"cuscusera,"* was then steamed over boiling liquid (mainly fish stock). The *"cuscusera"* and the pot containing the stock were sealed together with a roll of dough. The grains were finally mixed with some stock, then wrapped with cloth layers and allowed to absorb the stock's flavor and to plump up for a while.

I have beaten the odds here (in the U.S.) and have made *cuscus* with an improvised *"mafaradda"* and with semolina too finely ground to be suitable. Instead of dampening my fingers, I have sprayed water on the flour with an atomizer; to my surprise I have managed to produce a very fine-grain *cuscus,* which is to store-bought *cuscus* what freshly made pasta is to boxed pasta. But it is not something I would do often, and I do not expect that much dedication from anybody.

CUSCUS ALLA MANDORLA

couscous with almonds

serves 6

2 CUPS COUSCOUS	COMMERCIAL (SEE PAGE 123)
6 TABLESPOONS OLIVE OIL	
1 TO 2 TEASPOONS BLACK PEPPER	FINELY GROUND
1 BAY LEAF	OPTIONAL
1 TO 2 CUPS CHICKEN, BEEF, OR FISH STOCK	CLEAR, STRONG (SEE PAGES 72 AND 71)

¾ CUP (4 OUNCES) BLANCHED ALMONDS

SALT, TO TASTE

In a heavy medium bowl, mix the couscous with the oil and the pepper. Add the bay leaf, if desired.

Bring the 2 cups stock to a rolling boil, stir 1 cup into the couscous, cover with a lid, wrap with a thick cloth, or a few layers of kitchen towels, and set aside. Keep the remaining stock hot.

After 5 to 10 minutes check the couscous. If it is unpleasantly crunchy and tastes raw, stir in a little more stock, cover, and wrap as before. Check again after 5 minutes, adding more stock if it is still too crunchy and raw tasting. Add stock until the couscous grains are very firm but pleasant to chew. Be very conservative adding the stock; just a little too much can turn the couscous into mush.

Grind the almonds until they are as coarse as the couscous grain being used. Toss the couscous with the almonds, then cover as before.

Let stand 15 to 30 minutes in a warm place before serving. Add salt as needed.

T W O

SECONDI PIATTI

second courses

CARNI

meats

PESCI

fish

UOVA

egg dishes

1985

Remembering is the only way I can bring back to life things and people long gone. But returning to Palermo, my "home" town, I see that a lot of the past is still alive.

When in Palermo, it is a must for me to visit the Capo, the market I went to as a child. Strolling along Via Volturno, from the back of the Opera House (a sure tourist stop) and leaving the sea behind, one comes upon the Porta Carini, which is just before the Court House and the main entrance to the section of the city called "Capo." The Capo encompasses the street market, the object of my visit.

MIMMETTA
LO MONTE'S
CLASSIC
SICILIAN
COOKBOOK

•

100

Until twenty years ago, going to the Capo would have provided an extra bonus: watching a storyteller perform. The storyteller's spot was between Porta Carini and a line of *carrozzelle,* the typical horse-drawn carriages of Palermo, which, at the time, were a very common and popular means of public transportation. One can still see an occasional *carrozella* there, with a resigned-looking horse hitched to it, head down, waiting patiently for a fare. The horse stands almost motionless except for a wiggle of the ears, a flap of the tail, or a contraction of muscles to get rid of a fly, causing the carriage to roll very slowly a few inches forward, a few backward—just enough to make the dozing coachman open his eyes.

The storyteller stood on a stage built of wooden crates arranged side by side, and also piled up one on top of the other. A colorful canvas busily painted with vignettes hung as a backdrop, suspended from perches and wires. The storyteller, looking straight at the crowd gathered in front of his makeshift stage, propped one foot up on a crate, swung his head back, put his chin up, and brandished a long, slender stick. He resembled a general summoning his soldiers, ready to illustrate his battle plans.

His voice gave life to the naive paintings of the backdrop, which his stick, lashing over his shoulder, would hit forcefully, scene after scene. His voice sounded like the strings of a bass viol plucked by strong fingers, wobbling and shaking with indignation, passion and sorrow.

The dramas he told were centuries-old folk stories as well as current news reported by papers. The components were the same for each story: love, betrayal, and vengeance, skillfully romanticized by his performance. An old favorite was "La baronessa di Carini": the sad story of a young noblewoman slain by her father when he finds out about a love affair she has had.

The adventures of the bandit Salvatore Giuliano ("Turi" to us Sicilians), were something else that, no matter how many times repeated, caught the crowd's attention, causing many mouths to drop and many hearts to beat faster as our bold hero was betrayed and gunned down. Given the vast array of crimes that have plagued Sicily for centuries, the storyteller never ran out of subjects.

The storyteller's audience consisted of shoppers who flowed in and out of the market and invariably stopped and listened to the tales, even if only for a few minutes. Storytelling is a dying art, like many others. Having survived through wars and revolutions, preserved through centuries, it is seemingly unable to survive the century we live in—not for lack of aficionados, but for lack of artists to carry on the unique function of the storyteller.

The storyteller was the anchorman of the people of the streets and squares of Sicilian cities—the animator of real life soap operas. When he left, he took his tales with him.

I am glad I have been able to experience and enjoy the last sparks of this tradition of the past. I am told that small-town fairs still see a storyteller appear on occasion, but he is no longer a permanent feature, and his isolated performance is of little impact. My daughter, still under twenty, and other people her age, may never be part of a crowd gathered before the stage of crates to hear the storyteller's account of the lives and misfortunes of rich and poor.

A playful photo: Great-uncle Peppino plays the role of the donkey and is being handed a feeder by a friend of the family. Nonno Alfredo is standing at the other end of the cart. Grandmother Severino is in the photo as well. The children are my mother, aunts, uncles, and their cousins.

Sicilians, pressured by new "necessities" imposed by a consumer-oriented society in the name of progress, have been forced to change and to deprive themselves of some of their heritage. They have obtained materialistic comforts but have lost individual skills that tied them with the riches of many converging cultures. So now they get the news from a TV screen—information that I doubt is much more accurate, and certainly much less entertaining, than the storytellers' sagas.

But at times, unwilling to give up altogether the expressions of a past they love, Sicilians have come to compromise, as in the case of workers and street vendors who have adopted motorized vehicles in place of horse-drawn carts. These new vehicles, however (be they large trucks, or small three-wheelers), have been decorated in the same fashion as the traditional wooden carts. The bodies are painted with scenes from the "Carlo Magno" knight's folk stories. Ribbons and pompoms are attached to the rearview mirrors, rather than, as formerly, to horses' and donkeys' ears. Strings and bells festoon the metal hoods instead of manes. In Palermo, you will see a square, fringed flag bearing the image of Santa Rosalia (the patroness of the city) prominently displayed on vehicles' dashboards—better insurance against evil and accidents than any insurance company can provide.

The setting of the storyteller of Palermo I used to watch is fortunately unchanged, years and years after his disappearance. Right across from what was once his stage of wooden crates, there are still the same counters and carts, extensions of the narrow streets of the "Capo" market that spill onto the main street.

Displayed today are the same treats people snacked on while listening to and watching the storyteller's show: prickly pears and slices of watermelon, when in season; boiled ears, feet, and muzzles of pig and veal; boiled octopus; *fave "caliate"* (roasted fava beans); *"cubbaita"* (sesame seed and honey candy)—a whole battery of delicacies appreciated almost exclusively by Sicilians.

Take a few steps past those counters and carts and you are swallowed by the crowd of the market. The intensity of the human activity, the sounds, the smells, and the colors are overpowering. At night, incredibly bright lights suspended over the marble-topped tables are turned on, swinging under red and green awnings and adding a dazzling effect to the sense of drunkenness the market projects.

Whole swordfish and tuna, the huge bodies glistening, lie on the cool slabs of marble. The water used to cool the fish runs down and gathers into puddles on the polished stone paving. Constant squirts of water zip out of spouts on pans, filled with salt cod. Dogs, their bellies flat on the ground, sneak under butchers' counters and run off with discarded bones and pieces of fat. Snails creep out of huge baskets covered with burlap. They are small and white, an affordable delicacy.

Often an item on the festive table of Sicilians, the little snails, called *"babbaluci,"* are first put through a period of purge (to cleanse the digestive tract), then cooked with oil, garlic and parsley, or in a very light fresh tomato sauce. *Babbaluci* eating is almost a sport. The snails get sucked out of their shells or pulled out with the teeth, the most stubborn fished out with toothpicks.

Shoppers appraise the merchandise thoughtfully before making their choice. The exchange of money and goods happens rapidly, and shopping bags (sadly now made of plastic) are filled quickly. Only yesterday the *"coppo,"* a cornucopia rolled in a few seconds from very heavy paper or newspaper, was the only container offered in which to pack food.

Voices bounce back and forth, using dialect more forceful than Italian: *"Che frisca sta sarda"* (How fresh these sardines), *"Avi u sapuri du mari"* (It has the taste of the sea), fishmongers scream, pointing at sardines in a rainbow of greens and blues. *"Chi ssu belli sti pira, sunnu sanzeri, bianchi e duci comu li cosci d'una picciotta schietta"* (How beautiful these pears, they are smooth and solid, white and sweet, like the thighs of an unmarried girl) is the improvised lyric of a man selling fruit, along with *"Ceusa, ceusa, manciativilli, ca v'arrifriscanu"* (Eat mulberries, they'll cool you off). The huge mulberries, up to three inches long, blood-red, full of juice and slightly tart, are a delightful way to quench your thirst.

Butchers selling milk-fed veal assure ladies that it will melt in the mouth: *"Signora, si squagghia m'ucca,"* and fishmongers, to prove how alive their octopus is, slap it, causing an immediate reaction of contracting tentacles and suction cups: *"Taliassi che vivo, taliassi che vivo."*

Vendors can be gallant even when their merchandise gets put down by shoppers. Once, after I expressed doubt about the freshness of some fish, I was answered, *"Bedda di facci, ma nivura di cori"* (Beautiful face, but black-hearted).

Promises go with the merchandise. Vendors entice buyers with theatrical gestures, decorating their storefronts and counters, as well as their food, with seaweed, garlands,

MIMMETTA
LO MONTE'S
CLASSIC
SICILIAN
COOKBOOK

•

102

and bunches of evergreens and herbs; with price tags composed in careful collages of curlicued numbers and borders; with flowers and pompoms of colorful tissue paper.

In the shadows of the back of the stores, overseeing all this rukus, are photographs in oval frames of some tight-lipped man, father or grandfather, founder of the business, with a little light burning in front of the photographs. Very close by stands a peaceful-looking Saint Joseph. With his own little light, or even a whole series of little lights circling each frame, the saint holds a lily and Baby Jesus, whose chubby hand is in a graceful blessing posture.

Vendors emphasize the nature of what they sell, and the nature of butchered meat is blood, muscle, bone, and guts. There is no inhibition about, nor hypocrisy in, displaying the meat, and no habitual shopper is put off by the view. A Sicilian would be more ill at ease when dealing with a steak packaged in plastic than by watching a butcher take apart a beef hind and carve out the desired part.

Butchers hack, slice, grind, sharpen their knives, wrap and weigh, replenish their display. Trembling masses of liver lie on the counters. Slits along the bodies of kids and lambs are kept open with bamboo slivers, inserted across the flaps of the stomach opening, the guts spilling out of them. Tripe, roughly scrubbed and boiled, hangs with its folds and layers of beehived flesh, undulating at any vibration. Yards-long links of sausage tied in sections with raffia cascade from hooks, shining in their plumpness. Specks of pepper and grains of fennel seed mixed with the pink-and-white of the ground pork show through the casings.

In contrast with the violent sight of the butcher shops are the vegetable and fruit stands. Shelves are arranged in a terraced fashion, lined with red and green tissue paper and foil, overhanging with cutouts to form a light lace. Fruit and vegetables are arranged in an apotheosis of shapes and colors—a hymn to nature. Yellow, red, and green bell peppers give way to purple eggplants. Orange-pink *nespole* (loquats) are flanked by apricots flushed with red and by blood oranges, some cut in half, to show their russet pulp. The merchandise changes with the seasons, but its array never fails to stimulate the shopper.

"Panari" (baskets handwoven from twigs) hold merchandise that either won't fit on the shelves or is very precious. Figs fill some of the medium-size *"panari"* carefully lined with leaves from the same fig tree. Tubular-shaped *"panareddi"* (very small baskets) are filled with strawberries, true red, and as small as the tip of a child's finger.

Pale-green squash, two to four feet long, curl and stretch out of huge baskets called *"gerle."* Squash flowers in a delicate combination of soft orange and green are laid on shallow, wide *"panari."* The vendors never cease to praise their produce. Their eyes and their hands seem to fly from merchandise to the scales to the shoppers to the money, their fingers as quick as a magician's.

In every open market of Palermo there is at least one fast-food vendor. It is fast food the Sicilian way, hot and freshly cooked, and it is the only source of true Sicilian cuisine the visitor can draw from, unless a private home can be "tapped." Restaurants, for the most part, offer a questionable version of Sicilian dishes. And, surprisingly, the most expensive restaurants can only offer good continental-style cuisine.

The fast-food places, called *friggitorie* or *"panellari,"* offer no frills. You stand on the street while the sales counter breeches the opening of the establishment, making an insurmountable division between customers and the grottolike kitchen, originally white-tiled, now blackened by decades of smoke from fryers. Cauliflower and cardoons are dipped in batter and deep-fried. Baby fish and squid are deep-fried as well, their flour coating turning into a light golden crust.

Deboned sardines filled with a savory stuffing of bread crumbs, pine nuts, and currants are flavored with bay leaves, lemon juice, and orange juice, then prettily arranged in tight rolls in pans, neatly lined up, the tail fins sticking out. Croquettes of mashed potatoes and parsley, chick-pea-flour cakes, *"panelle"* and whole eggplants slit in large juliennes at one end and held together at the other, are fried. Like almost all of the fare offered, these foods are stuffed into soft, thin-crusted bread, and sold as fast as they come out of the boiling oil. A large dish filled with sea salt is within easy reach. You dip your fingers in and season the food to your liking.

As the market branches out into the side streets, its activity tapers off. Shops change from food establishments to artisans' workshops. The noise is left behind, and I am confronted by the almost deserted streets of old Palermo. The transition from the highly individualistic and vocal expression of the market to the still eloquence of the "Aspra" stone, articulated in different-styled buildings—Baroque, the distinctive Sicilian "Chiaramontano," and Norman—happens almost unnoticeably

I can find no excuse for the decay in the old section of Palermo. Every so often I read the words "horror" and "slum" associated with this part of Palermo in articles and travel books. It saddens me. The harsh judgment shows a cultural and emotional bias that discounts the architectural beauty of many buildings, beaten by time, war, and abandonment, but still there to manifest itself through graceful arches, exquisitely sculpted capitols, cornices, and consoles.

Sea monsters, medusas and shells, carved in stone and marble, fountains once kept alive with water, appear at the crossings of the narrow streets of the baroque city, or lean against crumbling palatial walls. Small round-bellied balconies cast shadows on the facades of their intricate ironwork. Peeking through cracks of old massive doors, one discovers elegant courtyards and majestic stair ramps that often climb up to a roofless dwelling. As scarred as it is, at least the old city heart is still there. Other parts of the city, such as the Art Nouveau district, have been completely destroyed, as have the citrus groves that once encircled Palermo.

MIMMETTA
LO MONTE'S
CLASSIC
SICILIAN
COOKBOOK

•

104

A Word About Second Courses

Second courses are dishes predominantly based on protein. The type of protein most commonly eaten changes according to one's social class and the environment. In the cities, for example, second courses are comprised mainly of beef, veal, and fish. To a smaller extent they include the usual fare of farms and villages; eggs, cheese, small game, lambs and kids.

A common Sicilian principle (not to be applied only to the upper class) is to eat protein sparingly, using vegetables and bread as flavor balancers and enhancers, as well as fillers. Consequently, the choice of a second course should be made by taking into consideration the vegetable one is going to serve it with. Some second courses are combined with enough vegetables not to need one as a side dish. Bread, however, is always served.

Between the first course and dessert, a second course should be eaten in moderation, without fulfilling the desire for food to the last degree: desserts are made for that!

The recipes here include old and new dishes, the traditional ones and the unusual ones as their sources have been. As in the past, they meet the taste and the need of different people and different occasions.

SECONDI
PIATTI

•

CARNI
meats

MIMMETTA
LO MONTE'S
CLASSIC
SICILIAN
COOKBOOK

•

106

BOLLITO

boiled meat

serves 6

There is no waste in Sicilian cooking. When stock is needed, a second course is born by using the meat cooked in the stock. With the addition of delicious and simple-to-make sauces, *Bollito* (Boiled Meat), served hot, is a very cozy dish in the winter. Served cold, it's a refreshing summer dish.

Prepare Beef Stock (see page 72). When the stock has simmered for at least 2 hours, remove the meat from the stock, along with the parsnips and carrots. Save the stock for other recipes. Slice the meat and arrange with vegetables on a platter.

SALSA AL DRAGONCELLO

tarragon sauce

yields about 1 ½ cups

This is a wonderful sauce to serve with roasted or boiled meats, such as *Bollito* (above), *Arrosto nell'olio* (see page 110), *Arrosto imbottito* (see page 111), and *Gallotta ripiena* (see page 147).

I CUP CHICKEN OR BEEF STOCK	STRONG, CLEAR (SEE PAGE 72) OR USE GOOD-QUALITY BOUILLON CUBES, DOUBLE-STRENGTH
½ POUND BREAD	VERY DENSE SANDWICH BREAD, WHITE OR SEEDLESS RYE; CRUSTS REMOVED
3 SPRIGS FRESH TARRAGON	STEMS REMOVED, OR I½ TEASPOONS DRY
8 FULL SPRIGS FRESH PARSLEY	STEMS REMOVED
4 TO 5 LARGE CLOVES GARLIC	
½ CUP RED WINE VINEGAR	
2 TABLESPOONS SHERRY	GOOD QUALITY, DRY
½ TO I TEASPOON BLACK PEPPER, TO TASTE	FINELY GROUND
SALT, TO TASTE	
I½ TEASPOONS SUGAR	OPTIONAL

Puree ½ cup stock, the bread, tarragon, parsley, garlic, vinegar, sherry, and pepper in a food processor. If sauce is too thick, add enough of the remaining stock to get a creamy but not runny consistency. Salt to taste. Add sugar, if desired.

SALSA ALLE NOCI

walnut sauce

yields about 1½ to 2 cups

Serve this simple, refreshing sauce with roasted or boiled meats, such as *Arrosto nell'olio* (see page 110) and *Arrosto inbottito* (see page 111).

I CUP WALNUTS	
4 TABLESPOONS CAPERS	PRESERVED IN VINEGAR; SQUEEZE OUT VINEGAR AND DISCARD IT
15 SMALL ANCHOVY FILLETS	(2 OUNCE CAN) PACKED IN OLIVE OIL; DRAINED WELL
¾ CUP CHICKEN STOCK	STRONG, CLEAR (SEE PAGE 72) OR USE WHITE WINE

Optional

¼ CUP LIGHT TUNA	PACKED IN OIL; DRAINED WELL

Process the walnuts, capers, anchovies, and tuna, if using, in a food processor with ½ cup of stock until grainy. Add as much liquid as necessary to get a creamy but not runny consistency.

MIMMETTA
LO MONTE'S
CLASSIC
SICILIAN
COOKBOOK

•

108

SALSA ALLA MENTA DI MARIA ANGELICA

maria angelica's mint sauce

yields about 1½ cups

Reading some of Maria Angelica's notes (she was my grandfather Alfredo's sister), I came across this recipe for mint sauce, in which she calls for *due soldi* (two pennies) of French bread. French bread was eaten by "I signori," the well-to-do people. It was delicate golden and crunchy, with a substantial white interior.

When I used white bread in this sauce, it yields a rather slimy result. Consequently, I use seedless rye bread instead, which is ironically similar to the very coarse dark bricklike bread the peasants ate.

3 SLICES BREAD	SEEDLESS RYE; CRUSTS REMOVED
I LARGE CLOVE GARLIC	
½ CUP FRESH MINT	LOOSELY PACKED LEAVES
½ CUP FRESH PARSLEY	LOOSELY PACKED LEAVES
¼ CUP RED WINE VINEGAR	
2 TEASPOONS SUGAR	
½ CUP OLIVE OIL	
I TEASPOON SALT	

Puree the ingredients in a food processor or blender.

Serve this sauce with fish and roasted or boiled meats such as *Bollito* (see page 106), *Arrosto nell' olio* (see page 110), and *Arrosto imbottito* (see page 111).

ARROSTO IN CASSERUOLA RAPIDO

quick pot roast

serves 6

3½ POUNDS BEEF	BONELESS RIB EYE OR NEW YORK STRIP OR USE ROUND OR EYE OF THE ROUND—WHICH WILL BE TOUGHER BUT VERY TASTY
2¼ CUPS RED WINE	DRY; PLUS 2 TABLESPOONS FOR DEGLAZING
¼ CUP SWEET MARSALA	(OR PORT) PLUS 2 TABLESPOONS FOR DEGLAZING
4 BAY LEAVES	
1 TEASPOON BLACK PEPPER	FINELY GROUND
¼ CUP OLIVE OIL	
½ TEASPOON SALT	

Marinate the beef in the wine, bay leaves, and pepper for 3 hours. Place the beef in a heavy pot, where it fits snugly. Pour in the marinade and the oil.

Bring ingredients to a boil over high heat, uncovered, and let it boil, turning the beef continuously, until all the liquid has evaporated, about 15 minutes. Keep the heat high at all times, adjust only if liquid dries out too quickly. The water content of the beef and the type of pot used affect liquid released: If the liquid does not evaporate within 15 minutes, remove the beef from the pot and let the liquid boil out until only drippings and oil are left; then return the beef to pot.

Cook the beef an additional 15 minutes, turning constantly, and adding small amounts of water from time to time, so that drippings do not burn. During the last 5 minutes of cooking, add salt.

Remove the roast from the pot. Add a little water, and a couple more tablespoons each of red wine and Marsala to the pot to deglaze it. Turn off the heat.

Cut the roast in thin slices, dribble the wine sauce on top, and serve.

ARROSTO NELL'OLIO

beef roasted in oil

serves 8

MIMMETTA
LO MONTE'S
CLASSIC
SICILIAN
COOKBOOK

•

110

The shape and the size of the pot used are essential to the outcome of this dish. The pot diameter must be such that the roast will fit closely to the sides, and pot depth must be such that the roast won't come above the middle of it.

3½ POUNDS BEEF LOIN   VERY LEAN, OR USE ROUND
10 CUPS OLIVE OIL
SALT, TO TASTE
BLACK PEPPER, TO TASTE   FINELY GROUND

Tie the beef with a string, with string loops ½-inch apart.

Bring the oil in a pot to the smoking point (325° to 350° F.). (Check temperature with a thermometer.) Place the pot in the middle of a large pan with high sides sitting on a counter. With the tip of a long barbecue fork, hold the roast by the string. Dip the roast into the oil and cover the pot immediately.

Some of the oil is likely to spill and splatter, so use caution. The function of the pan under the pot is to catch any oil that will bubble over, and holding the roast with a long fork will keep you out of reach of the splattering and bubbling oil. I also suggest the use of heavy gloves when placing the lid on the pot.

As soon as the bubbling subsides, cover the pot with several layers of cloth. The roast will be done and ready to be eaten as soon as the pot becomes lukewarm, quite a few hours later.

Remove the roast from the oil, remove and discard the string from the beef, and cut in thin slices. Sprinkle on salt and pepper to taste.

Serve with *Salsa alla menta di Maria Angelica* (see page 108); *Ammogghio* (see page 158); *Salsa alle noci* (see page 108); or *Salsa al dragoncello* (see page 107).

The leftover oil can be used for cooking meats, meat sauces, and vegetables.

ARROSTO IMBOTTITO

stuffed roast

serves 8

2 CLOVES GARLIC	CUT INTO A FEW JULIENNES
3 POUNDS BEEF EYE OF ROUND	VERY LEAN, PINK; SMALL IN DIAMETER
2 TABLESPOONS SHELLED PISTACHIOS	PREFERABLY RAW UNSALTED NUTS
I SPRIG PARSLEY	MAIN STEM DISCARDED, SEPARATED INTO SMALLER SPRIGS
2 THICK SLICES SALAMI	PREFERABLY HARD; JULIENNED (OPTIONAL)
OLIVE OIL	FOR COATING THE BEEF
¾ TEASPOON SALT	
½ TEASPOON BLACK PEPPER	FINELY GROUND

Preheat the oven to 375° F.

Set one-third of the garlic aside

Insert the blade of a knife, about 4 inches long and ¾ inch wide, through one end of the roast. Push the blade as far as it will go. Fill the cut with half the pistachios.

Make two more similar cuts (or three if you wish to stuff your roast with the salami as well), spacing them evenly, and stuff one with half the garlic, the other with half the parsley, the third with the salami.

Repeat the process at the other end of the roast. Wrap a string around the roast, with loops ½ inch apart. Rub the roast with plenty of oil, the salt, and the pepper. Insert the reserved garlic under the string, spacing it evenly.

Bake in the oven for 1 hour, remove from the oven, and cool for about 10 minutes. Remove string and thinly slice.

Serve this roast with *Salsa alla menta di Maria Angelica* (see page 108); *Salsa alle noci* (see page 108); or *Salsa al dragoncello* (see page 107).

STUFATO NERO
black stew
serves 8

Wild rabbit, the most frequently used meat for this dish in Sicily, is rarely available in the United States. Beef is a good substitute, since domestic rabbit is too delicate in taste and texture for this dish.

¼ PEEL OF ONE LARGE ORANGE	
1 SMALL ONION	CUT VERY SMALL
¾ CUP OLIVE OIL	
1¾ POUNDS BEEF ROUND TIP ROAST	VERY LEAN; CUT INTO 1-INCH CUBES
8 TO 10 PRUNES	PITTED
1 TEASPOON COCOA	UNSWEETENED
¾ CUP WHITE WINE	DRY
½ TEASPOON RED WINE VINEGAR	
⅙ TEASPOON SUGAR	
⅛ TEASPOON SALT	
¼ OUNCE BITTER CHOCOLATE	CUT INTO SMALL PIECES

Remove the peel from the orange with a vegetable peeler, making sure not to catch any of the white pith. Dip the peels into boiling water, and boil for 2 minutes. Drain, rinse well, and cut into very small slivers.

In a heavy pot, cook the onions in the oil, until aromatic. In the same pot, sear the beef over very high heat. Add the slivered orange peel, the prunes, cocoa, wine, vinegar, sugar, and salt. Cover and simmer 1 hour and 15 minutes, or until the beef is tender, stirring frequently.

Stir in the bitter chocolate. Taste the stew; it should have a very faint sour taste, if not add a little extra vinegar.

COTOLETTE TEDESCHE
german cutlets
serves 8

Cutlets can be served at room temperature. They make excellent sandwiches for picnics and snacks, served either hot or cold.

3 POUNDS BEEF EYE OF ROUND	VERY LEAN, SLICED LESS THAN ⅓ INCH
¾ CUP RED WINE VINEGAR	
2 EGGS	BEATEN LIGHTLY WITH A FORK
2 TO 3 CUPS BREAD CRUMBS	UNFLAVORED
CORN OIL	ENOUGH FOR A ¾-INCH LAYER IN SKILLET
½ TEASPOON SALT	

MIMMETTA
LO MONTE'S
CLASSIC
SICILIAN
COOKBOOK

•

112

In a large pan, marinate the beef slices in the vinegar for 30 minutes. Drain well, dip the beef into the eggs, and then coat with bread crumbs.

In a skillet with high sides, heat a ¾-inch layer of oil. As soon as smoke is barely visible fry the beef slices over high heat, without crowding, until golden brown, about 1½ minutes total, turning only once. For even browning, do not pierce the meat. Adjust the heat as necessary.

Drain the slices on a rack or on paper towels. Sprinkle with salt. Serve hot.

ARROSTO DI FILETTO AL FORNO

oven-roasted filet

serves 10 to 12

4 POUNDS BEEF FILET	VERY LEAN; AT LEAST 2½ TO 3 INCHES IN DIAMETER
4 CUPS RED WINE	DRY
2 LARGE CARROTS	SLICED
I LARGE ONION	SLICED
2 WHOLE BAY LEAVES	
4 FULL SPRIGS PARSLEY	
I TEASPOON BLACK PEPPER	FINELY GROUND
3 SMALL RED CHILI PEPPERS	DRY (OPTIONAL)
OLIVE OIL	ENOUGH FOR ⅓-INCH LAYER IN PAN(S)
I½ TEASPOONS SALT	

Tie the filet, keeping string loops ½ inch apart. Place the filet in container where it will fit very tightly (curve it to fit).

Marinate the filet for 12 hours in the wine with the carrots, onion, bay leaves, parsley, black pepper, and chilies, if you like a hotter taste.

Preheat oven to 450° F.

Remove the filet from the marinade. Set aside the marinade. In a shallow pan in which the filet will fit,* heat the layer of oil over high heat. As soon as smoke is barely visible, sear the filet all around. Transfer it to a shallow baking dish, and cook in the oven for 30 minutes. While baking, turn the filet four times for even browning. Add very small amounts of water to the bottom of the pan if the meat starts to burn.

Remove the herbs from the wine marinade and sauté them in the pan used for the filet, until the herbs are aromatic. Add the wine to the pan and reduce by half, over medium-low heat. Strain and add the salt to the sauce.

Remove and discard the string from the filet. Slice the filet—the thickness depends on your taste—and serve with the wine sauce trickled on top.

* IF SUCH A PAN IS NOT AVAILABLE, CUT THE FILET IN TWO SECTIONS AND USE TWO PANS. FOLLOWING THE SAME PROCEDURE TO SEAR, BAKE FOR 25 MINUTES INSTEAD OF 30, KEEPING THE SECTIONS WELL APART WHILE BAKING.

BRACIUOLETTE ALLE ERBE

herbed beef slices

serves 8

MIMMETTA
LO MONTE'S
CLASSIC
SICILIAN
COOKBOOK

•

114

3 TO 3½ POUNDS BEEF EYE OF ROUND	VERY LEAN, CUT INTO 40 SLICES
¼ POUND HAM	DANISH OR SIMILAR KIND, JULIENNED INTO 40 STICKS; 1½ INCHES LONG
½ POUND PROVOLONE	JULIENNED INTO 40 STICKS; 1½ INCHES LONG
10 SPRING ONIONS	CUT INTO 1½-INCH SECTIONS; TOUGH LEAVES REMOVED
¼ CUP FRESH THYME LEAVES	LIGHTLY PACKED
¼ CUP FRESH ROSEMARY LEAVES	LIGHTLY PACKED
2 TABLESPOONS CURRANTS	
OLIVE OIL	ENOUGH FOR ¼-INCH LAYER IN SKILLET
¼ TEASPOON SALT	
½ TEASPOON BLACK PEPPER	FINELY GROUND

In the center of each beef slice, place 1 stick of ham, 1 stick of provolone, some spring onion, herbs, and currants. Fold the edges of the two opposite sides of the beef over the filling (they should not meet in the middle) and roll tightly, from one unfolded end of the beef to the other. Place a metal skewer through each end, the Sicilian way,* so that the skewers are parallel. Pack the rolled beef tightly together on the skewers.

In a skillet, heat oil. Cook the skewered beef in batches, without crowding, or use two very wide skillets. The meat must get seared as quickly as possible, cooked over high heat for a total of 10 to 12 minutes. Turn a couple of times during that time.

Sprinkle with the salt and the pepper; serve immediately.

* FOR AN ILLUSTRATION OF SKEWERING THE SICILIAN WAY, SEE PAGE 134.

INVOLTINI DI MESSINA

messina meat rolls

serves 8

1 TABLESPOON OLIVE OIL	PLUS SOME FOR COATING
2 TO 3 CUPS BREAD CRUMBS	UNFLAVORED
1 MEDIUM ONION	CUT INTO VERY SMALL PIECES
1 CUP FRESH PARSLEY	LOOSELY PACKED LEAVES; CUT VERY SMALL
½ TEASPOON SALT	
1 TEASPOON BLACK PEPPER	FINELY GROUND
¾ CUP GRATED PARMESAN	
6 OUNCES GRUYÈRE	JULIENNED INTO 40 PIECES
8 TABLESPOONS (4 OUNCES) BUTTER	UNSALTED, CHILLED; CUT INTO 40 PIECES
3 TO 3½ POUNDS BEEF EYE OF ROUND	SLICED INTO 40 SLICES

Preheat the oven to 450° F.

In a heavy skillet, heat the oil and add 1 cup bread crumbs. Stir the crumbs over medium heat until pleasantly golden brown. Stir in the onion, then turn off the heat. Add the parsley, salt, pepper, and ⅔ cup Parmesan.

Divide the mixture among the beef slices, placing it in the center of each slice. Then place 1 piece Gruyère and 1 piece of butter on each. Fold the edges of the two opposite sides of the beef over the filling (they should not meet in the middle) and roll tightly, from one unfolded end of the beef to the other. Place a skewer through each end, the Sicilian way,* so that the skewers are parallel. Pack the rolls tightly together on the skewers.

Coat the meat rolls with some oil. Sprinkle them with the remaining Parmesan, then coat them with remaining bread crumbs.

In a very shallow pan, bake in the oven for 20 minutes, turning after 10 minutes of baking. Or, grill or broil the rolls (about 10 minutes per side).

* FOR AN ILLUSTRATION OF SKEWERING THE SICILIAN WAY, SEE PAGE 134.

CARNE E CARCIOFI

beef and artichokes

serves 10

OLIVE OIL	ENOUGH FOR ¼-INCH LAYER IN TWO SKILLETS
3 POUNDS BEEF LOIN	VERY LEAN; CUT INTO 1½-INCH CUBES
6 LARGE ARTICHOKES	TENDER, CLEANED; SLICED INTO ¼-INCH WEDGES (SEE PAGE 212)
4 POUNDS GREEN, RED, OR YELLOW BELL PEPPERS	SLICED INTO ½-INCH STRIPS
½ POUND PEARL ONIONS	FROZEN OR FRESH; PEELED, PARBOILED, WELL DRAINED
¼ TO ½ TEASPOON CAYENNE PEPPER	
BLACK PEPPER	
1 TEASPOON SALT	
½ CUP TOMATO JUICE	(OPTIONAL)

MIMMETTA
LO MONTE'S
CLASSIC
SICILIAN
COOKBOOK

116

In two very large skillets, heat a ¼-inch layer of oil. While heat is on high, add the beef, without crowding. Turn only as necessary for even browning. Remove and set aside as soon as beef is well seared.

Divide the vegetables equally between the skillets and stir until the vegetables are well coated with oil. Cook, over high heat, stirring occasionally, for about 5 minutes, or until pleasantly crisp. Add cayenne.

Return equal amounts of beef to each skillet, stir, and cook a couple of minutes (longer if you do not like your beef rare). Salt to taste. If you prefer a moister dish, add the tomato juice, letting it cook long enough to deglaze the skillet.

Serve immediately.

CARNE AI SETTE CONTORNI

meat with seven vegetables

serves 16

This dish takes more time to prepare, but it's well worth that time and it feeds a hungry group. It can be made in advance, refrigerated, and baked when needed. Make sure you bring it to room temperature before baking, then warm it for 20 minutes, or until hot, at 350° F.

Beef

5 POUNDS BEEF EYE OF THE ROUND ROAST   WELL TRIMMED
2 TEASPOONS SALT
2 STICKS (½ POUND) BUTTER   UNSALTED
I LARGE ONION   CUT INTO LARGE PIECES

Salsa alla pancetta (Bacon Sauce)

2 TO 4 OUNCES BACON   (PREFERABLY NITRATE FREE AND
    WITH VERY LITTLE FAT) DICED
I TABLESPOON OLIVE OIL
1½ CUPS WHITE WINE   DRY (USE GOOD TABLE WINE)
I TEASPOON FLOUR   UNBLEACHED, ALL-PURPOSE
1½ CUPS RESERVED BROTH   FROM COOKING THE MEAT; NOT
    REDUCED, COOLED

Vegetables

I POUND PARSNIPS   PEELED AND SPLIT IN HALF, PARBOIL
    AND REMOVE AND DISCARD HARD
    CORE; CUT INTO ¼-INCH SLICES
I POUND ASPARAGUS   TENDER TIPS ONLY
I POUND MUSHROOMS   IF VERY SMALL, LEAVE WHOLE; IF
    LARGE, CUT IN HALF OR QUARTER,
    AS NECESSARY TO BE BITE SIZE
4 CUPS OLIVE OIL
2 CELERY HEARTS   VERY THINLY SLICED
2 POUNDS FRESH PEARL ONIONS   OR USE FROZEN, PARBOILED
3 TO 4 CLOVES GARLIC   CUT INTO SMALL PIECES
2 CUPS FRESH TOMATOES   FLESHY AND RIPE, PEELED AND
    SEEDED; CUT INTO SMALL PIECES
I POUND NEW POTATOES   VERY SMALL
4 FULL SPRIGS PARSLEY   STEMS DISCARDED; CUT FINELY
I TEASPOON SALT
BUTTER   FOR COATING

NOTE: IF ASPARAGUS ARE NOT IN SEASON, SUBSTITUTE AN EQUAL AMOUNT OF PEAS. IF YOU USE FROZEN PEAS, PARBOIL THEM FIRST. IF YOU USE FRESHLY SHELLED SMALL AND TENDER PEAS, YOU WON'T NEED TO PARBOIL. SAUTÉ THE PEAS BRIEFLY IN A PAN WITH A THIN LAYER OF OIL. COVER AND COOK OVER LOW HEAT FOR 5 TO 10 MINUTES.

IF NEW POTATOES ARE OUT OF SEASON, CARVE SMALL-SHAPED POTATOES FROM LARGE ONES.

To prepare beef: Tie the beef with a string, keeping the string loops ½ inch apart. Place the roast in a pot in which it will fit snugly (you may bend the roast). Add the salt, butter, and onion. Cover with water, keeping the water level just above the meat. Bring to a boil, cover, and cook on low heat for 2 hours.

Uncover and cook over medium-high heat for another 30 minutes. Remove the meat and 1½ cups liquid from the pot. Set aside the 1½ cups liquid for the *Salsa alla pancetta*. If the remaining liquid is more than 2 cups, reduce it to 2 cups. Set aside the 2 cups of liquid for the vegetable mixture. After the meat has cooled off, remove the strings and discard them, then slice the meat into ¼-inch slices and set aside.

While the meat is cooking, start to prepare the sauce and the vegetables.

To prepare Salsa alla pancetta: In a medium saucepan, cook the bacon and the oil on low heat until the bacon starts getting slightly crisp; then add the wine.

In a bowl, dissolve the flour in some of the beef broth, then slowly stir in the rest of the broth. In a steady stream, add this mixture to the bacon-wine sauce, while stirring constantly. The sauce will thicken slightly. Set aside.

To prepare vegetables: Place the parboiled parsnips and asparagus into a very large bowl.

Clean the mushrooms under running water, stem-side down, running your finger over the caps very well. Cut off the stem ends. Heat a thin layer (about ½ cup) of oil in a large skillet. Add the mushrooms and cook over high heat, stirring until the mushrooms are aromatic and no liquid is left in the pan. Remove the mushrooms from the pan with a slotted spoon and place them in the bowl with the asparagus and parsnips.

If the pan is dry, add and heat a couple of tablespoons of oil. Add the celery and wilt it over low heat. Remove the celery and place it in the bowl with the other vegetables.

Cut the ends off the onions, dip in plenty of boiling water, and let them boil a couple of minutes. Drain and pop them out of their skins. (If using frozen onions, dip them in boiling water, just enough to separate them.)

Add a little more oil and the onions to the pan, and quickly cook over high heat until aromatic. Remove the onions and place in the bowl with the other vegetables.

If the pan looks scorched, you might want to get a clean one. Then add a very thin layer (a scant ½ cup) of oil and the garlic. Heat the pan and add the tomatoes. Cook briefly, about 5 minutes, over high heat. Add the tomatoes and garlic to the other vegetables in the bowl.

In a different skillet, fry the new potatoes over medium heat in approximately ½-inch oil until golden. Add the potatoes to the vegetables in the bowl along with the parsley, salt, *Salsa alla pancetta,* and 1 cup of the remaining meat liquid. Mix well.

Preheat the oven to 375° F. Butter a large, deep baking dish (about 14 by 10 inches). Place a layer of meat slices on the bottom. Cover with half of the vegetable mixture, then a layer of the remaining meat, and end with the remaining vegetables. Bake in the oven for 10 minutes.

Serve immediately.

MIMMETTA
LO MONTE'S
CLASSIC
SICILIAN
COOKBOOK

•

118

CARNE IN SALSA CRUDA

meat in raw sauce

serves 6

Please note that the first part of this recipe calls for preparation a day in advance.

I SMALL ONION	CUT INTO THIN STRIPS
3½ TEASPOONS SALT	
2 TO 2½ POUNDS EYE OF ROUND BEEF	VERY LEAN
4 TABLESPOONS (2 OUNCES) BUTTER	UNSALTED, OR USE OLIVE OIL
¾ CUP OLIVE OIL	
2 CUPS WHITE WINE	DRY
¼ CUP RED WINE VINEGAR	
¼ OF PEEL OF I LEMON	VERY FINELY CUT
¼ OF PEEL OF I LIME	VERY FINELY CUT
2 POUNDS FRESH TOMATOES	PEAR SHAPED; SEEDED; CUT WIDTHWISE, ONE-FOURTH OF THEM INTO VERY SMALL PIECES, SLICE THE REST INTO THIN ROUNDS
I CUP FRESH BASIL	LOOSELY PACKED LEAVES; CUT FINELY
20 FRESH MINT LEAVES	FINELY CUT
½ CUP PARSLEY	LOOSELY PACKED LEAVES; CUT FINELY

Soak the onion in 2 cups of water and 2 teaspoons of the salt for 12 hours. Rinse and drain well.

Tie beef with a string; keep loops ½ inch apart.

In a large skillet, sear the beef in the butter and 4 tablespoons of oil over high heat. Add the wine. Do not puncture the meat.

Add enough hot water to barely cover the beef. Add 1 teaspoon salt. Bring to a boil, lower the heat, and simmer, covered, for a couple of hours. Remove the beef from the liquid,* cool, and refrigerate. Remove the string from the beef and discard it. When thoroughly cold, slice ¼ inch thick.

In a large bowl, mix ½ cup oil with the vinegar, the remaining ½ teaspoon salt, the lemon and lime peel, the tomato pieces, onion, and the herbs.

Mix the beef slices with the sauce and arrange them on a serving platter, top with the tomato rounds. Serve cold.

* THERE'S NO NEED TO WASTE THE LIQUID THE BEEF WAS COOKED IN. REDUCE IT TO APPROXIMATELY ¾ CUP, ADD A DOLLOP OF FRESH, UNSALTED BUTTER, AND SERVE IT WITH ¾ POUND OF SPAGHETTI COOKED AL DENTE (SEE PAGE 31). TOP WITH PARMESAN CHEESE. THIS TASTY MEAL WILL SERVE 4.

CUSCUS CON CARNE E VERDURE

couscous with meat and vegetables

serves 10 to 16

With its Arabic heritage, *cuscus* is a dish typical of the cooking of the extreme west point of Sicily. As it often happens in ethnic islands, Sicilians have maintained a very old way of serving *cuscus,* which is with fish, rather than meat. Fish in that area is plentiful and particularly tasty.

Cuscus with meat has always appeared at special celebrations such as weddings. In the last few decades, the dish has almost disappeared. This recipe has been recreated from tales of several people from Pantelleria, Trapani, and Erice. Wine is my addition, to make up for the lighter taste due to the lack of fat in lean beef.

MIMMETTA
LO MONTE'S
CLASSIC
SICILIAN
COOKBOOK

•

120

MEAT TO ACCOMPANY THE *CUSCUS*

¾ CUP OLIVE OIL	
4 LARGE CARROTS	CUT INTO ½-INCH CUBES
2 LARGE HEARTS CELERY	CUT INTO ½-INCH PIECES
2 MEDIUM ONIONS	CUT INTO ½-INCH PIECES
5 POUNDS BEEF RUMP OR ROUND	VERY LEAN (OR LEAN PORK OR LAMB); CUT INTO ¾-INCH CUBES
2 TEASPOONS SALT	
¾ CUP WHITE WINE	DRY

VEGETABLES TO ACCOMPANY THE *CUSCUS*

PEPPERS

3 RED BELL PEPPERS	STEMMED, CORED, AND SEEDED
3 YELLOW BELL PEPPERS	STEMMED, CORED, AND SEEDED
6 MEDIUM ONIONS	
¾ TO I CUP OLIVE OIL	
¾ TEASPOON SALT	

STRING BEANS

I POUND FRESH STRING BEANS	
½ CUP (SCANT) OLIVE OIL	
2 CLOVES GARLIC	CUT INTO A FEW PIECES
¼ TEASPOON SALT	

SQUASH AND EGGPLANT

I½ POUNDS EGGPLANT	UNPEELED, ENDS CUT OFF; CUT INTO ½-INCH CUBES
4½ TEASPOONS SALT	
I⅓ CUPS OLIVE OIL	

5 CLOVES GARLIC	CUT INTO LARGE PIECES
2 POUNDS ZUCCHINI	CUT INTO ½-INCH CUBES
I POUND YELLOW SQUASH	CUT INTO ½-INCH CUBES
5 SPRIGS PARSLEY	CUT FINELY

Peas

2 10-OUNCE BOXES FROZEN PEAS	OR THE EQUIVALENT AMOUNT OF FRESH
½ CUP OLIVE OIL	
I SMALL ONION	CUT INTO VERY SMALL PIECES
½ TEASPOON SALT	

Optional

3 BUNCHES SPRING ONIONS	CUT INTO THIN ROUNDS

Cuscus

4 CUPS CUSCUS	
¾ CUP OLIVE OIL	
2 TEASPOONS BLACK PEPPER	FINELY GROUND
4 TO 6 CUPS LIGHT CHICKEN STOCK	(SEE PAGE 72) OR 2 TO 3 BOUILLON CUBES DISSOLVED IN 4 TO 6 CUPS WATER

To prepare the meat: In a large heavy pot, pour the oil. Add the vegetables and stir them around, over high heat, until aromatic.

Add the meat, stir it. Add water to barely cover the meat and vegetables. Add salt, cover, and cook over low heat until tender.

Remove the meat and the vegetables from the liquid to another container, cover, set aside.

Reduce the liquid, boiling it uncovered or partially covered, to half the original quantity. Add the wine, heat to a full boil, return the meat and the vegetables to it, cover, reduce the heat to low, and simmer about 30 minutes. Keep warm. While the meat is simmering, prepare the vegetables.

To prepare the peppers: Cut the peppers into squares a little smaller than 1 inch. Cut the onions so that the layers are about the same as the peppers.

Heat the oil in a very large skillet (you may want to use two, if your vegetables are going to be too crowded in your skillet). Add the vegetables and stir over high heat for a few minutes. Reduce the heat to medium high and continue stirring until the vegetables lose their crispness and are quite aromatic. Add the salt, stir, and set aside.

To prepare the string beans: Trim the ends from the string beans and cut in half. Place in plenty of water, bring to a boil, and let them boil 3 minutes, or until crisp, but not too stiff. Drain well.

In a skillet, heat the oil and the garlic until aromatic. Add the cooked beans and stir over high heat, for 1 to 2 minutes. Reduce the heat to medium and cook, stirring very often, until the beans look slightly "wrinkled." Add the salt, stir, and set aside.

To prepare the squash and eggplant: Place the eggplant cubes in a large bowl filled with water and add 3 teaspoons salt. Weigh the eggplants down in the water by placing a plate on top of them. Drain after 30 minutes, pressing lightly against a colander to remove excess water.

Add half the oil to each of two large skillets. Divide the garlic between them. Heat the oil and the garlic until aromatic. Add the vegetables (reserving the parsley), dividing an equal mixture of them between the skillets, stir over high heat for 2 to 3 minutes. Reduce to low, cover, and cook until tender (about 2 to 3 minutes). Uncover and cook, stirring, over high heat about 5 minutes. Add 1½ teaspoons salt, parsley, and stir. Set aside.

To prepare the peas: If using frozen peas, fill a large pot with water and bring to a full boil, add the peas, cover, and bring the water back to a boil quickly. As soon as the peas are separated, and the water is boiling, drain them.

In a skillet, heat the oil and the onion until aromatic; stir in the peas. Cover and cook until tender over low heat. Add salt and set aside.

To prepare the cuscus: In a large heavy bowl mix the *cuscus* with the oil and the pepper. Bring the stock to a rolling boil, stir 3½ cups stock into the *cuscus*. The liquid should be absorbed promptly. Cover with lid and with several layers of cloth to keep warm. Taste after 5 minutes. If still crunchy, add ⅓ cup more stock, cover as before, and taste again after 5 minutes. Repeat if necessary until pleasantly firm. Fluff with a fork before placing it in a serving dish.

(If you want to serve the *cuscus* a few hours after it has been cooked, spread it on a large ovenproof serving dish. Sprinkle on some water and stir. Cover with foil, and place in an oven preheated to 325° F. until hot, about 10 minutes.)

Serving the dish: To serve the *cuscus* with the meat and vegetables, arrange the vegetables in ovenproof dishes. In one large dish, put the peas on one side, the string beans on the other, and the peppers in the center. In another dish, place the squash and eggplants. Cover with foil and keep warm.

Spoon a small amount of the meat and the vegetables around the *cuscus* on individual plates. Spinkle small amounts of the juices from the meat over the *cuscus* and the spring onions to taste, if desired.

MIMMETTA
LO MONTE'S
CLASSIC
SICILIAN
COOKBOOK

•

122

Some General Advice on Preparing Cuscus

Cuscus can be made at home, from scratch, mixing semolina, water, salt, and oil. However, it is a very time-consuming process, and requires a skill acquired only with experience.

But there are several commercial cuscus brands that are very good, and that are quick to prepare. The only drawback is that the amount of water recommended in the cooking instructions generally yields a cuscus that is too wet, too dry, or too greasy, and you will need to adjust the quantity of liquid as you cook. Some of the brands I use, Sipa brand for example, absorb half as much liquid as the quantity suggested on the instructions.

The cooking liquid used for cuscus can be any kind of stock; making it with good quality bouillon cubes is perfectly acceptable. Using the fat called for in the recipes on the box is not always necessary. But if you use it, add it in a ratio of 3 tablespoons to 1 cup uncooked cuscus. Use olive oil, and not butter, as is often suggested in the box recipes. (Sicilians don't cook cuscus with butter.)

Test a small amount of cuscus, cooking it according to the box directions, to determine the quantity of liquid and fat to use. After being mixed with the liquid, cuscus should swell up some, but the grains should be quite firm and although they can be pressed together in little balls, they should not be sticky. If the cuscus is too hard and dry, increase the stock quantity. If it becomes soggy, sticky, or mushy, cut down on the liquid when you prepare the actual dish. It may be that the brand you are using does require a certain amount of fat for the grains not to stick together, so, if you haven't used it before, try adding some oil.

To cook cuscus: Bring the liquid to a boil. Place the cuscus in a heatproof heavy ceramic or similar bowl. Add the liquid to it, stir in the oil, if using, and then stir in pepper. Cover and keep warm.

Fluff with a fork after 10 minutes; taste. Add more liquid if necessary.

INSALATA DI CARNE

beef salad

serves 10

Refrigerate this dish for 12 hours before serving it.

MIMMETTA
LO MONTE'S
CLASSIC
SICILIAN
COOKBOOK

•

124

3 POUNDS BEEF BOTTOM ROUND	VERY LEAN
⅓ CUP LEMON JUICE	FRESHLY SQUEEZED
2 TEASPOONS Tabasco SAUCE	
½ CUP RED WINE VINEGAR	
2 TEASPOONS Worcestershire SAUCE	
1 CUP OLIVE OIL	
1½ TEASPOONS SALT	
1 SMALL ONION	CUT INTO VERY SMALL PIECES
1 CUP GREEN OLIVES	PREFERABLY ITALIAN OR GREEK,
	PITTED; CUT INTO A FEW PIECES
⅓ CUP CAPERS	PACKED IN VINEGAR, WELL DRAINED
½ CUP ITALIAN PICKLES	"GIARDINIERA" (PICKLES PACKED
	EXCLUSIVELY IN VINEGAR)
2 CUPS PARSLEY	LOOSELY PACKED LEAVES; CUT FINELY
1 CELERY HEART	LARGE, TENDER; CUT INTO VERY SMALL
	PIECES

Tie beef with a string, keeping the string loops about ½ inch apart.

Place the beef in a pot where it will fit snugly, cover with water, and bring to a boil. Cover, and simmer 1½ hours. Turn a few times while cooking.

Remove the beef from the liquid, set it aside to cool. Reserve the liquid for other uses (such as stock). Remove the string from the beef and discard.

During the time the beef is cooking and then cooling, prepare the sauce. In a bowl, mix together the lemon juice, Tabasco, vinegar, Worcestershire sauce, oil, and 1 teaspoon salt. Set aside.

Slice the beef a little thinner than ¼ inch thick. Coat the slices with the sauce.

In a bowl, mix the onion, olives, capers, pickles, parsley, and celery. In another bowl, alternate slices of beef and the herb mixture. Dribble any remaining sauce on top. If you wish, sprinkle on the remaining salt.

Refrigerate for 12 hours; serve cold.

ROTOLO DI TRITATO

ground beef roll

serves 12

4 EGGS	EXTRA-LARGE
6 OUNCES BREAD	WHOLE WHEAT
½ CUP MILK	
I MEDIUM ONION	CUT INTO VERY SMALL PIECES
I CLOVE GARLIC	CUT INTO VERY SMALL PIECES
¾ CUP FRESH PARSLEY	LOOSELY PACKED, CUT FINELY
25 MINT LEAVES	FINELY CUT
I TEASPOON SALT	
I TEASPOON BLACK PEPPER	FINELY GROUND
6 TABLESPOONS GRATED PARMESAN	
2 TABLESPOONS GRATED CACIOCAVALLO	OR PECORINO ROMANO
3 POUNDS GROUND BEEF	VERY LEAN ROUND
OLIVE OIL	FOR COATING
½ POUND MONTEREY JACK	(OR USE ANY MILD CHEESE) THINLY SLICED
20 OUNCES FRESH SPINACH	(OR FROZEN, PARBOILED; COOKED JUST ENOUGH TO SEPARATE) SQUEEZED WELL
½ POUND HAM	THINLY SLICED (OPTIONAL)
¼ POUND SALAMI	THINLY SLICED (OPTIONAL)

Preheat the oven to 350° F.

Hard boil 2 eggs, then cut them in quarters lengthwise.

Soak the bread with the milk, add the remaining 2 eggs, the onion, garlic, parsley, mint, salt, pepper, Parmesan, and caciocavallo. Mix well, then combine with the ground beef.

Cut two pieces of wax paper, 20 inches long. Oil them well, divide the beef mixture between them, and spread each in an even 10- x 12-inch layer.

Spread a layer of Monterey Jack or other mild cheese on the beef and then evenly distribute the spinach in small clumps. Line up 4 egg quarters along the short side of each layer. Layer beef mixture with the ham slices, and/or evenly distribute the salami in rows, if using. Then roll the beef layers, with the help of the wax paper, starting from the shorter end of the rectangle.

Wrap the rolls in foil, sealing them in well, and pierce the foil with a skewer in random spots around the rolls.

Cook in the oven for 1½ hours.

Cool; refrigerate. Serve cold; cut into ½-inch slices.

PASTICCIO DI CARNE E PATATE

baked meat and potatoes

serves 8 to 10

This dish can be prepared a day in advance. Make sure to bring it to room temperature before reheating at 325° F. for 20 to 30 minutes.

MIMMETTA
LO MONTE'S
CLASSIC
SICILIAN
COOKBOOK

•

126

4 OUNCES BREAD	WHOLE WHEAT
⅓ CUP MILK	
2 POUNDS GROUND BEEF	VERY LEAN ROUND
I TEASPOON SALT	
I TEASPOON BLACK PEPPER	FINELY GROUND
6 TABLESPOONS GRATED CACIOCAVALLO	OR PECORINO ROMANO
2 EGGS	EXTRA-LARGE
I LARGE ONION	CUT INTO VERY SMALL PIECES
2 TEASPOONS DRIED OREGANO	
2 TEASPOONS DRIED CHERVIL	
½ TEASPOON DRIED MARJORAM	
½ TEASPOON DRIED THYME	
½ TEASPOON DRIED ROSEMARY	
2¼ POUNDS POTATOES	ALLOW EXTRA FOR WASTE
¼ CUP OLIVE OIL	
I CUP TOMATOES	CANNED AND PEELED; SEEDED (OR USE EQUAL AMOUNTS OF FRESH, RIPE, SKINS ON)
BUTTER	UNSALTED, FOR COATING
⅓ CUP PROVOLA PICCANTE	(ABOUT I OUNCE) CUT INTO VERY SMALL CUBES OR SHREDDED

In a large bowl, soak the bread in the milk. Mix in the beef with ½ teaspoon salt, ½ teaspoon pepper, grated cheese, eggs, half the onion, and the herbs.

Peel the potatoes, cover with plenty of water. Bring to a boil and cook at a low boil until they are al dente, then cut them into ¼-inch rounds and place in another bowl. Mix in ½ teaspoon salt, ½ teaspoon pepper, the oil, and the remaining onion.

Cut the peeled tomatoes in coarse pieces. If you are using fresh ones, cut into thin slices, but do not peel.

Coat a 12-inch round baking dish, at least 2½ inches deep with a generous layer of butter.

Preheat oven to 350° F.

Lay the potatoes in the dish. Pat them down. Cover with the meat mixture, patting it down firmly. Finish with the tomatoes, distributing them evenly over the meat.

Bake in the oven for 1½ hours. In the last 15 minutes of baking, distribute the provola on top. Depending on the moisture of the potatoes and the meat, the cooking time might be a little longer. To check for doneness, insert a thin skewer through the potato layer. If the skewer meets no resistance, *pasticcio* is done.

SFOGLIATA ARROTOLATA DI CARNE E SPINACI

meat and spinach rolled in pastry

serves 12

Strudel dough

2⅔ CUPS FLOUR	UNBLEACHED, ALL-PURPOSE
6 TABLESPOONS OLIVE OIL	
1 CUP WARM WATER	

Filling

¾ CUP OLIVE OIL	
3 POUNDS GROUND BEEF	VERY LEAN
1 MEDIUM ONION	CUT VERY SMALL
7 EGG YOLKS	EXTRA-LARGE
2 POUNDS FRESH SPINACH	PARBOILED; SQUEEZE OUT EXCESS WATER, AT ROOM TEMPERATURE
1 CUP GRATED PARMESAN	
1 TEASPOON SALT	
1 TEASPOON PEPPER	
8 TABLESPOONS BUTTER	UNSALTED, MELTED

To make and stretch the pastry, use the above ingredients and follow instructions for *Strudel di mele,* page 331. Divide dough to make two rolls.

Preheat the oven to 350° F.

In a very large skillet, heat the oil; add and brown the meat and onion. Turn off the heat.

In a large bowl, mix 6 egg yolks with the spinach and the cheese. Mix in the meat, salt, and pepper.

Brush a cookie sheet with butter.

Spread some of the melted butter on the stretched dough. Spread half the meat mixture on it, roll, and transfer to the cookie sheet. Sprinkle the strudel with butter; pat gently to spread it.

Repeat the procedure with the remaining dough and meat mixture.

Bake in the oven for 50 minutes. Brush the rolls, if desired, with the remaining egg yolk, and bake 10 minutes longer. Let rolls rest 10 to 15 minutes, then slice before serving.

If you wish to make this dish in advance, bake a total of 50 minutes. Refrigerate, then crisp in the oven at 350° F. for 20 minutes.

PASTICCIO DI CARNE

meat pie

serves 12 to 14

This recipe, and the proceeding one, are both from the Duke's cookbook.

MIMMETTA
LO MONTE'S
CLASSIC
SICILIAN
COOKBOOK

•

128

Crust

1½ POUNDS FLOUR	UNBLEACHED, ALL-PURPOSE
½ CUP SUGAR	
¾ POUND BUTTER	UNSALTED
4 EGGS	EXTRA-LARGE; SEPARATED

Stuffing

1 POUND CHICKEN LIVERS	
¾ POUND SWEETBREADS	
1 POUND PARSNIPS	PEELED, BOILED UNTIL TENDER, HARD CORE REMOVED; CUT INTO VERY SMALL PIECES
5 TABLESPOONS (2½ OUNCES) BUTTER	UNSALTED, MELTED
3 TABLESPOONS DRY MUSHROOMS	SOAK IN COLD WATER 1 HOUR OR UNTIL PLUMP BUT NOT MUSHY; WASH VERY WELL, REMOVING ANY SAND OR DIRT; THEN DRAIN, AND CUT INTO VERY SMALL PIECES
2 TEASPOONS FRESH ROSEMARY LEAVES	CUT VERY SMALL
¼ CUP FRESH SAGE LEAVES	LIGHTLY PACKED; CUT VERY SMALL
1½ TEASPOONS POWDERED MARJORAM	(OR 1 TABLESPOON FRESH) CUT VERY SMALL
½ TEASPOON GROUND NUTMEG	
1 TEASPOON CELERY SEED	
1½ TEASPOONS SALT	
1½ TEASPOONS BLACK PEPPER	FINELY GROUND
½ CUP OLIVE OIL	
2 OR 3 ARTICHOKES	CLEANED (SEE PAGE 212); QUARTERED, SLICED VERY THIN (ABOUT 4 LEVEL CUPS, LOOSELY PACKED)
3 POUNDS BEEF EYE OF THE ROUND	TRIMMED TO REMOVE FAT; SLICED LESS THAN ¼ INCH THICK
FLOUR	UNBLEACHED, ALL-PURPOSE; FOR COATING

½ POUND CHEESE

PROVOLA (MILD) OR MONTEREY JACK;
THINLY SLICED

12 QUAIL BREASTS

BREASTBONE REMOVED

To make the crust: In a large bowl, mix the flour and sugar. Cut in the butter until roughly mixed. Add the egg yolks and mix with your fingers until it holds lightly together. Set in a cool place for 30 minutes.

Have on hand a 14- by 10- by 3-inch heavy baking dish.

Roll two thirds of the dough between two pieces of wax paper, to line the dish. Keep the remaining dough to top the pie. As you roll the dough, keep peeling off the top layer of wax paper, replace it, turn the dough over, and peel off the other layer, replace it, and roll until ¼ inch thick.

This dough is very fragile. To transfer it to the dish, peel off the top layer of wax paper, dust the dough well with flour, then invert into the dish and peel off the wax paper. The dough can be patched very easily—any tear or missing part can be repaired by pressing the edges together and adding little bits of dough when necessary. Brush the dough (the bottom) with egg white just before adding the filling.

To make the stuffing: Parboil the chicken livers for 5 minutes, then rinse and cut into very small pieces. Repeat the procedure with the sweetbreads.

In a large bowl, mix together the parsnips, sweetbreads, liver, and melted butter. Then add the mushrooms, herbs, spices, and salt and pepper.

In a large skillet, heat the oil. Add the artichokes and just enough water to moisten them. Cook over medium-high heat until crisp, but not hard. If there is water left, cook on high heat until it evaporates.

Coat the beef lightly with flour. Lay one third of the beef slices, then one third of the stuffing over the dough in the pan. Follow with one third of the beef, one third of the stuffing, the artichokes, cheese, and remaining beef.

Pack the remaining one third of the stuffing on the skinless side of the quail breast. Arrange the breasts, skin-side up, on the beef layer, in a regular pattern. Cover with the remaining crust, seal the edges together, and flute. Cut a few slits on the crust. Bake in the oven for 2 hours.

Eat when thoroughly cool, or chilled.

Can be made in advance and refrigerated.

"GRANATA" DI ANIMELLE

meat pie

serves 12

An intriguing aspect of this old recipe is that the meat serves as the pie shell, instead of a dough.

MIMMETTA
LO MONTE'S
CLASSIC
SICILIAN
COOKBOOK

•

130

½ POUND SWEETBREADS	
¼ POUND MUSHROOMS	
I POUND SMALL PARSNIPS	PEELED

Marinade

2 TABLESPOONS OLIVE OIL	
2 TABLESPOONS SHERRY VINEGAR	
¼ TEASPOON FENNEL SEED	
½ TEASPOON DRIED OREGANO	
I LARGE CLOVE GARLIC	THINLY SLICED
I½ POUNDS BEEF EYE OF THE ROUND	VERY THINLY SLICED (ENOUGH SLICES TO FULLY LINE, WITH SOME OVERLAP, A 12-INCH ROUND, 3-INCH DEEP BAKING DISH; CHOOSE THE LIGHTEST COLOR MEAT POSSIBLE—THE REDDER THE MEAT, THE TOUGHER IT WILL BE)

Meatballs

2 LARGE SLICES WHITE BREAD	SANDWICH-TYPE
3 TABLESPOONS GRATED PARMESAN	
I EGG	EXTRA-LARGE
3 TABLESPOONS HEAVY CREAM	
¼ TEASPOON GRATED NUTMEG	
¼ TEASPOON GROUND CINNAMON	
½ TEASPOON SALT	
¼ TEASPOON BLACK PEPPER	FINELY GROUND
I¾ POUNDS GROUND BEEF	LEAN
FLOUR	UNBLEACHED, ALL-PURPOSE; FOR COATING AND THICKENING

½ POUND MILD SAUSAGE	
½ POUND CHICKEN LIVERS	
¾ CUP OLIVE OIL	
I½ TABLESPOONS (¾ OUNCE) BUTTER	UNSALTED; PLUS SOME FOR COATING
8 LARGE GREEN OLIVES	PREFERABLY SICILIAN OR GREEK

⅓ CUP RAISINS
2 TEASPOONS SALT
BLACK TRUFFLE   PREFERABLY FRESH; GRATED (OPTIONAL)

Split the sweetbreads in half. Blanch, drain, rinse, and steam them for about 20 minutes. Allow to cool and then thinly slice.

Clean the mushrooms under running water, stem-side down, running your fingers over the caps. Cut the stem end and thinly slice.

In a large pot, cover the parsnips with water; boil until al dente. Thinly slice.

For the marinade: In a large bowl, mix together the marinade ingredients. Coat the beef slices with the marinade, cover, and refrigerate.

For the meatballs: Make a smooth paste of the bread, cheese, egg, cream, nutmeg, cinnamon, salt, and pepper. Add to the ground beef and mix very well. Shape some of the mixture into about 35 cherry-sized balls. Coat with flour, reserving the remaining mixture.

Preheat the oven to 325° F.

Place the sausage in a small frying pan with ½ inch of water. Pierce the links in several spots and cook over low heat about 20 minutes, turning frequently. When cool, remove the casing and slice the sausage into thin rounds. Discard the cooking liquid.

Coat the chicken livers with flour.

In a skillet, heat the oil. Brown the meatballs over moderately high heat. Remove from the pan and cook the liver very quickly in the drippings. Cut into small pieces.

Melt the butter in a skillet and cook the mushrooms in it. They will absorb the butter immediately. Keep the heat on medium high for a couple of minutes, stirring constantly. After turning the heat off, add the sweetbreads and the liver to the pan. Mix in the olives, the raisins, ½ teaspoon salt, and 1 tablespoon of flour.

Mix the meatballs with the sausage.

Butter a 12-inch round, 3-inch deep baking dish. Line it with the beef slices, overlapping them a little and forming a shell. Lay the parsnips over the beef slices and sprinkle with ½ teaspoon salt. Divide the reserved ground beef mixture into two parts, one a little larger than the other. Shape the smaller amount into very thin patties, and cover the parsnips. Evenly distribute the meat balls and sausage mixture over the parsnips. On top of this sprinkle your grating of truffle, if desired.

Use the mushrooms, sweetbread, and liver mixture for the next layer. Sprinkle with ½ teaspoon salt. Make the last layer with the remaining ground beef mixture. Pat it down gently and tuck over it the meat slices shell. Bake in the oven for 1 hour and 15 minutes.

Bring to room temperature. Let it rest 24 hours in the refrigerator. Unmold, turning upside down on a serving plate, serve at room temperature, slicing it in wedges, as you would a cake.

FEGATO DI VITELLA ALLA CIPOLLA

veal liver with onion

serves 6

You may want to cook this dish dividing the ingredients between two skillets, since the success of cooking liver is strictly related to the quickness of the cooking process.

MIMMETTA
LO MONTE'S
CLASSIC
SICILIAN
COOKBOOK

•

132

8 TABLESPOONS (4 OUNCES) BUTTER	UNSALTED
10 OUNCES COUNTRY HAM	¼-INCH THICK SLICES, CUT INTO STRIPS LESS THAN ¼ INCH WIDE
12 SPRING ONIONS	DISCARD THE GREENEST PART; CUT IN HALF LENGTHWISE
A FEW SPRIGS FRESH SAGE	ABOUT 20 LARGE LEAVES
1¼ TEASPOONS DRIED ROSEMARY LEAVES	
2 POUNDS VEAL LIVER	½ INCH THICK; CUT INTO 3-INCH PIECES
SALT, TO TASTE	
¾ TEASPOON BLACK PEPPER	FINELY GROUND

Melt the butter in the skillet(s). Add the ham, onions, sage, and rosemary. Cook, stirring over medium-low heat, until the onions wilt.

Increase the heat to high, add the liver, and cook it a little less than 1½ minutes per side. Salt to taste, and add pepper. Serve immediately.

ANIMELLE CON PISELLI

sweetbreads and peas

serves 4 to 6

1½ POUNDS SWEETBREADS	BLANCHED; CUT INTO WALNUT-SIZED PIECES
FLOUR	UNBLEACHED, ALL-PURPOSE; FOR COATING
⅔ CUP OLIVE OIL	
1 SMALL ONION	CUT INTO VERY SMALL PIECES
1⅓ CUPS WHITE WINE	DRY
1¼ POUNDS PEAS	FROZEN OR FRESH (IF FROZEN, SCALD IN BOILING WATER LONG ENOUGH TO SEPARATE THEM); DRAINED
1 TEASPOON SALT	
BLACK PEPPER, TO TASTE	FINELY GROUND

Lightly coat the sweetbreads with flour.

Coat a large skillet with the oil and heat it with the onions over medium heat until aromatic. Increase the heat to high and add the sweetbreads. Cook them for a few minutes, turning occasionally, add the wine, and deglaze the pan.

Lower the heat to simmer. Add the peas, salt, and pepper. Cover and simmer about 25 minutes. Remove the sweetbreads and reduce the sauce, cooking it, uncovered, over medium-high heat about 5 minutes, or long enough to thicken it. Return the sweetbreads to the pan; serve while very hot.

If you wish to prepare the dish in advance, after removing the sweetbreads from the pan, refrigerate them (and the sauce, not yet reduced, as well) until shortly before your meal. Bring them to room temperature on the countertop, and follow the above instructions.

LINGUA INFORNATA

baked tongue

serves 6 to 8

3 POUNDS BEEF TONGUE

4 TABLESPOONS (2 OUNCES) BUTTER   (OR USE OLIVE OIL) UNSALTED

½ TEASPOON SALT

½ TEASPOON BLACK PEPPER   FINELY GROUND

½ CUP GRATED PARMESAN

Place tongue in a pot with plenty of water to cover it, bring to a boil, and let it boil about 15 minutes. Drain and rinse the tongue.

Remove the skin, then place back in the pot, cover with plenty of water, and bring to a boil again. Simmer, covered, for 1½ hours.

Remove the tongue to a plate and let cool. (You may want to reserve the water it has cooked in to use as stock.)

Preheat the oven to 375° F.

Thinly slice the tongue a little less than ¼ inch thick.

In a medium-sized baking dish, melt the butter, toss the tongue slices in it until well coated. Add the salt and pepper.

Cover the bottom of the pan with a layer of tongue. Sprinkle with a third of the cheese, cover with tongue slices, more cheese, one more layer of tongue, and end with cheese.

Bake in the oven for 20 minutes and serve immediately.

SPIEDINI DI CARNE MISTA
skewered mixed meats
serves 8

These skewered meats can be cooked in the oven: Place them on a hot cookie sheet covered with olive oil. Put in oven preheated to 475° F. and cook 10 minutes, turn, and cook for 10 more minutes.

1 POUND SAUSAGE	ABOUT EIGHT 3- TO 4-INCH LONG LINKS
1¾ POUNDS BONELESS	
DUCK BREAST	SKINNED (THREE 5-POUND DUCKS YIELD
	APPROXIMATELY 1¾ POUNDS BONELESS BREAST) *
10 OUNCES CALF'S LIVER	½ INCH THICK
A FEW SPRIGS FRESH SAGE	
OLIVE OIL	FOR COATING
1 TEASPOON SALT	
BLACK PEPPER, TO TASTE	FINELY GROUND
BREAD CRUMBS	UNFLAVORED

MIMMETTA
LO MONTE'S
CLASSIC
SICILIAN
COOKBOOK

•

134

Thoroughly pierce the sausage with a thin skewer. Place into a pot, cover with plenty of water, bring to a boil, and cook 15 minutes. Drain. Cut each link in half lengthwise and crosswise.

Cut the duck breast in pieces to match the size of the sausage. Cut the liver in sixteen pieces.

Skewer the meat so that the liver is encased by two sections of sausage—sandwiched in between the flat sides of the sausage—and alternate that with pieces of duck, and sage leaves. Skewer the meats the Sicilian way, having two skewers, each running parallel through the ends of the meat. This keeps the meat from revolving when turning it. Pack the rolls tightly on the skewers.

Coat the skewered meat well with olive oil. Sprinkle with salt and pepper, coat with bread crumbs, and grill for about 6 minutes per side, or until done to taste.

Serve.

* NOTE: IF YOU HAVE RESERVED DUCK LEGS, YOU CAN USE THEM FOR *RAGU DI ANATRA* (SEE PAGE 43).

Skewer meats the Sicilian way; two skewers, each running parallel through ends of meat. Skewer so liver is sandwiched between sausage. Alternate with duck piece and sage leaf.

"BROCIOLETTINE" DI MAIALE

stuffed pork bundles

serves 6

2 EGGS	EXTRA-LARGE
8 OUNCES BREAD	DENSE WHITE SANDWICH-TYPE; CRUSTLESS
6 TABLESPOONS GRATED PECORINO ROMANO	
I TEASPOON FENNEL SEED	
2 SMALL RED CHILI PEPPERS	DRY, CRUSHED
½ TO ¾ TEASPOON SALT	
2 POUNDS PORK LOIN	BONELESS, VERY LEAN, SLICED THIN, AS PER SCALOPPINE (ABOUT 30 SLICES)
⅔ TO I CUP OLIVE OIL	
½ CUP WHITE WINE	DRY

Using your fingers, or a potato masher, mix together the eggs and bread in a large bowl. Mix in the cheese, fennel seed, chilies, and ½ teaspoon of the salt. Divide the filling among the pork slices—about a generous teaspoon each—placing it in the middle of each.

Fold the two opposite sides of the slices over the filling, and roll tightly. Skewer the Sicilian way,* with two skewers, inserting one at each end of each of the rolls, keeping them parallel. This keeps the meat from revolving when turning it. Pack the rolls tightly on the skewers.

In a very large pan, heat the oil. The pan should be large enough to accommodate all your skewers, or use two pans and divide the ingredients between them. Add the skewered bundles, cook over medium-high heat until lightly browned (usually a few minutes). But if the pork releases a lot of liquid, remove the bundles from the pan, increase the heat to high, reduce the liquid, and return the bundles to the pans. Keeping the heat on high, turn the meat only as necessary, for even browning.

Add the wine over high heat. Let it evaporate for a couple of minutes. Reduce the heat to low, cover, and simmer 20 minutes, turning the bundles a couple of times.

Remove the bundles from the pan(s). Cook the liquid in the pan, uncovered, until it is reduced to a nice thick sauce. Add salt to taste. Return the bundles to the pan, turning them in the sauce. Serve immediately.

* FOR AN ILLUSTRATION OF SKEWERING THE SICILIAN WAY, SEE PAGE 134.

PÂTÉ RUSTICO

rustic pâté

serves 10

BUTTER	FOR COATING
FLOUR	FOR DUSTING
I POUND CHICKEN LIVERS	WASHED AND WELL DRAINED
¾ POUND GROUND BEEF	VERY LEAN ROUND
¾ POUND GROUND PORK	VERY LEAN LOIN
2 OUNCES GROUND DANISH HAM	OR SIMILAR HAM
2 TABLESPOONS BUTTER	UNSALTED; MELTED
2 EGG YOLKS	EXTRA-LARGE
⅓ CUP FRESH SAGE	LOOSELY PACKED LEAVES; CUT FINELY
I TABLESPOON FRESH ROSEMARY LEAVES	CUT FINELY
I TABLESPOON JUNIPER BERRIES	CRUSHED
2 TABLESPOONS PINE NUTS	
I TABLESPOON FLOUR	UNBLEACHED, ALL-PURPOSE
½ TEASPOON SALT	
I TEASPOON BLACK PEPPER	FINELY GROUND
I MEDIUM PARSNIP	PEELED, PARBOILED, HARD CORE REMOVED, CUT LENGTHWISE INTO ⅓-INCH STICKS

MIMMETTA
LO MONTE'S
CLASSIC
SICILIAN
COOKBOOK

•

136

Preheat the oven to 375° F.

Line the bottom and the long sides of a 1-pound bread loaf pan with a doubled-up piece of foil, long enough to hang over the sides by a few inches. Coat the foil lining the pan, and the unlined pan sides, with butter, then dust with flour.

Remove the membrane and the fat from the chicken livers and discard. Cut the livers into very small pieces.

In a bowl, mix the livers with the other meats. Add the melted butter, egg yolks, sage, rosemary, juniper berries, pine nuts, flour, salt, and pepper. Mix thoroughly with your hands.

Start packing the meat mixture into the pan, distributing the parsnip sticks in the mixture, parallel to the long sides of the pan, cover the sticks with more mixture, then repeat until all mixture and sticks are used.

Bake in the oven for 2 hours. After the first hour, drain the juices collected in the pan. Reserve the juices. Before returning the pan to the oven, gently pack its contents by holding the foil that overhangs the pan, bringing the edges together, over the top of the pâté. Replace the foil away from the pâté top, and return to the oven.

Let the pâté cool on the counter. If the top is dry, baste it with the drained juices. Leftover juices can have other uses, such as flavoring risotto or stock, if desired. Remove it from the pan by pulling the overhanging foil. Chill. Serve, cut in thick slices.

AGNELLO DI CUSTONACI

custonaci lamb

serves 4 to 6

Every village in Sicily has its own way to cook lamb. This recipe comes from the town of Custonaci; the one following from the town of Gratteri, and the lamb stew is from Petralia.

4 POUNDS LEG OF LAMB	SHANK END, VERY LEAN; CUT INTO 6 OR 7 SLICES (INCLUDE THE LEG BONE)
¾ CUP OLIVE OIL	PLUS ENOUGH FOR ½-INCH LAYER FOR FRYING POTATOES
I TEASPOON SALT	
½ TEASPOON BLACK PEPPER	FINELY GROUND
40 SPRING ONIONS	DISCARD THE GREENEST ENDS
8 GOOD SIZED TOMATOES	CANNED AND PEELED, SEEDED; WELL DRAINED, CUT INTO SMALL PIECES
2 POUNDS POTATOES	(ALLOW EXTRA FOR WASTE) PEELED

Preheat the oven to 425° F.

Divide larger slices of lamb in two parts. All fat must be removed from the lamb to avoid the very strong, gamey taste it carries.

In a large baking dish, about 14 by 10 by 3 inches, pour a generous layer of oil. Coat the lamb with the oil and lay it in the pan.

In a bowl, sprinkle the salt and the pepper on the onions and tomatoes, toss with some oil, then spread over the lamb. Place in the oven and bake for about 30 minutes.

Remove the pan from the oven and pour the rendered liquid into a saucepan. Return the lamb to the oven for 15 more minutes. Boil the liquid, reducing it to about 1 cup. (If the liquid is already only 1 cup, do not reduce.)

Soak the potatoes in water for a few minutes, then rinse well, drain, and pat dry. (Remove the potatoes from the water only when ready to use them, or they'll discolor.)

In a frying pan heat ½-inch oil. Over low heat, fry the potatoes in small batches of a single layer, for about 10 minutes. You'll be able to fry the potatoes in only two batches if you use a 10-inch skillet. Increase the heat to high and fry until golden, turning the potatoes occasionally. Set aside.

Remove the lamb from the oven. Keep in the pan and add the liquid to the lamb. Spread the potatoes on top; serve from the pan immediately.

This dish can be prepared in advance. Before serving, warm the lamb and potatoes separately. (Spread the potatoes on a cookie sheet.) Bake both in a 425° F. oven for 10 minutes. Warm the reserved liquid on the stove, add to the lamb, and top with the potatoes. Serve.

AGNELLO DI GRATTERI

lamb from gratteri

serves 6

3 POUNDS BONELESS LEG OF LAMB	VERY LEAN
¾ CUPS OLIVE OIL	
I MEDIUM ONION	CUT INTO VERY SMALL PIECES
½ CUP WHITE WINE	DRY
½ POUND ASPARAGUS TIPS	
2 ARTICHOKES	CLEANED (SEE PAGE 212); QUARTERED AND SLICED INTO ⅓-INCH THIN WEDGES
I LARGE BULB FENNEL	QUARTERED, SLICED INTO ⅓-INCH WEDGES; THE TENDER, FEATHERY LEAVES CUT UP (SEE PAGE 204)
½ TEASPOON FENNEL SEED	
2 TEASPOONS SALT	
½ TEASPOON BLACK PEPPER	FINELY GROUND
¼ TEASPOON SAFFRON	OPTIONAL

MIMMETTA
LO MONTE'S
CLASSIC
SICILIAN
COOKBOOK

•

138

All fat must be removed from the lamb to avoid the very strong, gamey taste it carries. Cut the lamb in slices a little over ½ inch thick. Divide each slice into a few pieces (three or four, according to the size of the slice).

In a heavy pan, heat the oil and add the onion. When onions are aromatic, add and sear the lamb over high heat. Cover and cook over medium heat an additional 10 minutes.

Remove the lamb from the pan. Reduce the liquid to one third its original volume. Return the lamb to the pan and add the wine. Cook over high heat for a few minutes, turning the meat once.

Add the remaining ingredients to the pan except the saffron, stir well. Cover and cook over medium-low heat for 20 more minutes, stirring a few times. In the last 5 minutes, add the saffron if desired. To prepare saffron, crush the stigmas by placing them between wax paper and rolling over them with a rolling pin. Soak them in a spoonful of the liquid released by the lamb. Serve.

AGNELLO A "CIUCIDDU" (PETRALIA)

lamb stew

serves 4 to 6

¾ CUP OLIVE OIL

5 CLOVES GARLIC — LARGE

2½ POUNDS BONELESS LAMB — CUT INTO SMALL CUBES

¾ TEASPOON SALT

I TEASPOON BLACK PEPPER — FINELY GROUND

I½ TEASPOONS FENNEL
  SEED

2 EGGS — SMALL, SEPARATED

I LARGE BULB FENNEL — FEATHERY LEAVES INCLUDED (ONLY THE TENDER
ONES), CUT INTO ¼-INCH WEDGES (SEE PAGE
204)

In a large, heavy pot heat the oil. Add the garlic and the lamb. Sear the lamb, using high heat.

Add enough water to cover the lamb three quarters of the way up. Add salt, pepper, and fennel seed. Bring to a boil, place a lid on the pot, left ajar, and cook over low heat until the lamb is so very tender you can separate with a fork.

Add the fennel, cook until al dente. If there is more than half an inch of liquid in the pan, reduce it over high heat, uncovered, until about half an inch remains.

Beat the egg whites until very fluffy, add the yolks, and beat until mixed. Over low heat, stir the eggs into the pot with the lamb until creamy. Serve immediately.

"GALLO D'INDIA" RIPIENO

stuffed turkey

serves 14 to 16

MIMMETTA
LO MONTE'S
CLASSIC
SICILIAN
COOKBOOK

•

140

Traditionally *uova non nate,* unborn eggs, were used in this recipe. These are eggs which are still developing in the hen. I've substituted quail eggs for them. The type of pasta traditionally used was *anelletti,* a typically Sicilian pasta best suited for stuffings and timbales since it packs very well, holds up to prolonged baking, and is very pretty. Unfortunately, as with unborn eggs, it is very difficult to find today. But use it if you can find it.

Serve this dish as either a first or a second course.

12-POUND TURKEY	
¾ POUND MILD PORK SAUSAGE	
10 QUAIL EGGS	
2½ TEASPOONS SALT	
¾ CUP OLIVE OIL	
1 LARGE ONION	CUT INTO VERY SMALL PIECES
2 CLOVES GARLIC	
1 POUND BEEF ROUND	CUT INTO 2-INCH CUBES
1 POUND BONELESS PORK LOIN	VERY LEAN; CUT INTO 2-INCH CUBES
½ CUP WHITE WINE	DRY
12 OUNCES TOMATO PASTE	
10 OUNCES FROZEN PEAS	USE VERY SMALL ONES
¼ POUND PROVOLONE	PREFERABLY IMPORTED; CUT INTO VERY SMALL CUBES
¾ CUP GRATED PECORINO ROMANO	OR OTHER SHARP GRATED CHEESE
3 EGGS	EXTRA-LARGE
1 TEASPOON BLACK PEPPER	FINELY GROUND
1½ POUNDS PASTA SHELLS	MEDIUM SIZED; COMMERCIAL

Have the butcher debone the turkey, preferably removing bones from the first wing sections and the thighs, leaving the drumstick bones in. Reserve the carcass and giblets.

In a pot, cover the quail eggs with plenty of water, bring to a boil, and cook 5 minutes. Drain, dip the eggs in cold water for a few minutes, then shell and set aside.

Thoroughly pierce the sausage casing with a thin skewer. Place in a pot, cover with plenty of water, bring to boil, and cook for 10 minutes. Drain and set aside.

In a large pot, cover the turkey carcass and the giblets with plenty of water. Add 1 teaspoon salt; bring to a boil. Skim the surface and simmer for 1½ hours. Skim as needed. Remove and discard carcass and giblets. Set stock aside.

In a large pot, heat the oil, onion, and garlic. Cook over high heat until aromatic. Add and sear the beef, pork loin, and sausage. Add the wine; let it evaporate. Stir in the tomato paste. As soon as the mixture sizzles, add enough water to barely cover the meats. Stir, dissolving the tomato paste, and add 1½ teaspoons salt. Bring to a boil and let simmer, covered, until the meat chunks are tender enough to be shredded with a fork, about 1½ to 2 hours.

Parboil the peas.

Shred the meat chunks, crumble the sausage, and add the peas to the pot. Set the meat sauce aside to cool. After the ingredients have cooled some, stir in the cheeses, the three eggs, and the pepper.

In the meantime cook the pasta in the stock set aside. Cook very much al dente (see page 31). Pasta will be ready when cut in half and there is still a distinct white core. Do not add cold water. Drain very well (since shells trap liquid). Taste the pasta and adjust the salt if necessary. Mix the pasta with the meat sauce.

Stuff as much pasta and meat into the turkey as it will hold. Insert one quail egg into each of the wings and the thighs. Distribute the others evenly throughout the rest of the filling.

Preheat the oven to 325° F.

Stitch up the turkey (unwaxed and unflavored dental floss works very well). Make sure the stitches catch both the skin and the flesh, and that they are approximately ⅓ inch away from the edges of the skin, or they will not hold.

Coat the turkey with some oil, sprinkle with some salt and, if you wish, pepper. Tie a string around the turkey forcing it to stay in a "turkey" shape.

Pack any leftover pasta/meat mixture in another baking pan, coated with oil.

Bake the turkey for 3 hours. For the last 1½ hours, cover the turkey loosely with foil and baste it frequently. Bake the pasta for the last 45 minutes.

Let the turkey cool 30 minutes before serving it. Remove the string and discard. Cut off the drumsticks and the wings, then cut the body in half lengthwise. Cut each half into thick slices. If you wish, remove thin slices from the breast before cutting the body in half, but leave enough breast meat to encase the pasta/meat mixture. Serve along with the pasta and meat mixture baked separately.

"FRACASSÉ" DI POLLI

chicken fricassee

serves 6

4 WHOLE CHICKEN BREASTS	HALVED
2 TEASPOONS SALT	
6 TABLESPOONS (3 OUNCES) BUTTER	UNSALTED
4 TABLESPOONS OLIVE OIL	
2 SMALL PARSNIPS	QUARTERED AND THINLY SLICED
½ SMALL ONION	CUT INTO VERY SMALL PIECES
8 CELERY RIBS	TENDER; CUT INTO VERY SMALL PIECES
4 SPRIGS CORIANDER	STEMS REMOVED; CUT FINELY
4 FULL SPRIGS PARSLEY	STEMS REMOVED; CUT FINELY
10 TO 15 FRESH SAGE LEAVES	
6 TEASPOONS LEMON JUICE	FRESHLY SQUEEZED
4 EGG YOLKS	EXTRA-LARGE

MIMMETTA
LO MONTE'S
CLASSIC
SICILIAN
COOKBOOK

•

142

In a large pot, cover the chicken breasts with water. Add 1 teaspoon salt and bring to a boil. Skim the sediment from the surface. Let the chicken cook 15 minutes from the boiling point, keeping water at a low boil.

Remove the chicken from the liquid. Remove the skin, fat, and bones. Cut the chicken breasts in pieces a little larger than bite sized and set aside.

Return bones to liquid, but discard the fat and skin. Let the liquid simmer, uncovered, until reduced by about one third. Turn off the heat. Discard the bones. Skim again as necessary. Set aside the stock.

Add to a very large frying pan the butter and the oil (or use two large pans, and divide all the ingredients in half). Let the butter melt over low heat. Add the parsnips, onion, and celery and cook over medium heat, stirring, until pleasantly crisp and aromatic.

Stir in the chicken, coriander, parsley, and sage. Increase the heat to high, cook stirring for a few minutes, until the pan looks dry and the ingredients start sticking to it.

Add 1 cup of the chicken stock and 2 teaspoons lemon juice to the pan. Stir well, scraping the bottom of the pan to deglaze. Add one more cup of stock, let it come to a boil, and then reduce the heat to low. Remove 4 tablespoons liquid and set aside to cool.

Push the solid ingredients to the side of the pan. With the heat very low, simmer the liquid (if necessary, remove from heat for a short time).

In a bowl, mix together the egg yolks and the reserved 4 tablespoons of liquid. With ingredients still kept to one side of the pan, trickle the mixture into the liquid in the pan. Over very low heat, stir liquid very evenly and quickly—until the mixture thickens into a smooth, creamy sauce. Then mix the sauce with ingredients pushed to side of pan.

Remove the pan from the heat. Sprinkle in up to 1 more teaspoon salt, and mix in 4 more teaspoons lemon juice. Serve immediately.

For a richer dish with more sauce, increase the quantity of egg yolks and stock. Add up to four more yolks, adding ½ cup stock per additional yolk.

POLLO PICCANTE

hot chicken

serves 6

FLOUR	UNBLEACHED, ALL-PURPOSE; FOR COATING
2 POUNDS CHICKEN BREAST	(OR USE TURKEY BREAST) SKINLESS AND BONELESS, CUT INTO 1-INCH CUBES
6 TABLESPOONS BUTTER	(OR USE OLIVE OIL) UNSALTED
3 TABLESPOONS OLIVE OIL	
8 SMALL RED CHILI PEPPERS	DRY
20 FRESH SAGE LEAVES	(OR ½ TEASPOON DRY) GROUND
5 TABLESPOONS WHITE WINE	DRY
5 OUNCES BRANDY	OR USE WHISKEY
½ TEASPOON SALT	

Lightly flour the chicken.

In a very large skillet, warm the butter, oil, and chilies over very low heat about 5 minutes. Squeeze the chilies down in the pan, using a spoon. Turn the heat to high. Add the chicken, stir. Turn heat to medium-high and cook chicken turning only as necessary for even browning, for about 10 minutes. Adjust the heat if it is browning too quickly or too slowly.

Increase heat to high again. Add the sage, wine, brandy, and salt; stir for a couple of minutes.

Serve immediately.

"SOFFIELLO" DI POLLO

chicken soufflé

serves 6

Although its looks and consistency suffer some, this soufflé will still be good if served when it has lost its puffiness. To serve it at its best, you may want to have everything except for the egg whites prepared in advance. Beat and add the egg whites just before baking. Generally I use chicken left over from other dishes.

BUTTER	UNSALTED; FOR COATING
BREAD CRUMBS	UNFLAVORED; FOR COATING
½ POUND COOKED CHICKEN BREAST	GROUND
2 CUPS BECHAMEL	SEE PAGE 48
4 EGGS	EXTRA-LARGE
¾ TEASPOON SALT	
3 TABLESPOONS GRATED PARMESAN	
15 LARGE FRESH SAGE LEAVES	CUT INTO THIN STRIPS
¼ TEASPOON GROUND CINNAMON	

MIMMETTA
LO MONTE'S
CLASSIC
SICILIAN
COOKBOOK

•

144

Preheat the oven to 325° F.

Coat an 8-inch soufflé dish with the butter and bread crumbs.

In a large bowl, mix the chicken with the just made, still hot bechamel. When mixture is lukewarm, add the 4 egg yolks, salt, cheese, sage, and cinnamon, mixing well.

In a separate bowl, beat the egg whites to their peak. Gently mix one third of the egg whites into the chicken mixture. Then gently fold in the rest of the whites. Pour into the prepared dish. Bake in the oven for 45 minutes.

Serve immediately.

POLLO D' AUTUNNO

fall chicken

serves 12 to 14

Since this dish is served cold, it's a wonderful choice if you can prepare the food a day in advance.

Filling

2 POUNDS GROUND PORK	VERY LEAN; BONELESS LOIN PREFERRED
3 EGGS	EXTRA-LARGE
3 APPLES	TART; PEELED, CORED, CUT INTO VERY SMALL CUBES
I LARGE ONION	CUT INTO VERY SMALL PIECES
I CUP WALNUTS	COARSELY GROUND
1½ TEASPOONS FENNEL SEED	
I TEASPOON GROUND CINNAMON	
¾ TEASPOON GROUND CLOVES	
¾ TEASPOON GROUND NUTMEG	
1½ TEASPOONS GROUND CORIANDER	
2 LARGE SLICES BREAD	WHOLE WHEAT, SANDWICH-TYPE
2 TEASPOONS SALT	
2 TEASPOONS BLACK PEPPER	FINELY GROUND
3 CUPS CHESTNUTS*	PACKED IN WATER
BUTTER	UNSALTED
7-POUND CHICKEN	ROASTER; DEBONED

In a large bowl, mix together the filling ingredients, adding the chestnuts after everything else is thoroughly mixed.

Preheat the oven to 325° F. Coat a baking dish with butter.

Stuff the chicken, forcing the filling into the wings and the drumsticks first. Sew and tie the bird.

Place the bird breast-side up in the prepared baking dish and place a few flakes of butter on it. Bake in the oven for 3½ hours. After the first hour of baking, cover loosely with foil. Baste frequently.

Cool. Refrigerate until thoroughly cold. Remove and discard the thread. Cut in ½-inch slices.

Serve cold. This dish can be made 24 hours in advance.

* OF COURSE IF YOU WANT TO USE FRESH CHESTNUTS, YOU ARE WELCOME TO DO SO. YOU WILL NEED 2½ CUPS OF THEM AND SOME TIME TO GET RID OF THE SHELLS (BE CAREFUL NOT TO CUT YOURSELF). AFTER YOU HAVE REMOVED THE OUTER SHELL, DIP THE CHESTNUTS IN A PAN WITH BOILING WATER, TO REMOVE SKINS.

IN A POT, COVER THE PEELED CHESTNUTS WITH WATER, AND BRING TO A BOIL. SIMMER UNTIL TENDER, DRAIN, AND CUT THE CHESTNUTS IN A FEW PIECES.

POLLETTO ARROSTO

roasted cornish game hen

serves 1

1 SMALL CORNISH GAME HEN
3 TABLESPOONS LEMON JUICE   FRESHLY SQUEEZED
¼ TEASPOON GROUND CUMIN
⅓ CUP OLIVE OIL
¼ TEASPOON TABASCO SAUCE
BEEF OR CHICKEN STOCK   SEE PAGE 72
¼ TEASPOON SALT

MIMMETTA
LO MONTE'S
CLASSIC
SICILIAN
COOKBOOK

•

146

Preheat the oven to 450° F.

With a sharp knife, cut along the center of the hen's breastbone, gently lifting the flesh from it. Remove the bone. Also remove the thigh bones by first making two cuts in the flesh of the thighs, facing the inside of the bird along the thigh bones. Then break the joints with the drumstick bones. Lift the flesh gently away from the thigh bones. Cut ligaments and remove thigh bones. The drumstick bones remain in the bird.

In a bowl, combine 1 tablespoon lemon juice, the cumin, 1 tablespoon oil, and the Tabasco, and coat the hen with the mixture.

In an ovenproof sauté pan, heat a very thin layer of oil. Sear the butterflied hen over high heat, then bake in the oven for 20 minutes, skin-side up. Check the hen often, adding small amounts of stock to the bottom of the pan when necessary to prevent scorching.

Remove the hen from the oven and from the pan. Add the remaining 2 tablespoons of lemon juice, 3 tablespoons of stock, and the salt, and stir to deglaze the pan. Serve the hen topped with the pan drippings, adding more stock if you'd like more juices.

"GALLOTTA" RIPIENA

stuffed roast chicken

serves 10 to 14

A small young female turkey was traditionally used for this dish. *"Gallotta"* means female turkey. Using a roaster (instead of an average turkey) will help to replicate the tenderness of a young female turkey.

7-TO-8 POUND CHICKEN	ROASTER
3 POUNDS GROUND BEEF	VERY LEAN ROUND
2 EGGS	EXTRA-LARGE
2 TABLESPOONS RED WINE VINEGAR	
3 TABLESPOONS LEMON JUICE	FRESHLY SQUEEZED
LEMON PEEL	½ OF 1 LEMON, REMOVED WITH A POTATO PEELER; CUT INTO VERY SMALL PIECES
¼ TEASPOON GROUND NUTMEG	
¼ TEASPOON GROUND CINNAMON	
¼ TEASPOON GROUND CORIANDER	
¾ TEASPOON GROUND CLOVES	
1½ TEASPOONS BLACK PEPPER	FINELY GROUND
1½ TEASPOONS SALT	
2 CLOVES GARLIC	
½ CUP PINE NUTS	
10 QUAIL EGGS	HARD-BOILED (OPTIONAL)
½ POUND *PROSCIUTTO CRUDO* *	CUT INTO ¼-INCH THICK SLICES AND THEN IN STRIPS
5 BAY LEAVES	WHOLE
¼ POUND FULLY COOKED HAM	CUT INTO THIN SLICES AND THEN INTO 1-INCH STRIPS
3 CUPS *SALSA AL DRAGONCELLO*	SEE PAGE 107

Preheat the oven to 325° F.

Have your butcher debone the roaster, preferably removing the bones from the first wing section, the thighs, and the drumsticks—but leaving the last third of the drumstick intact.

In a large bowl, mix together the ground beef, eggs, vinegar, 1½ tablespoons lemon juice, the lemon peel, nutmeg, cinnamon, coriander, ¼ teaspoon cloves, 1 teaspoon pepper, 1 teaspoon salt, the garlic, and the pine nuts. Set aside.

* ITALIAN "RAW HAM," THE LITERAL TRANSLATION OF *PROSCIUTTO CRUDO,* IS WHAT AMERICANS CONSIDER TO BE "PROSCIUTTO." IN ITALIAN, *PROSCIUTTO* SIMPLY MEANS HAM. *PROSCIUTTO COTTO,* OR "COOKED HAM," IS MOST SIMILAR TO AMERICANS' DANISH HAM.

Open up the chicken, breast-side down. Stuff the wings and the drumsticks with some of the beef mixture and the quail eggs if you like, and lay some of the mixture evenly over the opened-up bird. Insert the strips of *prosciutto crudo,* forcing them into the beef mixture as far as they will go. Lay a few strips lengthwise on the beef layer, cover with rest of the beef and, if using, the remaining quail eggs. Lay the remaining ham strips over the beef, pressing them down into the beef.

Thread a large needle with unwaxed, unflavored dental floss. Close up the bird, and manipulate it so that there won't be bulges, overlap the skin edges a little along the back, and sew both skin and flesh with long overcast stitches. Do not pull the thread too much or it will tear the skin and the meat. Turn the bird breast-side up.

Sprinkle the surface of the chicken with the remaining lemon juice and the remaining salt, pepper, and cloves. Tie the drumsticks together from the ends, where the small piece of bone is left.

Tie a string around the chicken, criss-crossing it in three different spots: across the breast and wings, across the middle, and across the thighs. Insert bay leaves under the string at regular intervals. Cover with cooked ham strips.

Place the chicken in a lightly greased baking pan and bake in the oven for 1 hour. Baste with the drippings, loosely cover with foil, and bake 2½ hours longer, if your bird weighs about 7 pounds. If your bird is over 7 pounds, allow 15 extra minutes for each extra pound. Baste a few times during baking.

Remove the bird from the oven, cool. Remove the pan, reserving the drippings, remove and discard the thread, and refrigerate until thoroughly chilled. Cut into slices a little less than ½ inch thick. Decorate a plate with orange wedges and serve the bird with *Salsa al dragoncello.*

Note: You can make a stock with the carcass, neck, giblets, and pan drippings, to use in a *risotto* (see page 59) to serve with this recipe. Or, you can cook some tender peas in the drippings and then thicken the drippings with a little cornstarch and serve on the side.

MIMMETTA
LO MONTE'S
CLASSIC
SICILIAN
COOKBOOK

•

148

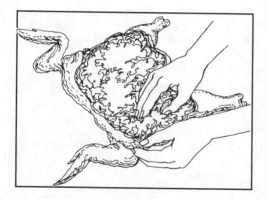

Stuff beef mixture (and quail eggs) into wings, thighs and drumsticks. Lay some mixture evenly over opened up bird.

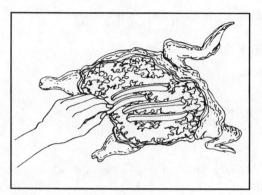

Insert strips of raw ham into wings, thighs and drumsticks. Lay a few strips lengthwise on beef mixture. Cover with remaining mixture (and quail eggs). Lay remaining raw ham strips on top, pressing them down into beef.

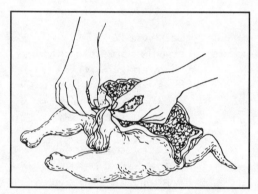

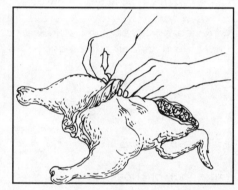

Stitch the bird closed, using unwaxed dental floss. Start from the back, overlapping the skin edges; use overcast stitches.

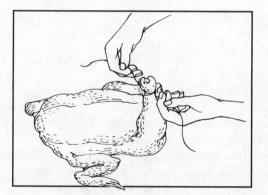

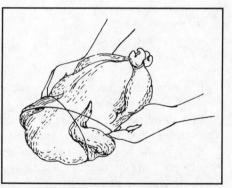

Turn bird breast-side up; tie drumsticks together from the ends where pieces of bone have been left.

Tie a string around the chicken, criss-crossing it in three different spots: across the breast and wings, across the middle, and across the thighs.

PETTI DI POLLO IN SALSA ALL' ARANCIA

chicken breast in orange sauce

serves 1

This is a very easy dish to make, taking very little time. You can also substitute squab breast, duck breast, or whole quail for the chicken breast. Just make sure to adjust cooking time to size of bird.

MIMMETTA
LO MONTE'S
CLASSIC
SICILIAN
COOKBOOK

•

150

6 TABLESPOONS BEEF OR CHICKEN STOCK	SEE PAGE 72
1 HEAPING TEASPOON DRIED PORCINI MUSHROOMS	SOAK IN ROOM TEMPERATURE WATER UNTIL PLUMP; WASH VERY WELL, REMOVING ANY SAND OR DIRT; THEN DRAIN AND CUT OFF SKIN; AND CUT INTO SMALL PIECES
1 TEASPOON CAPERS	PRESERVED IN VINEGAR; RINSED AND DRAINED
1 TEASPOON ORANGE PEEL	PARBOILED; CUT INTO VERY SMALL PIECES
1 TABLESPOON BUTTER	UNSALTED
1 TABLESPOON OLIVE OIL	
1 SMALL CHICKEN BREAST	SKINNED, DEBONED, TRIMMED OF FAT
¼ CUP ORANGE JUICE	
⅛ TEASPOON SALT	
BLACK PEPPER, TO TASTE	FINELY GROUND
½ SMALL ANCHOVY FILLET	PACKED IN OLIVE OIL; MASHED

In a small saucepan, simmer ¼ cup stock, the mushrooms, capers, and orange peel, covered, for 10 minutes.

In a sauté pan heat the butter and the oil until smoke is barely visible. Add the chicken breast and cook over medium heat about 5 minutes per side.

Remove the breast from pan and reduce the pan drippings to about one half (or reduce just long enough to boil out excess watery juices yielded by the breast). Return the breast to the pan. Over high heat, add mushroom sauce, orange juice, salt, and pepper. Cook the breast for 5 more minutes, adjusting the heat so that the sauce gets reduced by about one half during that time.

Mix the anchovy with the remaining 2 tablespoons stock; add to pan. Turn the breast in the sauce. Serve.

PETTI DI ANATRA AL MARSALA

duck breasts in marsala

serves 8

Please note that you will need to marinate the duck 12 hours in advance of preparing this dish.

6 WHOLE DUCK BREASTS	(APPROXIMATELY 4 POUNDS) BONELESS, SKINNED, FAT REMOVED
2 CUPS MARSALA	DRY
6 TABLESPOONS CURRANTS	
½ CUP OLIVE OIL	
½ TEASPOON SALT	
I TEASPOON BLACK PEPPER	FINELY GROUND

In a large bowl, marinate the duck overnight in 1 cup of Marsala and the currants.
Remove the duck from marinade. Remove any currants that stick to the duck.
In a shallow pan, pour the oil and heat almost until smoke is barely visible. Using high heat, sauté the breasts, uncovered, for 3 minutes per side.
Add the marinade and the second cup of Marsala. Deglaze, adding salt and pepper.
Remove breasts from pan and slice them lengthwise, following the grain.
Serve, sliced, with the pan juice trickled on top.
On the side, serve *Salsa ai pinoli* (see below).

SALSA AI PINOLI

pine nut sauce

yields ⅔ cup

¾ CUP PINE NUTS	
I TABLESPOON CAPERS	PACKED IN VINEGAR; WELL SQUEEZED
3 TABLESPOONS RED WINE VINEGAR	
I TEASPOON SUGAR	
¼ TEASPOON SALT	
I TEASPOON CURRANTS	

Puree all the ingredients but currants in a food processor. Add the currants and process until they are roughly cut.

QUAGLIE IMBOTTITE

stuffed quail

serves 6

Please note that you need to marinate fruits a day in advance of preparing this dish.

I CUP DRIED APPLE CHUNKS	LOOSELY PACKED
18 DRIED APRICOT HALVES	HALVED
1½ CUP Marsala	DRY
12 QUAIL	
¼ CUP OLIVE OIL	PLUS SOME FOR COATING
½ TO ¾ TEASPOON SALT	
¾ TEASPOON BLACK PEPPER	FINELY GROUND

MIMMETTA
LO MONTE'S
CLASSIC
SICILIAN
COOKBOOK

•

152

Preheat the oven to 425° F.

Marinate the apples and the apricots in the Marsala overnight.

Remove the breastbone, the rib cage, and the attached backbone from each quail.

Stuff each bird with some apples and three pieces of apricot. Set aside the remaining Marsala. Tie the drumstick ends together, using a string long enough to then wrap around the wings and the legs, forming a firm bundle.

In a skillet, heat the oil until smoke is barely visible. Over high heat, sear the quail, breast-side down.

When the birds are well-seared, place them in a low-sided baking dish, well coated with oil. The birds must not be crowded.

Bake in the oven for 20 minutes. Check the pan and add very small amounts of water to the bottom of it if it starts to burn, shaking the pan to distribute water evenly.

Take the dish out of the oven, sprinkle the birds with salt and pepper, remove them from pan, and set aside.

Add the reserved Marsala to the dish. With a spatula, scrape the bottom of the dish to help deglaze it. Remove and discard the strings from the birds.

Serve with the Marsala sauce poured over birds.

QUAGLIE ARROSTO IN CASSERUOLA

quail roasted in the pot

serves 4

½ TEASPOON SALT	
½ TEASPOON BLACK PEPPER	FINELY GROUND
8 QUAIL	IF BIRDS ARE VERY SMALL USE 12
16 FRESH SAGE LEAVES	

BUNCH OF CHIVES	ALLOWING AT LEAST 4 STRANDS PER BIRD
2 SPRIGS ROSEMARY	
8 SPRIGS PARSLEY	
2 CLOVES GARLIC	THINLY SLICED
¼ CUP OLIVE OIL	
⅔ CUP RED WINE	DRY
2 SLICES BACON	CUT INTO 8 PIECES (OR 12 IF USING 12 BIRDS)

Sprinkle the salt and pepper in and on top of the quail.

Mix all the herbs together with the garlic, and stuff the birds with the mixture.

In a heavy pot where the birds will fit in a tight layer, heat the oil. Quickly sear the quail over high heat. Add the wine, reduce the heat to low, place one piece of bacon on each quail, cover, and cook about ½ hour.

Turn the birds a couple of times while cooking, being sure to replace the bacon piece on top of them after doing so. At the end of the cooking time, if the sauce is watery, remove the birds from the pot, and boil down the liquid. Return birds to pot. Serve hot.

QUAGLIE AL MARSALA

quail in marsala

serves 4

½ TO ⅔ CUP OLIVE OIL	
8 QUAIL	IF BIRDS ARE VERY SMALL USE 12
8 SMALL SPRIGS FRESH ROSEMARY	
I CUP MARSALA	DRY
½ TEASPOON SALT	
BLACK PEPPER, TO TASTE	FINELY GROUND

Butterfly the quail by cutting along the breastbone and removing it.

In a very large skillet, heat the oil. Add 4 birds and 4 rosemary sprigs. The birds should not be crowded. Cook over high heat, 2 minutes per side. Remove these birds and repeat with the other four, keeping the heat on high.

Return all the birds to the skillet and add ½ cup Marsala and the salt. Keeping the heat on high, turn the quail in the wine quickly, then remove again from the skillet and set aside.

Add the remaining half cup Marsala to the skillet, deglaze the pan, and turn off heat. Pour the sauce over the quail.

Serve topped with the remaining rosemary sprigs and sprinkled with pepper.

You can also serve with *Salsa ai pinoli* (see page 151).

OCA SELVATICA RIPIENA

stuffed wild goose

serves 6

I CUP CONVERTED RICE	
6 TABLESPOONS (3 OUNCES) BUTTER	UNSALTED
I POMEGRANATE	REMOVE MEMBRANES; CLEAN
2 TEASPOONS ORANGE PEEL	SLIVERED FINELY
I TEASPOON GROUND CINNAMON	
¼ POUND DRIED FIGS	CUT INTO VERY SMALL PIECES
½ CUP WALNUTS	BROKEN INTO LARGE PIECES
½ CUP HAZELNUTS	COARSELY GROUND
I¼ TEASPOONS SALT	
I TEASPOON BLACK PEPPER	FINELY GROUND
3½- TO 4-POUND WILD GOOSE	CLEANED

MIMMETTA
LO MONTE'S
CLASSIC
SICILIAN
COOKBOOK

•

154

Bring ¾ cup water to a boil. Stir in rice. Cover, simmer until water is absorbed. Rice must be very firm.

In a large bowl, mix the rice along with 3 tablespoons butter, the pomegranate, orange peel, cinnamon, figs, walnuts, hazelnuts, ¾ teaspoon salt, and 1 teaspoon pepper.

Preheat the oven to 325° F.

Stuff the goose with as much of the mixture as necessary to fill it, packing it well.

Pack the remaining mixture in a baking dish well coated with butter (using part of 1 tablespoon), and top it with butter flakes (using the rest of the tablespoon).

Melt 2 tablespoons of butter.

Place the bird in a baking dish just a little larger than the bird itself and coat the bird with the butter, adding whatever butter is left to the baking dish. Sprinkle with ½ teaspoon salt, and pepper to taste. Cover the bird loosely with foil.

Place the goose in the oven and bake for 2½ hours. During the last 30 minutes of the bird's cooking time, place the dish with the leftover stuffing in oven. Once the bird is cooked, allow it to sit on the counter, still loosely covered with foil for 15 minutes before carving it.

To carve the bird, slit the skin around the drumsticks and the wings. Cut through the meat to the joints. Cut through the joints and set the wings and drumsticks aside.

Slit the skin along the crest of the breastbone and on each side of the breast, where the meat tapers off over the rib cage. Holding the blade very close to the breastbone, cut the meat away from it on each side. Slice each breast half into about sixteen thin slices—each one retaining its portion of skin. Set aside each slice in the order it has been removed so that in the end you can recompose the breast.

Cut the meat of the thighs away from the bone, leaving the pieces fairly large. Mound the stuffing of the carcass on the serving dish, with the meat arranged around it. Serve with the remaining baked stuffing.

Ragù *di polli*.
I polli si riempiono di *farsa* di vitello suffritta con
erbe , presciutto , funghi , tartufi , ed`aromi , e si
fanno cuocere nella stufa con lardo , presciutto , ed
erbe. Cotti si daranno con salsa di *acetosella*.

Ragù *di selvaggina*.
Steccata con aromi , rosmarina , salvia, si pone a
stufare con lardo , presciutto , oglio, lauro, targone,
ed aromi con un poco di vino ; e se venisse a dis-
seccarsi, si umidisce con altro vino , e con un poco
di brodo.

43

RAGÙ DI SELVAGGINA

game stew

serves 6 to 8

2 POUNDS VENISON	ROUND OR SIMILAR PART, VERY LEAN (NO SINEWY PARTS); CUT INTO 1-INCH CUBES
2 CUPS RED WINE	
10 CLOVES	WRAPPED IN CHEESECLOTH OR AN HERB CONTAINER
2 TEASPOONS DRY TARRAGON LEAVES	
12 LARGE FRESH SAGE LEAVES	
½ TEASPOON FRESH ROSEMARY LEAVES	
2 SMALL BAY LEAVES	
¾ CUP OLIVE OIL	
1 LARGE ONION	CUT INTO SMALL PIECES
4 LARGE CARROTS	CUT INTO 1-INCH SECTIONS
½ TEASPOON SALT	
½ TEASPOON BLACK PEPPER	FINELY GROUND

Marinate the venison for 1 hour in the wine, the cloves, and the herbs, turning it often. Reserve marinade when you remove venison.

In a heavy pot, heat the oil, add and sauté the onion and the carrots, until aromatic. Add the venison and sear over high heat.

Remove and discard 6 of the cloves from the marinade. Add the marinade, salt, pepper, and as much water as necessary to barely cover the meat. Cover and simmer on low heat for 1 hour and 15 minutes, or until the meat is tender.

Remove the venison and carrots from pot. Reduce the liquid to approximately ¾ cup.

Return the venison and carrots to the pot, stir, and reheat well.

FILETTO DI CERVO ARROSTITO NEL FORNO

venison filet roasted in the oven

serves 4

1¼ POUND VENISON FILET	2½ TO 3 INCHES THICK
10 LARGE FRESH SAGE LEAVES	
3 2-INCH ROSEMARY SPRIGS	
10 JUNIPER BERRIES	CRUSHED
2 CUPS RED WINE	HEAVY BODIED, SUCH AS A BAROLO
¼ TEASPOON BLACK PEPPER	FINELY GROUND
½ TO ⅔ CUP OLIVE OIL	
SALT, TO TASTE	

MIMMETTA
LO MONTE'S
CLASSIC
SICILIAN
COOKBOOK

•

156

Preheat the oven to 450° F.

Marinate the venison in the herbs, wine, and pepper for a couple of hours. Remove the meat from the marinade and drain very well, reserving the marinade.

In a large sauté pan, heat the oil until smoke is barely visible. Add the filet and sear very quickly. Reserve the pan with the drippings.

Transfer the filet to a wide, shallow baking dish, coated with olive oil. Bake in the oven for 20 minutes, turning after 10 minutes.

While filet is baking, add the marinade to the pan in which the filet was seared, and reduce mixture to approximately ⅔ cup. Add salt to taste.

Remove the filet from the baking dish at end of baking period, place on serving dish and thinly slice.

Transfer the sauce to the pan in which filet baked. Scrape the bottom of the baking pan well. Strain the sauce over the sliced filet. Serve.

PESCI
fish

A Word About My Fish Recipes

These recipes have been arranged in an order that reflects easiest to prepare dishes to more difficult to prepare ones. If you would like to find a variety of recipes to make for a certain kind of fish, please check the index for page numbers.

TRANCE DI PESCE CON "AMMOGGHIO"

fish steaks with "ammogghio"

serves 6

2 POUNDS TUNA, SWORDFISH, OR HALIBUT	SLICED INTO 6 1-INCH THICK SLICES
OLIVE OIL	FOR COATING
½ TEASPOON SALT	
½ TEASPOON BLACK PEPPER	FINELY GROUND
1 RECIPE "AMMOGGHIO"	SEE BELOW

Preheat the oven to 425° F.

Coat the fish with the oil, then sprinkle with salt and pepper. Lay the steaks, uncrowded, in a very low sided baking dish. Bake in the oven for 13 to 15 minutes or grill or broil the steaks (5 to 10 minutes per side). To test for doneness, insert a very fine skewer into the fish. If color is whitish and juices released are clear, then fish is done.

Top steaks with *"Ammogghio"* immediately after taking them out of the oven and serve.

MIMMETTA
LO MONTE'S
CLASSIC
SICILIAN
COOKBOOK

•

158

"AMMOGGHIO"

wrapping

serves 6

This topping is usually made to top grilled, broiled, or baked fish. *"Ammogghio"* is also delicious when served on hot bread slices, preferably very dense and homemade (see *Pane di casa,* page 240).

1 POUND FRESH TOMATOES	PEAR SHAPED, RIPE BUT FIRM, SKIN ON; CUT INTO VERY SMALL PIECES
2 LARGE CLOVES GARLIC	CUT INTO MINUTE PIECES
⅓ CUP OLIVE OIL	
¾ TEASPOON SALT	
½ TEASPOON BLACK PEPPER	FINELY GROUND
1 TEASPOON OREGANO	DRY LEAVES

In a bowl, mix together all the ingredients except the oregano. Rub the oregano between your hands and let it fall into the bowl. This releases the aroma of the herb. Mix. Serve at room temperature.

PESCE APPARECCHIATO

dressed-up fish

serves 8

This dish can be made in advance. Refrigerate the fish as soon as it is lukewarm after cooking. Bring it to room temperature before serving.

10 GREEN OLIVES	
3 POUNDS TUNA, SWORDFISH,	
OR HALIBUT	SLICED ¾ INCH THICK
FLOUR	UNBLEACHED, ALL-PURPOSE; FOR COATING
CORN OIL	(OR USE SIMILAR VEGETABLE OIL) ENOUGH FOR A 1-INCH LAYER
2 CUPS OLIVE OIL	
¼ SMALL ONION	CUT INTO VERY SMALL PIECES
1 CELERY HEART	INCLUDING THE LEAVES; CUT INTO VERY SMALL CUBES
4 LARGE TOMATOES	CANNED OR FRESH; PEELED; SEEDED, CUT INTO SMALL PIECES; RESERVE JUICE
½ TEASPOON SUGAR	
2½ CUPS RED WINE VINEGAR	
1½ TO 2 TEASPOONS SALT	
BLACK PEPPER, TO TASTE	FINELY GROUND
⅓ CUP CAPERS	PACKED IN VINEGAR, RINSED AND DRAINED

Scald the olives in hot water. Remove the pits and cut the olives into small pieces. Pat the fish into the flour until well coated.

In a very deep skillet, pour 1-inch layer of corn oil. Over high heat quickly brown the fish in the skillet. Turn once while cooking.

In two large skillets, pour the olive oil. Add the onion and celery; cook until aromatic. Add the tomatoes and cook over high heat until they sizzle. Stir in the sugar, vinegar, salt, pepper, capers, and olives. Place the fish into the pans.

Turn the heat to low and cook the fish, covered, 15 minutes. Halfway through the cooking, turn the fish (very gently so that it won't break) by inserting a spatula under it and easing it down on the other side with the help of a wooden spoon. If pans are dry, add the reserved tomato juice.

Let the fish rest a couple of hours before eating. Serve at room temperature.

TONNO ARROSTO

roast tuna

serves 6 to 8

3½ TO 4 POUNDS TUNA	CUT INTO ABOUT 1½-INCH THICK STEAKS
RED WINE VINEGAR	FOR COATING
½ TEASPOON SALT	
OLIVE OIL	FOR COATING
I RECIPE *SALSA ALLA MENTA DI MARIA ANGELICA*	SEE PAGE 108

Preheat the oven to 450° F.

Coat the slices of tuna with plenty of vinegar. Sprinkle on some salt, let them sit for ½ hour.

Coat the slices with oil. Place in a shallow baking pan, uncrowded. Bake in the oven for 10 to 15 minutes. Or grill or broil them about 5 to 10 minutes per side. To test for doneness, insert a very fine skewer into the fish. If color is whitish and juices released are clear, then fish is done.

Serve with sauce.

MIMMETTA
LO MONTE'S
CLASSIC
SICILIAN
COOKBOOK

•

160

PESCE ALLA MENTA

fish with mint

serves 6

2½ POUNDS SWORDFISH OR TUNA	CUT INTO 6 PIECES ABOUT ⅔ INCH THICK
I CUP RED WINE VINEGAR	
3 SPRIGS FRESH CORIANDER	STEMS DISCARDED
FLOUR	UNBLEACHED, ALL-PURPOSE; FOR COATING
½ CUP OLIVE OIL	
I SMALL ONION	THINLY SLICED
½ TEASPOON POWDERED CORIANDER SEED	
½ TEASPOON SALT	
3 GLOVES GARLIC	THINLY SLICED
⅔ CUP FRESH MINT	LOOSELY PACKED LEAVES
I TEASPOON SUGAR	

Marinate the fish in ⅔ cup vinegar at room temperature for about 30 minutes.

Coat the fish with the flour. In a large skillet over high to medium-high heat, heat the oil and cook the fish, about 2 minutes per side. When turning the fish, always gently turn it with a spatula.

Remove the fish from the skillet. Set aside. Then, over low heat, add the onion, and cook until wilted. Return the fish to the skillet. Add the powdered coriander seed and salt. Turn the fish well in the oil and cook over medium-low heat for 3 minutes, turning once while cooking.

Increase heat to high, add the remaining ingredients, turning the fish in the sauce. Turn the heat off and let stand 15 minutes before serving. The fish can be eaten at room temperature.

TONNO A RAGÙ

tuna ragout

serves 8 to 10

3 WHOLE CLOVES GARLIC	ONE CUT IN THIN SLIVERS
½ CUP FRESH MINT	LOOSELY PACKED LEAVES
4 POUNDS TUNA	ONE CHUNK (RESEMBLING A CAKE WEDGE), SKIN ON OUTSIDE OF WEDGE, CENTRAL BONE (AT NARROW POINT OF WEDGE) REMOVED
¾ CUP OLIVE OIL	
3 CUPS TOMATOES	CANNED AND PEELED; DRAINED; CUT INTO SMALL PIECES; RESERVE JUICE
2 TEASPOON TOMATO PASTE	
1½ TEASPOONS SALT	
2 TO 6 SMALL RED CHILI PEPPERS	DRY

Insert the garlic slivers and mint into the tuna, in between the layers of meat (from top of wedge, not sides). Tie the tuna with a string, running the string around the sides of the chunk, not from top to bottom, but from rounded, skin side of wedge to narrowed point (where bone would be). Keep the string loops ½ inch apart.

In a large pot, heat the oil and the whole garlic cloves until aromatic. Add the tomatoes and the tomato paste, cook over high heat for 10 minutes, uncovered. Add the tuna, salt, and enough of the tomato packing liquid to cover the tuna one third of the way up.

Add the peppers, cover, and cook over low heat for about 1 hour. The tuna should be turned several times while cooking.

Tie the tuna with a string. Run the string around the sides of the chunk, not from top to bottom.

The Introduction of Cod and Herring to Sicily

The prosperity enjoyed by Sicily during the Arab domination was maintained by the Normans and the Suebi in the eleventh through the thirteenth centuries, and Sicily took on a new luster. Sicilians—who had been politically fragmented in the Hellenistic period and who had been regarded as a colony by the Romans—were given a sense of political identity and gained a consciousness as an independent state which they still maintain.

The food brought by these new conquerors—such as cod and herring—fit in very well with the local eating customs, and was assimilated into the cuisine. To this day, no large market of Palermo is without barrels of herring or slabs of cod exuding a tangy smell.

MIMMETTA
LO MONTE'S
CLASSIC
SICILIAN
COOKBOOK

•

162

BACCALÀ AL POMODORO

salt cod with tomatoes

serves 6

Tuna, swordfish, halibut, and mahi-mahi can all be cooked in the same fashion. Reduce the cooking time of these fish to 10 minutes and do not soak in water or preboil. Salt should be added to taste. The fish should be cut into ¾-inch slices, approximately.

2 POUNDS SALT COD	(NET WEIGHT) LARGE PIECES, NO SKIN OR BONES
¾ CUP OLIVE OIL	
4 CLOVES GARLIC	CUT INTO LARGE PIECES
16 LARGE TOMATOES	CANNED AND PEELED; FIRM; DRAINED; SEEDED AND COARSELY CHOPPED; RESERVE JUICE
20 LARGE BLACK OLIVES	SICILIAN OR GREEK; WHOLE
3 TABLESPOONS RAISINS	
1 TEASPOON BLACK PEPPER	FINELY GROUND
½ CUP FRESH PARSLEY	LOOSELY PACKED LEAVES; CUT VERY SMALL

It is very important that the cod is of good quality. It should be thick and plump, and already store-treated to remove salt. To rinse off excess salt, let it sit in a pan with cold tap water for 1 hour, rinsing and changing the water as often as possible.

In large pot, bring 12 cups of water to a boil. Dip in the cod for about 30 seconds, then remove it from the water, and dip into plenty of cold water. Dip again in the boiling water, this time for only 15 seconds. Remove, then dip in cold water. Repeat last step once more. Place the cod in a pan with cold water; set aside.

In a large pot, pour the oil and add the garlic and heat until aromatic. With the heat on high, add the tomatoes, olives, and raisins. Cook about 5 minutes until the tomatoes sizzle, stirring only as necessary so as not to scorch them.

Add the cod, pepper, and enough of the reserved tomato juice to barely cover the cod. Bring to a boil, cover, and simmer for 20 minutes, or until the cod can be flaked with a fork into moist flakes.

Add parsley and serve.

PESCE SPADA AL FINOCCHIO

fennel-flavored swordfish

serves 6

1½ CUPS OLIVE OIL	
1¾ POUNDS SWORDFISH	CUT INTO ⅔-INCH THICK SLICES
2 MEDIUM BULBS FENNEL	TOUGH OUTER LAYER AND DARK GREEN FEATHERY LEAVES REMOVED; CUT INTO ⅓-INCH WEDGES (SEE PAGE 204)
1 MEDIUM ONION	CUT INTO VERY SMALL PIECES
6 SMALL ANCHOVY FILLETS	PACKED IN OLIVE OIL; DRAINED WELL, MASHED
BLACK PEPPER, TO TASTE	FINELY GROUND
⅓ TEASPOON SALT	OR TO TASTE
¼ CUP ALMONDS	SKINS ON, TOASTED (SEE PAGE 49), THEN COARSELY CRUSHED

In two very large sauté pans, divide and heat the oil. Add the swordfish slices and cook over high heat 2½ minutes per side. Remove from the pans and set aside.

Add the fennel to the pans, cook over medium-high heat, until pleasantly crisp. Add the onion and cook over high heat, stirring as needed, until the vegetables start browning. Stir in the anchovies, pepper, and salt, then return the fish to the pan, turning the slices gently to mix them with the vegetables (about 2 to 3 minutes).

Arrange on serving platter and sprinkle with almonds.

PESCE IN VERDURE

fish in vegetables

serves 10

Serve this fish along with *Cuscus alla mandorla* (see page 97).

MIMMETTA
LO MONTE'S
CLASSIC
SICILIAN
COOKBOOK

•

164

ONE 6- TO 7-POUND RED SNAPPER OR SALMON	CLEANED AND SCALED, WITH HEAD AND TAIL INTACT
OLIVE OIL	FOR COATING
2 TEASPOONS SALT	
2 TEASPOONS BLACK PEPPER	FINELY GROUND
1 TEASPOON GROUND CORIANDER	OPTIONAL
1 LARGE BULB FENNEL	TENDER, FEATHERY LEAVES INCLUDED; CUT INTO ⅓-INCH WEDGES (SEE PAGE 204)
4 LARGE CARROTS	PEELED; CUT INTO 3 SECTIONS, EACH CUT LENGTHWISE IN SLICES ABOUT ⅛ INCH THICK
2 SLENDER ZUCCHINI	SLICED AS PER CARROTS
1 LARGE CELERY HEART	CUT ABOUT THE SAME SIZE AS CARROTS
1 LARGE ONION	CUT INTO RINGS ¼ INCH THICK
6 FULL SPRIGS PARSLEY	FINELY CUT THE LEAVES; DISCARD THE STEMS
10 LARGE GREEN OLIVES	RINSED, PITTED
10 LARGE BLACK OLIVES	RINSED, PITTED
2 LARGE FRESH TOMATOES	RIPE BUT FIRM, CUT WIDTHWISE INTO ¼-INCH THICK ROUNDS
3 CLOVES GARLIC	SLIVERED (OPTIONAL)
2 SPRIGS FRESH MINT	OPTIONAL

Preheat the oven to 375° F.

Thoroughly wash the stomach cavity of the fish and run plenty of water through the head. Shake off the water.

Lay the fish in a baking pan, well coated with oil. Coat the fish, inside and out with oil, 1 teaspoon salt, and 1 teaspoon pepper. If using the coriander, add that too.

In a bowl, mix together the fennel, carrots, zucchini, celery, onion, parsley, olives, and half of the tomato slices.

Lay the mint and some of the garlic along the cavity, if desired. Fill the stomach cavity with as much of the vegetable mixture as will fit. Mound the remaining vegetables and garlic on top of the fish so that it is well covered.

Carefully line up the remaining tomato slices on the very top of the mound. Sprinkle the remaining salt and pepper over the vegetable mixture, and trickle some oil on top. Bake in the oven, allowing 10 minutes for each pound of the fish net weight.

PESCE ALLA SACCENSE

fish sciacca style

serves 8

You can substitute salmon or red snapper for the rockfish, if you prefer.

ONE 6- TO 7-POUND ROCKFISH	CLEANED, SCALED, HEAD AND TAIL INTACT
2½ TO 3 POUNDS NEW POTATOES	WASHED, UNPEELED
8 OR MORE LEEKS*	YOUNG, SLENDER
⅔ CUP CAPERS	PREFERABLY PRESERVED IN SALT
1½ CUPS OLIVE OIL	
2 CUPS BREAD CRUMBS	UNFLAVORED
6 SPRIGS PARSLEY	STEMS DISCARDED; CUT VERY FINELY
2½ TEASPOONS SALT	
1½ TEASPOONS BLACK PEPPER	(OR TO TASTE) FINELY GROUND
6 CLOVES GARLIC	THINLY SLICED

Preheat the oven to 425° F.

If you are afraid of too many bones, have your fish filleted for you. Regardless, pat dry the outside of the fish and the stomach cavity.

Boil the potatoes in plenty of water until al dente, about 15 minutes. Drain well. Dip the leeks in boiling water. Cook until barely limp. Drain well.

Rinse the capers to rid them of the salt, squeeze out any excess water. If the capers preserved in vinegar are the only ones available, soak them in water for about one hour and rinse very well, then squeeze out the excess water.

* TO CLEAN LEEKS, CUT DOWN TO ROOT—NOT THROUGH IT—IN TWO CUTS THAT CROSS EACH OTHER. SWISH IN WATER UNTIL DIRT IS WASHED OFF.

In a cast-iron skillet over medium heat, stir the bread crumbs in six tablespoons of oil until they are golden brown.

In a bowl, mix the bread crumbs with the capers, parsley, 1½ teaspoons salt, 1 teaspoon pepper, and the garlic.

In another bowl toss the potatoes and the leeks with ½ cup oil.

Coat the fish with oil, inside and outside. In a large baking pan, pour the remaining oil, add the fish, stuff it with a little less than one half of the bread crumb mixture and cover the fish or fillets with the rest. Place the potatoes and the leeks around the sides of the fish.

If you don't have a pan large enough to contain the whole fish, place some heavy foil under the head and tail to use as an extension of the pan. Or, detach the head and bake it on the side or in a different pan. If using two pans, divide the potatoes and the leeks between them.

Sprinkle the remaining salt and pepper on the vegetables.

Bake the fish in the oven for 20 minutes. Reduce the heat to 375° F. and bake 40 more minutes. For fillets, bake for 15 minutes, then at 375° F. for 15 more minutes.

Serve with *Salsa piccante* (see below).

MIMMETTA
LO MONTE'S
CLASSIC
SICILIAN
COOKBOOK

•

166

SALSA PICCANTE

hot sauce

yields 2½ cups

This is a zesty sauce to serve with fish, shrimp, or parboiled vegetables or as a dip for raw vegetables.

3 CUPS MAYONNAISE	HOMEMADE OR COMMERCIAL
3 LARGE CLOVES GARLIC	MASHED
15 SMALL ANCHOVY FILLETS	(2 OUNCE CAN) PACKED IN OLIVE OIL, WELL DRAINED, MASHED
CAYENNE PEPPER, TO TASTE	

In a food processor, puree one third of the mayonnaise, the garlic, and the anchovies. Stir in the remaining mayonnaise and the cayenne pepper. However, if you use homemade mayonnaise, don't use a food processor. Gently blend ingredients in a bowl. Serve at room temperature.

SARDE A BECCAFICO DI SCIACCA

"beccafico" sardines, from sciacca

serves 10

This recipe, along with *Pesce alla saccense*, is one of the many dishes told to me by our friend from Sciacca. Since sardines are almost impossible to find in any U.S. city, fresh or frozen, use frozen (fresh, if available) smelts instead.

3 POUNDS LARGE SARDINES OR SMELTS	WEIGHT WITHOUT HEADS OR GUTS (ABOUT 20 PER POUND)
1½ CUPS BREAD CRUMBS	UNFLAVORED
2 TABLESPOONS OLIVE OIL	PLUS SOME FOR COATING FISH
1½ CUPS FRESH PARSLEY	LOOSELY PACKED LEAVES; CUT FINELY
1 CLOVE GARLIC	CUT INTO VERY SMALL PIECES
1 TEASPOON FENNEL SEED	
¾ TEASPOON SALT	
1 TEASPOON BLACK PEPPER	FINELY GROUND
JUICE OF ½ LEMON	FRESHLY SQUEEZED
5 BAY LEAVES*	EACH CUT INTO FOUR PIECES

Preheat the oven to 375° F.

To debone fish, remove the back and stomach fins. Make a slit along the stomach to the tail, lift the bone gently, prying around with your fingers, and remove it by pulling it toward the tail while holding the flesh of the fish at the tail end. The tail fins should come off along with the bone.

Rinse under plenty of tap water, removing any bloody membrane that might still be attached to the stomach—not doing so might cause your dish to have an unpleasant odor.

In a cast-iron skillet over medium-high heat, roast the bread crumbs with the oil. Stir continuously until the bread crumbs are golden.

In a bowl, mix the bread crumbs, parsley, garlic, fennel seed, salt, and pepper.

In a plate, pour a generous layer of olive oil. Coat the butterflied fish with the oil, putting a generous teaspoon of the filling at the wide end of the fish. Tightly roll the fish up toward the tail end.

Place the fish in a low sided baking dish (see illustration, page 169). Symmetrically pack the rolls in it, side to side. Tail ends should face up, barely showing. If any filling remains, sprinkle it on top. Squeeze the lemon over the rolls. Insert the bay leaf pieces between the rolls, distributing them evenly.

Bake in the oven for 30 minutes. This dish can be eaten at room temperature.

* CALIFORNIA BAY LEAVES ARE MUCH MORE PUNGENT THAN MEDITERRANEAN ONES. HALFWAY THROUGH BAKING THE FISH, CHECK THE AROMA. IF OVERPOWERING, REMOVE THE LEAVES.

SARDE A BECCAFICO DI PALERMO

"beccafico" sardines, from palermo

serves 4

Beccafico is the name of a small bird. The sardines, when rolled, are about the size of, and resemble, these birds. Fresh sardines are very difficult to find. Smelts make a good substitute, their shape being similar if not their taste.

MIMMETTA
LO MONTE'S
CLASSIC
SICILIAN
COOKBOOK

•

168

I POUND LARGE SMELTS	NET WEIGHT, NO HEADS OR GUTS (ABOUT 2O PER POUND)
OLIVE OIL	FOR COATING
½ CUP BREAD CRUMBS	UNFLAVORED
I TABLESPOON CURRANTS	
I TABLESPOON PINE NUTS	
½ SMALL ONION	CUT INTO VERY SMALL PIECES
½ TEASPOON SALT	
½ TEASPOON BLACK PEPPER	FINELY GROUND
I TABLESPOON GRATED PARMESAN	
½ CUP FRESH PARSLEY	LOOSELY PACKED LEAVES, CUT FINELY
2 BAY LEAVES	EACH CUT INTO FOUR PARTS
½ LEMON	

It is perfectly all right to use previously frozen smelts. To debone them, follow instructions for *Sarde a beccafico di Sciacca,* (see above).

Preheat the oven to 375° F.

In a cast-iron skillet, pour a couple of tablespoons of oil. Over medium heat, stir the bread crumbs until golden.

In the pan with the bread crumbs mix the currants, the pine nuts, onion, salt, and pepper. Add the cheese and parsley when the mixture has lost some of its heat.

Spread some of the filling on each deboned fish, and tightly roll each from the head end to the tail end.

Tightly fit the rolls into a low sided baking dish, well coated with oil and lightly dusted with bread crumbs. Rolls should be side by side, tail ends will face up. Brush the top of the rolls with oil. If any filling remains, spread it on top of the rolls. Insert the bay leaf pieces between the rolls, distributing them evenly.

Bake in the oven for 20 to 25 minutes. After baking 5 minutes, squeeze the lemon over the rolls.

The fish can be eaten hot or at room temperature.

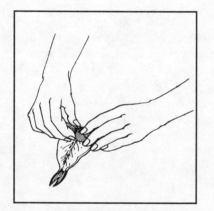

Roll fish with filling tightly, from head to tail end.

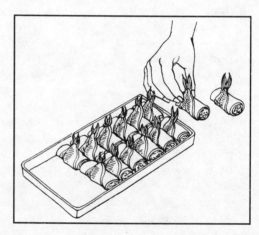

Fit rolls snugly; lie side by side, tail ends facing up.

"CARCIOFFE" CON SARDE A PASTICCIO

baked artichokes with sardines

serves 8

This recipe, like most artichoke recipes I have, is from my Grandmother Severina's notes. The recipe calls for fresh sardines, deboned and butterflied. I have substituted both smelts and canned sardines. I suspect very few people would be willing to debone and butterfly smelts; therefore, I suggest using canned sardines. It would be interesting to try the dish using mackerel fillets. I think your fish supplier could be talked into filleting mackerel, but I wouldn't try to talk him into butterflying smelts.

If you can find fresh sardines or smelts and want to try deboning them, see page 167.

MIMMETTA
LO MONTE'S
CLASSIC
SICILIAN
COOKBOOK

•

170

6 LARGE ARTICHOKES	TENDER, CLEANED (SEE PAGE 212)
I POUND SARDINES	CANNED IN WATER OR OIL (DO NOT USE SMOKED SARDINES) WITH A LOW-SALT CONTENT
¼ CUP LEMON JUICE	FRESHLY SQUEEZED
I CUP ALMONDS	SKINS ON, TOASTED (SEE PAGE 49); GROUND FINELY
¾ CUP BREAD CRUMBS	UNFLAVORED, TOASTED (SEE PAGE 217)
8 SMALL, FLAT ANCHOVY FILLETS	PACKED IN OIL; WELL DRAINED, MASHED
½ CUP FRESH PARSLEY	LOOSELY PACKED LEAVES; CHOPPED FINELY
½ TO I TEASPOON SALT	
½ TEASPOON BLACK PEPPER	FINELY GROUND
OLIVE OIL	FOR COATING
2 TABLESPOONS PINE NUTS	
2 TABLESPOONS CURRANTS	
A FEW BAY LEAVES	

Preheat the oven to 350° F.

Slice artichokes in ¼-inch wedges, soak them in acidulated water (see page 211). Drain, but allow them to retain some water.

In a bowl, mix the artichokes with the lemon juice. In another bowl, mix the toasted almonds, toasted bread crumbs, anchovies, parsley, salt, and pepper.

Choose a baking dish that will allow the artichokes to fit in three layers, alternated with the other ingredients. Coat the dish well with oil. Sprinkle some of the bread crumb mixture on the bottom of the dish, saving enough for three more layers. Alternate three layers each of artichokes, sardines, and bread crumb-almond mixture, ending with the crumb mixture, and sprinkling pine nuts and currants in between.

Arrange a few bay leaves on top of the pan. Cover loosely with foil and bake in the oven for 1 hour.

conseg`na

| OGGETTI CONSEGNATI | | | FIRMA | Annotazioni |
Lettere e pieghi	Bolgette	Pacchi	DEL RICEVENTE	

Carciofi con salsa a pasticcio

Si prendono quattro carciofi di taglia a fettine sottili si puliscano a filo tende si fa della mollica brust[...] si [...] con carciofi mond[...] la brustolita pignola e pattolina pepe e aroma. Dopo si mette un po d'olio in un [...] da [...] farmase tre o quattro [...] fagandoli sempre con la [...] pepirale bagandoli con due [...] poche gocie. Si cope con foglie d'alloro e di me[...] con [...] tutti [...] sopra. Le carciofi appena taglicte si mettano in acqua e [...] se sono due si d[...] [...] [...] scaldate.

Palermo, 29 (3-38, 4 (30) 0/86.

113/18

SPUMA DI SALMONE

salmon mousse

serves 12 to 14

2 EGGS	EXTRA-LARGE, HARD-BOILED; CUT IN ROUNDS
2 MEDIUM CARROTS	PARBOILED; CUT INTO THIN ROUNDS (OR 2 ARTICHOKES, CLEANED (SEE PAGE 212), PARBOILED, DRAINED WELL; SLICED VERY THIN)
2 ENVELOPES GELATIN	UNFLAVORED
2 CUPS CHICKEN STOCK	SEE PAGE 72
3 CUPS POACHED SALMON MEAT	SEPARATED INTO VERY SMALL SHREDS OR USE CANNED SALMON IF YOU DON'T WANT TO POACH
2 TABLESPOONS LEMON JUICE	FRESHLY SQUEEZED
1 TEASPOON PAPRIKA	
2 TEASPOONS SALT	
1 TEASPOON BLACK PEPPER	FINELY GROUND
1½ CUPS MAYONNAISE	
1 CUP SOUR CREAM	
1 CUP HEAVY CREAM	ALREADY WHIPPED TO A VERY STIFF STAGE

MIMMETTA
LO MONTE'S
CLASSIC
SICILIAN
COOKBOOK

•

172

Have two 1-pound bread loaf pans on hand.

In one, arrange half of the eggs and vegetables in a pleasing pattern on the bottom and along the sides.

In a pan, soften the gelatin in ½ cup of stock. Dissolve it over low heat, mix in the remaining stock (at room temperature).

In a bowl, mix together the salmon, lemon juice, paprika, salt, and pepper. Thoroughly mix in the gelatin, followed by the mayonnaise and the sour cream. Fold in the whipped cream.

Divide the mixture between the bread loaf pans. Chill. When almost set, arrange the remaining egg and vegetable slices on top.

To unmold, dip the pans in hot water for about 10 seconds. You might want to draw the mousse from the sides of the pan with your fingertips, with very light pressure. Turn over onto a serving dish. Repeat dipping the pans in hot water, if unsuccessful at unmolding the first time.

PÂTÉ DI TONNO IN GELATINA

tuna pâté in gelatin

serves 6 to 8

1¾ POUNDS TUNA	FRESH, PREFERABLY 1 CHUNK, NO DARK BROWN MEAT, NO SKIN OR BONES
OLIVE OIL	FOR COATING
⅔ CUP CRÈME FRAÎCHE	
1 CLOVE GARLIC	OPTIONAL
A FEW LEAVES FRESH MINT	OPTIONAL
4 ENVELOPES GELATIN	UNFLAVORED
7 CUPS CHICKEN STOCK	CLEAR, NO FAT, SALTED TO TASTE (SEE PAGE 72)
6 TABLESPOONS LEMON JUICE	FRESHLY SQUEEZED
2 TABLESPOONS RED WINE VINEGAR	
1 TEASPOON SALT	
1 TEASPOON BLACK PEPPER	FINELY GROUND

Preheat the oven to 375° F.

Rub tuna all over with oil. Place in a pan and bake in the oven for 30 minutes. Let cool.

In a food processor, puree the tuna with the crème fraîche, and, if desired, the garlic and mint, and chill.

In a pot, warm 5 cups chicken stock.

Soften 3 envelopes gelatin in 1 cup room temperature stock. Add it to the 5 cups warmed stock, along with the lemon juice and vinegar. Stir well, bring to a boil. Boil 30 seconds, turn off the heat.

Pour 1½ cups of the liquid into a 12- by 8- by 2-inch pan (approximately) and chill until well set. Keep the remaining gelatin mixture at room temperature and set aside.

In a pan, soften the remaining envelope of gelatin in the remaining cup of stock. Stir on medium heat until it comes to a boil. Add the salt and pepper, and let it cool. Fold the gelatin into the chilled tuna and crème fraîche mixture.

In the gelatin-coated dish, arrange the tuna mixture in a layer—keeping it away from the sides of the dish by about ½ inch. Pour the gelatin mixture over it and refrigerate several hours until thoroughly set.

To unmold the pâté, place it in a pan filled with hot water for 1½ minutes. Turn it over onto a cookie sheet, remove its pan, then turn it over again on a serving plate.

MIMMETTA
LO MONTE'S
CLASSIC
SICILIAN
COOKBOOK

•

174

e cipolle. ... mettendo la ... Quando ... che pollo, senza muovere ... con un *Coppino* di ... to fuoco, senza muovere ... con un *Coppino* di ... e disseccata, si umetterà con un nuovo si em... di acqua calda, o di acqua la *cassarola*, mettendovi pirà di brodo, o di acqua la *cassarola*, mettendovi un poco di sale e di pepe, pesato una cipolla stec-cata di cannella, di carofani, coriandri, ed un maz-zetto di erbe, come nel brodo chiaro, e covrendole, si faranno bollire le carni, e poi si *sgrassa*, e si chiarifica, come nel brodo chiaro.

Buidin.

Si pone il latte in una *cassarola*, con qualche panne anche di latte, pangrattato, zucchero, *rossi d'uova*, un pò di butiro, piccola uva passa, e piguuoli un poco di portogallo tritato, pistacchi anche tritati, cannella, e un poco di vainiglia. Si fa addeuzare a lento fuoco, e poi si passa dentro un altra *cassa-rola* unta di butiro, e polverata di pan grattato. Si fa cuocere al forno con la cruoal di soprà-

C

Caponate.

Dentro un'insalatiera di cretaglia si pongono i bi scotti di buon pane, bagnati nell'acqua *cirifogli*, broccoli

12

torzuti, o *cavalofiore*, o *carote*, a fette, prima bol-lite, menta e qualche altra erba odorosa, alici salate fette di *Tarantello* cotto e dissalzato, bocconi di pe-sce, di aragoste, ed altro, olive nere, capperini qualche poco di *butarico*, o *caviale* e qualche fette di *cocozzata* candita, ben accomoata con olio, e aceto guernito il piatto con fette di limone.

...suola.

Si fanno cuo... in brodo di sostanze, braciuolette di vitella ... mgelle petti di piccioli, e granelli in quart... fette di presciutto, cervellate in quarti pi-selli torz... carciofii prugnoli prima bolliti, tartufi, ton-selli ... e padelle, e qualche erbetta tritata, e quanto tutto sarà cotto con un poco di fio di farina si farà alquanto addensate, con aggiungervi poche gocce di limone.

Castagne Sciruppate.

Si scelgono le castagne grosse, e le più intate si leva ad esse con attenzione la corteccia, senza la pel-licola. Poi si pongono a fuoco di carboni, con po-chissima fiamma, e si portano a buona cottura, to-gliendo quelle, che si frangeranno. Indi si fanno asciu-gare sopra un panno, e posto in un vaso, non alto, o di rame, o di creta si covrono di giulebbe; e si fan-no così stagionare per un pajo di giorni a lento fuo-co. Dopo ciò con un pò di giulebbe più denso, e con qualche senso, s'innasprono, e si presentano.

CAPONATA DEL DUCA

the duke's salad

serves 3

This is another recipe taken from the Duke's old cookbook.

¾ POUND SHRIMP	UNSHELLED
3 SMALL ANCHOVY FILLETS	PACKED IN OLIVE OIL; DRAINED, MASHED
½ CUP OLIVE OIL	
3 TABLESPOONS RED WINE VINEGAR	
1 TEASPOON LUMPFISH CAVIAR	
6 LARGE BLACK OLIVES	SICILIAN OR GREEK, PITTED; CUT INTO A FEW PIECES
1 TABLESPOON CAPERS	PRESERVED IN VINEGAR; RINSED, SQUEEZED WELL
A FEW LEAVES FRESH MINT	
A SPRIG CHERVIL	OR USE A FEW LEAVES OF PARSLEY AND SOME TENDER FEATHERY LEAVES OF FENNEL
1 OUNCE CANDIED CITRON	OR USE MIXED CANDIED FRUIT; CUT INTO SMALL PIECES
BLACK PEPPER, TO TASTE	FINELY GROUND
½ POUND BROCCOLI	FLORETS, PARBOILED; SEPARATED INTO SMALL SECTIONS
1 LARGE CARROT	PARBOILED; CUT INTO THIN ROUNDS
1 CUP TUNA	VERY GOOD QUALITY; PACKED IN OIL, DRAINED WELL
1 LEMON	CUT INTO WEDGES
6 SLICES FRENCH BREAD	½ INCH THICK, TOASTED*

Dip the shrimp into a pot with plenty of boiling water. Drain as soon as they turn red. Shell.

In a bowl, mix anchovies with the oil and vinegar. Add the caviar, olives, capers, mint, chervil, citron, and pepper.

In the same bowl, toss the mixture with the shrimp, broccoli, and carrots. Mix in tuna gently.

Arrange the bread slices on a platter, top with the mixed ingredients and serve with lemon wedges.

* INSTEAD OF TOASTING THE BREAD, YOU CAN MAKE *FETTE DORATE* (SEE PAGE 76).

GAMBERI ALLA TERMINESE

shrimp from termini

serves 6

This is one of Nonna Severina's recipes, and is my favorite shrimp recipe.

2 POUNDS SHRIMP	UNSHELLED
⅔ TO ¾ CUP OLIVE OIL	
¼ TEASPOON SALT	OR TO TASTE
¼ TO ½ TEASPOON CAYENNE PEPPER	

Rinse the shrimp very well to make sure there is no "fishy" smell. Drain well.

In 2 very large skillets, divide and heat the oil over high heat. Add the shrimp and stir for a few minutes until the shells turn red and the shrimp meat turns white. Stir in the pepper. Serve hot.

MIMMETTA
LO MONTE'S
CLASSIC
SICILIAN
COOKBOOK

•

176

FRIED SQUID

calamari fritti

serves 4 to 6

1½ POUNDS SQUID	CLEAN PER INSTRUCTIONS (SEE PAGE 176)
2 LEMONS	CUT INTO WEDGES
2 EGGS	EXTRA-LARGE
2 CUPS FLOUR	UNBLEACHED, ALL-PURPOSE
CORN OIL	(OR USE A SIMILAR VEGETABLE OIL) ENOUGH FOR A ¾-INCH LAYER IN A FRYING PAN
SALT, TO TASTE	

Cut the hoods of the squid into ½-inch rings and leave the tentacles in clusters.

In a bowl, beat eggs with a fork, then toss the squid in the egg.

Toss no more than three pieces of squid at a time in the flour. Lay the pieces on a floured surface so that they don't overlap or touch.

In a frying pan, heat the oil until smoke is barely visible. Fry the squid over high heat until golden brown, turning once.

Serve immediately, sprinkled with salt, and with lemon wedges on the side.

Cleaning Squid

Fresh squid, that is, squid caught the night before one is going to cook it, is something I have not yet been able to find in this country. I will describe it anyway, just as one likes to talk about a utopia: The squid's skin is glistening and unbroken, the reddish blotches very distinct and lively. There is nothing limp about the squid; even the little "ear" flaps on the side of the hood do not hang lifeless. Above all, there is nothing fishy about its smell—you can touch it and then smell your hand without finding the penetrating unpleasant odor of stale or stagnant sea water. The squid available here, however, is what we have to cook. Taking a few extra steps in its preparation, such as parboiling or rinsing the squid repeatedly, will generally take care of the fishy smell.

The hood contains the digestive tract, the ink bladder, and the featherlike transparent cartilage that runs along the flat front part of the hood. By pulling the tentacles down and off, the digestive tract and the ink bladder almost invariably slip out of the hood. The cartilage is easily pulled out by grabbing its tip right at the edge of the hood opening. Squeeze the hood from the tip down to eliminate any considerable amount of digestive tract which might have remained in the hood. Run plenty of water inside it and further clean it by inserting your finger and running it around inside. Remove the digestive tract from the tentacles. Be very fastidious about cleaning any small parts which might stay attached to the tentacles, as the digestive tract carries a very unpleasant odor. Hidden by the tentacles is the "mouth"—a cartilage beak. Remove that, and if you wish, remove the eyes as well, especially if it is a large squid.

Rinse tentacles several times in cold water. If the squid still carries an unpleasant odor, dip squid in boiling water, remove it after a few seconds, rinse well with cold water. If you are going to fry the squid, use extra care in blotting out the water; water bubbles popping out of the pan is a very common hazard when frying squid.

One last word: Squid is often confused with cuttlefish—at least in restaurants with Italian menus. Cuttlefish, seppia in Italian, contains in its hood quite a solid white diamond-shaped bone instead of the feather-like cartilage. The hood is rounder than the squid's, and its side flaps do actually look like little ears. Large cuttlefish has to be skinned. The hood has to be cut longitudinally in order to remove the bone. Otherwise, it can be treated and cleaned just like squid, taking care not to break the ink sac. Also, the ink sac of cuttlefish contains a considerably larger amount of ink than the squid's.

CAPPESANTE IN PADELLA

scallops in the skillet

serves 6 to 8

⅔ TO ¾ CUP OLIVE OIL	
I LARGE ONION	CUT INTO ¾-INCH SQUARES
6 RED BELL PEPPERS	CUT INTO ¾-INCH SQUARES
2 POUNDS SEA SCALLOPS	
I TEASPOON OREGANO	DRY LEAVES
¾ TEASPOON SALT	
I TEASPOON BLACK PEPPER	FINELY GROUND

In a very large skillet, heat a generous layer of oil. Add the onions and peppers and cook over medium heat until the onions begin to brown. Lift the peppers and onions from the skillet and set aside.

Increase the heat to high. As soon as the pan is very hot add the scallops, cook for 5 minutes, turning only as necessary for even cooking. Return the vegetables to the pan, stir in the oregano, salt, and pepper. Serve.

MIMMETTA
LO MONTE'S
CLASSIC
SICILIAN
COOKBOOK

•

178

LUMACHE AL ''PIC PAC''

"pic pac" snails

serves 6 to 8

"Pic pac" is the name for the quickly cooked tomato sauce served with these snails. It is a must to use a wide pan, so that the tomato will get seared very quickly.

7 DOZEN LIVE SNAILS	THE SIZE OF A CHERRY
⅔ CUP OLIVE OIL	
I VERY SMALL ONION	CUT INTO VERY SMALL PIECES
3 CLOVES GARLIC	CUT INTO LARGE PIECES
2 SMALL RED CHILI PEPPERS	DRY
12 LARGE TOMATOES	CANNED AND PEELED, SEEDED; CUT INTO SMALL PIECES
½ TEASPOON SALT	
¾ CUP FRESH PARSLEY	LOOSELY PACKED LEAVES; CUT VERY SMALL

Prepare the snails following the instructions on page 180. Remove the snails from shells, removing the last segment (that often remains in the shell), which is the digestive tract. Leave the little sac which is whitish in color.

In a wide pan, heat the oil, onion, garlic, and chili peppers until aromatic. Add the snails and cook for a few minutes over medium heat, stirring very often.

Increase heat to high and remove the chilies if you prefer a mild taste. Add the tomatoes and the salt, stir for 3 minutes, lowering the heat if tomatoes stick to the pan. Add the parsley, then serve.

I "Babbaluci"

It is nearly the middle of July: all the shutters on the west side of the house are closed. Their slats crackle, shaken by the *scirocco,* the hot, dry wind from Africa. From the street, the muffled noise of an occasional car or bus reaches me.

It is nap time for Father and Mother, and silent time for my brother, the maid, and me. After the main meal of the day, everybody is required to retire to his or her own room, and absolutely no noise is allowed.

There is not much one can do without making any noise except read and draw. I have stretched out on my bed; the heat is making me tired, but not sleepy. If I come close to the wall, I can feel the heat of the sun transfused through the stone.

Time never goes by: every minute is like a lead weight to be pushed forward with great effort. However, thinking is another thing one can do without making any noise. Lying down, I think about the forthcoming vacation with relief. We'll leave town after the *festino,* the celebration of our patron saint, Santa Rosalia, which means we'll be leaving very soon. The *festino* will start tomorrow and will be concluded on the fifteenth by the most stunning fireworks at *la marina.* Along this promenade by the sea, people will leave mountains of discarded shells—of pumpkin seeds, peanuts, snails—and other litter from the food eaten in connection with the festival.

Giovanna's room is next to mine; I hear her stirring. She must be preparing to go to the kitchen to make coffee for Mother and Father to ease their awakening. I hear the kitchen door being opened and —a second later—"Signora, signora!" Giovanna's voice rings out like a fire-alarm bell.

I am in the kitchen instantly, followed by Mother and Father. We all stand at the door to contemplate three kilos of small white snails which have crept out of the basket where they were left to purge (to cleanse the digestive tract), and have invaded the kitchen. Ceiling, walls, cabinets, the refrigerator, the stove, and of course, the floor —the reason for which we have halted at the door—are covered with snails. Where I don't see snails, I see a network of that fine, magically iridescent ribbon that marks their itinerary.

"Maria, *che disastro!*" None of us is called Maria—the name stands for the Virgin Mary, invoked by Mother (who is otherwise not at all religious) to witness unusual and serious happenings. I laugh, but discreetly, as I know Giovanna is in trouble, and wait to hear what else Mother has to say. "You didn't secure the cloth on top of the basket carefully enough." Mother's voice, addressing the maid, is thin and cold.

Father laughs openly; he seems particularly amused by the puzzled way our boxer sniffs at the snails on the floor. Actually, when Giovanna first screamed I thought the dog had done something bad in the kitchen. I start singing a song in Sicilian dialect about snails: "Have you ever seen snails fly, while pushing stone slabs with their horns, had I not been so quick to recall them, you couldn't believe what damage they would have done."

Giovanna tiptoes through the snails, clears a few from the stove, and makes coffee. Now I have my pastime for the evening; to recapture the snails. "Not the ones on the ceiling," says my mother, and, the drama gone from the air, she leaves the kitchen.

The snails will be cooked tomorrow, as planned, at the get-together with relatives and friends that marks the first day of the Santa Rosalia celebration. Mother will tell her sisters the snail story and sigh a lot about how long it will take to clean their tracks, while she eats the little devils, pulling them out of their shells with a pin, and then sucking shamelessly the delicious juices from the shell.

I will tell the story to my cousins, except for one part that nobody knows but me. I actually think it was I who didn't tie down the cheesecloth carefully enough on the basket when I snuck into the kitchen to get a couple of snails to have a snail race in my room. I couldn't think of a quieter afternoon activity than that, but as the song goes, there is a lot of trouble snails can cause.

MIMMETTA
LO MONTE'S
CLASSIC
SICILIAN
COOKBOOK

•

180

Preparing Live Snails

My story, I ''Babbaluci,'' connected snails with a saint (Santa Rosalia). This association is proof once again of the oddity of the Sicilian soul. There may also be some oddity in the way Sicilians handle and cook snails, but the end result is deliciously different. My mother taught me, and she ought to know well—did I mention that her name is Rosalia?

Place the live snails in a container with plenty of holes. Traditionally the container used was a basket, but a colander will do—and will be easier to clean.

Sprinkle the snails with unflavored bread crumbs—one tablespoon for two pounds of snails. Cover the container with cheesecloth and secure this well around the edge. Let the snails sit at room temperature for twenty-four hours to give them time to purge (to cleanse the digestive tract). The most convenient place to rest snails is the drainboard of your sink, or the sink itself.

Rinse the snails well with room-temperature water and place them in a pot with enough room-temperature water to cover them. Keep the pot securely sealed with cheesecloth. Depending on the temperature, it will take the snails from as little as one minute to a couple of hours to come out of their shells: when they do, you will see snails clinging to the cheesecloth. It is best to leave the snails undisturbed in order to keep them from retreating into their shells. As soon as they come out of the shells, place the pot on a burner, using the lowest heat possible to cook the snails. Any snails that still cling to the cheesecloth after a few minutes of slow heating can be returned to the water by lowering the cheesecloth into it for a minute, before resecuring it.

By the time the water reaches 105° F., the snails will be in some sort of nirvana and will have no inclination to leave the water. At this point, remove the cheesecloth.

> As soon as the water reaches 115° F., increase the heat to high and bring the water to a boil. Boil the snails for 3 minutes, drain, and rinse very well.
>
> My mother says that at no time while handling live snails should you use salt, which would cause them to shrivel up and retreat into their shells. I'm not sure if this is true!

LUMACHE CON PAN GRATTATO

snails with bread crumbs

serves 6 to 8

7 DOZEN LIVE SNAILS	THE SIZE OF A CHERRY
⅔ CUP OLIVE OIL	
1 CUP BREAD CRUMBS	UNFLAVORED
½ TEASPOON SALT	
¾ TEASPOON BLACK PEPPER	FINELY GROUND
3 CLOVES GARLIC	CUT INTO VERY SMALL PIECES
¾ CUP FRESH PARSLEY	LOOSELY PACKED LEAVES; CUT INTO VERY SMALL PIECES

Prepare the snails following the instructions on page 180. Remove the snails from their shells, removing the last segment (that often remains in the shell), which is the digestive tract. Leave the little sac which is whitish in color.

In a cast-iron skillet, heat the oil over medium-high heat. Add the snails and bread crumbs, and cook, stirring constantly, for 6 minutes. Add the salt and pepper. Adjust the heat if the bread crumbs brown too quickly.

Remove from the heat, stir in the garlic and parsley, serve immediately.

Different Names for Snails

The Sicilian dialect word for snails is *"babbaluci,"* and it is believed to be of Arab origin. However, some say that it comes, instead, from the contraction of two words, *bava* meaning slime, and *"luci"* meaning shine. The word *"babbaluci"* is also applied in an affectionate way to a baby when teething or having a cold. Sicilians' liking for the word is displayed colorfully by a proverb in our dialect: *"Babbalucia sucari e fimmini a vasari 'un ponnu mai saziari"* (Snails to suck and women to kiss, one can never have enough of). The Italian word for snails is *umache*.

LUMACHE AGLIO E OLIO

snails with garlic and oil

serves 6 to 8

7 DOZEN LIVE SNAILS	THE SIZE OF A CHERRY
⅔ CUP OLIVE OIL	
¼ TEASPOON SALT	OR TO TASTE
¼ TEASPOON BLACK PEPPER	FINELY GROUND
¾ CUP WHITE WINE	DRY
4 CLOVES GARLIC	CUT INTO VERY THIN SLICES
½ CUP PARSLEY	LOOSELY PACKED LEAVES; CUT INTO VERY SMALL PIECES

MIMMETTA
LO MONTE'S
CLASSIC
SICILIAN
COOKBOOK

•

182

Prepare the snails following the instructions on page 180. Remove the snails from their shells, removing the last segment (that often remains in the shell), which is the digestive tract. Leave the little sac whitish in color.

Heat the oil in a pan large enough to cook all the snails without crowding. Add the snails and cook over medium heat for about 7 minutes, stirring very often. Expect to see some foam developing, which will cook out after the first few minutes.

At the end of cooking, add the salt, pepper, and wine, stirring over high heat for a few seconds. Remove the pan from the heat and add garlic and parsley.

Serve immediately.

The Most Commonly Eaten Snails in Sicily

"Babbaluceddi," *or* "babbaluci du fistino," *very small snails—smaller than a cherry. They are white and are found very easily in the summer in fields, where they cluster on dried grass.*

"Crastuni," *a large snail with brown stripes, found in fields.*

"Attuppateddu," *a large snail, dark brown, its opening covered by a membrane. This snail is found a few inches underground. After the first fall rains, the snail comes to the surface: it is then called* crastuni niuru *(large black snail).*

UOVA
egg dishes

FRITTATA AL PAN GRATTATO

bread crumb frittata

serves 4 to 6

½ CUP BREAD CRUMBS	UNFLAVORED
¾ CUP GRATED PARMESAN	
I SMALL ONION	CUT INTO VERY SMALL PIECES
12 FRESH SAGE LEAVES	CUT VERY SMALL (YOU CAN ALSO USE
	2 PARSLEY SPRIGS, CUT VERY SMALL)
5 EGGS	EXTRA-LARGE, SEPARATED
½ CUP OLIVE OIL	

In a bowl, mix together the bread crumbs and cheese.

In another bowl, mix the onion and sage.

In another bowl, beat the egg whites to stiff peaks. Beat in the yolks. Lightly mix in the onion and the herb, then fold in the bread crumb–cheese mixture. The consistency will be rather heavy.

In a 10-inch heavy skillet, heat the oil. Move the skillet around so that the oil coats the sides of it. There should be enough oil that you can see it flow around.

Pour in the egg mixture. Cook on medium heat for about 3 minutes, adjust the heat so that you get a good solid light crust on the bottom of the pan without burning it. To turn over the frittata, insert a long spatula under it, then flip it. Cook for another 5 minutes on low heat.

You may find it easier to fry the batter in two batches, in a smaller skillet.

"SHASHOUKA"

"shashouka"—a vegetable-egg dish

serves 3

MIMMETTA
LO MONTE'S
CLASSIC
SICILIAN
COOKBOOK

•

184

One of my mother's friends whose family came from southwestern Sicily shared her *"Shashouka"* with me. The name reveals its North African origin. Looking at a map, one can see that a trip from the coast of Tunisia to the coast of Sicily facing it is a very short one. Exchanges between the two coasts are frequent (although not always amiable when it comes to fishing rights). *"Shashouka"* somehow landed in Sciacca and, accompanied by country bread, has made quite a few suppers easy for overworked housewives with small food budgets who are faced with large families with large appetites. The vegetables for *"Shashouka"* can be cooked in advance, refrigerated, then warmed up to cook with the eggs.

1¾ POUNDS BAKING POTATOES	
2 LARGE BELL PEPPERS	FLESHY; 1 RED OR YELLOW, 1 GREEN OR BOTH GREEN
1 MEDIUM ONION	
3 LARGE TOMATOES	CANNED AND PEELED, SEEDED; CUT INTO SMALL PIECES
⅔ TO ¾ CUP OLIVE OIL	
½ TEASPOON SALT	OR MORE
6 FRESH LEAVES BASIL	WHOLE
1 SMALL RED CHILI PEPPER	DRY, WHOLE
6 EGGS	EXTRA-LARGE

Peel the potatoes and cut them into ½-inch cubes. Cut the peppers into ½-inch strips and the onions into ¼-inch slices.

In a large skillet, heat the oil over high heat. Add and cook the potatoes, peppers, and onions, while stirring. When aromatic, add the tomatoes. Let cook a couple of minutes; add the salt, basil, and the hot pepper. Cover the skillet, turn the heat to very low, and let the vegetables simmer until done, up to 1 hour and 10 minutes. While cooking, stir several times.

Taste and correct the amount of salt. Turn the heat to medium low. Break in the eggs (over the vegetables), cover, and cook until the yolks are covered with a thin white film, about 3 to 4 minutes.

Remove the hot pepper, after squeezing it into the vegetables, pressing down with a spoon.

Arrange the eggs in a serving dish, surrounded by the vegetables.

Serve immediately.

UOVA ALL'AGIRINA

eggs of agira

serves 4

8 EGGS	EXTRA-LARGE
I SMALL ONION	CUT INTO VERY SMALL PIECES
½ TO ⅔ CUP OLIVE OIL	
I CUP STRONG, CLEAR CHICKEN OR BEEF	
STOCK	SEE PAGE 72
½ TEASPOON SALT	
¼ TEASPOON BLACK PEPPER	FINELY GROUND
2 SPRIGS PARSLEY	DISCARD STEMS, CUT FINELY
2 TABLESPOONS LEMON JUICE	FRESHLY SQUEEZED

Hard-boil the eggs. Cut through the white, from the tip to the bottom and then around. Remove the yolks, whole. Cut the whites into long, thin strips.

In a medium-size skillet, cook the onion in the oil until aromatic. Add the eggs, stock, salt, and pepper. Bring to a boil. Cover and cook very slowly, about 30 minutes. Some of the yolks will have dissolved in the stock at the end of the 30 minutes.

Turn off heat, stir in parsley and lemon juice.

Serve immediately.

CACIO ALL' "ARGENTERA"

"argentera" cheese

serves 2

This is a typical peasant dish that everyone loves because it's so tasty and easy to make. Bread is a must to eat along with this dish. French bread is the closest to the kind of bread that traditionally is served with it in Sicily. Traditionally, the dish is made with aged caciocavallo, but since this cheese is so hard to find, I've substituted provolone for it.

⅓ CUP OLIVE OIL	
½ POUND PROVOLONE	SHARP, IMPORTED
I CLOVE GARLIC	VERY THINLY SLICED
I TEASPOON OREGANO	DRY
⅛ TEASPOON BLACK PEPPER	FINELY GROUND
3 TABLESPOONS RED WINE VINEGAR	

Cut the provolone into two slices, ½ inch thick each.

In a very heavy skillet (preferably not cast-iron) heat the oil. Over medium heat, add the cheese and cook 3 minutes. Insert a spatula under the cheese, turn it over, and cook 3 more minutes. Add the garlic during the last minute. Add the remaining ingredients to the pan.

Serve immediately, topping the cheese slices with the pan drippings.

FRITTATINE CON RICOTTA

omelettes fried with ricotta

serves 1

This is an old favorite of Sicilian farmers: Eggs and ricotta are always on hand. Depending on which version you serve, the omelettes can be lunch, brunch, breakfast, supper, or dessert.

MIMMETTA
LO MONTE'S
CLASSIC
SICILIAN
COOKBOOK

•

186

Savory version

2 EGGS	EXTRA-LARGE
1 TABLESPOON GRATED CHEESE	PECORINO ROMANO OR CACIOCAVALLO
½ CUP RICOTTA	SCANT, REMOVE EXCESS MOISTURE BY BLOTTING WITH PAPER TOWEL
2 FRESH SAGE LEAVES	CUT VERY SMALL (OR ⅛ TEASPOON GROUND SAGE), OPTIONAL
¼ CUP OLIVE OIL	

In a bowl, beat the eggs for a minute with a fork, until well blended. Beat in the grated cheese.

In another bowl, mix the ricotta with the salt, and, if using, the sage.

In a small cast-iron skillet, heat the oil. Pour in the eggs, moving them around so that the bottom of the pan is well covered. Cook over medium-low heat until the bottom is very firm.

Place the ricotta evenly along the middle of eggs. Fold one side of the omelette onto the other and flip. Cook on low heat a couple more minutes. Serve hot along with French bread.

Sweet version

2 EGGS	EXTRA-LARGE
2 TEASPOONS SUGAR	
SALT	A VERY SMALL PINCH
½ CUP RICOTTA	SCANT, REMOVE EXCESS MOISTURE BY BLOTTING WITH PAPER TOWEL
¼ CUP OLIVE OIL	
CINNAMON	A SPRINKLE
CONFECTIONERS' SUGAR	A SPRINKLE

In a bowl, beat the eggs for a minute with a fork, until well blended. Beat in 1 teaspoon sugar and salt. In another bowl, mix the ricotta with the remaining sugar. In a small cast-iron skillet, heat the oil. Pour in the eggs and use the same procedure for frying, as in the savory version.

Place the ricotta evenly along the middle of the eggs. Fold one side of the omelette onto the other and flip. Cook on low heat a couple more minutes.

Serve hot, topped with a sprinkle of cinnamon and sugar.

You can prepare as many *frittatine* as you want in advance. Line them up in a heatproof dish to reheat. Warm them in a 375° F. oven, 10 minutes or until hot. If you are cooking the sweet version, sprinkle on the sugar and cinnamon just before serving.

Of course, wine is always served with meals. Here are some tips about wines, translated from Grandfather Alfredo's cookbook.

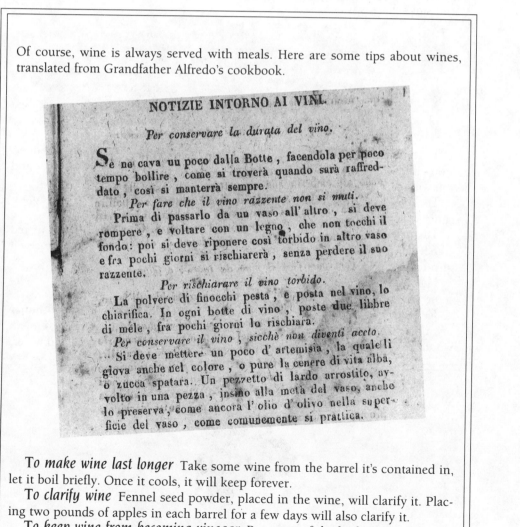

NOTIZIE INTORNO AI VINI.

Per conservare la durata del vino.

Se ne cava un poco dalla Botte, facendola per poco tempo bollire, come si troverà quando sarà raffreddato, così si manterrà sempre.

Per fare che il vino razzente non si muti.

Prima di passarlo da un vaso all'altro, si deve rompere, e voltare con un legno, che non tocchi il fondo: poi si deve riponere così torbido in altro vaso e fra pochi giorni si rischiarerà, senza perdere il suo razzente.

Per rischiarare il vino torbido.

La polvere di finocchi pesta, è posta nel vino, lo chiarifica. In ogni botte di vino, poste due libbre di mele, fra pochi giorni lo rischiara.

Per conservare il vino, sicchè non diventi aceto.

Si deve mettere un poco d'artemisia, la quale li giova anche nel colore, o pure la cenere di vita alba, o zucca spatara. Un pezzetto di lardo arrostito, avvolto in una pezza, insino alla metà del vaso, anche lo preserva, come ancora l'olio d'olivo nella superficie del vaso, come comunemente si prattica.

To *make wine last longer* Take some wine from the barrel it's contained in, let it boil briefly. Once it cools, it will keep forever.

To *clarify wine* Fennel seed powder, placed in the wine, will clarify it. Placing two pounds of apples in each barrel for a few days will also clarify it.

To *keep wine from becoming vinegar* Put some of the herb artemisia in the container, which will be good also for the color. Or, put ashes from the alba grape vine, or ashes from the spatara squash in the container.

A little piece of roasted lard, wrapped in some cloth, placed halfway in the wine container will also work and, of course, the most commonly practiced method —covering the surface of the wine with olive oil.

To *find out if there is water in the wine* Place a bamboo stick which has been previously dipped in oil into the wine: if there is water in the wine, the drops will adhere to the bamboo. If the bamboo comes out as originally put in, that will be sign that there is no water.

If a wild apple or pear, placed in the wine floats, then the wine is pure. If the fruit sinks there is water.

> *Per eonoscere se nel viso vi sia dell' acqua*
>
> Si pone nel vino una canna bagnata nell' olio: se vi sarà acqua, le gocciole dell' acqua resteranno attaccate alla canna; se uscirà come si è posta, sarà segno di non esservi dell' acqua. Se un pomo, o un pero selvatico posto nel vino, resterà di sopra, il vino è puro, se al fondo, vi è dell' acqua.

To *separate water from wine* Place a bit of liquid alum in the wine container. Stop up the container with a sponge soaked with olive oil, tilt the container and you will see the water running out that way.

To *keep wine safe from thunder and lightning* One must cover the container with an iron lid and branches of laurel.

To *turn red wine into white wine, and white into red* The ashes of red grapevine placed in white wine will turn it red, the ashes of white grapevine will turn the red into white.

How *not to get drunk* Before one drinks, one should eat raw almonds and some raw cabbage while drinking a glass of olive oil.

Remedies *to Revive the Drunkard* If you eat cabbage marinated in honey or drink a glass of very potent vinegar, drunkenness will go away. Of course it would also be very effective to stick the head of the drunkard in very cold water.

T H R E E

CONTORNI

side dishes

VERDURE
vegetables

PANE
bread

1949

As I get older, afternoons seem to get more boring. On school days I am very seldom allowed to have playmates over or go to see them. Once I am finished with my homework, there isn't much else to do but quarrel with my brother or hang around the kitchen and talk to the maid while she prepares our supper. The one from Sardinia talked and cooked strangely. She called the faucet *"grifon,"* a mythological bird, but she could make some delicious turnovers.

Now we have Giuseppina. She can make very good *spiedini* of ground beef, currants, and pine nuts. I don't think there is a single night we don't have potatoes. I don't mind that. They can be cooked in so many ways that they are never boring. I could eat fried potatoes supper after supper without ever getting tired of their deliciously soft, steamy, hot insides, encased by the skin-thin oil-fragrant crust.

Once in a while Mother and my grandparents trade maids: Giuseppina went to work for Nonno Alfredo, while Paolina, who had been with Nonna Adelina for a while, came back with us. I was very sad when Giuseppina left, not only because she was nice and a decent cook, but because she used to buy "soap opera" magazines that Mother absolutely forbid me to look at, and which I read thoroughly as soon as Mother left the house.

I never understood this hopscotch strategy of maid movements among relatives, but on this occasion I caught an explanatory conversation between my mother and one of her sisters. We had to take Paolina because she was so stupid, and my Grandfather Giovanni so short-tempered, that he had threatened to kill her if she committed another idiocy.

Paolina is a terrible cook. No wonder Grandfather couldn't stand her. She is not able to keep track of time. Her pasta is always overcooked, her sauces scorched, and anything she puts in the oven burned. She sits at the kitchen table and stares into space while pots boil over and smoke comes out of the stove. She does not notice these things because she is more concerned with her boyfriends. Discussing her dates with her takes care of my entertainment for part of the evening.

I must say that although she isn't very bright, she is very pretty. She has lots of curly light-brown hair that she gathers in two puffy buns on top of her head. She has pale blue eyes, and she wears bright red lipstick. Some of her suitors are from out of town. Together we read their love letters, and she never fails to let me read the ones she writes back. The experience came in handy when, after Paolina left the household, we got Giovanna, who is very smart, but who can't write.

MIMMETTA
LO MONTE'S
CLASSIC
SICILIAN
COOKBOOK

•

190

1953

I take care of Giovanna's correspondence. She, too, has some suitors from out of town. I do not overdo it. Giovanna would be very embarrassed if her suitors knew that she couldn't write, so I use clichés and childlike writing typical of people who haven't gone to school for long. Giovanna is a good, plain cook. The food she used to eat in her mountain village consisted of wild vegetables, and for us she mixes them with flour, then fries them in olive oil into thick, large cakes. She treats me like a spoiled child, not noticing that years have gone by and I'm not so little.

1958

I am in my last year of high school, working hard and losing weight because I am so worried about my final exams.

Giovanna insists on carrying me to bed at night in her arms, as if I were a baby. She wakes up at dawn, making sure that I have a hot cup of espresso in bed to help me to wake up and get ready to go to school. When I come out of the bathroom, she has my school uniform laid out and my shoes polished.

I am seventeen. I feel I have to start making decisions on my own, but the family thinks I shouldn't have that privilege. They have decided for me that although I am not old enough to choose what to do with my life I am old enough to get married.

I am dragged by Mother to have tea and meet my prospective husband. It is a miserable meeting. I obstinately keep my head turned to avoid seeing my prospective husband's face, or my mother's face. Finally Mother gets embarrassed enough to leave. She reports my inexcusable behavior to my father, saying that I have certainly ruined any chance of marrying that one person—Thank God, I think. The only explanation I can give for my being so ill-mannered is that I do not wish to get married, ever. I say this to avoid further discussion, but in my mind I decide right then that nobody is going to determine the turns my life might take for me.

My biggest problem up until this time has been a mild antagonism toward my brother and my mother. I have also decided that fat is ugly, and having shed mine in my very early teens, I am determined not to put it back on ever again. I love food, but I hate overeating. I think it cheapens good food. Thin now, I get teased with phrases like *"A carni sta bedda a atta,"* that is, in Sicilian dialect, "Flesh looks attractive on the pussy cat." I do indulge in fast food, but I stay slim.

This attitude seems to bother my mother, who is heavyset, most of all. Grandmother Adelina tells me I may get "weak of chest" (*debole di petto*), a nice way to say tuberculosis, if I don't eat properly. But she is also the only one in the family who sees me as not just being programmed to get married and have a family. I give her the poems I wrote as a child. She tells me that writing is the only dignified way for a woman to earn a living.

Grandmother Adelina is a terrible cook, but she has enough sense to stay away from cooking, which suits her just fine: She can afford help to cook for her. She finds the activity boring unless it is social, such as getting together with her sister-in-law and cousins to prepare special meals.

Grandmother Adelina.

A Word About Side Dishes

Side dishes are an integral part of a Sicilian meal, and they complement second courses. Some side dishes can be served as a meal in themselves. These dishes include combinations of ingredients (predominantly vegetables), which satisfy all nutritional needs, and are generally served with large amounts of bread.

Vegetables are a very important part of the Sicilian diet. Before the advent of modern technology, vegetables and fruits were strictly seasonal. Given our mild climate, there was never a winter without a fresh green vegetable of some sort, but the best times for vegetables were spring and summer.

The appearance or disappearance of a vegetable or a fruit marked the beginning or dying of a season, or a variation in the weather pattern. A sudden summer rain would fill the markets with wild fennel and wild greens, a very wet fall, with mushrooms. We had less but we had more, as flavors were full, and vegetables were not expensively grown in greenhouses.

Today, vegetables with as much character as those of old Sicily are hard to find, making the reproduction of some dishes a real challenge (but not an impossibility).

Bread is the most significant food link Sicilians have with one another and with the past. To make good bread is an art Sicilians have, and the bread produced responds to the different needs of the people who are going to eat it.

Construction workers will lunch on white French-type bread stuffed with the product of some fast-food counter. Farm workers will chew on bread—the dark, heavy kind that will last days (baked once or twice a week)—drawing out all the sweetness of the unrefined flour with slow and pensive mouth motions. Olives, dried sausage or cheese are eaten very sparingly along with this bread.

Often the very poor will eat bread accompanied only by the flavor "of the knife"—a "pani e cutieddu" lunch, as it is jokingly called. Teething babies—rich or poor—are given the heel of French bread or the crusty hard part of the heavy country bread.

MIMMETTA
LO MONTE'S
CLASSIC
SICILIAN
COOKBOOK

•

192

VERDURE
vegetables

INSALATA COTTA

cooked salad

serves 8

2 TO 3 LARGE BELL PEPPERS	RED OR GREEN; FLESHY
¾ CUP OLIVE OIL	
2 POUNDS STRING BEANS	PARBOILED AND DRAINED
I POUND CARROTS	PARBOILED AND DRAINED; JULIENNE SAME SIZE AS THE STRING BEANS
6 SPRING ONIONS	DARKEST GREEN PART DISCARDED; CUT INTO THIN STRIPS
I CUP FRESH PARSLEY	LOOSE LEAVES; CUT FINELY
I TEASPOON OREGANO	DRY
I TEASPOON SALT	
½ TEASPOON BLACK PEPPER	FINELY GROUND

Preheat the oven to 400° F.

Bake the peppers on a cookie sheet in the oven for 1 hour and 10 minutes, turning them at least once. Cool, peel, seed, and julienne them. Set aside.

Heat ½ cup oil, over high heat, in a large skillet. Add and cook the beans for a few minutes, while stirring.

Remove the beans from the skillet. Add the rest of the oil to the skillet and cook the carrots over high heat for a few minutes. Set aside.

While the beans and carrots are still hot, mix the remaining ingredients together in a large bowl.

Serve at room temperature.

INSALATA ALLA MENTA

mint salad

serves 6

⅓ CUP OLIVE OIL	
¼ CUP RED WINE VINEGAR	
¾ TO 1 TEASPOON BLACK PEPPER	FINELY GROUND
1 LARGE HEAD ROMAINE LETTUCE	CUT INTO ½-INCH WIDE RIBBONS
20 FRESH MINT LEAVES	CUT SMALL
⅛ TO ¼ POUND RICOTTA SALATA (SALTED RICOTTA)	SHREDDED
A SPRINKLE SALT	RICOTTA SALATA CAN BE VERY SALTY SO TASTE THE SALAD BEFORE ADDING ANY SALT

MIMMETTA
LO MONTE'S
CLASSIC
SICILIAN
COOKBOOK

•

194

In a bowl, mix the oil, vinegar, and pepper.
Toss with the lettuce, mint, and cheese just before serving.
Taste, and, if necessary, add a sprinkle of salt.

CONDIMENTO PER INSALATA ALL'ARANCIA

orange salad dressing

yields about ⅔ cup

This is a wonderful dressing to use on green salads, or on very thinly sliced fresh artichoke hearts. Or use this on any salad made with sliced oranges, Belgian endive, or raw fennel cut in very thin wedges, served by themselves or in any combination.

⅓ CUP OLIVE OIL	
⅓ CUP ORANGE JUICE	FRESHLY SQUEEZED
1 TABLESPOON LEMON JUICE	FRESHLY SQUEEZED
LEMON PEEL	A FEW SLIVERS; VERY FINELY CUT
¾ TEASPOON SALT	
½ TEASPOON BLACK PEPPER	FINELY GROUND
⅓ CUP FRESH PARSLEY	LOOSELY PACKED LEAVES; CUT FINELY
¼ CUP FRESH CORIANDER	LOOSELY PACKED LEAVES; CUT FINELY

In a bowl, mix together all the ingredients. The sauce tastes best when used immediately.

INSALATA CRUDA DI CARCIOFI E FINOCCHI

raw artichoke and fennel salad

serves 4 to 6

2 OR 3 ARTICHOKES	CLEANED AND PREPARED (SEE PAGE 212); THE ARTICHOKES MUST BE SLICED *JUST* BEFORE SERVING THE SALAD, OR THEY WILL DISCOLOR
1 LARGE BULB FENNEL	(OR 2 SMALLER BULBS) WELL ROUNDED, CLEANED (SEE PAGE 204)
JUICE OF 2 LEMONS	FRESHLY SQUEEZED
CONDIMENTO PER INSALATA ALL'ARANCIA	SEE PAGE 194 (OMIT LEMON JUICE)
1 ORANGE	PEELED; CUT INTO THIN SLICES WIDTHWISE, SEEDED (OPTIONAL)

Cut the artichokes and the fennel into quarters, lengthwise. Thinly slice them.

In a bowl, toss the artichokes with the lemon juice. Drain.

In a serving bowl, mix the artichokes and fennel with the *Condimento per insalata all'arancia*. Add the orange slices, if desired.

INSALATA DI GRANO

wheat salad

serves 8 to 10

This is my version of a traditional peasant dish eaten on the Day of Santa Lucia. In order to cook wheat, you'll need three days' advance preparation.

MIMMETTA
LO MONTE'S
CLASSIC
SICILIAN
COOKBOOK

•

196

4½ CUPS COOKED WHEAT	SEE PAGE 265
6 SPRING ONIONS	DARKEST GREEN PART DISCARDED; CUT INTO THIN ROUNDS
I CUP FRESH CORIANDER	LOOSELY PACKED LEAVES; CUT FINELY
I CUP FRESH PARSLEY	LOOSELY PACKED LEAVES; CUT FINELY
⅓ CUP LEMON JUICE	FRESHLY SQUEEZED
½ CUP ORANGE JUICE	FRESHLY SQUEEZED
¼ CUP OLIVE OIL	
I½ TEASPOONS SALT	
I TEASPOON BLACK PEPPER	FINELY GROUND

In a bowl, mix the cooked wheat with the onions, coriander, and parsley. Add the remaining ingredients just before serving.

INSALATA DI CARDONI E POMODORO

cardoon and tomato salad

serves 6

2 TABLESPOONS CAPERS	PRESERVED IN VINEGAR; WELL SQUEEZED
¼ CUP RED WINE VINEGAR	
⅔ CUP OLIVE OIL	
½ TEASPOON SALT	OR MORE, DEPENDING ON THE SALTINESS OF THE CAPERS
¾ TEASPOON BLACK PEPPER	FINELY GROUND
I POUND CARDOONS	PARBOILED (SEE PAGE 197); CUT INTO PIECES A LITTLE LARGER THAN ½ INCH
I POUND FRESH TOMATOES	FIRM BUT RIPE, CUT INTO CUBES A LITTLE LARGER THAN ½ INCH

In a food processor or blender, process the capers, vinegar, oil, salt, and pepper until capers are minced. Taste and correct the salt, if necessary. In a large bowl, mix with the vegetables.

Serve.

Cardoni
(Cardoons)

Cardoons are seldom found in regular supermarkets, unless the area has a very strong Italian-American population. While part of the artichoke family, cardoons look like very large celery heads. Their taste is faintly artichokelike (the solid core is the part which has the most distinct artichoke taste), while their consistency is celerylike.

Raw cardoons are bitter: parboiling them eliminates the bitterness.

To prepare a cardoon to parboil it, separate the ribs until you reach the tender, smaller ribs of the core. Leave those attached. The ribs have ridges just like celery, with strings running through them. Pull the strings from the ribs separated from the core, then cut each rib in half, widthwise. Slightly loosen up (without detaching them) the ribs of the core. Wash the cardoon well.

To parboil, bring a lot of water to a rolling boil in a pot. Add to it the juice of half a lemon and the squeezed half itself; one half for every 2 pounds of cardoon to be parboiled.

Add the cardoon. Boil until pleasantly crisp (al dente) and taste to check firmness. The core and the ribs which you have separated closer to the core will be ready earlier than the outer, tougher ribs and must be removed from the water before the rest. These are easy to distinguish because they are larger. Dip these ribs in cold water and drain as soon as cool.

Keep cooking the tougher ribs until they are al dente. Drain, dip in cold water to cool, then drain again.

Remove and discard the leafy part of the inner core ribs—and any leafy part of the ribs—these parts are hopelessly tough. Use the cardoons immediately or store in the refrigerator for a few days.

A Meal of Caponata di Patate

When I am in Sicily, I often appear for lunch, unannounced, at my uncles' and aunts' summer places on the coast. There I have been surprised with *Pasta con minestra di patate* and *Caponata di patate*. Both are considered everyday fare—nothing unusual about them—as normal as the natural beauty enjoyed while eating our lunches in the balmy air, with the view of the sea, in the midst of the triumphant colors of the bougainvillea climbing from the garden below, and of the soft, restful blue blooms of the plumbago, hovering against the walls. The herbs of the minestra are picked from the garden, just before it is cooked. The *Caponata di patate* sums up many of the characteristics of Sicilian cooking: sweet-and-sour, pleasant to eat in the summer heat, with contrasting flavors and textures.

MIMMETTA
LO MONTE'S
CLASSIC
SICILIAN
COOKBOOK

•

198

CAPONATA DI PATATE
potato caponata
serves 8 to 10

4 POUNDS BOILING POTATOES	ALLOW EXTRA FOR WASTE
OLIVE OIL	ENOUGH FOR DEEP FRYING
1½ TO 2 TEASPOONS SALT	
2 LARGE ONIONS	CUT INTO ½-INCH SQUARES
1 LARGE CELERY HEART	CUT INTO VERY SMALL CUBES
1 CUP RED WINE VINEGAR	
3 TABLESPOONS SUGAR	
½ CUP GREEN OLIVES	PITTED; CUT INTO COARSE PIECES
½ CUP CAPERS	RINSED WELL AND DRAINED
1½ CUPS *SALSA DI POMODORO*	
PASSATA	(SEE PAGE 39) USE ONLY PARSLEY AND
	BASIL AS HERBS; DO NOT STRAIN

Peel and dice potatoes. In a bowl, cover well with water. Soak for about 5 minutes, drain, rinse, and drain again.

In a skillet, fry the potatoes in 1-inch oil. Potatoes should be uncrowded. Fry at first over medium-low heat, for about 5 minutes. Then over to high heat, fry until the potatoes are light golden, occasionally turning them. Sprinkle with 1½ teaspoons salt.

In a very large skillet over medium-low heat, cook the onion and the celery in 1 cup of oil, stirring frequently, until aromatic. You can use the oil from the potatoes. Increase the heat to high, add the vinegar and sugar. Cook, while stirring, for a couple of minutes. Add the remaining ingredients except the remaining salt. Stir well, taste, and add the salt if necessary.

Serve at room temperature. *Caponata* can be eaten immediately, or refrigerated for several days.

Remembering Italian Potatoes

Le bambole Lenci—*Mother is standing third from left.*

A POTATO STORY

Once upon a time there was a little Italian girl. She had thick braids, and she squinched up her nose when she smiled. She loved the whole world: people, animals, flowers, and food. Maybe she loved food a little too much, and she loved potatoes a little more than any other food.

One day all the town's children were invited to a "mardi gras" masked party, given by the richest and skinniest girl in town, the daughter of the only Fiat dealer. The little girl wanted to go dressed as a *bambola Lenci,* a felt doll popular with all Italian girls, and her heart was broken when a mean little boy suggested she ought to go dressed as a potato, since she looked like one.

She stopped smiling and stopped loving the whole world, and she swore she'd never eat potatoes again. She undid her braids, so that her hair would hide her body, and she hid until one day a good fairy heard her crying. The fairy didn't have to ask her why she was crying—good fairies know everything. She parted the hair in front of the little girl's eyes with her magic wand and gave her a mirror to look at herself, and to the surprise of the little girl, she discovered that the image in the mirror was not one of a potato but was that of a slender wild asparagus.

The little girl thanked the fairy, started smiling, and started eating potatoes again, but she also went to a Jane Fonda exercise class, and she stayed slender, and she lived happily ever after. If you are wondering what happened to the mean little boy, he grew up to be a grouchy man, whom not too many people liked.

Potatoes have hardly ever been the subject of a fairy tale, and by the same token the potatoes have rarely been considered as having the potential of being turned into unusual dishes. Forgive, though, my very personal fantasies about potatoes, and follow me through some more realistic facts on them.

MIMMETTA
LO MONTE'S
CLASSIC
SICILIAN
COOKBOOK

•

200

Potatoes started out as unattractive, bumpy tubers that grew in a very secluded area of the world, the Andes. As unattractive as they might have been, they were to become one of the Incan marvels that the whole world benefited from. From the middle of the sixteenth century, when European travelers and explorers first took notice of potatoes, to the time they actually became a staple in the diet of the old world inhabitants, a good two hundred years went by. During this time potatoes were looked upon with suspicion, liked by few, despised by most, and even accused of causing leprosy.

By the eighteenth century potato culture had spread all over Europe. In Ireland potatoes had become indispensable to the nutrition of the entire population. Commonly thought of as a vegetable used in northern European countries, in the nineteenth century potatoes had already been quietly adopted in Italy as a starchy component of a meal, interchangeable with wheat, rice, or corn.

Today, from north to south, potatoes are handled by Italians in very imaginative ways: Often used to stretch more expensive food, mixed with a variety of ingredients, they are turned into timbales, croquettes, fritters, breads, and desserts. They respond to scooping out, filling, molding, and reshaping: Bland and amorphous per se, they can mellow and balance out other flavors. To an inventive cook, they are what clay is to a gifted potter.

The fact that potatoes are a starch doesn't keep Italians from mixing them with other starches, such as rice, pasta, and beans. The result can be a wholesome *minestre* that once eaten gives an incredible feeling of contentment and reassurance. Potatoes seem to feed the soul as well as the body.

Among people interested in Italian cuisine outside of Italy, potatoes have been overshadowed by dishes more readily identifiable as Italian, such as pasta, veal, and eggplants. Potatoes have remained in the twilight of the known repertoire of Italian cuisine: On the food stage, they have been the grunt workers and technicians, while pasta has played the primadonna and gotten all the applause.

Italians themselves have treated potatoes as the stepchild of the vegetable world, or at best like a plain country cousin, whose virtues are very convenient—and whose presence in the house is quite comforting. This cousin is able to sew, mend, and cook, take care of children, grow a vegetable garden in flowerpots on the terrace, but is discouraged from showing herself when guests come: "Dear old Matilde, she is so sweet, never lost her country habits; very shy, up with the sun and down with the sun."

I myself grew up with potatoes. Just as pasta was the staple of my middle-of-the-day meal, potatoes were the staple of my supper. In the instructions Mother gave the maid for the evening meal, the word *patata* was always included. The various Giuseppinas, Marias, Paolinas, and Giovannas, our maids who rotated in the household, were not allowed to do much for the main meal in the middle of the day. But they were free to construct the menu for the evening meal, which was considered unimportant unless one was entertaining. Since the maids came from different villages of Sicily, a few even from Sardinia, they brought quite a contribution to operation "potato camouflage," and broke the monotony of the family recipes.

Aside from fried potatoes and potatoes baked in olive oil, rosemary and onions (all old favorites), we had potato croquettes, potato beignets, frittata with potatoes, potato salads, potato timbales, potato soups, potato stew—the list could go on and on. It seems that we never ran out of potatoes or of ideas of what to do with them. I ate them enthusiastically no matter how presented, but at some point I started developing an animosity toward them—in fact, I would have been very happy had they stayed in the Andes along with Machu Picchu.

Plain, harmless, innocent potatoes started having a psychological effect on my life, and as incredible as it may sound, even took on Freudian implications in my relationship with my parents: For one thing, between the ages of nine and thirteen, I was referred to as "potato" or *naso a patata* (potato nose). I must admit, sturdy and evenly padded all over, I did look like a potato, and so did my nose, not having much of a bridge—a round little ball smack in the middle of my face. And then there was my mother, with a slim body and the most perfect nose, adored by my father for her beauty.

Too much is too much. Potatoes went out of my life, and stayed out of it even after I became, if not exactly a slender wild asparagus, then at least the thicker cultivated type, and my nose finally grew a bridge. But when I started writing my first cookbook, I had to recognize that potatoes have a role in Sicilian and Italian cuisine (yet the number of recipes in that book which include potatoes is disproportionately small compared to the abundance of potato eating I have done).

My reconciliation with potatoes took place in their country of origin—Peru. That seems quite appropriate and an amusing trick of fate: One of my many uncles lives there, and he is a strong believer that good food is half of good living (I'll let you imagine what he thinks the other half is). His Peruvian Indian cook put together fantastic potato dishes, using the yellow-fleshed kind, which is the favorite in Italy as well, and tastier than the white-fleshed variety used in the United States.

After that eye (and stomach) opener, I started noticing that potato recipes recurred in many of my notes taken during trips to Sicily. They had been given to me by just about everyone—relatives, friends, or acquaintances—whom I had pinned down and urged to talk about food. The recipes also emerged from all the handwritten notebooks that people so generously have given me, happy to share something so dear to them. The most exciting find: potato recipes were in the old yellow cookbook I inherited from Grandfather Alfredo.

PATATE ROSOLATE AGRODOLCE

sweet and sour browned potatoes

serves 4

These potatoes can also be made in advance and refrigerated. Bring to room temperature before serving.

2 POUNDS MEDIUM-SIZE BAKING POTATOES	ALLOW EXTRA FOR WASTE
2/3 TO 3/4 CUP OLIVE OIL	
4 MEDIUM ONIONS	CUT INTO 1/4-INCH STRIPS
I CUP RED WINE VINEGAR	
I TEASPOON SALT	
2 TABLESPOONS SUGAR	

MIMMETTA
LO MONTE'S
CLASSIC
SICILIAN
COOKBOOK

•

202

In a pot, cover the potatoes with plenty of water and bring to a boil. Boil for 20 minutes, uncovered. Drain, peel the potatoes, and chill.

Cut each potato in half, widthwise, and quarter each half into four parts (or three, according to the size of the potato).

In a skillet, heat the oil. Then add the potatoes and fry over high heat, turning them until evenly brown, about 2 to 3 minutes. Cook the potatoes in two batches. Set them aside.

Add to the oil the onion and cook over low heat until wilted and aromatic. Increase the heat to high. Add the vinegar, salt, and sugar. Cook, while stirring, for 1 to 2 minutes, then pour over the potatoes.

Serve at room temperature, after potatoes have cooled for at least 2 hours.

PATATE "IN INSALATA"

potato salad

serves 4

2 POUNDS SMALL BOILING POTATOES	(ALLOW EXTRA FOR WASTE) PEELED
WHITE WINE	DRY; ENOUGH TO COVER POTATOES
3 OUNCES BREAD	WHITE, DENSE SANDWICH-TYPE; CRUST REMOVED, ROUGHLY CRUMBLED
1/3 CUP FRESH PARSLEY	LOOSELY PACKED LEAVES
1/4 TEASPOON FENNEL SEED	
1/4 TO 1/2 TEASPOON MARJORAM	DRY, POWDERED
1/2 TEASPOON CHERVIL	DRY LEAVES

½ TEASPOON TARRAGON	DRY LEAVES OR THE FRESH LEAVES FROM
	A 6-INCH SPRIG
6 SMALL FLAT ANCHOVY FILLETS	PACKED IN OLIVE OIL, WELL DRAINED
1½ TABLESPOONS LEMON JUICE	FRESHLY SQUEEZED
2½ TABLESPOONS RED WINE VINEGAR	
½ CUP PLUS 2 TABLESPOONS OLIVE OIL	
½ TEASPOON SALT	
½ TEASPOON BLACK PEPPER	FINELY GROUND

In a large pot, cover the potatoes well with white wine. Add 1 cup of water and bring to a boil. Let the potatoes boil until done, but firm, about 20 minutes. You can use very small, unpeeled new potatoes, but don't cook as long. Drain and cool.

Slice the potatoes in rounds, about 1½ inches thick (leave the new potatoes whole). Arrange in one layer on a plate.

In a food processor or a blender, puree the remaining ingredients. Spoon some sauce (it will be thick) on each potato slice. (Toss new potatoes with the sauce.)

Serve at room temperature.

FAGIOLINI AL PAN GRATTATO

breaded green beans

serves 6

These beans are best served at room temperature.

⅓ CUP BREAD CRUMBS	
⅓ CUP PLUS 2 TEASPOONS OLIVE OIL	
1¾ POUNDS GREEN BEANS	PARBOILED; CUT INTO 1½- TO 2-INCH
	SECTIONS
1 CLOVE GARLIC	CUT INTO VERY SMALL PIECES
5 SMALL ANCHOVY FILLETS	PACKED IN OLIVE OIL; WELL DRAINED,
	MASHED
⅛ TEASPOON SALT	OR TO TASTE

In a heavy skillet over medium heat, toast bread crumbs in 2 teaspoons of oil, until golden brown.

In a skillet, sauté the beans on high heat in the remaining olive oil for a few minutes. Turn off the heat, stir in the garlic and the anchovies.

Add the bread crumbs just before serving. Add salt to taste.

MIMMETTA
LO MONTE'S
CLASSIC
SICILIAN
COOKBOOK

•

204

About Fennel

Finocchio, *fennel in English, is widely used in Italy. The kind found most commonly is Florence fennel. It has a round white bulb, with green leaf stalks and feathery green leaves.*

In Sicily, where the bulb-like fennel is used both raw and cooked, wild fennel is largely used as well. Wild fennel is considered both an herb and a vegetable. It looks very much like dill, but I would never substitute dill for it, since the flavor is very different. Fennel seed, also used frequently in Sicilian cuisine, comes from wild fennel. I have seen—and become very excited at the sight of—wild fennel growing in California.

When buying Florence fennel, always choose round bulbs. When the bulbs are elongated, they are overgrown and past their peak. Overgrown fennel is fibrous and almost inedible. Disregard the size of the fennel bulb; as long as it is round and fresh, it will be tender.

To clean fennel: Remove the tough outer leaf stalks. After the stringy and spongy parts are removed, they can be used to flavor soups. Quarter the fennel bulb and wash. Cut following the recipe instructions. The outer feathery leaves and the green leaf stalk ends bearing them are very tough and should be discarded. The feathery leaves attached to the inner leaf stalks are tender and should be used for color and flavor.

FINOCCHI PER CONTORNO
fennel as side vegetable
serves 6

½ CUP OLIVE OIL	
2¼ POUNDS FENNEL	QUARTERED; CUT INTO ⅓-INCH WEDGES; KEEP TENDER FEATHERY LEAVES (SEE ABOVE)
1½ CUPS FRESH PARSLEY	LOOSELY PACKED LEAVES; CUT SMALL
½ TEASPOON SALT	
1 TEASPOON BLACK PEPPER	FINELY GROUND
½ CUP MILK	
¼ TO ⅓ CUP GRATED PARMESAN	OPTIONAL

In a large skillet heat the oil over high heat. Add and cook the fennel, while stirring, for a few minutes. Add the parsley, salt, pepper, and milk. Cover and cook until the fennel is barely soft, about 5 to 10 minutes, depending on its tenderness.

Fennel can be served at room temperature or warm. Sprinkle the Parmesan on it, if desired, preferably if you are planning to serve it warm.

FINOCCHIO ALL'ARANCIA

orange fennel

serves 6

This dish is best made in advance, even 24 hours, and reheated.

2 LARGE BULBS FENNEL	QUARTERED; THINLY SLICED, KEEP TENDER FEATHERY LEAVES (SEE PAGE 204)
JUICE FROM 1 ORANGE	FRESHLY SQUEEZED
JUICE FROM 1 LEMON	FRESHLY SQUEEZED
2 TABLESPOONS PINE NUTS	
2 TABLESPOONS CURRANTS	
½ CUP BREAD CRUMBS	UNFLAVORED
6 TABLESPOONS OLIVE OIL	
2 TEASPOONS OR MORE SALT	
1 TEASPOON BLACK PEPPER	FINELY GROUND

Preheat the oven to 375° F.

In a bowl, mix together all the ingredients. Place mixture into an 8-inch pan and bake in the oven for 20 minutes. Reduce the temperature to 300° F. Stir the ingredients, cover, and bake for 20 more minutes. Serve hot.

INDIVIA BELGA ALL'ARANCIA

orange-flavored belgian endive

serves 1

1 TABLESPOON OLIVE OIL	
1 SMALL BELGIAN ENDIVE	CUT INTO ½-INCH THICK WEDGES
1 ORANGE SLICE	½ INCH THICK
SALT, TO TASTE	
BLACK PEPPER, TO TASTE	

In a small sauté pan, heat the oil. (Choose a size pan so that endive will not be crowded.) Over high heat, add the endive and cook until barely wilted—a couple of minutes.

Add the orange slice and cook about 1 minute, turning it once. Remove from the heat, sprinkle with salt and pepper, and serve.

CESTINI DI POMODORI

tomato baskets

serves 4

MIMMETTA
LO MONTE'S
CLASSIC
SICILIAN
COOKBOOK

•

206

The tomatoes can be made 24 hours ahead of time and warmed before serving.

1½ POUNDS FRESH TOMATOES	(ABOUT 8) RIPE, BUT FIRM
¼ CUP GRATED PARMESAN	
2 OUNCES PROVOLONE	SHARP (IMPORTED); CUT INTO THIN SLICES TO COVER THE TOMATO TOPS
1 SMALL ONION	CUT INTO VERY SMALL PIECES
1 CLOVE GARLIC	CUT INTO VERY SMALL PIECES
¾ CUP FRESH PARSLEY	LOOSELY PACKED LEAVES; CUT FINELY
¼ TEASPOON SALT	
¼ TEASPOON BLACK PEPPER	FINELY GROUND
2 TABLESPOONS BUTTER	UNSALTED

Preheat the oven to 350° F.

Coat a baking dish with ½ tablespoon butter.

Cut off the very top of each tomato, carefully hollow it out, without piercing the outer layer. Discard insides.

In a bowl, mix together the Parmesan and the diced provolone, the onion, garlic, parsley, salt, and pepper.

Fill the tomatoes with the mixture, top the filling with the remaining butter.

Place the tomatoes in the prepared dish. They should fit tightly.

Bake in the oven for 1 hour and 20 minutes. In the last 10 minutes, top with the cheese slices.

Serve hot.

CAPPELLE DI FUNGHI RIPIENE

stuffed mushroom caps

serves 4 to 6

12 LARGE MUSHROOMS	FLESHY, CAPS ABOUT 3 INCHES IN DIAMETER; CLEANED (SEE PAGE 59)
2 CLOVES GARLIC	CUT INTO VERY SMALL PIECES
½ CUP OLIVE OIL	
3 TABLESPOONS BREAD CRUMBS	TOASTED (SEE PAGE 217)
½ TEASPOON SALT	
½ TEASPOON BLACK PEPPER	FINELY GROUND
3 FULL SPRIGS PARSLEY	CUT FINELY, STEMS DISCARDED
3 TABLESPOONS LEMON JUICE	FRESHLY SQUEEZED

Optional

2 SMALL FLAT ANCHOVY FILLETS	PACKED IN OLIVE OIL; WELL DRAINED, MASHED

Remove the stems from the mushrooms and peel them, if necessary. Cut very small. In a skillet, briefly cook the stems and the garlic in one tablespoon oil and very little water, covered, over low heat, until tender. Uncover and cook over high heat until the liquid has dried out and the vegetables start to be aromatic and lightly brown. Turn off the heat. Mix in the bread crumbs, salt, pepper, parsley, and, if using, anchovies.

Sauté the caps in a wide pan (you may have to use two), in the remaining oil over high heat, turning them. When they become lightly golden, turn heat down. Turn caps bottom-side down. Add 2 to 3 tablespoons of water to the pan, along with the lemon, and cook covered until al dente. The cooking time depends on the type of mushrooms used. Test for doneness with a thin skewer. The mushrooms are ready when the skewer encounters "soft" resistance when inserted.

Turn the caps bottom-side up in a serving plate and sprinkle with the bread crumb mixture. On top, trickle the drippings from the mushroom-cooking pan. Serve hot or at room temperature.

SPIEDINI DI PEPERONI

bell pepper rolls

makes 8 rolls

8 LARGE BELL PEPPERS	FLESHY; GREEN, RED, OR YELLOW
OLIVE OIL	FOR COATING
8 TABLESPOONS PROVOLONE	SHARP (IMPORTED); SHREDDED
2 FRESH TOMATOES	PEAR SHAPED, RIPE BUT FIRM, SEEDED; CUT LENGTHWISE INTO ¼-INCH SECTIONS
A SPRINKLE SALT	
A SPRINKLE BLACK PEPPER	FINELY GROUND
8 FRESH BASIL LEAVES	

MIMMETTA
LO MONTE'S
CLASSIC
SICILIAN
COOKBOOK

•

208

Preheat the oven to 425° F.

Cut off the ends of the peppers, reserve for another use. Remove the seeds and place the peppers, on their side, on a cookie sheet. Bake in the oven for 1 hour. Turn once after about 30 minutes.

Let the peppers cool, then remove the skin gently without tearing the flesh of the peppers. It is better to leave a few stubborn pieces of skin on than to break up the peppers. Cut the peppers along one side, so that they can be flattened out in a long, wide strip.

Coat both sides of the strips with oil. Lay them skin-side down. Spread a tablespoon of provolone on each and distribute the tomato juliennes along the strips, parallel to the short sides. Sprinkle the peppers with salt and pepper. Add a basil leaf to each.

Roll the peppers very tightly and skewer the Sicilian way, having two skewers, each running through the ends of peppers. Keep the skewers parallel and pack the rolls tightly together, the end of each roll packed between the flanking rolls, so each roll remains compact (doesn't start unraveling).

Bake on a lightly oiled cookie sheet in the oven for about 12 minutes.

Let the peppers cool a few minutes before removing the skewers.

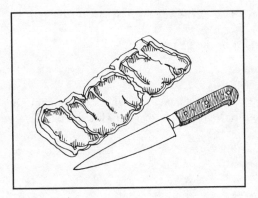

Cut the peppers along one side, down to the bottom; flatten out in a long wide strip.

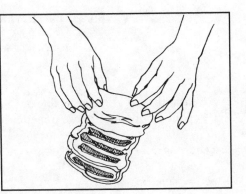

Roll the prepared strips very tightly.

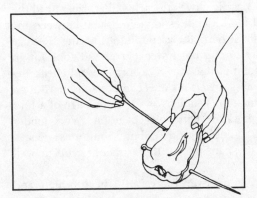

Skewer the Sicilian way, having two skewers each running through ends of peppers.

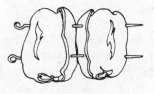

Keep skewers parallel and pack rolls tightly together.

CARCIOFI SALTATI IN PADELLA

artichokes sautéed in the pan

serves 6

Use this dish as a side vegetable or to top pasta. As a pasta topping, it yields enough for ¾ pound of pasta. Choose trenette (linguine), spaghetti, or rotini for the pasta.

8 LARGE ARTICHOKES	TENDER, CLEANED (SEE PAGE 212); SLICED INTO ⅓-INCH THICK WEDGES
⅔ CUP OLIVE OIL	
6 CLOVES GARLIC	CUT INTO LARGE PIECES
2 CUPS FRESH PARSLEY	LOOSELY PACKED LEAVES; CUT VERY SMALL
½ TO 1 TEASPOON SALT	
½ TO 1 TEASPOON BLACK PEPPER	FINELY GROUND

MIMMETTA
LO MONTE'S
CLASSIC
SICILIAN
COOKBOOK

•

210

To cook the artichokes, use two large skillets (do not use uncoated cast-iron). Add a ¼-inch layer of oil (roughly ⅓ cup) and 3 garlic cloves to each skillet. Heat until the garlic is lightly aromatic and colored. Add the artichokes, dividing them between the two skillets and over high heat, cook while stirring for a couple of minutes. Reduce the heat to medium-low, add to each skillet ½ cup hot water. Cover and cook for an additional 5 to 10 minutes. During the cooking time stir occasionally, and check the consistency several times. To test for doneness, insert a skewer in the solid part of an artichoke wedge: it should encounter moderate resistance, or see if the edge of a fork will cut the artichoke without too much pressure; better yet, taste one. Very tender artichokes will require a minimum amount of cooking time (about 5 minutes). Cooking time will increase proportionately to the hardness of the artichokes, up to well over 10 minutes.

As soon as the vegetable is pleasantly crisp, uncover, increase the heat to high, and let the liquid reduce until the artichokes and garlic sizzle, stirring frequently, to prevent scorching. Turn off the heat. Add the parsley, salt, and pepper. Serve.

To serve as a pasta topping, cook the pasta (see page 31). Reserve some of the drained water.

Immediately toss the pasta with the artichokes; if the pasta clumps together, add small amounts of the reserved water to loosen it.

Artichoke Delights

Artichokes have been my toughest antagonists—tougher than eggplants. I still remember my first American artichoke—that thing was so tough and unyielding, and I was so unprepared for it, it practically brought me to tears and destroyed the dream of tenderness and lightness for the side dish I had planned.

But an artichoke is not what it appears to be. Under those thorny scales is a prince of vegetables. To emerge and sparkle, all it waits for is a loving hand that can skillfully rid it of its inconveniently rough exterior and turn it into a most manageable vegetable, far more versatile than you have known up till now.

The average American thinks that artichokes, when fresh, can only be boiled or steamed to the point of grayness in taste and color. This is not just due to lack of creativity on the part of the American cook. Until a few years ago there was not much else you could do with the fresh artichokes offered at local produce counters. An artichoke lover possessed by the overwhelming desire of sinking his teeth into an artichoke dish could only resort to commercially packaged products.

Finally, though, artichoke growers saw the light and decided that the artichoke, like all flowers, should be picked before full bloom. There are many varieties of artichoke plants. The ideal variety of plant produces artichokes that are large when still young. Getting a small artichoke doesn't necessarily mean that it is a young, tender one.

In Italy, markets offer quite a variety of artichokes: very, very small; small; medium; large; very large; with leaf tips slightly open, or tight together; with thorns and without. (As an aside, what we commonly refer to as artichoke leaves, are actually scales.) It is the variety of the plant that determines the size of the artichoke and how it looks: No matter what type of artichoke the plant produces, artichokes are never allowed to grow so large that the size is detrimental to their tenderness.

Artichokes grow to an ideal size: When picked at the right time, almost the whole vegetable is edible; the only parts to be discarded are two to four layers of outer leaves, the thorny tips, and the choke. The choke itself, if the vegetable is young and fresh, is not wiry, and it is quite possible to eat it.

Good things in life do not come easy: This applies to artichokes, too. Boiling an artichoke is the easy way out of dealing with it. Whatever taste and consistency is left by the boiling process is promptly erased by dipping the artichoke in one of the following things: vinaigrette sauce, ketchup (yes, I have seen that, too), or melted butter. I do not object to dipping artichokes in ketchup so much as I object to dipping them in melted butter: that I find as sacrilegious as the use of butter with seafood or fish, or the use of fresh pasta with a seafood sauce. Artichokes deserve olive oil, and so does the human body, to keep the cholesterol down and the digestive tract healthy —the last a belief that may not have medical backing, but that is part of the Sicilian credo: no butter with seafood or with fish.

Anyone who finds out what an artichoke is really like unspoiled by prolonged cooking will think his taste buds have gone crazy, and will of course have a hard time believing that fresh artichokes can be eaten by the forkful, mixed with many other vegetables, pasta, rice, meats, and fish—their taste a delicate balance of faint bitterness and sweetness, carried by a nutty consistency.

The recipes here were inspired by my Grandmother Severina's recipes. She was an artichoke lover. The recipes are very old, and with the exception of one—*Carciofi saltati in padella*—have fallen into oblivion.

Artichoke Preparation

To have an artichoke dish turn out well is not an easy task, mainly because of an element beyond our control: finding artichokes that are both tender and fresh.

The freshness of an artichoke can be told by the leaves: they should be of a uniform "army" green, unmarred by brown spots, and when pressed together and slightly shifted, they should squeak. The tenderness is harder to determine: generally, too big an artichoke is going to have a very wiry choke and tough leaves. Otherwise, gently pry away from the artichoke core one leaf of the third or fourth layer. If the leaf uncovered is very pale green, almost white, two thirds of the way up, you can be reasonably sure that you are holding a tender artichoke. You can also try the fingernail test: a fingernail should easily leave an imprint on the stem. Of course, if anyone is caught checking artichokes by this method in the grocery store, I will deny suggesting such a thing. Freshness is a contributing factor to tenderness.

To remove the tough parts of the average artichoke available in supermarkets, and still be left with as much meat as possible to work with, follow the procedure described below (and your good judgment). The preparation process will require some patience and practice before mastering it, and a good grip on one's emotions. You will have to overcome any irrational feeling that so much of the artichoke is being thrown away. Anyone who feels that way is encouraged to try to ingest any of the parts destined to be discarded. If successful, it may only mean one thing: too much is indeed being thrown away, due to inexperience. If anybody feels bad about wasting the insignificant amount that can be scraped from the inner part of even the toughest leaves discarded, she can set those leaves aside and use them for whatever they may be good for—boiling them, feeding a goat, putting them in the refrigerator and throwing them away a month later, or adding them to the mulch pile.

A **quick tip**: The fresher the artichoke, the more discoloring power it will have. I really do not mind the artichoke turning dark as much as I mind my fingers getting stained. Rubbing the cut surface of a halved lemon on the vegetable and on the fingers will minimize the problem as the preparation process goes on.

To **begin preparation**: Of the outer layers of leaves, only the very bottom of their inner part—which keeps the leaves attached to the stem—is edible. Keeping that in mind, snap off the first layer of leaves. Then, snap off the following 2 or 3 rows of leaves, progressively leaving a little more of the leaf attached; that is, the part lightest in color. After the first two or three rows, leaves should get much lighter, and more tender. Keep snapping them off just above the dark stringy part, leaving the pale green part attached. As soon as the leaves are a pale green almost all the way up to

MIMMETTA
LO MONTE'S
CLASSIC
SICILIAN
COOKBOOK

•

212

the tip, cut off the tip of the artichoke, as much as one third of the way down.

The stem of the artichoke is edible, and should be removed only if the recipe calls for whole artichokes standing up. In that case, the stem can be cooked on the side.

Once the artichoke tip is cut off, proceed to peel away the fibrous outer layer of the stem and of its base where the leaves have been snapped off. Rub the stem and the base with lemon. At this point the artichoke is ready to be used for any recipe, the choke and inner leaf ends to be removed in the manner the recipes call for. For recipes for whole artichokes, pry the outer layers of leaves away from the core leaves, which will still be bearing spines. Loosen up the core leaves with a small knife blade, rotating the blade around the leaves, then pull them out. Hollow out the artichoke bottom "cup," scooping the choke with a coffee spoon inserted through the opening created by having pulled out the core leaves. In case you have trouble identifying the choke, it looks like fuzz packed together, and it has different degrees of texture—from goose down to barbed wire. Tender artichokes contain the soft fuzz, which actually can be eaten.

For recipes calling for the artichoke in wedges, quarter the artichoke, from the stem down: using the blade of a very sharp knife, bend the small inner leaves still bearing spines toward the choke, and cut them off. This should be done so that most of the leaves remain attached to the artichoke. If this process is hard to picture, just pull off the leaves, but do not complain about waste. Remove the choke with the upper part of the knife blade.

To minimize discoloration, submerge the artichokes, after they are cut, in water acidulated with lemon juice—2 to 3 tablespoons to 8 cups of water. Before soaking the artichokes, check the recipes: for some recipes acidulated water is undesirable, while other recipes indicate that water trapped between the scales is needed for the cooking process.

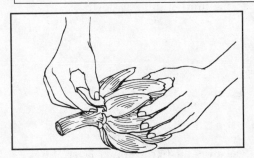

Snap off the first layer of leaves.

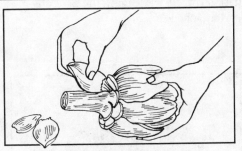

Snap off the following 2 or 3 rows of leaves, progressively leaving a little more of the leaf attached.

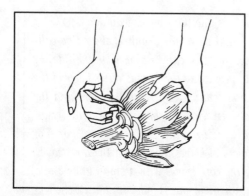

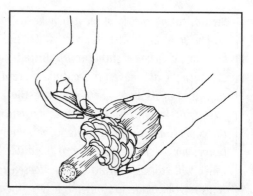

As you snap off more layers, apply pressure from all of your fingers to help snap and then tear off leaves.

MIMMETTA
LO MONTE'S
CLASSIC
SICILIAN
COOKBOOK

•

214

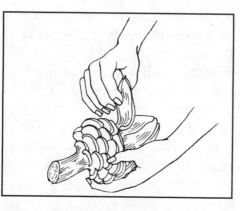

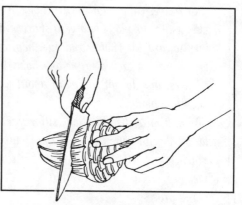

Keep snapping the leaves off above the dark stringy part, leaving the pale green part attached.

Cut off the tip of the artichoke, as much as one-third of the way down.

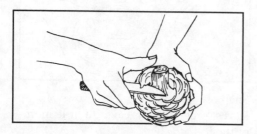

Peel away the fibrous outer layer of base, where the leaves have been snapped off.

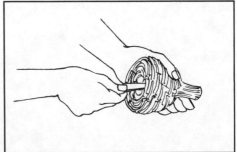

For recipes calling for whole artichokes: Pry the outer layers of leaves away from the core leaves, which will still be bearing spines.

Loosen up the core leaves with a small knife blade. Rotate the blade around the leaves, then pull them out.

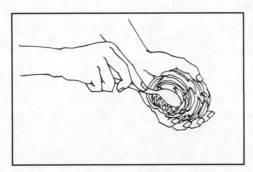

Hollow out the artichoke bottom "cup" to remove the choke.

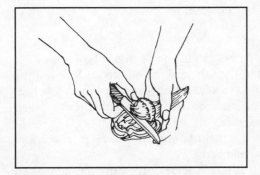

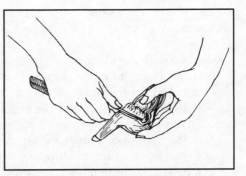

For recipes calling for artichoke wedges: Using the blade of a very sharp knife, bend the small inner leaves still bearing spines toward the choke, and cut them off.

Remove choke with upper part of the knife blade.

CARCIOFI ALLA MANDORLA

artichokes in almond sauce

serves 8

MIMMETTA
LO MONTE'S
CLASSIC
SICILIAN
COOKBOOK

•

216

8 LARGE ARTICHOKES	TENDER, CLEANED (SEE PAGE 212); CUT IN HALF, LENGTHWISE, CHOKE AND THORNY TIPS OF INNER LEAVES REMOVED
2 TABLESPOONS LEMON JUICE	FRESHLY SQUEEZED
1 TEASPOON SALT	
¼ CUP OLIVE OIL	
1 TABLESPOON FLOUR	UNBLEACHED, ALL-PURPOSE
2 TEASPOONS SUGAR	
⅔ CUP BLANCHED ALMONDS	VERY FINELY GROUND
BLACK PEPPER, TO TASTE	FINELY GROUND

Use two skillets, in which the artichoke halves can fit snugly in one layer.

Beat the lemon juice with 1 cup of water, the salt, and the oil; divide between the two pans. Add the artichokes. Bring the liquid to a boil, cover, and cook over low heat for about 20 minutes, or until the artichokes are al dente (test with skewer; when inserted, it should meet with moderate resistance).

In a heatproof dish, arrange the artichokes, cut-surface up, in one layer, cover, and keep warm. Transfer the pan drippings into one pan.

In a bowl, mix the flour with the sugar, and stir in some of the drippings to make a smooth paste.

Stir the paste into the rest of the drippings in the pan. Cook over medium-low heat until paste thickens. Turn off the heat. Stir in the almonds and spoon the sauce over the artichoke halves.

Serve warm sprinkled with black pepper, or at room temperature.

"CARCIOFFE" IMBOTTITE

stuffed artichokes

serves 8

8 LARGE ARTICHOKES	TENDER; CLEANED (SEE PAGE 212)
8 SMALL SPRIGS PARSLEY	
8 CLOVES GARLIC	PEELED; CUT IN HALF
¾ TO 1 CUP OLIVE OIL	
2 TABLESPOONS LEMON JUICE	FRESHLY SQUEEZED
½ TEASPOON SALT	

Filling

½ CUP BREAD CRUMBS	UNFLAVORED
½ CUP WHOLE ALMONDS	SKINS ON; TOASTED
1 TABLESPOON PINE NUTS	
1 TABLESPOON CURRANTS	
10 BLACK OLIVES	PREFERABLY SICILIAN OR GREEK, PITTED; CUT INTO SMALL PIECES
8 SMALL FLAT ANCHOVY FILLETS	PACKED IN OLIVE OIL, WELL DRAINED; MASHED OR CUT VERY SMALL

Cut off the stems very close to the bottom of the artichokes, and reserve them. Remove the inner leaves, scoop out the chokes. Gently loosen up the leaves.

To toast the almonds, toss them with a couple tablespoons oil in a heavy cast-iron skillet. Stir over medium heat, stirring constantly until the almonds crackle. Immediately remove from the pan. Blot with paper towels. Grind almonds finely when cool.

Pour ¼-inch layer of oil into a stove- and oven-proof pan. The artichokes should fit in it close together, standing up, stem-side down. Fit the artichokes in, and place a sprig of parsley and 2 garlic halves inside each.

With a fork beat together ½ cup of water, 2 tablespoons oil, lemon juice, and the salt and trickle over the artichokes and in between the leaves.

Cook the artichokes, covered, on stovetop over low heat for about ½ hour, or until pleasantly crisp. (Using a skewer to test, insert it through the bottom part of the artichokes. It should encounter moderate resistance. Also, taste a leaf: if it is hard and not cooked through after the 30 minutes of cooking, while the bottom part is, turn the artichokes leaf-side down. If the water has dried out, add ½ cup more. There must be at least ½ cup liquid in the pan during cooking time. Cover and cook until done.

As soon as the artichokes have reached an even and pleasant crisp stage, uncover, turn the heat up, and, artichoke-bottoms down, reduce the liquid, if any, until only drippings are left.

Preheat the oven to 425° F. To toast the bread crumbs, stir in a cast-iron skillet, over medium heat with a tablespoon of oil until golden. In a large bowl, mix together the filling ingredients. Divide the filling among the artichokes, placing it in between the leaves.

Cook the artichokes in the oven for 5 minutes. Serve hot or at room temperature.

CARCIOFI PICCANTI

savory artichokes

serves 6

4 LARGE ARTICHOKES *	TENDER, CLEANED (SEE PAGE 212); CUT INTO WEDGES LESS THAN ¼ INCH THICK
OLIVE OIL	FOR COATING
2 CUPS *SALSA DI POMODORO PASSATA*	(SEE PAGE 39) DO NOT STRAIN, USE PARSLEY AS HERB
1 TEASPOON OREGANO	DRY
¼ TEASPOON SALT	
3½ OUNCES SARDINES	PACKED IN OIL, WELL DRAINED, DEBONED; DO NOT USE SMOKED SARDINES
½ CUP PROVOLONE	(IMPORTED); SHREDDED
½ POUND MOZZARELLA	THINLY SLICED

MIMMETTA
LO MONTE'S
CLASSIC
SICILIAN
COOKBOOK

•

218

Preheat the oven to 375° F.

Use a baking dish that will accommodate the artichokes as well as the other ingredients, in two layers. Generously coat the dish with oil.

Mix the tomato sauce with the oregano and salt.

Spread one third of the tomato sauce on the bottom of the dish; cover with half the quantity of artichoke wedges. Spread on top of it the sardines, and then half the quantity of the provolone and of the mozzarella, followed by half of the tomato sauce that is left. Cover with the rest of the artichokes, cheeses, and tomato sauce.

Bake in the oven for 35 to 40 minutes. Serve hot.

* IF THE ARTICHOKES ARE NOT VERY TENDER, DIP THEM IN A POT OF BOILING WATER AND COOK BRIEFLY, UNTIL QUITE AL DENTE. DRAIN WELL.

CARDONI DI CAPODANNO

new year's eve cardoons

serves 6

This old recipe is very unusual because it calls for butter. Sicilians never serve butter with artichokes and cardoons, but use olive oil instead.

10 SMALL ANCHOVY FILLETS	PACKED IN OLIVE OIL, WELL DRAINED; MASHED

10 TABLESPOONS (5 OUNCES) BUTTER	UNSALTED; MELTED
½ TEASPOON BLACK PEPPER	FINELY GROUND
2 POUNDS CARDOONS	(SEE PAGE 197) PARBOILED; CUT INTO
	PIECES APPROXIMATELY 3 INCHES LONG
	AND ¾ INCH WIDE

In a bowl, add the mashed anchovies to the melted butter along with the pepper. Stir well.

Dip the parboiled cardoons in boiling water. When thoroughly hot, drain.

Arrange the cardoons on a serving platter. Spoon the butter mixture on top.

CARDONI AL GRATIN

gratin of cardoons

serves 6

While I have not suggested it, my mother firmly believes that fresh parsley should be part of the bread-crumb mixture and that this dish should be topped with small flakes of butter before baking it. Feel free to do so!

¼ CUP PLUS 2 TABLESPOONS OLIVE OIL	
½ CUP BREAD CRUMBS	UNFLAVORED; PLUS MORE FOR COATING
½ CUP GRATED PARMESAN	
1 OUNCE SHREDDED PECORINO ROMANO	
2 POUNDS CARDOONS	(SEE PAGE 197) PARBOILED; CUT INTO
	STICKS APPROXIMATELY 1½ INCHES
	LONG AND ⅓ INCH THICK
¼ TEASPOON SALT	
1 TEASPOON BLACK PEPPER	FINELY GROUND

Preheat the oven to 350° F.

Coat a baking dish, approximately 12 by 8 inches, with oil. Coat with bread crumbs.

In a heavy cast-iron skillet, over medium-high heat, stir around ½ cup bread crumbs and 2 tablespoons oil, until lightly toasted. Cool. Mix the toasted bread crumbs with the cheeses.

In a bowl, toss the cardoons with the remaining oil, salt, pepper, and two thirds of the bread-crumb mixture. Pack it into the baking dish. Sprinkle the remaining bread-crumb mixture on top.

Bake in the oven for 50 minutes.

VERDURE ALLA PASTELLA

vegetables in batter

serves 6

MIMMETTA
LO MONTE'S
CLASSIC
SICILIAN
COOKBOOK

•

220

This recipe is a Sicilian "fast-food" dish, and can be eaten for lunch, stuffed in Frenchlike bread. Instead of zucchini, you can use very tender artichokes, cut in thin wedges (no hard parts), parboiled cauliflower, or boiled cardoons.

Pastella

10 TABLESPOONS FLOUR	BLEACHED
½ TEASPOON BAKING SODA	
⅛ TEASPÓON SALT	
5 TABLESPOONS WATER	AT ROOM TEMPERATURE
¼ TEASPOON LEMON JUICE	
2 TABLESPOONS OLIVE OIL	SCANT
CORN OIL	ENOUGH TO DEEP FRY
1 POUND ZUCCHINI	4 SMALL ONES, CUT WIDTHWISE INTO THREE SECTIONS, THEN EACH SECTION CUT INTO 6 WEDGES

To make pastella: In a bowl, mix the flour with the baking soda and the salt. Mix the water, lemon juice, and olive oil, and add to the flour mixture. Beat with a whisk until smooth.

In a skillet, heat a 1-inch layer of corn oil until smoke is barely visible.

Coat some zucchini with the pastella. Fry it on high heat until it is golden brown. Do not crowd the zucchini in the oil. Remove the zucchini from the pan and blot out the excess oil with paper towels. Repeat until all the zucchini is cooked.

Serve immediately.

ZUCCHE IMBOTTITE

stuffed squash

serves 8

ABOUT 2½ POUNDS ZUCCHINI	4 LARGE ONES (THIS IS ONE OF THE FEW INSTANCES WHERE LARGE ONES SHOULD BE CHOSEN) INSTEAD OF SLENDER, SMALL VEGETABLES
1 EGG	LARGE
¼ CUP GRATED PECORINO ROMANO	
1 CUP FRESH PARSLEY LEAVES	CUT FINELY
10 LARGE SAGE LEAVES	CUT FINELY
⅛ TEASPOON GROUND CLOVES	
¼ TEASPOON GROUND NUTMEG	
¼ TEASPOON GROUND CORIANDER	
2 TABLESPOONS RAISINS	
2½ CUPS WHITE BREAD	CRUSTLESS; CUT INTO SMALL PIECES, LOOSELY PACKED
½ TEASPOON BLACK PEPPER	FINELY GROUND
½ TEASPOON SALT	
⅔ CUP OLIVE OIL	
1 SMALL ONION	DICED INTO VERY SMALL PIECES
¼ POUND BLACK OLIVES	PREFERABLY SICILIAN OR GREEK

In a large pot, bring some water to a rolling boil. Dip the zucchini (ends uncut) in. Bring the water back to a boil as fast as possible, and boil the zucchini for 10 minutes. Drain, dip in cold water, drain zucchini again, and cool.

Cut the zucchini in half, crosswise. Remove the seedy core, leaving the uncut end whole. Stand the halves, cut-side down, in a colander to drain for about 1 hour.

In a bowl, mix together the egg, cheese, parsley, sage, cloves, nutmeg, coriander, raisins, bread, pepper, and ¼ teaspoon salt. The mixture should be very firm. Divide the mixture into eight parts and stuff the zucchini with it, mounding over the opening of the zucchini, if necessary.

In a skillet large enough to accommodate the zucchini in one layer, heat the oil and the onion. When the onion is aromatic, add the zucchini, olives, and the remaining salt and cook over medium-high heat for a few minutes, turning them a few times. Cover and cook for 30 minutes over low heat, turning zucchini every now and then.

Serve hot.

PIZZA DI MELANZANE

eggplant pizza

serves 10

2 EGGPLANTS	(ABOUT 2½ POUNDS) UNPEELED; ENDS CUT OFF, SLICED INTO ¾-INCH ROUNDS
½ TO ⅓ CUP OLIVE OIL	
4 OUNCES PROVOLONE	SHARP, (IMPORTED); CUT INTO VERY SMALL PIECES
10 LARGE BASIL LEAVES	(OR USE 1 TEASPOON DRY) CUT INTO A FEW PIECES
1 LARGE CLOVE GARLIC	CUT INTO VERY SMALL PIECES
12 FRESH TOMATOES	PEAR SHAPED, VERY RIPE (OR THE CORRESPONDING AMOUNT OF ANY SHAPE RIPE TOMATOES, EXCEPT CHERRY; IF NOT AVAILABLE, USE FIRM, CANNED, PEELED ONES)
8 OUNCES MOZZARELLA	THINLY SLICED

MIMMETTA
LO MONTE'S
CLASSIC
SICILIAN
COOKBOOK

•

222

Put the eggplants in a pot with plenty of water, bring the water to a boil, and let eggplants boil 1 minute. Remove from the heat and drain in a colander, arranged so that the pieces rest on their skin sides for at least 10 minutes. Squeeze each slice gently to release more moisture.

Preheat the oven to 375° F.

Choose a baking dish with a 2-inch side, which can accommodate the eggplant slices in one layer, very close together. Pour enough oil in the dish to cover the bottom in a thin layer. Arrange the slices of eggplant in the pan, turning them over once, so that the top side is slightly oiled.

Cover the eggplant with the provolone, then evenly distribute the basil and garlic over the cheese. Lay the tomatoes on top and trickle a couple of tablespoons of oil over them.

Cover with the mozzarella slices, turning the slices over once so that the top surface will be moistened by the oil and juice from the tomatoes.

Bake in the oven for 40 minutes. Serve hot.

POLPETTE DI MELANZANE

eggplant fritters

makes about 16 fritters

1¼ POUNDS EGGPLANT	CHOOSE A SKINNY, LONG EGGPLANT, OR BUY LARGER EGGPLANTS AND REMOVE THE SEEDY PART; PEEL THE EGGPLANT(S) AND CUT INTO 1-INCH CUBES
2¼ TEASPOONS SALT	
⅓ TO ½ CUP OLIVE OIL	
¾ CUP BREAD CRUMBS	UNFLAVORED
1 EGG	EXTRA-LARGE
¼ CUP GRATED CACIOCAVALLO OR PECORINO ROMANO	
¼ CUP FRESH PARSLEY	LOOSELY PACKED LEAVES; CUT VERY FINELY
8 LARGE BASIL LEAVES	CUT VERY FINELY
½ CUP FLOUR	UNBLEACHED, ALL-PURPOSE (OR ¼ CUP MIXED WITH ¼ CUP SEMOLINA)
CORN OIL	OR A SIMILAR VEGETABLE OIL, ENOUGH FOR ¾-INCH LAYER

In a large bowl, soak the eggplant in plenty of water and 2 teaspoons salt, placing a plate on top of the eggplant to prevent it from floating. Drain after 30 minutes.

Cook the eggplant in a skillet coated with a thin layer of olive oil, over very low heat until very soft, about 45 minutes. Stir a few times.

In a bowl, mash the eggplant using a fork or a potato masher. Mix in the bread crumbs and a scant ¼ teaspoon salt. Cool some, and mix in the egg, cheese, and herbs.

In a large pan, drop the mixture by the heaping tablespoonful into the flour. Flip it over gently and shape it into oval patties, each a little over ½-inch thick.

In a skillet heat ¾-inch corn oil until smoke is barely visible, over high heat. Fry the fritters for about 1½ minutes until brown, flipping once during that time. If they get brown faster than that, or if they do not brown within that time, adjust the heat.

Serve hot.

Fritters can be fried a few hours in advance, then laid out on a cookie sheet, and refrigerated. Bring them to room temperature on the counter. Crisp them in a pre-heated 450° F. oven, until the fritters sizzle, about 5 minutes.

TORTINO DI FAGIOLINI

baked string beans

serves 6

MIMMETTA
LO MONTE'S
CLASSIC
SICILIAN
COOKBOOK

•

224

2 POUNDS STRING BEANS	
I POUND BAKING POTATOES	ALLOW EXTRA FOR WASTE
I LARGE ONION	CUT INTO VERY SMALL PIECES
4 TABLESPOONS OLIVE OIL	YOU MAY SUBSTITUTE OLIVE OIL FOR THE AMOUNT OF BUTTER ABOVE, USING A TOTAL OF IO TABLESPOONS OLIVE OIL
6 TABLESPOONS (3 OUNCES) BUTTER	UNSALTED
2 EGGS	EXTRA-LARGE; LIGHTLY BEATEN
6 TABLESPOONS GRATED PARMESAN	
I TEASPOON SALT	
BREAD CRUMBS	UNFLAVORED, FOR COATING

Preheat the oven to 400° F.

Dip the beans in plenty of boiling water. Let boil a few minutes, or as long as necessary to be al dente. Drain and cut into ½-inch pieces.

Boil the potatoes in plenty of water. Cook 20 to 30 minutes, depending on the size, then peel and coarsely mash them.

In a large skillet, cook the onion slowly in the oil and 4 tablespoons butter (or more oil) until aromatic. Add the string beans and stir for a couple of minutes. Turn off the heat. Mix in the potatoes. Let the vegetables cool some.

Add the eggs, Parmesan, and salt to the vegetables. Stir well. Coat a medium-sized baking dish with oil, then bread crumbs. Spoon in the string bean mixture, smooth the top, and sprinkle with bread crumbs. Dot with the remaining butter or trickle 2 tablespoons oil on top.

Bake in the oven for 30 minutes.

PURÈ DI ZUCCA ROSSA ALLA MENTA

mint-flavored butternut squash

serves 6 to 8

4 SMALL BUTTERNUT SQUASH	SPLIT IN HALF, LENGTHWISE, SEEDS AND STRINGS REMOVED
⅓ CUP OLIVE OIL	
4 CLOVES GARLIC	THINLY SLICED
2 TABLESPOONS SUGAR	
¾ CUP RED WINE VINEGAR	
½ CUP FRESH MINT	LOOSELY PACKED LEAVES
1 TEASPOON SALT	
BLACK PEPPER, TO TASTE	FINELY GROUND

Preheat the oven to 425° F.

Place the squash, cut-side down, in a baking dish coated with oil. Bake in the oven until soft, about 30 minutes.

Scrape the flesh from the peel and mash roughly. Return to the pan.

In a skillet, heat the oil and the garlic, until aromatic. Add the sugar, vinegar, mint, salt, and pepper. Turn off the heat. Mix with the squash and serve hot.

ZUCCA AL POMODORO

butternut squash with tomato

serves 6

6 LARGE TOMATOES	CANNED AND PEELED; RESERVE SOME OF THE PACKING JUICE
1¾ POUNDS BUTTERNUT SQUASH	PEELED; DICED
3 OUNCES PECORINO ROMANO	CUT INTO VERY SMALL PIECES
1 MEDIUM ONION	CUT INTO VERY SMALL PIECES
1 TEASPOON OREGANO	DRY
½ TEASPOON SALT	
¼ CUP OLIVE OIL	

Seed the tomatoes, reserving the juice and cut into very small pieces. Add enough of the packing juice to the reserved juice to make ⅔ cup. Pour into a pot and add the tomatoes and the remaining ingredients. Bring to a boil, cover, and simmer until done, about 15 minutes or until squash is soft; cubes should keep shape. Check often—you may want to add small quantities of water. Serve hot.

PURÈ DI CECI

chick-pea puree

yields about 8 cups

This puree should be served warm or at room temperature, as a side dish for meats. You can also serve the puree as a topping for *Patate imbottite infornate* (see page 234), at room temperature as a vegetable dip, or as a spread on dense country bread (see *Pane di casa,* page 240). Note that you will need to soak the chick-peas a day in advance of preparing this dish.

I POUND CHICK-PEAS	
I MEDIUM ONION	CUT INTO LARGE PIECES
½ TO ¾ CUP PINE NUTS	
2 TO 4 LARGE CLOVES GARLIC	
¼ TO ½ CUP OLIVE OIL	
1½ TO 2 TEASPOONS SALT	
I TO 2 TEASPOONS WALNUT OIL	OPTIONAL

Sort and rinse the chick-peas in cold tap water, then soak in plenty of cold tap water for 24 hours. Change the water and rinse at least once during the 24 hours. Drain and rinse well.

Place the chick-peas and onion in a pot, add enough water to be about 2 inches above them. Bring to a boil and cook, covered, at a low simmer until tender, at least 2½ hours. During the cooking time add water as needed to cover the ingredients. Drain, reserving the water.

Let the chick-peas cool some; then puree in food processor along with the pine nuts and garlic, adding enough of the reserved water to reach a thick, creamy consistency. Blend in oil and salt to taste and, if using, the walnut oil.

MIMMETTA
LO MONTE'S
CLASSIC
SICILIAN
COOKBOOK

•

226

Longing for Fava Beans

"If you meet a Greek and a wolf, shoot the Greek and let the wolf go."

In spite of this saying about Greeks (which in fact I think was originated by the feelings Sicilians had toward the Albanians who settled in Sicily at the end of the 1500s, and who were referred to as "the Greeks"), I started rooting for the Greeks against the Romans from elementary school on.

Through the rather simplified history the nuns taught me, it became clear that the Romans were the villains. I could never forgive them for besieging Syracuse for two years—it took them that long to break down the defense system engineered by Archimedes—and for killing Archimedes himself during the sack of the town.

Syracuse was the capital of Sicily during the Roman Empire, and the residence of its praetors. From the size of the kitchens and of the banquet rooms of the beautiful villa of Piazza Armerina, which is very close to Syracuse, and from the writings of Romans of the time, we can safely assume that eating was one of the main preoccupations of the new rulers.

The Romans introduced new flavors brought from the Middle East and the Orient, such as anise and cloves and—a very significant fact—a change in the style of the cuisine. Dishes started appearing which, rather than being made up of one main ingredient flavored in a straightforward way with the addition of olive oil and herbs, were a combination of main ingredients—fish and meats together—and were flavored more heavily with spices and herbs. They could be considered the predecessors of *pasticci* and *torte.*

Vegetables often mentioned during Roman times were asparagus, onions, and fava beans, all of which are consumed in large quantities by Sicilians today. A very common peasant dish called *"maccu,"* which is believed by many to have been in existence prior to Roman times, derives its name from a Latin word that means "smash," and that is indeed very descriptive of the dish: a puree of dried fava beans.

In the United States I have seen fava beans rise from total obscurity to become the pet legume of fancy restaurants. Yet the rare references to fava beans in cookbooks written in English (by people who aren't Mediterranean) describe them as a second-class vegetable, the Cinderella of the beans, and apt to satisfy only the inhabitants of Third World countries.

The fava bean is in fact a very effective way to stave off hunger in many poor countries: the bean, allowed to grow to its potential, becomes very large and gives a very good yield. Of course, once it has become large and has started turning yellow, the fava bean can only be conveniently used dried. In Sicily, favas—which are very easy to grow in the right habitat (on hilly ground, in cool but not freezing weather)—are equally enjoyed by rich and poor in their different stages: very small, larger (but still green and tender), and dried.

When I first came to this country, dried favas could be found in ethnic specialty stores, though fresh ones did not exist. Twice in the sixties, fresh favas unexpectedly appeared in the supermarket where I used to shop. It was the mystery vegetable that baffled both checkout-counter employees and shoppers. I hoarded the fava beans along with some Latinos who had also spotted them, and feasted on them.

Many more years went by, and again there was no trace of favas. Then they started appearing in gourmet stores, and, from the price, one would have never guessed that they were food of the poor. The price was not the only problem, however. A more serious one was that the beans had been cultivated by someone who did not understand favas. They had become too large to be a delicacy, too small to be a staple. Picking them at the right time is crucial.

To this day favas remain misunderstood, since people do not seem to know when to pick them or how to cook them. In the fanciest restaurants, I have been served favas cooked in the most insipid ways. Maybe it takes over two thousand years of tradition —centuries of cultivation—to understand this simple legume.

In Sicily, from generation to generation, we have eaten fava beans. What I know about growing and picking favas is what I learned on one of the estates belonging to my paternal grandfather. The caretaker would tell us when the beans were ripe, and the family would make a special trip to have a meal of which favas were the main element.

I remember diving with my brother into the huge heaps of dried favas kept in the storage room in the farmhouse, pretending they were gold coins—we were influenced by the Walt Disney cartoon character Scrooge—and invariably getting hives from some sort of herb that got harvested along with them. I remember the flowers of the bean, white with a little black eye, that unobtrusively dotted the fields.

Once I moved to the States, for years it was impossible for me to return to Sicily during the right season for favas. I have to confess that I became so obsessed with the desire of tasting some that, coming back from one of these trips, I, a law-abiding citizen, decided to smuggle in my pockets two handfuls of dried favas, determined to plant them in the front yard of my town house and to grow them against all the odds.

The guilt and the anxiety I felt going through customs were terrible. The favas in my pocket rattled like maracas at the least movement. I thought I would have heart failure when a female customs officer starting looking intensely at my coat, and then asked where I had bought it. I had to show her the label—Bonwit Teller—and in the process the favas displayed their musicality pretty loudly. She did not notice, as she was so preoccupied with catching me for having bought an expensive coat abroad and trying to smuggle it in without paying duty tax. She let me go with a very sour observation: "Only the best for you." It took me a while to recover.

After that I experienced remorse. What if I was introducing a fungus, bacteria, or other pest that would destroy some form of vegetable life in the United States? I survived the remorse and planted the favas in my front yard, carefully following my father's instructions: Make a hole in the ground a few inches deep, put in three beans —or was it two?—to beat the odds, and cover them.

MIMMETTA
LO MONTE'S
CLASSIC
SICILIAN
COOKBOOK

•

228

Well, in due time the plants came out, grew, and flowered. I was in heaven, but pretty soon it became obvious that the favas were not—they thought they were in a swamp. My amorous looks could not make up for the wrong climate. It became too hot too soon, and the humidity was excessive. My crop consisted of a total of three pods. My daughter Vivien shares my same passion for favas. Those three pods received from the two of us treatment and respect that not even a fresh truffle would have gotten. We sat together in the shade, inhaled the scent released by the pods while we cracked them, and very slowly chewed the tiny favas. They were few, but they were perfect.

The only other time when, outside of Sicily, I had a chance to eat fava beans picked with my own two hands, was in Peru. I was being driven outside of Cuzco to visit some ancient ruins. I was letting my eyes search the immense landscape of the high plains, green and luscious, so different from anything I had seen before. At some point, in that incredible extension of greenery, something started looking incredibly familiar. *Fave!* I screamed, and ordered the Peruvian driver to stop immediately. He did not think favas were something to get excited about: Food raised to keep a few million poor Indians alive was food to shun once one made a good living as a driver. But you know these *turistas,* they are crazy, and you have to humor them. So he stopped.

From the right and left of the road the favas went on, as the ground dipped and raised as far as my eyes could see. I noticed a man outside a little shack made of twigs, and some children. I did not know much Spanish—but neither did he, like many Indians in the high plains. So we resorted to talking with our hands. He understood right away that I wanted some favas. He refused to take any money, and with a very eloquent and gracious gesture of his hand he invited me to help myself. I picked a bunch as large as my fist could hold and gave the children, whose curious eyes had never left me, some *soles,* then went back to the car. We smiled and waved to each other as the car drove away. The favas were delicious, picked at the moment when their distinctive flavor had peaked to perfection.

The fava recipes here I learned from my mother, who learned them from her father and from her maternal grandfather. Some, she admitted, she had never cooked herself, but she remembered eating them as a child. Favas with fennel, favas with *zucca rossa* (similar in taste to butternut squash), and favas with pasta—she called them Nonno's recipes, and it was my questioning that brought them back to her memory, along with the smile of someone who had rediscovered a portion of a happy past now stored away but still very much alive.

FAVE E FINOCCHIO

fava beans and fennel

serves 4

If the skin covering the favas is tough, it must be removed before cooking. Once the skin is removed, the favas' cooking time should be shortened, to keep them from disintegrating.

⅔ CUP OLIVE OIL	
½ MEDIUM ONION	CUT INTO SMALL PIECES
2 CUPS FAVA BEANS	SHELLED (SEE ABOVE), SMALL, TENDER, ABOUT 2 TO 3 POUNDS UNSHELLED
¾ POUND FENNEL	(NET WEIGHT) TOUGH OUTER RIBS AND RIB ENDS REMOVED, QUARTERED, CUT WIDTHWISE INTO ⅓-INCH SLICES (SEE PAGE 204)
½ TO ¾ TEASPOON SALT	
¼ TEASPOON BLACK PEPPER	FINELY GROUND

MIMMETTA
LO MONTE'S
CLASSIC
SICILIAN
COOKBOOK

•

230

Pour oil into a medium size pan, add onion and heat. Add fava beans and fennel, stir over high heat briefly (about 1 to 2 minutes). Add salt and pepper, reduce heat to low, and cook, covered, 15 minutes. Uncover, increase the heat to high, and stir around a few minutes until the liquid released by the vegetables dries out almost entirely. Serve.

Preparing Fava Beans

Fava bean pods should be picked, if one wants to eat the beans raw or use them as a side-dish vegetable, when they are about ¾-inch wide. The pod is then bright green and fleshy: rounded swellings along it indicate where the beans are. I open the pod, cracking it in a spiral that follows the swellings, pulling out the beans as I do so. The interior of the pod feels velvety and moist. It is a must to use fava beans while fresh, otherwise they will either mold or dry out. When they dry out, the skin that covers them becomes very tough. The bean itself looks like a lopsided fingernail; to also be able to eat the skin of the bean they should not be any wider than a half inch.

One is seldom able to buy pods that match in size, but since different sizes of favas can be used for different dishes, it is a good idea to buy them in large quantities and to sort through the beans, reserving the small ones for certain recipes, and the large ones for others. And let us keep hoping, while doing our sorting, that some fava bean grower will understand the proper way to handle them!

CAVOLO IMBOTTITO

stuffed cabbage

serves 8 to 10

Please note that you will have to prepare the risotto before you can complete preparing this dish.

2½ CUPS *ARBORIO* , ITALIAN RICE	OR GOOD-QUALITY JAPANESE RICE
2 TABLESPOONS (1 OUNCE) BUTTER	UNSALTED
2 TABLESPOONS OLIVE OIL	
5 TO 6 CUPS CHICKEN OR BEEF STOCK	STRONG, CLEAR, LIGHTLY SALTED, (SEE PAGE 72)
2 ZUCCHINI	(ABOUT ½ POUND), SLENDER; CUT INTO ½-INCH ROUNDS
½ CUP HEAVY CREAM	
1 CUP FRESH PARSLEY	LOOSELY PACKED LEAVES; CUT VERY SMALL
⅔ CUP GRATED Parmesan	
PEEL OF 1 LEMON	GRATED
¼ TEASPOON SALT	
½ TEASPOON BLACK PEPPER	FINELY GROUND
1 HEAD CABBAGE	ABOUT 2¼ POUNDS
CORN OIL	FOR COATING

Make a *Risotto rapido* (see page 59) using the ingredients called for here: the rice, butter, olive oil, stock, and zucchini. Once the risotto is ready, turn off the heat. Add the cream, parsley, cheese, lemon peel, salt, and pepper. Set aside.

In a pot, cover the cabbage with plenty of water, and bring to a boil. Keep at a low boil, covered, for 30 minutes. Remove the cabbage from the water, let it cool just enough to be able to handle it without burning your hands.

Remove the outer leaves that have torn, and start rolling back the cabbage leaves one by one, pulling the edge away gently, until you reach the core, which will be still cold and uncooked. Remove it (should be the size of a small orange).

Fill the core space with the rice mixture. Pull back the first row of leaves around it. Spoon some rice between each row of leaves, making sure it reaches down to where the leaves are attached to the stem, and that it is evenly spread.

Preheat the oven to 375° F.

Mold the cabbage into an even, roundish shape, and coat well with olive oil. Wrap in foil, bake in the oven for 1½ hours. Open the top of the foil wrap to expose the top third of the cabbage. Bake for 15 more minutes.

Cool at least 15 minutes before slicing. Serve sliced in wedges.

CAVOLETTI DI BRUXELLES ALL'UVETTA

brussels sprouts with raisins

serves 8

2½ POUNDS BRUSSELS SPROUTS	STEM BOTTOM AND OUTER LEAVES REMOVED
⅔ TO ¾ CUP OLIVE OIL	
1 LARGE ONION	CUT INTO VERY SMALL PIECES
½ CUP RAISINS	
½ CUP WALNUTS	BROKEN INTO COARSE PIECES
½ TEASPOON SALT	
¼ TEASPOON BLACK PEPPER	FINELY GROUND

MIMMETTA
LO MONTE'S
CLASSIC
SICILIAN
COOKBOOK

•

232

In a pot, dip the sprouts in plenty of boiling water. Boil until al dente—depending on the size it could take 5 to 15 minutes. The sprouts should be drained as soon as a thin skewer can go through them with a moderate amount of resistance. The sprouts should be firm, not soft.

In a very large skillet, heat the oil until smoke is barely visible. Add the onion and stir around briefly (about 1 minute). Add the sprouts, raisins, and walnuts, and cook on high heat 5 to 8 minutes, stirring frequently. Adjust the heat if bottom of pan gets burned.

Turn off the heat; add salt and pepper.

Serve hot.

RAPE AFFOGATE

smothered turnips

serves 4

1¼ POUNDS TURNIPS	(ABOUT 3) PEELED; SLICED INTO ⅓-INCH WEDGES
½ TO ⅔ CUP OLIVE OIL	
1 TEASPOON CORIANDER	GROUND
1 TABLESPOON CURRANTS	
1 TABLESPOON ALMONDS	SKINS ON; SLICED

Sauté the turnips in the oil over medium heat, in a pan where they won't be crowded, for 1 minute. Add the remaining ingredients and ¼ cup water. Cover and simmer for 10 minutes.

Uncover, increase the heat to high, and sauté the turnips for a minute after the liquid has dried out.

Serve.

PATATE IMBOTTITE FRITTE

fried stuffed potatoes

serves 6

Patate imbottite fritte and Patate imbottite infornate are both recipes I have worked out from Grandfather Alfredo's cookbook. Recipes meant for the elite, these dishes are now available to everybody. I prefer to prepare this dish when I have leftover risotto.

6 MEDIUM BAKING POTATOES	ALLOW 2 EXTRA FOR WASTE
3 EGGS	EXTRA-LARGE; SEPARATED
½ CUP GRATED PARMESAN	
½ TEASPOON BLACK PEPPER	FINELY GROUND
½ RECIPE RISOTTO RAPIDO	(SEE PAGE 59) OMIT ONION AND MUSHROOMS FROM RECIPE
FLOUR	UNBLEACHED, ALL-PURPOSE, FOR COATING
BREAD CRUMBS	FOR COATING
CORN OIL	ENOUGH FOR A 2-INCH LAYER TO DEEP FRY

Place the potatoes in a pot in enough water to cover them. Bring to a boil and boil over medium to medium-high heat, uncovered, for 20 minutes. The skins should not split and potatoes should be fairly firm. Peel, then lay the potatoes on their flattest side and cut them in half, lengthwise. With a small, pointed knife, cut out the interior of the potato, so that you will have a shell a little less than ½-inch thick.

In a bowl, mix the egg yolks, Parmesan, and pepper with the risotto. If the risotto is room temperature, rather than refrigerator cold, it will be easier to mix. If you made fresh risotto, wait until it is lukewarm before mixing.

Molding the risotto into them, round out the potato halves again to a full potato shape, letting rice side bulge out to match the half potato. Lightly flour, coat with egg white, and then with bread crumbs.

With the potato scraps, and with any excess rice, you can make very quick croquette and *Arancine*. Mash the potato scraps with any leftover egg white from the coating. Add a touch of salt, and if you wish, a touch of Parmesan. Shape very small croquettes, and coat them with bread crumbs. Roll the rice in balls, the size of a small walnut. Coat them with egg white and bread crumbs.

Deep fry in very hot oil at high or medium-high heat until golden brown (if you see the crust turning dark too quickly, adjust the heat). Serve hot.

This dish can be made in advance (refrigerate if more than 3 to 4 hours in advance), and reheated on cookie sheets, at 350° F. about 10 minutes, or until it sizzles.

PATATE IMBOTTITE INFORNATE

baked stuffed potatoes

serves 4

In the Duke's original recipe, *bottarga,* or salted tuna fish egg, was called for in place of caviar. Today in Sicily, the fish eggs are as much of a delicacy (and almost as expensive) as caviar.

MIMMETTA
LO MONTE'S
CLASSIC
SICILIAN
COOKBOOK

•

234

2 POUNDS NEW POTATOES	(ABOUT 4 LARGE) ROUND SHAPED, OR USE BAKING-TYPE; SELECT THE MOST ROUNDED ONES
½ TO I TEASPOON SALT	
4 SMALL FLAT ANCHOVY FILLETS	PACKED IN OIL; WELL DRAINED, FINELY MASHED
2 OUNCES CAVIAR	GOOD-QUALITY LUMP FISH-TYPE
½ TEASPOON FENNEL SEED	
I½ TEASPOONS GROUND CORIANDER	
2 TEASPOONS CHERVIL	DRY LEAVES
⅔ CUP FRESH PARSLEY	LOOSELY PACKED LEAVES, CUT FINELY
8 TABLESPOONS OLIVE OIL	
I CLOVE GARLIC	CUT VERY SMALL (OPTIONAL)
I TABLESPOON BLACK PEPPER	FINELY GROUND
½ POUND LENTILS	SORTED, RINSED
I½ TEASPOONS GROUND CUMIN	

Preheat the oven to 375° F.

Cover potatoes well with water in a pot, bring the water to a boil and cook, uncovered, about 35 minutes. Peel.

It is very important that your potatoes are not water logged. The potatoes should be cooked through but still firm, and should have very few blemishes, if any.

Cut the potatoes in half, remove the very tip of the rounded bottoms, so that the halves will have a small flat surface to sit on without rolling. Hollow out the potatoes (from the largest cut side) to obtain shells a little less than 1 inch thick. Set aside the trimmings. Sprinkle with a little salt in and out, coat the outside with oil, and set aside.

Put the potato trimmings through a ricer or vegetable strainer and mix it with the anchovies, caviar, fennel seed, coriander, chervil, parsley, 4 tablespoons of oil, pepper and, if using, garlic. Taste and add salt if necessary. Then fill the potato halves level with the edges of the shell. For looks, pipe the rest on top of the potatoes with a pastry tube covering only the filling already in the shells.

Place in a well-oiled baking dish and bake for 30 minutes.

In a pot, cover the lentils with water so that the water is 1½ inches above the level of the lentils. Add ½ teaspoon salt, bring to a boil, and cook over medium-low heat, with the lid slightly ajar. Check and stir frequently. Add hot water as soon as the initial water has been absorbed, so the lentils are barely covered (you do not want the lentils to be swimming in the water, just covered enough to keep them from getting scorched). The lentils will be cooked half an hour after they have reached the boiling point. Stir in the cumin.

Put the lentils through a vegetable strainer to puree them. If you have too much liquid, drain them before straining, and add the liquid as needed to reach the consistency of a creamy, but not runny, puree. If you wish, puree the lentils in a food processor. I prefer to strain them so that the skins do not get into the puree.

Mix 4 tablespoons of oil into the puree.

Pass the puree around at the table, to be spooned on top of the potatoes.

PIZZA BIANCA DI PATATE

"white" potato pizza

serves 8

4 POUNDS BAKING POTATOES	(NET WEIGHT PEELED); CUT INTO ¼-INCH ROUNDS, COVERED WITH WATER
¼ CUP FRESH ROSEMARY	LOOSELY PACKED LEAVES
½ TEASPOON SALT	
1 TEASPOON BLACK PEPPER	FINELY GROUND
½ CUP OLIVE OIL	PLUS SOME FOR COATING
A FEW ANCHOVY FILLETS	CUT INTO SMALL PIECES (OPTIONAL)
1 MEDIUM ONION	THINLY SLICED (OPTIONAL)
½ CUP GRATED PECORINO ROMANO	OR PARMESAN FOR A LIGHTER TASTE

Preheat the oven to 375° F.

Drain the potatoes, leaving a little moisture. In a bowl, toss the potatoes with the rosemary, salt, pepper, oil, and, if using, the anchovies and onion.

Coat a baking dish, 12 by 9 by 2 inches deep, with oil. Alternate the potatoes and the cheese in three layers each, starting with the potatoes.

Cover dish with foil, bake in the preheated oven for 40 minutes. Test for doneness by inserting a skewer; it should find little resistance. If the potatoes are still hard, bake until the potatoes are fairly soft, but still firm. Uncover, increase the heat to 425° F., and bake 20 more minutes, or until the edges brown. Serve.

PANE

bread

MIMMETTA
LO MONTE'S
CLASSIC
SICILIAN
COOKBOOK

•

236

PANE DI MARIA ANGELICA

maria angelica's bread

serves 10

This bread can be kept unrefrigerated for several days. Serve slices slightly toasted before eating.

1 POUND FLOUR	(ABOUT 3½ TO 4 CUPS) UNBLEACHED, ALL-PURPOSE
3 TABLESPOONS SUGAR	
1 TABLESPOON YEAST	GRANULAR
1¼ CUPS MILK	LUKEWARM
4 TABLESPOONS (2 OUNCES) BUTTER	UNSALTED, MELTED, PLUS ADDITIONAL TO COAT PAN
½ CUP PINE NUTS	
⅓ CUP CURRANTS	
1 TEASPOON FENNEL SEED	
1 EGG	EXTRA-LARGE

In a bowl, mix the flour with the sugar. In another bowl, dissolve the yeast in 2½ tablespoons warm water, add to the flour, and beat with wire beater until grainy. I use a Kitchen Aid countertop mixer at speed 2 (low). Add the milk and butter, beat with the flat dough beater for 5 minutes, speed 2. Add the pine nuts, currants, fennel seed, and egg, and beat 2 more minutes, speed 2. The dough should be soft.

Generously butter a ring pan and place the dough in it. Let it rise, covered, in a warm place, until it has more than doubled.

Preheat the oven to 375° F. Bake in the oven for 40 minutes. Cool some before eating.

PANINI CRESCIUTI

"grown" rolls

makes 12 rolls

While I spent time with some friends, at their country home in the southwestern wine land of Sicily, I heard a lot of talk about *Panini cresciuti*. I liked the name of the dish, and the enthusiasm that lit up everybody when it was mentioned, but when I asked for the recipe, nobody could, or would, tell me the exact ingredients and quantities. I got more "maybes" than I could afford in experimenting with a recipe. Unexpectedly, I found a recipe in an old handwritten book, which I was allowed to photocopy. The enthusiasm raised by the sole mention of *Panini cresciuti* was justified and the breads were as likeable as their name.

I POUND POTATOES	ALLOW EXTRA FOR WASTE (SEE *PIZZA DOLCE DI PATATE* RECIPE, PAGE 308, FOR PREPARATION INSTRUCTIONS)
2 TABLESPOONS YEAST	GRANULAR, AT ROOM TEMPERATURE
2 TABLESPOONS MILK	TEPID
I POUND FLOUR	(ABOUT 3½ TO 4 CUPS) UNSIFTED, UNBLEACHED, ALL-PURPOSE
I TEASPOON SALT	
4 TABLESPOONS (2 OUNCES) BUTTER	UNSALTED, MELTED
3 EGGS	EXTRA-LARGE
I OUNCE ITALIAN, HARD SALAMI	OR PEPPERONI; CUT INTO 12 1½-INCH LONG STICKS
4 OUNCES PROVOLA PICCANTE	(SHARP ITALIAN CHEESE) CUT INTO CHUNKS ABOUT 1½ INCHES LONG
CORN OIL	OR SIMILAR VEGETABLE OIL, ENOUGH FOR A 2-INCH LAYER TO DEEP FRY

237

The potatoes can be cooked and riced one day ahead of time, refrigerated, and brought to room temperature before using.

In a small bowl, mix the yeast and milk. Wait until yeast is softened, then stir, pushing it against the sides of the bowl, until it forms a thick paste.

In another bowl, mix the flour and salt. Add the potatoes, butter, and eggs. Beat for 5 minutes with a wire beater at speed 4 (medium-low) (if you are using a Kitchen Aid mixer). Add the yeast paste and knead with the hook, at speed 2 (low), for 5 more minutes. You might have to rearrange the dough in the bowl for a more effective kneading. The dough should be pliable, not sticky, and pleasantly soft.

Roll the dough in a 2½-inch diameter roll and cut into 12 rounds. Shape the rounds between the palms of your hands like a large egg. Use your finger to make a lengthwise hole at one end, large enough to fit one piece each of salami and cheese. Press around the hole to close it, *or* flatten the rounds a little, place in the center of each the salami or pepperoni piece and cheese chunk. Then fold the edges over to seal, pressing them together, smooth like a large egg. Do not push the cheese and salami stuffing too far into the dough, causing the dough on the bottom to be too thin a layer to coat it.

Lay the rolls on a floured cloth, cover them with another floured cloth, and place somewhere warm to rise. They will be ready to fry when they are 1½ times their original size.

Heat 2 inches of oil in a deep fryer (I use a cast-iron pot), to medium-low, 270° F. Fry the rolls, uncrowded (to have room to expand), turning them very often (about every 30 seconds), until they are a deep golden brown, about 8 minutes.

Drain on paper towels. Serve hot. Do not puncture the rolls while frying them.

The rolls can be made 24 hours ahead of time, refrigerated, and then warmed up on a cookie sheet, in an oven preheated to 400° F. for about 8 minutes, or until they are crisp and they sizzle.

The rolls also freeze well, and can be heated frozen on a cookie sheet, in a 400° F. preheated oven, for 10 minutes or until crisp and sizzling.

MIMMETTA
LO MONTE'S
CLASSIC
SICILIAN
COOKBOOK

•

238

Discovering *Pastizzo di Mohamed Ibn Timnah*

My journey through the labyrinth of our culinary tradition has led me to some interesting discoveries. One has been to find out that the recipe for the *Pastizzu di Mohamed Ibn Timnah*, a round bread loaf, hollowed out, filled with various ingredients, and then baked—thought by everybody to be documented by only one writing of undetermined origin—exists instead in two versions on page thirty-six of my precious Duke's cookbook. Mohamed Ibn Timnah was an emir from Catania. The recipes reported by my little old cookbook make use of the loaf in the same fashion, while naming the dish in less exotic ways: one is *Pagnotte di grasso ripiene* and the other is *Pagnotte brusche di magro*. I have not included these recipes here, because their tastes are so eclectic, people today might not find them palatable (not to mention that their execution is long and complicated). Nevertheless, it is interesting to see the original recipes. For any cook who wants a challenge (and can read Italian, of course), be my guest, and try to make them, following the Duke's instructions.

Pastiera di grano.

Ben cotto il grano, o il farro, in acqua o in brodo, che sarà meglio con un poco di sale, o in stecco di cannella, e cortecce di aranci; che poi si levano raffreddato che sarà si unirà alla sua dose di zucchero, o di giulebbe, che sarà migliore, ai *gialli* di uova, al cedro e cocozzata in piccioli pezzi, ed a qualche *natta* di latte, con poc'acqua di fiori, e di cannella, e questa dose si metterà sulla pasta frolla o mezza frolla, e si covrirà a *liste* : e cotta si mangerà o calda, o fredda. Volendola diversificare, vi si potrà aggiungere della *provola* fresca grattata, ed un poco di *caciocavallo*, che sarà egualmente eccellente : Si può fare dello stesso modo ancor di riso, che non dovrà esser molto cotto.

Pagnotte di grasso ripiene.

Prima si gratta la superficie della pagnotta di pane, e poi si toglie da sopra un pezzo di corteccia, sicchè possa levarsene la *mollica*. Indi si riempie di un *ragucino* fatto di fegatelli, animelle, presciutto tritato e funghi prima bolliti, qualche frutto di mare, piselli, carciofi, se sieno di stagione, erbette ed aromi. Poi si ricovre il buco con la stessa corteccia toltane, e si fanno insuppare le pagnotte nel latte, ed acqua di cannella, dopo di che si covrono di *gialli* di nova, di butiro liquefatto, e di parmigiano grattato, e si fanno assodare nel forno.

Pagnotte brusche di magro.

Dopo grattate le pagnotte come sopra, si riempiono di *ragù*, di erbe, funghi prima bolliti, tartufi, frutta di mare, alici salse, chiapperini, olive nere senz'osso, tarantello tritato, prima bollito, e disalzato, piselli, carciofi, asparani nella stagione, e bocconcini di pesce : e poi chiuse come si è detto, si fanno insuppare nel latte di mandorle con cannella. Indi coverte di mandorle all' *amberlino*, pestate, cannella, e pane abbrustolito, e polverizzato, si fanno cuocere al forno.

PANE DI CASA

homemade country bread

yields two 8-inch round loaves

Hot thick slices of this bread are delicious topped with *"Ammogghio'* (see page 158) or *Purè di ceci* (see page 226).

3 CUPS FLOUR   (ABOUT ¾ POUND) UNBLEACHED, ALL-PURPOSE
I TABLESPOON SUGAR
1½ TABLESPOONS YEAST
2½ CUPS WARM WATER
2½ CUPS SEMOLINA FLOUR   ABOUT I POUND
2½ TEASPOONS SALT
2 CUPS WHEAT BRAN

MIMMETTA
LO MONTE'S
CLASSIC
SICILIAN
COOKBOOK

•

240

In a ceramic bowl, mix 1 cup of unbleached flour with the sugar and the yeast. Stir in 1 cup warm water, until reasonably smooth—don't worry if it's a little lumpy. Cover and set aside, letting it stand at room temperature until the mixture has doubled in size and is bubbly, about 15 minutes.

Mix the remaining flour and the semolina with the salt: Place it in the bowl of your countertop mixer. Add the yeast-flour mixture and the remaining 1½ cups warm water. Mix well, using the hook on a Kitchen Aid or similar countertop mixer at speeds 1 and 2. Once the ingredients are mixed, beat for about 8 minutes using speed 2. Depending on the quality of the flour used, you may need a little more water; however, dough is supposed to be stiff.

Transfer the dough to a floured countertop and dust with flour. Place in a heavy ceramic bowl, cover, and let rise to more than double—depending on the temperature for about 1 to 2½ hours.

Transfer the dough to a lightly floured counter and punch it down. Cut into two pieces, flatten into rounds, and tuck the edges of the rounds in. Lay on a large cookie sheet dusted lightly with a mixture of semolina and unbleached flour, tucked edges-side down. Very lightly dust the tops of the loaves with the same flour mixture. Using a razor blade and a sweeping motion, score the top with four ¼-inch deep cuts. Intersect the cuts to form a square with sides that go past the corners. Cover loaves with a cloth. Let them rise up to about 2½ times their size.

Preheat the oven to 400° F.

Place a small pan with water on the bottom of the preheated oven. Bake the loaves in the oven for 40 minutes. The crust should be light brown and should feel very solid when tapped. Reduce the heat to 350° F. and bake for 15 more minutes.

Cool on a rack after having punched quite a few holes in the crust with a thin skewer.

To make sour dough bread: Set aside a ball of dough the size of a small orange when making *Pane di casa*. Place in a container and let it sour for 24 hours before following instructions for *Pane di casa*.

Baking Bread on Grandfather's Farm

The land of "Cannavata"—Nonno Giovanni's estate where we went most often because of the very comfortable house—grew wheat, sesame seeds, vegetables and also cultivated vineyards. The oven to bake the bread—a wood oven of course—was in a rather unusual place; a corner of the oldest stable of the farmhouse.

I remember only two openings to the stable: two small solid doors, one toward the inner courtyard of the complex, one to the outside courtyard, toward the road that led to the farm. There was no artificial light in the stable, so the only time one could see to its other end was when the fire was burning and the door of the oven was open.

At one far end of the stable there was a small room, where milk-fed lambs and kids were raised in total darkness. Chickens used to lay eggs in the straw of the mangers, instead of in chicken coops, a fact that irritated the women on the farm enormously. The bread was baked among the squawking of the chickens (which were constantly being chased away), the mooing of the cows, and the snorting of an occasional mule. The smells of the fire, the bread, and the stable combined in a uniquely pleasant way. The men—Grandfather included—took large loaves of bread with them when they went to work in the fields.

F O U R

DOLCI

desserts

DOLCI DA CUCCHIAIO
spoon desserts

DOLCI DA CREDENZA
cupboard desserts

TORTE
cakes

CROSTATE
pies

1945

MIMMETTA
LO MONTE'S
CLASSIC
SICILIAN
COOKBOOK

•

244

I am old enough to go to school. It is a nuns' school called The Servants of the Sacred Heart. Their citrus orchard and the one of the Jesuits' school my brother attends are separated by a wall. At recess, when it doesn't rain (that is, most of the time) we are allowed to run around in the garden, which is very close to the orchard. But we are absolutely forbidden to go near the wall because there are "boys" behind it. Once in a while, one of the *grandi* (older students) is punished because she is caught throwing or retrieving messages wrapped around a stone and tossed over the wall.

It is nice to breathe some fresh air after having been locked up in the lunchroom, which smells like hard-boiled eggs, tomato sauce, and tangerine peel.

I have learned to read and write very quickly. In the morning, before entering the classrooms, we have to go to church and say prayers in Latin. The church we go to is a *cripta*, built underground below the "good" church open to the public.

It is very damp and cold here. Of course, the nuns don't care, covered up as they are with all that clothing. The only thing they don't have covered is the central part of their faces, and their waxy fingers. My legs get numb from the cold, with red and white blotches. I get very bored saying the same prayers day after day, so I have learned to move my lips without saying anything. In the meantime, I practice my reading of the names that are inscribed on the marble slabs that cover the walls of the *Cripta*. They are the names of Italian soldiers killed during the First World War. Each name is followed by the date of the soldier's birth, and the date and place of his death. Lots of them seem to have died at Caporetto or Carso.

Great-grandfather Saverio and Great-grandmother Rosalia got very old and have died. Great-grandmother Rosalia was Father's grandmother, and he loved her very much. He spent the summers in her care when he was a little boy, in her house in a very small town. The trip to that town was very long, and to keep him quiet he was given cinnamon sticks to suck on. I liked the stories he told me of all the things he got to do when he stayed with her. For example, he rode pigs. He also went to collect honey with "Don Calorio Pipitone," the *uomo d'onore* of the village, and to hunt rabbits with a ferret. One day the ferret was sprayed by a toad, or some kind of poisonous animal. Don Calorio asked everybody in the hunting party, including Father, to pee on the ferret to counteract the poison.

When Father was a little boy, he was blond, with straight bangs that covered his forehead. And he wore sailor dresses with pleated skirts, knee-high socks, and lace-up boots. His mother, whose name was Domenica, died when he was very small. So Grandmother Adelina is not his real mother, although I think of her as my real grandmother. I have been called Domenica, in remembrance of Papa's dead mother. But it doesn't seem that anyone wants to remember her, because everybody feels very uncomfortable calling me that. Adele is my second name, and Grandmother Adelina gives me a present on the day of Saint Adele but ignores Saint Domenico's day.

The nuns call me Adele, because they think Domenica is not refined enough for their high-class school. They should be the ones to really appreciate the name, as it means "she who belongs to God." They do not like my nickname, "Mimmetta." Father calls me "Micina," which means "little cat." Uncle Gianni calls me "Micetta," which also means "little cat." Other relatives call me "Mimmina." Nonno Alfredo calls me "Mimmettina," the diminutive of the diminutive of the diminutive of my real name.

My mother believes firmly that Domenica is a name that brings bad luck. She tells me that in the Lo Monte family, any woman with that name doesn't make it to thirty. That fact is a good reason to call me another name; still my relatives should make up their mind and stick to just one.

My first communion.

1947

Grandfather Giovanni is kidnapped: it happens during the summer, at harvest time, at one of his country estates. He spends twenty-four days in a cave, his eyes bandaged, sleeping on straw, without washing. Grandmother stays sick in bed the whole time. Father says it is because she hates having to pay the ransom money, not because she is worried about Nonno. When he comes back home, I hear him say, "Those sons of bitches fed me bread and salami the whole time I was there."

Many words Grandfather says cause Grandmother to make a funny little guttural sound, followed by a reproachful-sounding "Giovanni." Sometimes she doesn't make any sound at all, but only crosses herself. While he was in the cave, Grandfather probably missed his yogurt. It is made for him in the house, so he always has a fresh supply.

Some astounding things the Lo Monte grandparents have in their home are the refrigerator and the stove. They are huge, and they are American, left behind by the Americans themselves who took over the house as one of their officers' quarters. Grandmother still is furious over their having thrown her brocade-covered living-room furniture out onto the terrace. No harm done, really. The terrace is covered, and after all, now she has the best refrigerator and stove in town.

The stove has two ovens, one so large that a whole lamb can fit into it. Every now and then I see lambs or kids hanging head down on the kitchen terrace. Andrea, the driver, slits their skin here and there, and zip, zip, zip, he pulls it off, just as easily as Mother pulls off my skin-tight winter underwear. Donna Peppina scrubs the skins, the pretty ones, and then puts salt on them and keeps them in the open air until they don't smell anymore. They make nice little rugs to step on when getting out of bed on cold winter days.

MIMMETTA
LO MONTE'S
CLASSIC
SICILIAN
COOKBOOK

•

246

*Grandfather Giovanni Lo Monte
(left) with a friend.*

My Great Aunt Ciccina.

1948

Father, since the kidnapping, feels that Sicily is not a safe place to raise a family. He goes to Argentina to seek ways to establish himself there, and then send for us. He comes back after a year. He was very homesick, and whatever project he worked at there failed. He never really gets over it.

I missed him while he was gone. When he returned, he told me about Argentina, how lovely Evita Peron is, how wide the streets are in Buenos Aires, and how delicious the beef is. From his trip, he brought alligator skins and suede coats: "the prettiest coat for me," just like the ones Indians wear, with fringes hanging down.

My Grandfather and a group of his friends.

No matter how delicious meat was in Argentina, Father seems glad to be eating Mother's food again. The food she cooks for him is often different from the food we eat. He has a very delicate stomach, but after he is done with his meal, he also helps himself to ours. Eating this way doesn't seem to hurt his stomach. I do not mind, except once in a while when there is fried *neonata*, one of my favorite dishes, and boiled *neonata* for him, he eats so many of our nice golden cakes of baby fish that, if I want seconds, all there is left is the boiled fish.

Sometimes on holidays we go to buy desserts from a convent where the *Madre Badessa* (the former Mother Superior) used to be an aunt of Grandfather Alfredo's. My mother used to say her parents had squandered all their money "literally eating it up," so they had no money left to give her a dowry. Without a dowry, she couldn't have married well, and the only alternative to remaining a spinster was to enter a convent and to be a "spouse of Christ."

She also got to be in charge of many little orphans whom the convent sheltered for charity. Those orphans made that charity very well worth while because they worked their little fingers stiff, embroidering and making the pastries the convent sold.

The convent's desserts are beautiful and fragrant. The nuns and orphans make *conchiglie*, the lightest shell-like pistachio marzipan wrappings, pale green, filled with ground squash preserve; *Genovesi*, golden crumbly crusts filled with the smoothest custard; *cannoli*, brown and flaky, filled with the whitest and finest ricotta cream you can dream of.

But much as I like pastries, I hope Father puts enough money aside for me to have a dowry, because I wouldn't enjoy being locked up in a convent watching over orphans.

I shouldn't worry about that. Father is planning on marrying me off, I know for sure, because every now and then he brings home some beautiful embroidered white linen and says, "This is for your trousseau."

A Word About Desserts

I dolci *are the coronation of a meal, the final show-off creation. Dessert is a course that requires skill and time to prepare. Nothing can be more frustrating than to fail at its preparation and nothing more rewarding than to succeed at it.*

Desserts in the past used to be divided into two main categories: dolci da cucchiaio *(spoon desserts) and* dolci da credenza *(cupboard desserts). The first defined desserts to be eaten with the spoon, soft and short-lived. The second defined desserts of hard consistency and with a long shelf life.* Torte *(cakes) and* crostate *(pies) were somewhere in between the two, most cakes being closer to the* dolci da cucchiaio, *but not quite so fragile, and most pies closer to the* dolci da credenza, *but not quite so durable.*

In recent times, such a war has been waged on the most common ingredients of desserts—sugar, butter, cream, and eggs—that many people feel at least a twinge of guilt when eating them. Mothers have been accused of getting their children hooked on sugar. (In my opinion, one can only accuse Mother Nature, because a newborn baby instinctively loves the sweet taste of sugar, not to mention the fact that mother's milk is naturally sweet.) Dairy products have been shown as villains, busy clogging human arteries, their nutritional values ignored (Mother: Think of all the eggs, milk, and cheese you insisted I eat to grow strong and healthy!). Dairy products hide in containers claiming "lower this" and "lower that."

Before you know it we will have genetically engineered chickens and cows that will produce no-cholesterol eggs and milk. I think that the makers of artificial sweeteners and diet foods are creating all these rumors just to sell their products.

All kidding aside, my instinct has always told me to stay away from food products that are the fruit of chemistry and processing, and to eat in moderation. So let us overcome the guilt about eating dessert and be rational: One serving of most desserts in this book have about one tablespoon of butterfat, less than one egg, and less than two tablespoons of sugar. One can eat them, be happy, and enjoy all the benefits .

Persistence, patience, luck, and family bonds are the ingredients to be found in my traditional dessert recipes, along with those mentioned above, as well as almonds, preserves, and flour. Flavors become part of

MIMMETTA
LO MONTE'S
CLASSIC
SICILIAN
COOKBOOK

•

248

the thoughts and feelings tied to family life: for Sicilians away from home, to eat a food sorely missed and to savor a flavor from the past is to reunite with one's own land and traditions. For those people who love desserts and aren't Sicilian, these recipes will represent some of the most enticing, aromatic, and rich desserts to be tasted anywhere. But if my argument to eat these dolci *has not been convincing, you can always eat fruit, a very Italian way to conclude a meal.*

DOLCI DA CUCCHIAIO

cupboard desserts

CREMA AL MANDERINO
tangerine pudding

serves 6

Wonderful by itself, this pudding can also be used to fill and top *Pan di Spagna* (see page 296) plain, or with the addition of berries.

I CUP SUGAR	SCANT
¼ CUP CORNSTARCH	
I CUP TANGERINE JUICE	FRESHLY SQUEEZED
4 EGG YOLKS	EXTRA-LARGE
3 CUPS MILK	

In a medium-sized saucepan, combine the sugar and cornstarch. Add 2 to 3 table-spoons tangerine juice. Blend in the egg yolks and gradually stir in the remaining juice and the milk. The mixture should be smooth.

Cook over medium heat. Stir well down to the bottom, from the center to the sides, back to the center, always in the same direction, without stopping until the mixture begins to thicken. The mixture will thicken as the temperature approaches the boiling point. Let it boil, still stirring, for about 30 seconds, and remove it from the heat.

Pour the pudding into serving dish(es) while still hot. Decorate with berries when cool, if desired.

Serve chilled, with plain cookies.

SPUMA DI SUSINE NERE

plum "foam"

serves 8

MIMMETTA
LO MONTE'S
CLASSIC
SICILIAN
COOKBOOK

•

250

2¼ POUNDS DARK RED PLUMS	SMALL, OVAL SHAPE, RIPE, BUT FIRM; CUT IN HALF LENGTHWISE, PITTED
1½ ENVELOPES GELATIN	1½ SCANT TABLESPOONS, UNFLAVORED
½ CUP SUGAR*	
1 TEASPOON GRATED LEMON PEEL	
1 CUP HEAVY CREAM	

Place the plums in a heavy, medium-sized pot and gently mash with a wooden spoon. Cover and place over very low heat. Cook for 10 minutes, removing the lid to mash the plums with the spoon from time to time. When the plums have rendered enough liquid to cover the fruit, replace the lid and cook for 20 more minutes.

Remove from the heat and put through a vegetable strainer (using the smallest hole fitting). Reserve the first cup strained. Strain until only the peel is left. The puree will be very loose, and you should have enough for 3½ cups.

Mix the gelatin and sugar in a bowl. To dissolve the gelatin and sugar, add the reserved cup of puree little by little. Add this mixture to the remaining 2½ cups puree. Place in a pan, bring to a boil, and then turn off the heat. Add the lemon peel. Let the mixture cool to room temperature. (Stirring it frequently will hasten the process.) When cool, refrigerate for 30 minutes, stirring at least twice. Do not let the mixture gel.

In a very cold bowl, beat the cream until very stiff. (It should be pretty solid, not foamy.) Fold one third of the cream into the plum mixture. When well mixed, fold in the remaining cream. Refrigerate for 30 minutes. Fold thoroughly, return to the refrigerator for 30 more minutes, fold again. Spoon in 8 small bowls and refrigerate at least 3 hours until set.

* ½ CUP OF SUGAR COMBINED WITH DECENTLY SWEET PLUMS WILL GIVE A RATHER TART MIXTURE.

MELONE AL CAFFÈ

coffee-flavored melon

serves 8

I HONEYDEW MELON	ABOUT 6 POUNDS, RIPE
I CUP COFFEE	VERY STRONG ESPRESSO
I CUP LIGHT RUM	
I TABLESPOON SUGAR	

Cut the melon in half, widthwise, and remove the seeds and the pulp. Use a melon baller to cut the flesh. Mix the melon balls with the coffee, rum, and sugar. Stir to blend. Divide between the two halves.

Chill. Stir well before serving.

FRUTTA FRITTA

fried fruit

serves 6 to 8

This recipe is one I recreated from the Duke's cookbook.

4 LARGE, FIRM PEARS	OR USE SMALL, THIN-SKINNED, TREE RIPENED FIGS (ALLOW 4 TO 6 PER PERSON)
PASTELLA (BATTER)	(SEE *VERDURE ALLA PASTELLA*, PAGE 220) USE SAME AMOUNT
CORN OIL	ENOUGH FOR I- TO 2-INCH LAYER TO DEEP FRY
POWDERED SUGAR	FOR SPRINKLING

Peel, core, and cut each pear in twelve wedges.

Heat a layer of oil 1 inch deep (more for figs) until smoke is barely visible. Dip the fruit into the batter, then fry in batches, if necessary, over high heat until golden brown. Do not crowd the fruit in the oil. Blot the excess oil with paper towels. Repeat.

Serve hot, sprinkled with sugar.

Just as Grandfather Alfredo's cookbook tells us how to preserve wines, it also discusses preserving fruit:

Delle pera.

Le pera sementine, bargamotte, fiorentine, e buone — cristiani, sono le più atte a conservarsi, colte alquanto acerbette nel maggior caldo del giorno, si debbono esporre al Sole per quattro volte, poi si deve bagnare il fiore con pece dileguata calda, ponendole in una stanza dove sievi del fuoco badando che nel solajo l' uno non tocchi l'altra. Si conservano ancora tenendole in luogo nulla umido sull' alga marina asciutta, chiudendo così la stanza, che non v'entri l' aria. Si possono co' fili ligati alli piccioli, tuffar due volte nell' acqua marina bollente, senza fermarcele ponendole dopo per asciugarle all' aria levandole dopo sei giorni, e così conservarlo in una stanza, ove si faccia del fuoco.

About Pears To preserve pears year-round, pick pears a little underripe, at the hottest moment of the day. You must then expose them to the sun four times, then you must cover the bottom part of the pear, where the flower was, with molten tar and place the pears in a room where there is always a fire going, being careful that pears do not touch one another.

Another way to preserve pears is to put them in a place not at all humid, over well-dried seaweed, and lock the room, making sure that no air will circulate. Also, you may tie them by the stem and dip them in boiling sea water twice, without allowing them to stay in it for long. Afterwards, place them to dry in the air for six days and then put them in a room with a fire always going.

Delle Prugna.

Quelle che han molta polpa, come sono le Damaschine, le Mirabolane, le Pernigone, e li Prugnoni tondi sono le più atte a conservarsi. Si deve cavare

About Plums The best to preserve are the ones that are very plump and round in shape. Remove the bottom from a brand-new barrel. Inside the barrel drive quite a few nails and little pieces of wood in the shape of a cross. Then pick the plums at noon, expose them to six days of not-too-strong sun, then tie each plum to a little nail, so that when barrel is turned upside down they are suspended without touching one another. Then seal the barrel, wrap it in straw, place it in a mound of sand, and in a cold room rather than in a damp one.

FOR PRESERVING FRUIT, THE AUTHOR STRONGLY ADVISES PEOPLE TO DIP PEACHES, APRICOTS, AND *LAZZERRUOLE* IN MOLTEN WAX, BUT HE WORRIES ABOUT PEOPLE NOT BEING ABLE TO REMOVE THE WAX, SO HE SUGGESTS THE FOLLOWING:

Dip the fruit in a container filled with snow. When ready to use the fruit, the wax will crack very easily when cold and will be easily removed.

MIMMETTA
LO MONTE'S
CLASSIC
SICILIAN
COOKBOOK

•

252

MOSTARDA

wine dessert

makes 6 small molds

Eat *Mostarda* either chilled or, immediately after being prepared, as a pudding. In the latter case, there is no need to wet the bowls.

7½ CUPS RED OR WHITE WINE	DECENT DRY TABLE WINE
½ CUP MOLASSES	UNSULFURED
PEEL OF 1 ORANGE	ZEST ONLY, NO WHITE PART; BLANCHED AND RINSED
½ CUP HONEY	
6 TABLESPOONS CORNSTARCH	
A PINCH GROUND CLOVES	
¼ TEASPOON GROUND CINNAMON	
¼ CUP PISTACHIOS	RAW, UNSALTED, SHELLED; TOASTED IN A 375° F. PREHEATED OVEN FOR 5 MINUTES; CUT COARSELY
3 TABLESPOONS WHOLE ALMONDS	SKINS ON; CUT COARSELY, TOASTED AS FOR PISTACHIOS

In a small, heavy saucepan, bring the wine, molasses, and orange peel to a boil. Let it simmer, partially covered, until reduced to about two thirds. Add the honey and let it simmer some more, until reduced to four cups.

Remove the orange peel and cut into very fine julienne strips (enough to fill 2 teaspoons). Add to the wine mixture and discard rest of peel. Let the wine mixture cool.

In a medium saucepan, mix the cornstarch with the cloves and the cinnamon. Add a small quantity of wine mixture, stirring until it is a smooth paste. Thin it out, adding the rest of the wine mixture, a little at a time, stirring well.

Cook over medium heat, stirring constantly, down to the bottom, from the center to the sides, back to the center, always in the same direction. The mixture will thicken as the temperature approaches the boiling point. Continue cooking, stirring, past the boiling point, for 2 minutes. The mixture should be very thick.

Remove from the heat and add the pistachios and the almonds. Dip six 3-inch china bowls in water. Shake off the excess water, and divide the mixture among them. When cool, run the point of a knife around the top edge of the *Mostarda*. Let it rest, unrefrigerated and loosely covered, for 24 hours.

Press your fingers lightly on top of the *Mostarda* at the edges and draw it toward the center. This should detach it from the bowls so that you can unmold it. If the *Mostarda* splits while you are drawing it from the sides of the bowls, let it rest a few more hours, and try again.

Place the unmolded *Mostarda* on a wire rack, cover, and store in a cool place for at least a month. The desired consistency is rather rubbery.

"CIAMBUGLIONE"

moscato wine nut pudding

serves 4

¼ POUND PISTACHIOS   (OR USE PINE NUTS) SHELLED, UNSALTED
1 CUP MOSCATO   OR USE A SIMILAR WINE SUCH AS MALAGA
5 EGG YOLKS   EXTRA-LARGE
½ TEASPOON ORANGE FLOWER WATER
¼ CUP SUGAR

MIMMETTA
LO MONTE'S
CLASSIC
SICILIAN
COOKBOOK

•

254

In a large pot of boiling water, blanch the pistachios. Remove the skins. Pat dry and process into a paste in a food processor.

In a bowl, add some wine to the nut paste. Beat until smooth. Keep adding the rest of the wine, and stirring, so that there are no lumps.

Mix in the yolks, orange flower water, and sugar.

In a small, heavy nonreactive saucepan over low heat, heat the mixture stirring evenly and constantly, in one direction, well down to the bottom, from the center to the sides and back to the center until thick, about 20 minutes. The mixture will set and be quite firm once it cools.

While still hot, divide the pudding among four small glass bowls. Serve chilled.

About Pistachios

Pistachios, the most noble of nuts, were probably first cultivated in Sicily by the Romans. Plinio, in his *Natural History,* Book XIII, Chapter V, reports that Vitellio introduced pistachios to Rome toward the end of Tiberio's empire (1st century A.D.).

The pistachio likes a dry climate that alternates warm hours with chilly hours, and found Sicily to be a welcoming land. Pistachio plants are male and female. The trees, the male in particular, can become imposing, growing to thirty feet in height, while their trunks can reach a circumference of over four feet. Their growth is very slow, and their flowers, which bloom in clusters, are very sensitive to cold and look rather inconspicuous, as they have no petals.

In Sicily, the pistachio is cultivated at altitudes between 900 and 2,400 feet. It blooms after the second half of April, safely beyond early spring temperature drops. The leaves are compounded, arranged in feather fashion, in odd numbers (three to five), similar to rose leaves, but much coarser in texture. The color of the bark changes from the ash gray of the trunk and the older branches to the yellowish cream color (depending on the variety of the tree), of the new growth of the past year. This new growth is also tinted with red.

There are many varieties of pistachio trees. The most sought after are the ones producing fruit whose shells naturally split open at the apex when ripe. The dried hull reminds me of the skin of some lizards—leathery, thin, and textured in a dotted fashion. The shell is a cream color. The seed, wine-red on the rounded (dorsal) side and silver-green on the flat (ventral) side, when split presents the typical pistachio green. A pistachio that shows a yellow interior when split is old and/or rancid, and its delicate taste is gone, along with the green color that plays quite a part in its appeal.

Sicilians who regard pistachios as the perfect nut could never comprehend why anybody would want to salt and bake them, let alone dye them red. The only place I have seen pistachio shells dyed red is the States. It is a crazy thing to do. The habit might come from a distorted sense of aesthetics people may have (or that merchants think people may have): that a fake red shell is more attractive than, therefore preferable to, a natural cream-white one. This custom may also originate from the fact that the color red is typical of the plant, since it recurs in the tree branches, in the nut hull and in the skin of the nut itself. A shot of red where it does not belong is also, most likely, a practice used to convince the American consumer that the nuts are fresh, since the color fades from the skin as the nut gets older.

The seed, when used in its natural state, often livens up roasts (see *Arrosto imbottito,* page 111), and farcies, but it is in connection with desserts that pistachios have become unforgettably associated with Sicilian cuisine. In some desserts they contribute just a sprinkle, in some they are one of the main ingredients, and in some, such as the recipe for *ciambuglione* (see page 254), they are the main ingredient.

Pistachios became the mark of the nuns' very peculiar style (and taste), of pastries.

The nuns of the convents manipulated the nut to feature its color in addition to its taste. In their hands pistachio paste became the shell of pastries or their filling, or incredible, lifelike bunches of grapes, olives, almonds in the hull, or fava beans.

Today, unfortunately, pistachio paste has been replaced in almost all instances by almond paste dyed green, given the cost of the pistachio and the very laborious time-consuming task of removing its reddish skin.

RICOTTA AL CACAO

cocoa-flavored ricotta

serves 6 to 8

You can use this to fill and top *Pan di Spagna* (see page 296), or to top *Torta al cacao* (see page 304).

2 POUNDS RICOTTA	DRAINED, DO NOT PAT DRY
3 TABLESPOONS COCOA	UNSWEETENED
½ TEASPOON VANILLA	
¾ TO I CUP SUGAR	
2 OUNCES SEMISWEET CHOCOLATE	CUT INTO COARSE PIECES

In a food processor fitted with the metal blade, combine the ricotta, cocoa, vanilla, and sugar. Process until very creamy.

Serve in individual dessert bowls with the chocolate pieces sprinkled on top.

MIMMETTA
LO MONTE'S
CLASSIC
SICILIAN
COOKBOOK

•

256

ZABAJONE AL CAFFÈ

coffee-flavored zabajone

serves 6

I was astonished when I first saw *zabajone* served as dessert in Italian restaurants in the States. Until then I had thought of it as breakfast or a snack, which my mother would give me when she thought I needed the extra calories.

It was made with the freshest eggs from the farm, never allowed to thicken, and it was drunk from the breakfast *scodella* filled with the *zabajone* instead of the usual *caffè e latte* or *latte e cacao*.

9 EGG YOLKS	EXTRA-LARGE
½ TO ⅔ CUP SUGAR	
⅔ CUP ESPRESSO	
⅓ CUP DRY MARSALA	OR USE DRY SHERRY

In a small bowl using an electric beater, beat the egg yolks and sugar until very light (about 15 minutes).

In a medium-sized saucepan, heat coffee and Marsala over moderate-high heat until it reaches the boiling point. Don't let it boil. Reduce the heat to very low—or remove from burner—and start adding the yolks in a ribbon, stirring constantly in the same direction, and very rapidly, until all of the yolk mixture has been added.

Increase the heat to low—return mixture to burner if you removed it—and keep stirring for 5 more minutes. Stir well down to the bottom, from the center to the sides, back to the center, always in the same direction. Increase the heat to medium and continue stirring until the mixture thickens. Turn off the heat and stir about 30 seconds longer. Let the mixture cool slightly. Pour into cups. Chill.

Serve with cookies, whipped cream, or plain.

A Word About Scodella

A milk scodella is a peculiar Italian vessel. China or ceramic, it holds two cups of liquid easily. No Italian household with children is without one.

As children, Italians have to drink—to the last drop—liquid contained in the scodella, accompanied by the thick slices of bread and butter which complete breakfast. That liquid might be milk, or even, on occasion, zabajone. Growing up, most Italians get weaned from the scodella and graduate to the common cup. A few, especially men, do not. My father was one of those who did not.

When he visited me here in the States, I could not convince him that to drink his caffè e latte from a regular cup, simply filling the cup twice, was the same thing as drinking from the scodella.

"How come in America you cannot buy a 'lattera'?" he asked. The selection of words was not casual: "America" implied rich and advanced, and "lattera," said in Sicilian dialect, indicated the banality of the object. Close to losing his patience, he relaxed when, after a long search, a small pyrex mixing bowl was accepted to perform as the scodella. We moved on to solving a greater problem: the quality of the bread. Thank goodness, milk, coffee, butter, and jam got very high grades.

COPPE DI PAN DI SPAGNA E CASTAGNE

"pan di spagna" and chestnut cups

serves 6

I RECIPE *PAN DI SPAGNA* I   SEE PAGE 296
1¾ POUNDS CHESTNUTS   OR USE I POUND CANNED PLAIN CHESTNUT
                                  PUREE
5 TABLESPOONS BUTTER   UNSALTED, AT ROOM TEMPERATURE
⅓ CUP SUGAR
⅛ TEASPOON SALT
½ CUP RUM
3 OUNCES SEMISWEET CHOCOLATE
2 TABLESPOONS CORN OIL

MIMMETTA
LO MONTE'S
CLASSIC
SICILIAN
COOKBOOK

•

258

Have 6 flat-bottomed bowls, about 6 inches in diameter, on hand. (If you do not have such bowls, you can use dessert plates.)

Bake the *Pan di Spagna* in a 9- or 10-inch square pan. Cut into four layers. Reserve two layers for other use, cut each of the others into 9 squares.

If using fresh chestnuts, add to a large pot and cover with plenty of water. Bring to a boil and cook over high heat for 20 minutes. Remove the outer shell and peel while still hot. Discard any chestnuts with blemishes. You should then be able to measure 1 pound of chestnuts (the rest have been allowed for waste). Puree the chestnuts through a strainer or ricer.

In a food processor fitted with the metal blade, process the chestnuts (or chestnut puree) with the butter, sugar, salt, and ¼ cup of the rum until smooth, about 15 seconds.

Melt the chocolate in a double boiler, add the corn oil, and stir until very smooth.

To make one chestnut cup you will need three cake squares. For each cup, alternate, in a bowl, starting with the cake, three layers each of the cake and of the chestnut puree, moistening the cake with the remaining rum (depending on your taste, you can add more or less rum than the ¼ cup left).

For a nice touch, the chestnut mixture can be piped through one of those little pastry gadgets onto the top of the last cake layer. Trickle the melted chocolate on top. Serve chilled.

MONTE BIANCO

white mountain

serves 6

I POUND SHELLED AND PEELED CHESTNUTS   SEE PAGE 258
I CUP MILK
I SCANT TABLESPOON COCOA
⅓ CUP SUGAR
⅛ TEASPOON SALT
I CUP HEAVY CREAM
¼ TEASPOON VANILLA

In a saucepan, combine the chestnuts with the milk, cocoa, ¼ cup of the sugar, and the salt. Simmer, stirring frequently, until the chestnuts are very soft, about 30 minutes. Add small quantities of milk as is necessary to keep the mixture moist.

Remove from the heat and mix in 2 tablespoons of the cream and the vanilla. Finely mash using an electric mixer or by hand. Strain through a vegetable strainer, using attachment with hole size close to spaghetti. Hold the strainer above a flat serving dish, so that the mixture will come out in spaghettilike strands, in a light mound on the plate.

Correct the shape of the mound using light strokes of a fork. Whip the remaining cream, adding the remaining sugar as the cream reaches the soft peak stage. Whip until very stiff—the Italian way—to the point at which the cream starts losing volume. Arrange the cream around the base of the "mountain" and on the top.

If you wish, decorate the dessert by drawing a fork over the cream around the bottom up toward the top, and vice versa. You can also sprinkle a very small amount of cocoa powder over the "mountain."

The mashed chestnut mixture can be prepared a couple of days in advance and the finishing touches added the day the dessert is needed. (The mixture must be kept refrigerated.)

UOVA "MORENE"

black eggs

serves 5

In a notebook of a family friend from Sciacca, I found a detailed recipe for *Uova "morene."* Until now, the recipe was undocumented, known only by its name and by a partial, hearsay description of its ingredients. The recipe comes from an area of Sicily where the Arab influence has prevailed over every other.

This dessert is simple to make, but the *frittatine* are very fragile to handle and you might tear some at first. Don't be discouraged. Also note that the rolls should be put together while both the filling and the *frittatine* are still warm.

MIMMETTA
LO MONTE'S
CLASSIC
SICILIAN
COOKBOOK

•

260

Bianco mangiare

1¼ CUPS MILK
3 TABLESPOONS CORNSTARCH
3 TEASPOONS SUGAR
½ TEASPOON VANILLA

Frittatine

⅔ CUP ALMONDS	SKINS ON
3 EGGS	EXTRA-LARGE
3 TABLESPOONS SUGAR	
3 TEASPOONS COCOA	
UNSALTED BUTTER	FOR THE *FRITTATINE*

Make a very stiff *bianco mangiare* with the milk, cornstarch, and sugar (see *Crema di latte,* page 324). Stir in vanilla when you take it off the heat. Set aside.

Toast the almonds for 12 minutes on a cookie sheet in an oven preheated to 375° F. Grind the almonds to the consistency of coarse bread crumbs as soon as they cool off.

In a medium bowl briefly beat together (just to mix) the eggs, sugar, cocoa, and ground almonds. Generously butter a 7-inch (approximately) frying pan (I use a small cast-iron one very successfully). Heat it moderately, pour in about 3 tablespoons of the egg mixture, and make it flow as evenly as possible to cover the bottom of the pan, holding the pan steadily from the handle and inclining it while rolling it.

Reduce the heat to low and cook until the edges are noticeably dry and the center is still moist, about 4 minutes. Very gently insert a spatula under the *frittatina,* and lay it, fried-side down, on a marble surface or on a china plate. Keep the pan well greased.

Repeat the procedure to make four more *frittatine.* Stir the egg mixture well before pouring it into the pan, since the almonds and sugar tend to settle on the bottom. While cooking the new ones, spoon 4 tablespoons of the *bianco mangiare* onto each of the ones already cooked. Spread it evenly, keeping it ½ inch away from the edge, and then roll the *frittatina,* just tight enough not to squeeze out the filling.

Refrigerate until chilled. Cut off the ends of rolls, then slice each roll into five to six sections. Lay them flat on a serving dish (the ends are not as pretty to present, but they are as good to eat). Serve well chilled. They are best 24 hours after having been prepared.

You might want to serve *Monte bianco* (see page 259) on the side, and/or sprinkle some cinnamon on the slices.

TIRAMI SU

give me a lift

serves 6

A combination of cream cheese, sour cream, and crème fraîche is an excellent substitute for mascarpone, the cheese used in Italy for this dessert. Mascarpone is seldom available, often not very fresh, and always very expensive.

5 EGG YOLKS	EXTRA-LARGE
½ CUP SUGAR	
½ POUND CREAM CHEESE	AT ROOM TEMPERATURE
½ CUP WHITE RUM	
10 OUNCES SOUR CREAM	
5 OUNCES CRÈME FRAÎCHE	
2 EGG WHITES	EXTRA-LARGE
¾ CUP COFFEE	VERY STRONG ESPRESSO (SEE PAGE 273)
6 OUNCES LADYFINGERS	
COCOA	UNSWEETENED, FOR TOPPING

Beat the egg yolks and sugar until light. Add the cream cheese and beat until almost smooth—there will be a few very small lumps. Beat in 5 tablespoons rum. Fold in the sour cream and crème fraîche. Beat the egg whites until they form stiff peaks and very gently fold them into the mixture. Refrigerate at least 2 hours.

Mix the coffee with the remaining rum. Take a dish, where the ladyfingers can be fitted in two layers. Cover the bottom of it with a layer of ladyfingers, then sprinkle with half of the coffee. Gently fold through the chilled cheese mixture, then spoon half of it onto the ladyfingers layer. Cover with the remaining ladyfingers, sprinkle with the remaining coffee, and top with the remaining cheese mixture. Sift some cocoa powder on the top.

Refrigerate a few hours before serving. (It is quite good served immediately, but standing improves the consistency.)

FRITTELLE DI CASTAGNE

chestnut pancakes

serves 6

I make this recipe when I am using larger amounts of chick-peas in other recipes. It's not worth the trouble of preparing chick-peas solely for the small amount called for here. Nevertheless, I have given preparation instructions below.

MIMMETTA
LO MONTE'S
CLASSIC
SICILIAN
COOKBOOK

•

262

4 OUNCES BOILED CHICK-PEAS	
SALT	
4 OUNCES WALNUTS	
½ CUP SUGAR	
A FEW LEAVES FRESH MINT	OR USE ½ TEASPOON DRY
¼ TEASPOON GROUND CLOVES	
¼ TEASPOON GROUND NUTMEG	
¼ TEASPOON GROUND CINNAMON	
4 OUNCES CHESTNUT PUREE	CANNED, UNSWEETENED
4 EGGS	EXTRA-LARGE
2 EGG WHITES	EXTRA-LARGE
OLIVE OIL	FOR FRYING

Soak the chick-peas in plenty of water for at least 24 hours, changing the water every 12 hours, and rinsing well. Cover with a few inches of water, salt lightly (½ teaspoon for 1 pound chick-peas). Bring to a boil, simmer, covered, for 2 hours, at a low boil, or until tender. At the end of the cooking time, to further tenderize them, uncover, and cook at a rolling boil for a few minutes.

In a food processor fitted with the metal blade, process the chick-peas, walnuts, sugar, mint, cloves, nutmeg, and ¼ teaspoon cinnamon until smooth.

In a bowl, mix the chestnut puree, eggs, egg whites, and chick-pea mixture by hand or at low speed with mixer until well blended.

Very lightly oil a heavy 9-inch skillet (I like to use cast-iron). Have the heat on very low and spoon in 2 tablespoons of the mixture for each *frittella*. You should be able to cook three at a time. Flatten it out a little, vibrating a spatula on top of it.

Let them cook for 5 minutes. Turn, and cook 4 to 5 more minutes. You may have to adjust the heat if, during the first 5 minutes of cooking, the *frittelle* are still too soft to turn, or too brown. Keep warm.

Serve hot, sprinkled with cinnamon and, if you wish, some sugar.

TORTA TURCA

turkish torte

serves 10 to 12

For pastry layers
½ POUND FLOUR (ABOUT 2 CUPS) UNBLEACHED, ALL-PURPOSE
I TABLESPOON SUGAR
I TABLESPOON BUTTER UNSALTED
2 EGGS EXTRA-LARGE
CORN OIL FOR FRYING

For filling and assembly
6 TABLESPOONS CORNSTARCH
5 CUPS MILK
¾ CUP PISTACHIOS SHELLED, RAW, UNSALTED
I OUNCE SEMISWEET CHOCOLATE IN SMALL PIECES
6 STRIPS CANDIED ORANGE PEEL CUT INTO VERY SMALL PIECES; PLUS A FEW
ADDITIONAL STRIPS FOR DECORATION

For the pastry, knead together the flour, sugar, butter, and eggs until you obtain a very pliable and smooth dough. Add a little water if the dough is too hard to knead. Divide the dough into 12 pieces, roll them out with a pasta machine into rectangles, about 4 inches wide and 7 inches long.

Pour about ½-inch oil in a skillet. Heat until smoke is barely visible. Fry the rectangles of dough one by one, on medium-high heat, until golden, about 1 minute. (You may want to use two skillets to speed the process.) As soon as bubbles form on the dough, turn. Keep turning every few seconds. Keep the oil level close to ½ inch. Remove and lay on paper towel.

In a saucepan, mix the sugar and cornstarch. Stir in some milk to form a smooth paste, then thin with the remaining milk. Cook, stirring constantly, well down to bottom of pan, from center to sides, back to the center, always in the same direction until thick. Stir about 30 seconds longer, remove from heat, and let cool. When at room temperature, mix in half of the pistachios, half the chocolate, and the orange peel.

Cover the bottom of a rectangular tray with four layers of pastry, spread on one third of the filling, then cover with the pastry. Repeat twice. Sprinkle the reserved pistachios and chocolate on the top layer, and decorate with orange peel strips.

The pastry and filling can be made in advance. But assemble only 2 hours before serving.

"Cuccia" for Santa Lucia

As December thirteenth, the day of Santa Lucia, approached, about a week in advance the maid and I, as I finished my homework, would sit at the dining-room table and, under a strong light, pour the wheat little by little into trays, spreading it around to pick out all the little impurities. We pushed it to one side of the tray until we had a clean little mound, and so we went on, in a quiet competition, to determine who would receive the honor of having cleaned the most wheat.

By the ninth of December, a huge amount of wheat was ready to be soaked. On the twelfth it would be cooked in the evening, then wrapped up in woolen blankets. The next morning, no matter how early I arose, Mother was already in the kitchen. The wheat, still warm, was offered to me in a bowl, the precious golden beads sweetened by ricotta. That would be my very special breakfast that day, and while I was eating, *Zio Gianni* would show up with a container in which he put a good amount of the *cuccia*. He too was offered a bowl of it to eat with his favorite cream and some espresso. That morning, many early risers would show up, as *Mamma* was the one in the family who cooked the wheat and supplied it to the rest of the extended family. But *Zio Gianni*, who was the true glutton, was always the first to arrive with the excuse that he started making house calls to his patients very early in the morning.

As the day progressed, a member of each family household would show up. One of my little cousins who lived across the street from us came to get her family's share; Andrea would get *"cuccia"* for the *Nonni Lo Monte,* but he would also bring us a small, valuable container filled with *vino cotto* in exchange. All our visitors praised the tenderness of the kernels and the quality of the ricotta. They would eat, praising my mother's cooking, with everyone having a preference as to how to sweeten the wheat: half *bianco mangiare,* half ricotta, cinnamon, a sprinkle of chocolate bits, *zuccata,* no *zuccata* at all, chocolate pudding, and a thing I always found revolting in association with wheat—coffee pudding. *Vino cotto* was my favorite sweetener, and I would manage unobtrusively to hide away some of it (with my father's complicity, as it was also his favorite).

Mamma never forgot to give plenty of *"cuccia"* to the door keeper's family and to the greengrocer. They always returned the kindness by giving us chick-pea soup, which was the way of the poor to honor the Saint. I regarded this culinary custom with the greatest respect, not snubbing it at all—and I never had any competition in eating the soup, being the only one in the family who seemed to appreciate it. In fact, I have always loved the simplicity of taste of many things which were available only in very poor households, and that at home would appear very seldom, almost as a condescending concession to some popular custom. Sicilians are epicureans; eating becomes a carnal pleasure, and although saints and holy days are traditionally celebrated in some places with fasting, our households always celebrate with eating: this fact may seem blasphemous if you consider it from a truly religious point of view, but it explains how even atheists have their favorite saints to whom they are devoted!

MIMMETTA
LO MONTE'S
CLASSIC
SICILIAN
COOKBOOK

•

264

"CUCCIA"

whole kernels of wheat, sweetened with various additions

for serving number see notes below

"Cuccia" is a dessert very dear to me. It is made for the day of Santa Lucia, the Saint of the Light. She protects sailors and eyesight. Ever since I can remember, on the day of Santa Lucia, December 13, I have eaten *"Cuccia"* for breakfast. It has also concluded my lunch, as an afternoon snack, as the perfect end to a dinner, and as a late evening treat, just before going to bed. The Saint must have blessed my eyesight many times, given the devotion with which I have eaten this dish, and the huge quantities of it I have cooked and distributed among friends.

"Cuccia" is a very cultural dish, which many people at first do not know how to eat. They draw out all the cream and are left with a bunch of firm little balls in their mouth, not too sure of what to do with them. The secret is to chew the cream along with the wheat. Now that health food is appreciated by more and more people, *"Cuccia"* is not looked upon as strangely as it was years ago, and I think the Saint is going to get a few more devotees.

I POUND WHOLE WHEAT KERNELS	YIELDS ABOUT 7½ CUPS COOKED KERNELS
COLD TAP WATER	FOR SOAKING AND RINSING KERNELS
½ TEASPOON SALT	

Make sure the wheat kernels are whole and that they are sold for consumption, not for seeds. Preferably, buy soft wheat, the same that's used for cake flour or white bread. Hard durum wheat is less suitable.

Sort and rinse the wheat. Place it in a large bowl, and add water to the rim of the bowl, well above the wheat level.

Soak the wheat for two to three days, changing the water and rinsing the wheat well every 24 hours.

Cook the wheat, preferably in the evening because it has to rest through the night (if you want to have it for breakfast the morning of Santa Lucia). To cook it, place in a heavy pot, add 7 cups of water and the salt, cover, and bring to a boil. Let the wheat simmer about 1½ hours, or until the kernel skins split slightly. Drain most of the water, leaving just enough to keep the wheat moist.

Wrap the pot, well sealed with the lid, in a cloth, and then in a blanket (an old quilt will do). You want at least 2 layers around the pot to keep the heat in, and to let the wheat further tenderize and steam open, through the night.

In the morning, unwrap the pot and scrape off the top layer of wheat, which will look dry. Underneath, you'll discover that the kernels have popped open, letting some of the white interior show through the brown skin.

If you cook *"Cuccia"* past the point when the kernels split, the starch will come out, resulting in a sticky porridgelike mass, rather than well-separated grains. So pay attention to the cooking time.

You can keep the layer you have scraped off for wheat salad. The rest of the wheat, right after it has cooled off completely, can be mixed with *Crema di ricotta per "cuccia"*(see page 267), *Crema di latte* (see page 324), or *Budino di cioccolata* (see page 270). I like to combine my wheat with a mixture of the first two.

Vino cotto (see below) is another way of sweetening the wheat.

Mix the wheat with whatever addition, in the quantity to be consumed. If refrigerated already mixed, the wheat becomes rather hard.

Notes on Serving Portions

Three cups *"Cuccia,"* mixed with 2 pounds *Crema di ricotta per "cuccia"* will serve 8 to 10 people. (People have to be "broken in" before eating a good serving. You can change the ratio of "cuccia"-ricotta to your individual taste.)

Three cups *"Cuccia"* mixed with the full amount of the *Budino di cioccolata* will serve 8 to 10. Four cups *"Cuccia"* mixed with the full amount of the *Vino cotto* recipe will serve 8 to 10. Three cups *"Cuccia"* mixed with 3 times the amount of *Crema di latte* will serve 8 to 10. In all, use ⅔ cup sugar.

MIMMETTA
LO MONTE'S
CLASSIC
SICILIAN
COOKBOOK

•

266

VINO COTTO

cooked wine

enough to dress 4 cups

The original *Vino cotto,* as made in Sicily, is unobtainable but I have been able to come very close to its taste using this very simple method.

8 CUPS RED WINE	DRY
½ CUP MOLASSES	LIGHT, UNSULFURED
½ CUP HONEY	
2 TO 4 TABLESPOONS CORNSTARCH	

In a large saucepan, bring the wine and the molasses to a boil. Simmer, partially covered, until reduced to 4 cups. Stir in the honey and cook over low heat, stirring for a couple of minutes. Remove from the heat and cool to room temperature. Mix a small amount of the cooled wine mixture with the cornstarch, dissolving it, and then adding enough of the wine mixture to thin it out. Stir the cornstarch mixture into the remaining reduced wine. Using the least amount of cornstarch will yield a consistency closest to the true *Vino cotto,* which is like a dense liquid. More cornstarch will yield a puddinglike consistency.

Return the wine to the heat and bring to a boil, stirring constantly over medium to medium-low heat. The mixture will thicken at the boiling point—in different degrees depending on the amount of cornstarch used. Remove from the heat and cool. Mix with 4 cups *"Cuccia"* just before serving.

CREMA DI RICOTTA PER "CUCCIA"

ricotta cream for "cuccia"

enough for 3 cups "cuccia"

2 POUNDS RICOTTA	WELL DRAINED, PATTED WITH LAYERS OF PAPER TOWELS UNTIL MOISTURE IS ABSORBED
1 CUP SUGAR	
¼ TEASPOON GROUND CINNAMON	
2 OUNCES SEMISWEET CHOCOLATE	CUT INTO BITS

In a food processor with a steel blade, run together the sugar, ricotta, and cinnamon until very smooth. Mix in chocolate.

Mix with the *"Cuccia"* just before serving, and only in the amount you think will be consumed. The wheat, mixed with the ricotta cheese (or any other cream or dressing), tends to toughen when refrigerated.

RISO PARADISO

"paradise" rice

serves 8

½ CUP ITALIAN *ARBORIO* RICE	OR A GOOD-QUALITY JAPANESE RICE
4 CUPS MILK	
1 STICK CINNAMON	ABOUT 3 INCHES LONG
4 EGG YOLKS	EXTRA-LARGE
⅓ CUP SUGAR	SCANT
¾ TEASPOON VANILLA	

In a large, heavy saucepan, combine the rice and the milk. Bring to a boil, stirring frequently, reduce the heat, and simmer, uncovered, along with the cinnamon stick, until done, about 20 minutes. (Time is unpredictable; tasting some grains periodically is the only way to determine the doneness. Rice should be firm, but not crunchy.)

Beat the yolks with the sugar and the vanilla on a high speed, about 10 minutes. While the rice is still on low heat, start adding the yolk mixture in a thin ribbon, stirring constantly. Stir well down to the bottom, from the center to the sides, back to the center, always in the same direction, until all the mixture has been added.

Keep on the heat, stirring up to 4 minutes, until the mixture reaches the consistency of a light custard (the mixture must not boil). At first the surface will be covered by a white, light foam. As the mixture approaches the right consistency, the foam will gradually dissipate and be limited to the edges; the mixture will be pale yellow.

Transfer to a serving dish or fill eight individual cups. Chill before serving.

DOLCI

267

BUDINO DI RISO E RICOTTA

rice and ricotta pudding

serves 10

Ricotta-cream filling

4 CUPS RICOTTA	DRAIN EXCESS LIQUID
1 CUP SUGAR	
1 TEASPOON LEMON PEEL	GRATED
1 OUNCE SEMISWEET CHOCOLATE	CUT INTO SMALL PIECES

Rice pudding

1⅛ CUPS ITALIAN *ARBORIO* RICE	OR A GOOD-QUALITY JAPANESE RICE
6 CUPS MILK	
¾ CUP SUGAR	
3 EGGS	EXTRA-LARGE
¾ TEASPOON VANILLA	
BUTTER	UNSALTED, FOR COATING BAKING DISH
FLOUR	FOR DUSTING
1 TEASPOON GROUND CINNAMON	OPTIONAL

MIMMETTA
LO MONTE'S
CLASSIC
SICILIAN
COOKBOOK

•

268

To make the ricotta cream: Beat with electric beater or process in food processor with a steel blade the ricotta with the 1 cup of sugar. Beat until creamy. Mix in the lemon peel and the chocolate. Set aside.

To make the rice pudding: In a large saucepan, combine the rice, milk, and sugar. Bring to a boil over low heat, uncovered. Simmer for 20 minutes from the boiling point, uncovered, stirring frequently. Remove from the heat.

Reserve about 4 tablespoons of the rice pudding liquid in a small bowl. Cool along with the pudding, about 20 minutes.

Beat the eggs and the 4 tablespoons of the reserved liquid until blended. Do not overbeat. Trickle into the rice, stirring well. Add the vanilla.

Preheat the oven to 325° F.

Generously butter a round, 12-inch wide, 2½-inch high baking dish and dust with flour. Spread about half of the pudding on the bottom, spread the ricotta cream over it, and cover with the remaining rice pudding.

Bake in the oven for 1 hour and 15 minutes. Serve hot or cold, sprinkled with cinnamon, if desired.

RISO NERO

black rice

serves 8

¼ POUND HAZELNUTS

4 CUPS HOT WATER

1 CUP SUGAR

1 CUP ITALIAN *ARBORIO* RICE

6 TABLESPOONS COCOA

2 OUNCES BITTERSWEET CHOCOLATE

ABOUT 1 CUP

OR A GOOD-QUALITY JAPANESE RICE

Preheat the oven to 375° F.

Spread the hazelnuts on a cookie sheet. Toast in the oven for 7 minutes. Remove from the oven and roll energetically on a hard surface to detach the skins. If some of the skin stays on nuts (as it will) let it be. Grind the nuts in a food processor until oil starts to show. Some of the nuts will be in a paste, some still grainy.

In a large saucepan, combine the ground-up hazelnuts. Add ¼ cup of the water. Stir and continue adding water until the water and nuts form a smooth mixture. Add the rest of the water and bring to a boil. Stir in the sugar and the rice. Let it simmer, uncovered, until the rice is halfway done.* Stir in the cocoa and the chocolate. Keep the mixture simmering, uncovered, stirring very often until the rice is done (firm but not crunchy). The mixture should not be dry. Add some water, if necessary.

Add the cinnamon, if desired. Transfer to a serving dish and refrigerate until ready to serve. The rice is best if eaten at least 12 hours after prepared, and can be refrigerated for a few days.

Serve chilled.

---

* THE COOKING TIME OF THE RICE IS UNPREDICTABLE. A FAIR ESTIMATE OF HALFWAY DONE WOULD BE 15 MINUTES, AND 5 TO 10 MORE MINUTES TO BE DONE, BUT THE ONLY WAY TO BE SURE IS TO TASTE.

BUDINO DI CIOCCOLATA

chocolate pudding

serves 6

4 OUNCES SEMISWEET CHOCOLATE
2 TABLESPOONS CORNSTARCH
½ CUP SUGAR
¼ CUP COCOA
4 CUPS MILK
6 EGG YOLKS   EXTRA-LARGE; EGG-WHITE MEMBRANE
                                                           REMOVED, STIRRED

I TEASPOON VANILLA
SLICED ALMONDS FOR DECORATION

MIMMETTA
LO MONTE'S
CLASSIC
SICILIAN
COOKBOOK

•

270

Melt the chocolate in a double boiler. Keep warm while preparing the pudding.

In a saucepan, combine the cornstarch, sugar, and cocoa. Stir in enough milk to form a very smooth paste. Add the yolks and mix well. Add the remaining milk in a thin stream, while stirring.

Cook, stirring constantly, on medium-low heat. Stir well down to the bottom, from the center to the sides, back to the center, always in the same direction, until the mixture begins to thicken and boil. Stir over low heat 1 minute longer. Remove from the heat; stir in the vanilla and the melted chocolate.

If serving as a pudding, pour into individual cups while hot. Decorate with sliced almonds. Serve chilled.

If the pudding is to be used to dress *"Cuccia"*, chill. Mix with 3 cups of *"Cuccia"* after removing the film formed on top and just before serving. Sprinkle, if desired, with bits of semisweet chocolate.

Sicilian Delights, Arabic Tastes

Among the dishes that bear a strong Arab influence, and sometimes the Arab name, are many desserts, such as the ever famous Sicilian Easter dessert, *cassata* (from the Arabic *quas-at,* meaning round bowl), the sesame seed and honey bars, *cubbaita* (from *qubbayata*), and the wonderful ices flavored with the essence of fruit and flowers, *sorbetti* (*sciarbat* in Arabic), which are now called *gelati* in modern Italian. In fact, it was through Sicily that ice cream made its way to Europe. Caterina dei Medici is said to have taken a Sicilian ice cream maker with her to France, and, later on, toward the end of the 1600s, the Sicilian Procopio dei Coltelli opened the Café Procope in Paris, which soon made Sicilian ice cream famous.

The most delicate and refined *gelato* I have ever tasted is the one flavored with the scent of jasmine blossoms, still using the Arabic word *"scursunera,"* in the Sicilian dialect. Second best is the cinnamon sorbet, and the combination of the two is like a preview trip to the paradise promised by Mohammed. From Palermo, two incredibly smooth and rich *gelati,* made with milk in which grains of rice or coffee beans which have been soaked in milk, can also be linked to the Arab tradition. Strawberry *gelato* is also one of my favorites.

GELATO DI FRAGOLA

strawberry gelato

serves 6

3 CUPS STRAWBERRIES	USE ONLY RED OUTER LAYER; MEASURE AFTER DISCARDING THE WHITE SPONGY INTERIOR
½ CUP SUGAR	

Puree the strawberries in a food processor. Place the sugar in a small saucepan. Stir in 4 tablespoons water and cook, uncovered, over low heat until dissolved. Stir occasionally.

Add the sugar syrup to the puree in the food processor. Process until well mixed, about 1 minute. Transfer to a shallow freezerproof container. Cover tightly and place in the freezer. Check after 2 hours. Scrape any ice crystals that have formed with a fork, stir well, and return to freezer. Repeat every couple of hours, at least three more times. Each time the mixture will be more solid: after scraping it with the fork, mash it with a potato masher. After the last round of scraping and mashing, pack it down with your hands.

The *gelato* can be kept in the freezer for several weeks.

Walking Along La Marina

Semifreddo, like gelato, is one kind of Sicilian ice cream, which reminds me of celebrations at *La Marina,* the promenade by the sea in Palermo. When I was a child, we would eat sweets as we walked along, during festivals such as the one honoring Santa Rosalia. Patrician palaces still line the land side of *La Marina.* That sidewalk used to be the open *salotto* (drawing room), of the cream of Palermo's society, who—in the balmy nights—crowded its cafés, eating the ice creams—*pezzi duri, semi-freddi, bombette*—Palermo is famous for.

MIMMETTA
LO MONTE'S
CLASSIC
SICILIAN
COOKBOOK

•

272

SEMIFREDDO DI CASTAGNE

chestnut "semifreddo"

serves 8

3 EGG YOLKS	EXTRA-LARGE
⅓ CUP SUGAR	
8¾-OUNCE CAN CHESTNUT SPREAD	A GENEROUS ¾ CUP
1½ CUPS WHIPPING CREAM	

Beat the yolks and sugar until very light (10 to 15 minutes). Beat in the chestnut spread. Place in the top of a double boiler, over hot water. Cook over low heat, stirring constantly, well down to the bottom, from the center to the sides, back to the center, always in the same direction. Stir for 10 minutes. Cool on the counter, stirring occasionally while it is cooling. Transfer to a large bowl.

Line the long sides and the bottom of a 1-pound loaf pan with a doubled-up strip of heavy duty foil, long enough to overhang a few inches over both sides.

Whip the cream until very stiff (the beaters should leave definite marks; the cream will have lost some volume).

Gently stir 3 heaping tablespoons of cream into the chestnut mixture until well mixed. Fold in the remaining cream by thirds. Place in the prepared pan. Cover very tightly, then place in freezer at least 12 hours before serving.

To serve, remove from the freezer, run a knife blade between the *semifreddo* and the unlined sides of the pan, to detach. Pull from the foil, invert on a platter, peel off the foil, slice, and serve. *Semifreddo* will keep in the freezer for several weeks.

SEMIFREDDO DI CAFFÈ

coffee "semifreddo"

serves 16

6 EGGS   EXTRA-LARGE, SEPARATED
⅔ CUP PLUS 2 TABLESPOONS SUGAR
⅓ CUP TRIPLE-STRENGTH HOMEMADE
   ESPRESSO*
1 PINT WHIPPING CREAM

Beat the yolks with ⅓ cup plus 1 tablespoon sugar until very light (10 to 15 minutes). Place in the top of a double boiler over medium-low heat, over hot water. Trickle in the coffee, stirring evenly and constantly, well down to the bottom, from the center to the sides, back to the center, always in the same direction. Keep stirring until the mixture thickens, 10 to 15 minutes. Adjust the heat, if the mixture on the bottom and on the sides of the double boiler tends to dry out and stick in spite of the stirring. Place in the refrigerator to cool. Do not allow to chill.

Lightly whip the cream. Start adding the remaining sugar while beating. Beat until very stiff (until the beater leaves very definite marks—the cream will have lost some volume). Refrigerate.

Beat the egg white to stiff peaks. Have the egg yolk-coffee mixture in a large bowl. Fold a third of the cream into it. Alternately fold in the egg white and the remaining whipping cream, in about three additions each. Work rapidly.

Place the mixture in two 1-pound loaf pans, lined (see *Semifreddo di castagne,* page 272), and cover. Place in the freezer at least 12 hours before serving.

To serve, remove from the freezer, run a knife blade between the *semifreddo* and the unlined sides of the pan to detach. Pull from the foil, invert on a platter, peel off foil, slice, and serve. *Semifreddo* will keep in the freezer for several weeks.

* TO MAKE TRIPLE-STRENGTH ESPRESSO, PACK COFFEE GROUNDS IN THE FILTER OF A "TOP OF THE STOVE" ESPRESSO COFFEE POT. CHOOSE A GOOD QUALITY COFFEE, ROASTED TO A CHOCOLATE BROWN COLOR. COFFEE TOASTED TO BE BLACK IS NOT THE WAY ITALIAN ROAST OR ESPRESSO COFFEE IS SUPPOSED TO BE; IT IS SIMPLY BURNED COFFEE WHICH HAS LOST ANY AROMA. COFFEE SHOULD BE GROUND JUST A LITTLE COARSER THAN TURKISH. FILL THE BOTTOM PART OF COFFEE POT TO ABOUT ½ INCH BELOW THE VALVE WITH WATER. ALLOW ONLY HALF OF THE WATER TO COME UP VERY SLOWLY, USING LOW HEAT. COFFEE SHOULD BE VERY, VERY DARK AND VERY, VERY CONCENTRATED.

TRIONFO DELLA GOLA

the triumph of gluttony

serves 10

MIMMETTA
LO MONTE'S
CLASSIC
SICILIAN
COOKBOOK

•

274

The delicious deep pink of the watermelon pudding, along with its refreshing taste, make you savor the sweetness of the squash preserve and the delicacy of the pistachio nuts, while the thin layer of Pan di Spagna gives it body.

I RECIPE *PAN DI SPAGNA*	SEE PAGE 296
I SMALL WATERMELON	ABOUT 7 POUNDS
I TO 4 TABLESPOONS SUGAR	
7 TABLESPOONS CORNSTARCH	
I TABLESPOON ORANGE FLOWER WATER	
I CUP *CONSERVA DI ZUCCA*	SEE BELOW
I CUP PISTACHIOS	RAW, UNSALTED, SHELLED; COARSELY GROUND

Cut *Pan di Spagna* into layers approximately ⅓-inch thick. Use one cake layer for this recipe and reserve the others for another use.

Make watermelon juice by crushing the watermelon with your hands over a colander. Filter the juice through a mesh colander. You should have about 4 cups. If it is not a very sweet melon, add the full amount of sugar; if a very sweet melon, use a lesser amount.

In a medium saucepan, dissolve the cornstarch in some of the watermelon juice. Add the remaining juice and cook over medium heat, stirring constantly, well down to the bottom, from the center and to the sides, back to the center, always in the same direction, until the juice thickens. Stir in the orange water and remove from the heat.

Mix 1½ cups of the hot thickened watermelon juice with the *Conserva di zucca* and ½ cup of the pistachios. Let both the plain thickened juice and the one mixed with nuts cool. Use a platter with an edge. Place the cake layer on it. Spoon the mixture with the nuts on the layer. Place it in the freezer for a few minutes, to chill. Add the plain thickened juice, spooning it on top gently. Sprinkle the remaining half of the pistachios over it.

Chill in the refrigerator before serving.

More Sicilian Delights, Arabic Tastes

A lot has been written about Sicily, and a good deal by Sicilians themselves. Even when the goal or topic has not been food, some information about it has seeped through the lines. In 1800, Michele Amari, a patriot who fought for Italian independence, wrote a very detailed five-volume history of the Arab rule in Sicily. In *I Musulmanni in Sicilia,* he tracks back to the Arabs the many pastries made in Sicily by frying fermented dough. The Arabs combined ground almonds and sugar, initiating the great traditions of Sicilian marzipan, substituting at times pistachio for almonds for a finer texture and a richer flavor.

Sicilians have kept the taste by combining ingredients in a manner whose end result is unmistakably Arabic, even when a precise reference cannot be made. Examples of such combinations are the *Trionfo della gola* (see page 274), and *Cuscus dolce* (see page 276)—two desserts which take you into a dimension of sheer pleasure, removed from time and reality.

CONSERVA DI ZUCCA

squash preserve

about 1 cup

Squash preserve is used to fill pastries and cakes, and is added to many Sicilian desserts such as *Trionfo della gola* (see page 274), *Crostata di Valverde* (see page 322), "*Minni di virgini*" (see page 279), and *Bocconcini* (see page 284).

In her cookbook notes, grandfather's sister, Maria Angelica, recommends to expose the squash to "sunlight, moonlight, and starlight, if there is any," after the squash has been candied in a long process that seemed to involve a little magic.

I POUND CHAYOTE SQUASH   PEELED, QUARTERED, REMOVE CORE (SEEDS); CUT INTO SMALL ⅓-INCH CUBES

½ POUND SUGAR

Mix the sugar and the squash in a small saucepan. Cook over very low heat, covered, for about 5 minutes and stir. The squash at this time should have released quite a bit of liquid (if not, cook a little longer, until the liquid is released).

Cook the squash, covered with the lid ajar, on medium heat for 30 to 40 minutes, or until the liquid is reduced to a light syrup. Cool, place in a jar, and refrigerate if you are going to keep the preserve for over a few days.

If the preserve syrup crystallizes while stored, warm it up gently as needed.

CUSCUS DOLCE

sweet couscous

serves 6

The milk-pistachio pudding binds together the coarse grains of *cuscus*, with the faintly smoky taste of the ground, toasted almonds.

½ CUP MILK
⅔ CUP COUSCOUS
I TABLESPOON SUGAR
⅛ TEASPOON SALT
½ CUP WHOLE ALMONDS WITH SKINS

Pudding

3 TABLESPOONS CORNSTARCH
2½ CUPS MILK
¼ CUP SUGAR
½ CUP RAW PISTACHIOS SHELLED, UNSALTED

Topping

2 TABLESPOONS ORANGE MARMALADE

MIMMETTA
LO MONTE'S
CLASSIC
SICILIAN
COOKBOOK

•

276

Preheat the oven to 375° F.

In a large saucepan, bring ½ cup of milk to a boil. Turn off the heat. Mix in couscous, sugar, and salt. Cover and let rest for 5 minutes. Uncover and stir with a fork. Break up the couscous clumps with your fingertips until they turn into loose grains. Spread to cool.

Toast the almonds on a cookie sheet in the preheated oven for 10 to 15 minutes. (The size of the almonds is the main factor affecting the length of cooking.) Allow to cool. In a food processor fitted with the metal blade, grind the almonds until they are the same size as the couscous grain.

Combine the couscous with the almonds. Spread out on a 9-inch glass pie pan or similar container. Set aside.

In a food processor fitted with the metal blade, grind the pistachios until they are the same size as the couscous grains.

For the pudding: In a saucepan, dissolve the cornstarch in a small amount of milk, thin it out with the rest of the milk and add the sugar. Cook on medium to low heat stirring constantly and evenly well down to the bottom from the center to the sides, always in the same direction until the mixture thickens. Let it cool, then stir in the ground pistachios.

Spread the pudding on the couscous. Dot with the orange marmalade. Serve by spooning it out, at room temperature or slightly chilled.

DOLCI DA CREDENZA
spoon desserts

GENOVESI

genovesi

yields nine, 3½- to 4-inch filled pastries

Crust

1¾ CUPS FLOUR	UNBLEACHED, ALL-PURPOSE
½ CUP PLUS 2 TABLESPOONS SUGAR	
9 TABLESPOONS (4½ OUNCES) BUTTER	UNSALTED, CHILLED
2 EGG YOLKS	EXTRA-LARGE
PEEL OF ½ LEMON	FINELY GRATED
2 TABLESPOONS BRANDY OR BOURBON	OR AS MUCH AS NECESSARY TO GATHER THE DOUGH IN A SOFT BALL

Filling

6½ TEASPOONS CORNSTARCH	
3 TABLESPOONS SUGAR	
1¾ CUPS MILK	
3 EGG YOLKS	EXTRA-LARGE, BEATEN LIGHTLY
½ CUP LEMON PEEL	FINELY GRATED

POWDERED SUGAR

For the crust: Combine the flour and sugar in a medium bowl. Cut in the butter until the mixture looks like coarse crumbs. Cut in the egg yolks and the lemon peel until well distributed.

Add 2 tablespoons of brandy, and handling the dough lightly with your fingers, mix it in. Add more brandy if the dough does not gather easily into a ball. Set aside in a cool place, wrapped in wax paper.

For the filling: Combine the cornstarch and sugar in a medium saucepan. Pour in enough milk to make a smooth, thin paste. Add the remaining milk, egg yolks, and lemon peel. Stir well. Place over medium heat, stir well down to the bottom, from the center to the sides, back to the center, always in the same direction, without stopping until the mixture begins to thicken. When it reaches the boiling point, turn off the heat, stir a couple more minutes, and set aside. Let cool completely before using to fill the pastry.

To assemble the pastry: Preheat the oven to 375° F.

Divide the dough into 2 equal parts. Roll each out, between wax paper, into a rectangle, approximately 8 by 16 inches. Cut into sections, about 4 by 4 inch square. Spoon the filling in the center of eight of the squares (about a heaping spoonful each); cover the filling with the other squares.

Tap down the dough with your fingers around the filling, sealing the top square edges down where they meet with the bottom square. Further seal the pastry with either a ravioli wheel or a round pastry cutter-sealer. (With the leftover dough cuttings, you can make another "genovese.")

Transfer to a cookie sheet and bake in the oven for 15 minutes. Increase temperature to 400° F. and bake 5 more minutes. Let pastry cool a little. While still warm, remove from the cookie sheet. Serve, still warm, sprinkled generously with powdered sugar, or at room temperature, sprinkling the sugar on just before serving.

The pastries can be made 2 days in advance, refrigerated, crisped up in an oven preheated to 375° F. for 10 to 15 minutes, and served warm or at room temperature, sprinkled with powdered sugar.

MIMMETTA
LO MONTE'S
CLASSIC
SICILIAN
COOKBOOK

•

278

"MINNI DI VIRGINI"

virgins' breasts

yields about 20 pastries

For as long as people remember, the nuns have made pastries called *"minni di virgini"*—virgins' breasts—which are almond pastries in the shape of nice little compact breasts. When I was little, I remember that when you placed an order for them at the convent, you couldn't use that name. You had to call them *panotti*. Street boys would go to the order grate every now and then and ask for a pair of *"minni di virgini,"* just to get the nuns angry.

Crust

1 POUND ALMONDS	(ABOUT 4 CUPS) BLANCHED; VERY FINELY GROUND
1½ CUPS FLOUR	BLEACHED
1 POUND SUGAR	
3 EGGS	EXTRA-LARGE
2 OR 3 EGG WHITES	EXTRA-LARGE, TO COAT THE PASTRY AND MAKING HANDLING EASIER

Filling

1 CUP *CONSERVA DI ZUCCA*	(SEE PAGE 275) OR USE ¾ CUP GROUND HONEY DIPPED PAPAYA MIXED WITH ¼ CUP GROUND CITRON

Preheat the oven to 300° F.

Mix together the crust ingredients, using a countertop mixer, a hand beater, or your hands. The dough is going to be very soft, but will hold together. Moisten your hands with the egg white, and pick an amount of dough comparable to an egg (remember, you should come out with another 19 of them). Shape it in your cupped hand like a ball, hollow it enough to put in about ½ tablespoon filling, and fill it. To close, draw the dough up over the filling, in a little tip, the size of a hazelnut. Place them pastry-tip up on a cookie sheet, well coated with butter, leaving 1½ to 2 inches space in between.

Bake in the oven 45 minutes. Cool. To keep, place in a tin lined with wax paper. The pastries will last for a couple of weeks.

In Search of the Nuns' Perfect Pastries

The involvement of religion with food has been deeply rooted in the structure of Sicilian religious communities since Norman times. While the Normans were in power, convents and monasteries proliferated and took it upon themselves to preserve recipes along with Christianity. Nuns dedicated their skills to one particularly genteel branch of cuisine: desserts.

Besides pistachios, the nuns' pastries included a number of basic traditional ingredients: flour, sugar, honey, eggs, lard, butter, milk, ricotta, almonds, squash, citron, orange and lemon peel, cinnamon, cloves, and, a latecomer from the Spaniards, chocolate. Ingredients were handled in secret ways that along with elements particular to the different convents, made each convent famous for its own specialties.

Keeping formulas secret when creating a dish—or any product useful to mankind —is something I can understand as long as the people holding the key to the secret make sure it is passed on to someone of their choice in order that the recipes do not die out. Nuns guarded their recipes with the same ardor with which they guarded their chastity. I can sympathize with that: they counted on their chastity as one of the ways to earn the joys of heavenly life, and on their secret recipes to make their earthly life more prestigious and to give them badly needed income.

During the many summers spent as a child and as a teenager in Erice, I had developed a special attachment to the pastries made there by the nuns of the convent of San Carlo. Thousands of miles away I was haunted by the opulence of their almond desserts (see *Bocconcini,* page 284), the no-nonsense hardness, the mysterious scent of their *Mustazzola* (see page 293), and the delicate tenderness of Donna Gemma's *Genovesi* (see page 277). Donna Gemma was a former helper, turned traitor, of the nuns; being very entrepreneurial, she had set up shop for herself.

When I started, years ago, to try to find out how some of those desserts were made, the thought of infiltrating the convent as a helper crossed my mind. Unfortunately, to be eligible one had to meet some rigid requirements: to be female, very modest, absolutely chaste, very religious, and born in the area. Of all these, I only met one. My second-best possibility was to ingratiate myself with one of the helpers of the nuns. Yet another possibility was to eat the pastries at any given opportunity, and to figure out on my own the way to make them—from their smell, their looks, their taste, and their consistency. The research, no matter how it was conducted, required several trips to Erice.

Erice can now be reached very easily from Palermo, my hometown, where I always make my base. The highway is extremely comfortable and fast—how different from the first trip taken there in the summer of 1946. The exodus from the city took place in Nonno Lo Monte's "Bianchi," a great lady among the Italian cars. In it were Mother, myself, and Brother, the car driven by the chauffeur, Andrea, jam-packed with our belongings. We were followed by my father's "Topolino" (little mouse)—another classic Italian automobile—driven by Father, and just as full.

I remember my Uncle Enzo, who lived across from our city home, coming to say good-bye at the curb and laughing at the jumbled assortment of objects filling the cars. He said, "All you are missing is a birdcage," to which I responded by pulling out a tiny cage with my *cardellino* (finch), Pucci, and saying coldly, "We have that too." I would not part from Pucci for anything in the world. He had followed my first pet bird, a sparrow caught by Mother when a fledgling, who was so tame that he never needed a cage. Most of the time he roosted on a pretty basket, and once in a while he flew

MIMMETTA
LO MONTE'S
CLASSIC
SICILIAN
COOKBOOK

•

280

around the house. Pucci was also very tame; at the end of dinner he was allowed to hop around the table to peck at the bread crumbs.

The trip had all the makings of an expedition, with an inordinate amount of clothes, kitchenware, linen, and even some small pieces of furniture (folding chairs, etc.). There were also food provisions for the stay in the village and food for the trip.

The road climbed from sea level to about 2,000 feet. It was in a terrible state of disrepair. I remember Andrea mumbling to himself, "If I catch one of those holes I'll break a *balestra* [old type of suspension], or if I hit one of those bumps I'll break the 'carter.' " The car wheezed and huffed uphill. When the road finally leveled, it ran at the side of narrow, rugged canyons, so deep that even in full daylight they were menacing with shadows.

Soon after the trip started I was made to eat. The choice was cutlets or *frittata* stuffed in crunchy bread. That was my mother's way of preventing car sickness. "Eating stabilizes your stomach," she said. She also recommended that we always look straight ahead.

All of a sudden the gorge we were in would start opening up, the sun would chase away the shadows, and the road would slope down. Again my eyes could see the spacious, open land of farms and vineyards, birds courting in flight, and a turquoise strip of sea. Mother pointed very excitedly at some vague shape on a far elevation and said triumphantly, "*Ecco* Erice!" From that point on it took another two hours, but now that we had seen the village we were more lighthearted about the trip. Every now and then the sight would disappear and when it reappeared it was in greater detail, until the battlements of the castles would show.

Andrea helped to unload the cars; normally phlegmatic, he now seemed unusually hurried, and would not even stop to eat. All he wanted to do was to start the journey back soon enough to reach Palermo before sundown.

My more recent trips to Erice in search of recipes have taken a little over an hour and a half. The first was, as far as the pastry hunt went, a disaster. I found the huge convent doors locked. Walking past them on that same street I smelled something very familiar—the scent of marzipan pastry with the typical faint trace of bitter almond. The smell took me beyond a portal into a courtyard. There, through a wide-open door, in a room rustically equipped with tables made of unfinished boards that use throughout time had polished, stood a masonry coal-burning stove counter and a masonry oven in a corner.

Two dark figures were busy mixing what looked like flour. They seemed so completely absorbed in their work that I did not want to ask them any questions. Other people were there, and they appeared to be waiting. They looked like city people. I found out through one of them that it was possible to buy the pastries I was smelling, but that I had to be patient, as they were still in the oven. The women must not have been too absorbed in their mixing because one said abruptly, "There aren't any left to sell, they are all sold out." I pleaded that I had come all the way from Palermo just to buy some, I lived in the States, and God knows when I would have another chance. Not a word from the two black figures. But one of the people waiting made me a very generous offer; he would let me have some of those he had reserved.

After such an unhappy beginning, my expectations of getting any recipes were not very high. The pastries came out of the oven, and there was another wait for them to cool. I got my little package—a small, white cardboard tray wrapped in brown paper—waited for the crowd to thin out, and then very cautiously asked the two women if they could tell me how they made the *bocconcini*. The one who had spoken to me earlier said, "It is a secret I'll take with me to my grave." Well, I thought, the way you look, that may happen very soon. I walked away with my package, determined to dissect the *bocconcini* with such care that they could not hold any secrets from me.

My next disappointment was just across the village square and around the corner. Donna Gemma's courtyard door was locked. A passerby informed me that I could still find the *genovesi* made by people Donna Gemma had trained in a little store close by. Tacked on her door was a strip of black cloth; she evidently had died. The strip was not too faded yet, so it must have been only a few years before. Regardless, the *genovesi* I found were delicious and still had an oven freshness.

The next trip was much luckier. The two huge door halves of the convent were open. Those doors gave access to a grottolike hall that functioned as a waiting room. Three rows of brown painted wooden benches were on the right, and on the left the floor was paved with polished stones. There were two windowlike openings on the right wall, screened with a double grating of iron. Across from the doors was a smaller door, locked, and next to that two halved barrellike wooden fixtures set in the wall. Through them was conducted the exchange of money for goods. That was the maximum security system of the convent, to keep the sanctity of the place untouched by intruders.

No one was in the atrium. The routine was to go and knock at the smaller door and wait patiently until some undefined figure could be seen through one of the grate-protected openings. One would then place an order for the desserts. After another patient wait, the figure would appear again. The smaller barrel would rotate slowly and present the concave side. The money was to be placed there. The barrel would again turn, and after that the large barrel would be set in motion and the package with the ordered dessert would appear in the concave side.

I knocked at the small door. After a brief wait I saw the shape of a nun through the grate. I asked her for some *"mustazzola"* and *bocconcini*. Much to my surprise I heard the latch slide open and she invited me in. My hostess was a small, very old nun, to whom age had given the innocent and defenseless look of a child. She spoke to me in dialect, using the confidential form of "tu." She led me through one side of the cloister to a huge, dark room, the convent pastry laboratory. On a long table were some almond pastries decorated with dainty marzipan flowers and leaves that showed their delicate pink and green through a veil of sugar glaze.

She invited me to sit at the table across from her. I still did not know why I had been invited in. She explained, "I let you in because you don't look like all 'those others.' You must be a good girl, you don't paint your face." Later on, as we talked about almonds, preserves, cookies, and life changing, she mentioned that now she was alone in the convent. That was why, she said apologetically, she did not have a variety of pastries to offer.

MIMMETTA
LO MONTE'S
CLASSIC
SICILIAN
COOKBOOK

•

282

Alone. It was then that I realized what I had sensed was odd since the moment I had walked in the waiting hall. The entire place was empty with the exception of that small nun and myself. The nun had spent most of her life there, away from the world, but a life that until now had not known solitude. Each moment of it had been filled by the company of her sisters and their common activities, from praying and pastry making to the most humble chores. Until recently there had been one other sister, but she had been "called by the Lord." My presence gave the remaining nun a little companionship. My questions regarding her pastry making she accepted for what they were: not an attempt to steal something, but an attempt to preserve something.

She had no written recipes; she gave me a description of some almond pastries in the old-fashioned style "a little bit of this and a little of that." When I left the convent and heard the door shut behind me, I felt that I had been offered a glimpse of a life hidden to the world until just before its extinction.

Some time later, a woman from the village who worked for a family of friends took pride in giving me a recipe for *genovesi*. Some of the ingredients were accurately stated, some very vague.

My approach on figuring out the recipes by myself has been the most successful with the reinforcements offered by the little nun and the woman from Erice, and some very unusual handwritten notes from another convent. No convent allows out written information or will admit to having any, but in this case the recipes were written by a nun who left the religious life and became the cook for a family from Palermo. The recipes were meant to stay secret and within that family; however, a cousin of mine, Luciana, became part of it through marriage, and thanks to her affection for me decided to share them.

BOCCONCINI

morsels

makes 12

Bocconcini di pasta reale —

Mandorle senza guscio g. 500
Zucchero   g. 500
Si fanno pestare Le mandorle
per pasta reale — Si scioglie a
fuoco lo zucchero in 1 bicchiere

MIMMETTA
LO MONTE'S
CLASSIC
SICILIAN
COOKBOOK

•

284

BUTTER	FOR COATING
½ POUND ALMONDS	(ABOUT 2 CUPS) BLANCHED
5 OUNCES POWDERED SUGAR	(ABOUT ¼ CUP) PLUS SOME TO SPRINKLE
	ON *BOCCONCINI*
1 TABLESPOON PISTACHIOS	RAW, UNSALTED; COARSELY GROUND
2 EGG WHITES	EXTRA-LARGE
1 EGG YOLK	EXTRA-LARGE
3 TABLESPOONS *CONSERVA DI ZUCCA*	(SEE PAGE 275) NO SYRUP

Preheat the oven to 400° F.

Butter a large cookie sheet and set aside.

In a food processor fitted with the metal blade, process the almonds until they have the consistency of very coarse cornmeal. Do not overgrind, as that draws out the oil. Add the sugar and process very briefly, then scrape down the bowl. Add one half of an egg white and the egg yolk, and process again very briefly. Put the almond mixture in a bowl and stir it with a fork very thoroughly.

Mix together the ground pistachio and the squash preserve.

Moisten your hands with the remaining egg white and form the almond mixture into a roll. Divide it in twelve equal parts. Keeping your hands always moistened with the egg white, shape each portion in a flat round, approximately 2 inches in diameter.

Divide the preserve-pistachio mixture among the rounds. Keeping your hands moistened with the egg white, gather the edges of the round over the filling, packing the almond dough to form small balls.

Place the balls on the prepared cookie sheet. Bake in the preheated oven for 10 minutes. Remove from the oven and as soon as the *Bocconcini* are cool enough to handle, detach from the cookie sheet with a sharp blade. Gently mold the top into a domelike shape.

When cool, sprinkle with powdered sugar. Store in a tin box lined with wax paper. They will keep well for a week.

PALLINE DI SCORZA D'ARANCIA

little orange peel balls

yields 24

2 LARGE NAVEL ORANGES
¾ CUP SUGAR   PLUS ADDITIONAL FOR ROLLING THE BALLS

Peel the oranges by cutting off the "poles," and then slicing down, through the peel only, from pole to pole, divide into six or seven sections. Ease the sections from the flesh of the orange, leaving as much of the white attached to the peel as is possible. Soak the peels in cold water for 3 days, rinsing them well and changing the water once a day. Coarsely grind.

In a small saucepan, combine the ground orange peel, sugar, and ¼ cup water. Bring to a boil over high heat, reduce the heat to low, cover, and cook for 20 minutes.

Uncover, increase the heat to high, and cook, stirring constantly, until the mixture is dry enough to be gathered on one side of the pan.

Remove from the heat and spread the mixture on a plate. Once cooled, but still slightly warm, form balls the size of a large hazelnut, pressing the mixture together with your fingertips and rolling it between your palms. It will take a little practice and patience to find the best way to compact the mixture together and shape it.

Roll the balls in some sugar and set aside on the counter, uncovered, for a couple of hours. Store in a wax paper-lined tin. To keep longer than a week, refrigerate.

QUARESIMALI

lenten cookies

yields 18 large cookies

BUTTER	FOR COATING
3¼ CUPS FLOUR	UNBLEACHED, ALL-PURPOSE
1½ CUPS SUGAR	
1½ TEASPOONS BAKING POWDER	
1¾ CUPS WHOLE ALMONDS	WITH SKINS
3 EGGS	EXTRA-LARGE

MIMMETTA
LO MONTE'S
CLASSIC
SICILIAN
COOKBOOK

•

286

Preheat the oven to 300° F.

Lightly butter a large cookie sheet.

In a large bowl, combine the flour, sugar, and baking powder. Add the almonds and eggs, and handle the dough until well blended. If sticky, add small amounts of flour until you can form a breadlike shape 16 inches long. The dough should have the consistency of a thick cookie dough.

Place the dough on the prepared cookie sheet and bake in the oven for 1 hour. Remove from the oven and cool to lukewarm. Using a serrated knife, trim the ends and cut into eighteen slices, each a little over ½-inch thick. Place the slices on the cookie sheet, standing up. Handle with care. They can crumble easily at this stage.

Return to the oven, and bake for 1 more hour, at 300° F. During the last 15 minutes, turn the slices down, so that they will lay flat. Leave them in the oven, after the second baking period, with the oven turned off, for ½ hour.

Cool. *Quaresimali,* well wrapped and sealed, will last for a few weeks.

NOTE: DURING THE FIRST BAKING PERIOD, YOU MIGHT GET A LITTLE WORRIED SEEING YOUR BREADLIKE FORM LOSING ITS SHAPE AND SPREADING OUT. IT WILL EVENTUALLY RISE AND TAKE A CURVED SHAPE. AFTER THE FIRST COOKING PERIOD, THE DOUGH WILL STILL BE SOMEWHAT RAW AND SOFT, ALLOWING YOU TO CUT IT WITHOUT CRUMBLING.

"CUBBAITA"

sesame seed and honey bars

yields 8

½ CUP HONEY
1 CUP SESAME SEEDS
OLIVE OIL   FOR COATING

Place the honey in a medium skillet over low heat, allowing it to dissolve to a light syrupy liquid. Add the sesame seeds, increase the heat to medium, and cook, stirring constantly until the honey caramelizes, about 10 minutes. As the honey turns a deep golden brown, the sesame seeds will also turn darker.

Lightly coat a marble or formica surface with olive oil. Transfer the mixture to it. With a wide, long knife blade coated with olive oil, smooth and lightly press on the mixture. If it sticks to the knife, scrape it off and return it to the rest of the mixture, wait a few seconds, and try again, with a blade freshly coated with oil. The mixture can be molded as long as it is warm. Shape it, flattening and pressing it with the blade into a rectangle, approximately 6½ by 6 inches. While still warm cut off the raggedy edges. Then cut it parallel to the long sides, in two equal parts. Cut again, this time across, to form eight bars.

Place in an airtight container as soon as *"Cubbaita"* cools off and keep in a cool place. Of course, the bars can be eaten right away!

Eating Sweets with Santa Rosalia

When one attempts to trace the facts about the origins of traditions and habits of my island and my people, he or she finds that information from different sources has become fused together through the centuries. We have created what I like to call "fantastic history"; a history imbued with pragmatic mysticism. These terms sound contradictory, but they reflect the Sicilian soul: a crucible of contradictions. The researcher has to forget the rigidity of historical documentation and weigh information according to his or her own liking and fascination with the topic. The story of Santa Rosalia is a good example of such a "fantastic history."

Rosalia was born in the twelfth century, the daughter of the Duca Sinisbaldo di Quisquina, and the niece of Willem II, known as "William the Good." She renounced the privileges and luxuries of her position, and—still a teenager—went to live in isolation and prayer in a cave in an arid mountain that flanks Palermo.

Centuries later, in 1624, while a tremendous plague was ravaging the city, the saint appeared to a hunter in a dream, revealing where her remains could be found. The bones, found in the cave on the fifteenth of July of that year, were taken through the city, and the plague ceased. The cave immediately became a sanctuary: the mountain, once called Hertke, was renamed Pellegrino, because of the pilgrimage many made to the site. To this day, Santa Rosalia is revered as the patron saint of Palermo, and she has her own celebration, the *Festino,* every July fifteenth.

This account of Santa Rosalia has a pretty solid historical basis (there was indeed a plague which ended after the procession of the bones), with the exception of the dream: The hunter, scouting around, probably discovered the bones; the Palermitani were well aware of the existence of the cave and of the story of the maiden's life. And, apparently, the bones were found to be animal bones.

Goethe, in his *Viaggio in Italia,* gives what is perhaps the most famous description of the sanctuary and the statue of the saint, sculpted in white marble by Gregorio Tedeschi in 1625. My description comes from my impressions as a child. The sanctuary was one of the sites I would go to on weekends with my father during our own special times together. I remember the coolness of the place, the peacefulness and the soothing, sweet smell of rock and clean earth dampened by clear water trickling from the natural vault and walls. I remember the flicker of the votive candles and the gleam of the silver surfaces of reproductions of organs and other human body parts healed by the saint. Hearts, breasts, arms, and legs were displayed with candor, evoking both the frailty of human beings and their reverence to the saint. The *ex voto,* the silver replicas of varying sizes, were and are still considered symbols of gratitude to Santa Rosalia for having healed the ailing individual.

In the sanctuary I experienced total stillness of time and action, along with stupor, staring at the figure of the saint, adorned with jewels and lying in a flirtatious pose, but at the same time irradiating innocence, and seemingly very happy in her alcove overflowing with the jewels that could not fit on her body.

This was the hidden world of the mountain, where the maiden Rosalia, the golden child of a noble family and the darling of a king's court, chose to live and die.

Monte Pellegrino to us Palermitani is like a person: the sanctuary its soul, within which one can hear, see, and communicate without sounds, images, or words. The exterior—light-colored rock, speckled with orange lichens—is the body, exposed to the sun, the wind, and the heat, struggling to survive. On the outside, right at the bottom of the steps leading to the sanctuary, we bask in the sun, and feast on things most non-Sicilians consider odd or second-rate food. We never seem to have enough of all kinds of toasted nuts, carobs, fava beans, chick-peas, and pumpkin seeds. Candy made with sugar, honey, nuts, and sesame seed is joyfully crunched, and little white snails—*"babbaluci"*—get sucked out of their shells with a skill only experience can give.

So here we are, honoring a Norman saint—who loathed carnal things and loved ascetic life—eating predominantly Saracen snacks (the sesame seed-and-honey cake still bears the Arab name *"cubbaita"*), while in the sanctuary the *"santuzza"* lies covered by jewels she didn't want in real life.

MIMMETTA
LO MONTE'S
CLASSIC
SICILIAN
COOKBOOK

•

288

AMARETTI AL CACAO

cocoa amaretti

yields about 20

BUTTER	FOR COATING
⅔ CUP ALMONDS	
½ CUP PLUS 1 TABLESPOON SUGAR	
2 TABLESPOONS COCOA	
FLOUR	UNBLEACHED, ALL-PURPOSE; FOR COATING
1 EGG WHITE	LARGE

Optional

⅛ TEASPOON GROUND CLOVES	OR LESS
⅛ TEASPOON GROUND CINNAMON	OR LESS
ALMONDS	BLANCHED; SLIVERED, FOR DECORATION

Preheat the oven to 375° F.

Coat a large baking sheet with butter and set aside.

In a food processor fitted with the metal blade, grind the almonds finely. Overgrinding will draw out the oil. Add and briefly process the sugar, cocoa, and, if using, the spices. Add the egg white and process until the ingredients form a ball. Gather the dough and roll it out onto a floured work surface.

Sprinkle the dough with flour and flatten it between two pieces of wax paper. The dough will be very sticky. Very lightly roll it, using as little pressure as possible on the rolling pin. Roll out to a 6- by 7½-inch rectangle. Turn the dough often while it's between the wax paper, peeling off the paper and adding additional flour to prevent it from sticking until rolled to the desired size. The dough can be molded easily, pushing the sides with the blade of a long thin knife, to shape.

With a very sharp long blade knife, cut the rolled-out dough into 20 squares. Decorate with the slivered almonds if you wish. Carefully lift and place the squares on the prepared cookie sheet.

Bake in the preheated oven for 15 minutes. Remove from the oven and detach from cookie sheet while still hot. Return to turned-off oven and let them dry there for 1 hour.

Thoroughly cool, then store in a tin lined with wax paper.

CAPELLINI FRITTI AL MIELE

fried capellini with honey

yields about 20 rounds

Until I resurrected it, this charming dessert was one of the dishes that had fallen victim to time and was no longer made. Recently, I have topped the capellini with maple syrup instead of honey. Delicious!

½ POUND ANGEL-HAIR PASTA (CAPELLINI)	COMMERCIAL
2 TABLESPOONS OLIVE OIL	PLUS MORE FOR COATING PANS
1⅓ CUPS HONEY	
2 TABLESPOONS PISTACHIO	RAW, UNSALTED; COARSELY CRUSHED

MIMMETTA
LO MONTE'S
CLASSIC
SICILIAN
COOKBOOK

•

290

In a large pot of boiling well-salted water, cook the pasta (see page 31). Drain, and dip immediately in plenty of cold water to bring to room temperature. Drain very well, and toss with oil. Spread in a wide pan.

Heat two medium cast-iron skillets (working with two will hasten the process). Coat bottoms well with oil. Loosen up the cooked capellini strands with your fingers and add ½ cup of the pasta to each skillet.

Spread the pasta to form a 5-inch round. It will be a thin lacy-looking layer. Cook over medium-low heat about 1 minute. Press down with a spatula to compact it and cook 2 more minutes. Turn over, press down again, and cook for 2 more minutes. Remove. Repeat, adding oil as needed. The pasta should yield about 20 light golden, moderately crisp rounds. Adjust the heat to obtain such results within the 5-minute cooking time. Do not stack the capellini rounds or they will lose crispness.

If you like your capellini to be extra crispy, spread them on cookie sheets and crisp in a preheated 450° F. oven for 2 minutes. The capellini rounds can be prepared ahead of time (up to a couple of days) before they are needed. Refrigerate, then crisp in oven.

In a small saucepan, heat the honey. Trickle on the capellini and sprinkle with pistachios. Serve immediately.

ZEPPOLE FRITTE

fried zeppole

makes 18

My recipe for *Zeppole* came from my own nostalgia of this doughnut-shaped, fried potato dough, which *Mamma* made a few times, and which I never had enough of. Once I made my peace with potatoes, I felt the urge to fry a batch of *Zeppole,* and experience again the pleasure of the special way their soft interior melts in your mouth, coming through the honey-coated, delicately crisp exterior.

1 POUND POTATOES	ALLOW EXTRA FOR WASTE
¼ CUP TEPID MILK	
2 TABLESPOONS YEAST	GRANULAR, AT ROOM TEMPERATURE
1 POUND FLOUR	(ABOUT 3½ TO 4 CUPS) UNSIFTED, UNBLEACHED, ALL-PURPOSE
¼ TEASPOON SALT	
3 TABLESPOONS (1½ OUNCES) BUTTER	UNSALTED, MELTED
4 EGG YOLKS	LARGE
CORN OIL	OR SIMILAR VEGETABLE OIL; ENOUGH TO DEEP FRY
⅔ CUP HONEY	

Rice the potatoes. The potatoes can be cooked and riced one day ahead of time, refrigerated, and brought to room temperature before using.

In a small bowl, combine the milk and yeast. When the yeast is softened, stir it into a thin paste by mashing it against the sides of the bowl with a spoon. Add ⅔ cup flour and knead until you can gather it into a smooth ball. Set it into a floured bowl, cover, and place in a warm place to rise.

Mix the salt with the remaining flour. Add the riced potatoes and the butter and mix with wire beater at speed 4 for 5 minutes (I use a Kitchen Aid countertop mixer). Add egg yolks and beat with the hook, on speed 2 (low speed), about 3 minutes. As soon as the yeast ball has increased to about 1½ times its volume, add it to the potato mix, and beat with the hook beater, speed 2 (low speed) for 8 minutes.

If mix is *very* sticky, add 1 to 2 tablespoons of flour. However, the dough should be very soft and lightly sticky.

Gather the dough and place it in a bowl lined with a lightly floured napkin. Cover it and let it rise in a warm place for 1½ to 2 hours. The dough is ready to use when the volume increases by about half.

Heat a couple of inches of oil in a deep fryer to 270° F. (I use a cast-iron pot.) The heat should be medium-low to keep it at that temperature.

In the meantime, divide the dough into three equal sections, and each section in six parts. Roll each section out into an 8-inch long stick, shape as a ring, overlapping the ends in a cross, so that about 1 inch of each sticks out. Fold the ends over, on the opposite sides, and press gently. Lay on a floured cloth. Fry them, uncrowded with space to expand, for about 6 minutes, turning them very often, until deep honey colored. (Do not puncture.)

Drain on paper towels. Cool. Warm the honey and pour it over the *Zeppole* arranged in a serving dish.

Zeppole can be made up to 24 hours in advance, and stored, covered, at room temperature. About 1 hour before serving, crisp them in a preheated 400° F. oven, for 4 minutes.

Or, they can be frozen and crisped for about 8 minutes in a preheated 400° F. oven, until they fizzle. Cool and just before serving, pour on the honey. Or, pass around a bowl of hot honey for individuals to serve themselves.

MIMMETTA
LO MONTE'S
CLASSIC
SICILIAN
COOKBOOK

•

292

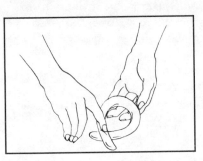

Shape each 8-inch long dough stick into a ring. Overlap the ends in a cross, so that about 1 inch of each sticks out.

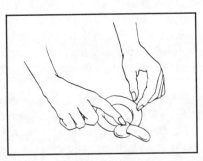

Fold the ends over, on the opposite sides, and press gently.

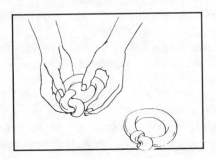

"MUSTAZZOLA"

old-fashioned cookies

yields 12 very large cookies

"Mustazzola" is a tough cookie! If you do not have extra-hard teeth, do not even attempt to bite on it without previously soaking it in some Marsala.

⅓ CUP ALMONDS	SKINS ON
OIL	FOR COATING
3½ CUPS FLOUR	BLEACHED, ALL-PURPOSE
⅔ CUP SUGAR	
1 TEASPOON BAKING POWDER	
¾ TEASPOON GROUND CLOVES	

Lightly toast the almonds in an oven preheated to 375° F. for 5 minutes. Cool. Grind to the consistency of the bread crumbs. Do not overgrind. Overgrinding will draw the oil out of the almonds.

Lower oven to 300° F. Lightly oil a cookie sheet and set aside.

In a large bowl, mix the flour, sugar, baking powder, and cloves. Add small amounts of water, up to ¼ cup, while kneading until you obtain a firm but pliable dough. Roughly mix in the almonds. Place in a countertop mixer bowl and knead with the dough hook at speed 1 (very low) for about 5 minutes.

Roll the dough on a lightly oiled surface to a 15- by 6½-inch rectangle. Press a very long knife blade on the dough to make diagonal shallow parallel indentations. Repeat the opposite way to form a very small diamond pattern. Cut the dough in twelve 6½-inch sticks.

Place on the prepared cookie sheet and bake in the oven for 2½ hours. Turn off heat. Leave in the oven with the door closed until the oven cools off.

Meditating on "Mustazzola"

Pane "vinesco" and "Mustazzola" are certainly not airy, sophisticated desserts, but they are true *dolci da credenza*. Maybe I like them because of the memory of infancy I get from them, because they are so earthy and rough, because eating becomes an engaging activity in itself.

When I was a little girl spending the holidays in Erice, I remember holding a 50-lire coin in my fist and running up a very narrow, steep alley, terraced in cobblestones, to Don Andrea's grocery shop. The convent, where we normally bought sweets, was too far and I was not allowed to go alone. The store was in an old church, the sales area in the entrance, separated from the nave and the altar by a wood partition. Don Andrea kept his supplies in the back. He wore a steel-gray cotton coat and was always very friendly. His wife was a very thin, pale woman, and the children, two little boys, looked just like her, fair and fragile. The wife helped fill the orders, but she was mainly busy with the children, who were cranky most of the time.

I would hand my coin over to Don Andrea, take a *"mustazzolo"* in exchange, and with a firm grip on it, started crunching on the barely sweet hard dough immediately. Once in a while the humidity would get to the *"mustazzolo"* in spite of the big glass jar it had been stored in, and I found it disappointingly soft. Nevertheless, it always took me twice as long to go back home, in spite of the way being now downhill, because *"mustazzolo"* always absorbed me in a sort of chewing meditation, which I lingered over.

MIMMETTA
LO MONTE'S
CLASSIC
SICILIAN
COOKBOOK

•

294

Rediscovering Pane "Vinesco"

While I was trying to figure out, mainly from memory, a recipe for *"Mustazzola,"* I came up with a very old-fashioned cookie I had forgotten about. As soon as I ate it, I recognized the old taste, something tried seldom as a child, and never found again. My memory had set it aside, but it was very quickly revived as I chewed on one of what I thought could turn out to be a *"mustazzolo."* The new-old cookie is pane *"vinesco,"* as it is called in the Duke's cookbook. I was completely unaware I was using a recipe similar to the Duke's! The fact that I stumbled onto baking a cookie written in the Duke's cookbook is just a coincidence, but I like to think about it as another little miracle, another taste from the past come to life.

PANE "VINESCO"

wine bread

yields 16 very large cookies

⅓ CUP ALMONDS

3 TABLESPOONS OLIVE OIL

2½ CUPS WHITE WINE   DRY

¼ CUP MOLASSES   UNSULFURED

½ CUP HONEY

1 TEASPOON GROUND CLOVES

3½ CUPS FLOUR   BLEACHED, ALL-PURPOSE

Lightly toast the almonds in the oven, preheated to 375° F., 8 to 10 minutes. Cool. Grind to the consistency of bread crumbs. Overgrinding will draw the oil out of the almonds.

Lower the oven to 300° F. Lightly oil a cookie sheet and set aside.

Bring the wine to a boil. Over medium heat, dissolve the molasses and the honey in it. Stir in the cloves. When the wine mixture is at a very low boil, add the flour and work it in until roughly mixed, about 2 minutes. Spread the dough on a kneading surface (preferably marble), well coated with some of the oil. When the dough is cool enough to handle, knead in the remaining oil. Keep kneading until smooth, about 5 minutes. Add the almonds and knead until evenly distributed.

Divide the dough into two equal pieces; roll each to a rectangle about 12 by 4½ inches. Cut each rectangle to form eight 4½-inch long sticks. Place them on the prepared cookie sheet, uncrowded. Bake in the oven for 1 hour and 45 minutes. *Pane "vinesco"* should be chewy, and can be kept in an airtight container in a cool place for several weeks.

TORTE
cakes

PAN DI SPAGNA I (DI MAMMA)
bread from spain
yields a 10-inch wide, 2½-inch high round base cake

MIMMETTA
LO MONTE'S
CLASSIC
SICILIAN
COOKBOOK

•

296

BUTTER	FOR COATING
FLOUR	FOR DUSTING
1½ CUPS CORNSTARCH	
1 TABLESPOON BAKING POWDER	
6 EGGS	EXTRA-LARGE, SEPARATED
¼ TEASPOON CREAM OF TARTAR	
1⅛ CUPS SUGAR	

Preheat the oven to 350° F.

Coat a 10-inch wide, 3-inch high round aluminum baking pan with butter and dust with flour.

Into a small bowl, sift ¼ cup cornstarch with the baking powder. Set aside.

In a large bowl, beat the egg whites until foamy. Add the cream of tartar. Continue beating until well whipped but not stiff. Add the sugar in a thin stream, beating until stiff and glossy.

Add the yolks, beating to blend well. Add the remaining plain cornstarch by the heaping tablespoonful, beating to blend after each addition. Finally add the cornstarch mixed with the baking powder. Scrape the bowl a couple of times while beating.

Pour into the prepared pan and immediately bake in the oven for 55 minutes. Let the cake cool in the turned-off oven for 30 minutes, with the door ajar. Finish cooling on the countertop. Unmold when at room temperature (do it very gently; the top of the cake is covered by a thin crust that crumbles very easily).

Serving suggestions: You can cut it into 3 to 4 layers, sprinkle with ⅓ cup orange juice mixed with ⅓ cup white rum or vodka, and fill between the layers and cover the top with tangerine pudding and berries or, after sprinkling with orange juice, fill with rum, and cover with sweetened whipped cream (1 pint) and berries.

You can moisten the layers with ½ cup dry Marsala and fill between the layers and the top with *Crema di ricotta per "cuccia"* (see page 267), using the amount called for in the recipe.

You can moisten *Pan di Spagna* with ⅓ cup white rum, then fill between the layers and top it with *Ricotta al cacao* (see page 256).

Or use it in *Coppe di pan di Spagna e castagne* (see page 258) or for *Torta ai marroni* (see page 304).

PAN DI SPAGNA II (DI LOLA)

bread from spain

yields a 10-inch wide, 2-inch high, round base cake

This recipe yields a firmer version of Pan di Spagna I.

BUTTER	FOR COATING
FLOUR	FOR DUSTING
1⅓ CUPS CORNSTARCH	
I TABLESPOON BAKING POWDER	
4 EGGS	EXTRA-LARGE, SEPARATED
¼ TEASPOON CREAM OF TARTAR	
¾ TEASPOON VANILLA	
¾ CUP SUGAR	

MIMMETTA
LO MONTE'S
CLASSIC
SICILIAN
COOKBOOK

•

298

Preheat the oven to 375° F.

Coat a 10-inch wide, 3-inch high round aluminum pan with butter and dust with flour.

In a small bowl, sift ⅓ cup cornstarch with the baking powder. Set aside.

In a large bowl, beat the egg whites until foamy. Add the cream of tartar. Beat until well whipped but not stiff. Add the sugar in a thin stream, beating until stiff and glossy.

Add the vanilla and yolks; beat to blend well. Start adding the cornstarch—first the plain one, then the one mixed with the baking powder—by the tablespoonful, beating to blend after each addition. Scrape the bowl a couple of times, while beating.

Pour into the prepared pan. Bake immediately in the preheated oven for 40 minutes. Let the cake cool for 30 minutes in the turned-off oven with door ajar. Finish cooling on countertop. Unmold when at room temperature (do it very gently; the top of the cake is covered by a thin crust that crumbles very easily).

Serving suggestions: Cut into four layers—reserving two for other uses. Moisten the remaining layers with a sprinkling of white rum, fill between the layers and top with *Ripieno di cioccolata e pasta reale* (see page 301), doubling the recipe.

Use for *Torta Savoia* (see page 303). Also, see *Pan di Spagna I* (page 296) for other suggestions.

PAN DI CASTAGNE

chestnut bread

serves 8 to 10

BUTTER	FOR COATING
FLOUR	FOR DUSTING
6 EGGS	EXTRA-LARGE, SEPARATED
¾ CUP SUGAR	
1⅓ CUPS CORNSTARCH	
1½ CUPS CHESTNUT FLOUR	
4½ TEASPOONS BAKING POWDER	
½ CUP MILK	
½ CUP CORN OIL	
WHIPPED CREAM	FOR TOPPING
SEMISWEET CHOCOLATE	GRATED, FOR TOPPING

Preheat the oven to 350° F.

Coat a 12-inch round baking pan with butter and dust with flour.

In large bowl, beat the egg yolks and sugar until light, about 15 minutes.

In a separate bowl, combine the cornstarch, chestnut flour, and baking powder. Beat into the yolk mixture, alternately with the milk and the oil.

In a large bowl, beat the egg whites until stiff peaks form. Fold in the yolk mixture and one third of the egg whites. Gently fold in the remaining beaten whites.

Pour into the prepared pan. Bake in the oven for 40 minutes, until the sides pull from pan and the center springs back when lightly touched.

Serve topped with whipped cream and grated semisweet chocolate.

A Sicilian Almond Harvest

The almond tree, if not already cultivated in Sicily when the first Greeks arrived, was certainly intensely cultivated during Greek colonization. The tree thrives where little else will grow, in rocky soil under very dry conditions.

The tree blooms in February. Isolated trees are a touch of grace and life that spring from the most barren terrain of the countryside. However, when the trees cover a valley and through their blossoms you can see the most majestic Greek temples emerge —as in "La Valle dei Templi" in Agrigento—the image of such a combination holds so much beauty that it will stay with you forever.

It is a brief moment of glory, for the lightest breeze will shake the petals to the ground, leaving behind the first stage of the fruit.

There are many varieties of almond trees, all self-sterile, and to bear fruit, different varieties of trees must be planted together. Sicilians start enjoying almonds when they are not yet fully developed. While the fuzzy, green hull is still tender, the shell soft, and the kernel at a gelatinous stage, almonds are picked and eaten as a delicacy or to be candied by confectioners. Almonds become a part of every Sicilian's life soon after birth: the baptism is celebrated by offering sugar-coated almonds, pink for baby girls, blue for baby boys. Sugar-coated almonds, in different colors according to the occasion, mark each successive important step of a Sicilian's life: communion, graduation, wedding, and anniversaries.

As soon as the fruit is fully developed, and before the hull starts drying out, almonds still in the hull reappear on the table early in the summer. Hull and shell are split by using very little pressure on the nutcracker: the kernel is extracted, and the pale-yellow supple skin that covers it is peeled off—the skin is very bitter—but once removed you can eat a tenderly crunchy, moist morsel of the most delicate taste, whiter than the whitest of pearls.

Hazelnuts and walnuts are eaten at this stage as well, before they dry out, though walnuts are presented without the hull because it is troublesome to remove.

As August advances and the fruits have been harvested, the almond trees in the Valley of the Temples, bearing only some parched leaves that reflect the heat and the lack of water, look neglected and attract very little attention—they let the temples dominate. It takes a Sicilian like myself—aching a little more than I am willing to admit from the distance put by life between a world that is mine because of birth and a world that I live in because of choice—to recognize their dormant beauty.

During my last visit to the valley at that time of the year, I was happy to stare at the temples from below. I picked a few almonds that were still stubbornly attached to the trees, and I found shelter from the sun in the only shade available—one of the niches dug into the rock of the Christian necropolis. There I cracked my almonds with a stone and let the time go by—cracking, peeling, and eating—waiting for the non-

MIMMETTA
LO MONTE'S
CLASSIC
SICILIAN
COOKBOOK

•

300

Sicilians who were traveling with me, and who had kept on climbing to the most highly placed temple, to come down again.

Cracking dry almonds is something I have done a lot of. When I was a child we received bagsful from the country, and I helped the maid with that chore during the idle evening hours. This is how I learned to recognize the best varieties, the *"muddisa"* (meaning "the soft one" in Sicilian dialect), and the *"cavalera"* (meaning cavalier in Sicilian dialect). This last one was the most prized; the shell was soft, as was the shell of the first one and therefore easy to crack—but it contained a larger kernel.

We used nutcrackers, as well as a hammer and a piece of rough marble on which the almond was placed and then struck with the hammer. This last method had to be used when, once in a while, we'd get a batch of the very hard-shelled variety impossible to crack with a nutcracker. The hammer method took some skill, since the almonds, if not hit the right way, would skid and shoot away like bullets. We then packed the almonds away in glass jars and saved the shells to add to the coals when grilling food.

It is no wonder that we had this endless supply of almonds to crack: Sicily has about twenty million almond trees, which is close to one fifth of the number of trees existing in the world. Yet I don't like to look at the almond tree as a statistic. To me it symbolizes the continuity of the Greek culture in the Sicilian culture of today.

RIPIENO DI CIOCCOLATA E PASTA REALE

almond paste and chocolate filling

enough to cover one 9-inch layer

Serve this recipe with *Pan di Spagna II* (see page 298), *Torta al cacao* (see page 304), or *Torta di nocciole* (see page 308).

4 OUNCES SEMISWEET CHOCOLATE
3 TABLESPOONS CORN OIL
¼ CUP WHITE RUM
3½ OUNCES ALMOND PASTE

In a double boiler, melt the chocolate, then stir in the oil. In a medium bowl, combine the rum with the almond paste. Beat in the chocolate-oil mixture. If too thick to spread, add more rum. Spreading is easier if the filling is used immediately.

MIMMETTA
LO MONTE'S
CLASSIC
SICILIAN
COOKBOOK

•

302

Gateau biscuit al cacao

Si fa a freddo; si prendono duecento grammi di burro freschissimo che si riduce battendolo in crema. Vi si aggiungono grammi duecento di zucchero fino e due torli d'uova. Quando la pasta è bene omogenea vi si versa, mettendolo a cucchiaio, una fortissima infusione di cacao molto calda, un bicchiere da tre once.

Si guarnisce l'interno e il fondo d'una forma di carta bianca attorno della quale si dispone uno strato di biscotti asciutti; poi si versa uno strato di crema, che si ricopre ancora una volta d'uno strato di biscotti e così di seguito; si carica il coperchio d'un peso e si mantiene almeno due ore in un posto fresco, avanti di levarlo dalla forma.

TORTA SAVOIA

savoia torte

serves 12

1 LAYER PAN DI SPAGNA II   ¾-INCH THICK (SEE PAGE 298)
26 OUNCES BITTERSWEET CHOCOLATE
¾ CUP HEAVY CREAM

Have *Pan di Spagna* layer set aside on a flat, large platter.

Melt 10 ounces of chocolate with 6 tablespoons of cream in the top of a double boiler set over hot water. Spread half of it on the *Pan di Spagna* layer, cover with a sheet of wax paper, and flip the chocolate-covered *Pan di Spagna* over. Spread with the remaining melted chocolate and cover with another sheet of wax paper.

Place a flat round tray on top of the cake, move it around so that the chocolate will even out. Leave the tray on top of the cake and place a cast-iron skillet on top of it—about the same size as the cake—to weigh it down. Refrigerate until thoroughly cold.

Melt 10 ounces more of the chocolate and the remaining cream in the double boiler. Take the cake out of the refrigerator and cut through the middle of the *Pan di Spagna* layer. You now have two layers of *Pan di Spagna,* each coated on one side with chocolate.

Put the layers chocolate-side down, leaving the wax paper under them. Spread each with equal parts of melted chocolate, cover with wax paper, again use the tray to even out the chocolate, stack the two chocolate-coated rounds—keeping the wax paper on to cover the chocolate. Top with the tray, weigh down with the cast-iron skillet, and place in the refrigerator.

When thoroughly cold remove from the refrigerator. Very carefully, leaving each chocolate-coated side covered with the wax paper, cut through the *Pan di Spagna* sandwiched between chocolate. You now have four layers of very thin *Pan di Spagna,* coated with chocolate on one side.

Place one layer, *Pan di Spagna*–side down, on a sheet of wax paper. Peel off the wax paper from the chocolate-coated side. Stack on it a second layer, *Pan di Spagna*–side down. Peel off wax paper. Repeat with the other two layers.

Leave the cake at room temperature until the chocolate starts softening. Cover the top chocolate coating with wax paper, place the tray on it, and press it down so that the layers will adhere together. Refrigerate.

Melt the remaining 6 ounces chocolate in the top of the double boiler over hot water. Spread some of the sides, smoothing it well. Trickle the rest on the top, in an uneven design. Refrigerate until 10 to 30 minutes before serving—the time depends on the room temperature; the chocolate should be allowed to soften only slightly.

TORTA AL CACAO

cocoa cake

serves 10

8 TABLESPOONS (4 OUNCES) BUTTER	UNSALTED, ROOM TEMPERATURE
8 EGG YOLKS	EXTRA-LARGE
1½ CUPS SUGAR	
1 CUP FLOUR	UNBLEACHED, ALL-PURPOSE
1½ TEASPOONS BAKING POWDER	
1 TEASPOON VANILLA	
⅔ CUP COCOA	

MIMMETTA
LO MONTE'S
CLASSIC
SICILIAN
COOKBOOK

•

304

Preheat the oven to 350° F.

Coat a 10-inch pan with butter and dust with flour.

In a large bowl, using a K.A counter-top mixer on medium-high speed (speed 6), beat the butter, egg yolks, and sugar until very light, 10 to 15 minutes. Sift together the flour and baking powder and add it to the egg mixture by the tablespoonful, blending well after each addition. Add the vanilla.

Scrape the bowl, add the cocoa by the tablespoonful, and scrape the bowl again. Beat a few seconds to blend well. The batter will be very thick. Spoon it into the prepared cake pan and evenly spread it over the bottom of the pan.

Bake in the preheated oven for 40 minutes. Check cake after 35 minutes; if edges look very dark, remove from oven.

Let cake cool some, then unmold while still slightly warm.

Serve at room temperature plain, topped with whipped cream, or with *Ricotta al cacao* (see page 256), halving the quantity.

TORTA AI MARRONI

chestnut cake

serves 16

6 OUNCES SEMISWEET CHOCOLATE	
2 POUNDS CHESTNUT PUREE	CANNED AND UNSWEETENED
1½ CUPS WHIPPING CREAM	
½ CUP WHITE RUM	
1½ TEASPOONS VANILLA	
1 TABLESPOON COCOA	
⅛ TEASPOON SALT	
3 LAYERS *PAN DI SPAGNA I*	A LITTLE THINNER THAN ½ INCH (SEE PAGE 296)

In the top of a double boiler set over hot water, melt the chocolate and keep warm.

In a large bowl, beat together the chestnut puree, ½ cup cream, the rum, vanilla, cocoa, and salt. Beat in two thirds of the melted chocolate, keeping the remaining chocolate warm.

Whip the rest of the cream until very stiff. Fold one third of the cream with the chestnut puree mixture, then fold in the rest.

Spread a little less than one third of the chestnut mixture on the first layer of cake, add the second layer, and repeat. Top with the third layer of *Pan di Spagna* and spread the remaining chestnut mixture on top of it and on the sides of the cake.

Dribble the remaining chocolate on the top and on the sides of the cake in a thin stream, to form an irregular weblike pattern. You might have to warm up the chocolate several times to keep it flowing as desired.

Chill and serve.

DOLCE DI CHIARE D'UOVO

egg white cake

serves 12

BUTTER	FOR COATING
FLOUR	FOR DUSTING
1 TEASPOON BAKING SODA	
1¼ CUPS CORNSTARCH	
¾ CUP RAISINS	
½ CUP WALNUTS	CHOPPED INTO SMALL PIECES
1 OUNCE SEMISWEET CHOCOLATE	CUT INTO SMALL PIECES
1¼ CUPS EGG WHITE	
½ TEASPOON CREAM OF TARTAR	
¾ CUP SUGAR	
2 TEASPOONS LEMON PEEL	FINELY GRATED
POWDERED SUGAR	FOR DUSTING

Preheat the oven to 375° F.

Coat a 10-inch ring pan with butter and dust with flour.

Sift the baking soda with the cornstarch. In a medium bowl, mix the raisins, walnuts, and chocolate.

In a large bowl, beat the egg whites until foamy, add the cream of tartar, and beat until well whipped but not stiff. Add the sugar in a thin stream; beat until stiff and glossy.

Add the cornstarch-soda mixture by the tablespoonful, beating long enough after each addition to blend it well. Blend in the lemon peel. Fold in the raisin-walnut-chocolate mixture.

Spoon the batter into the prepared pan, evenly distributing it. (The batter will be very stiff.) Gently level the top with a flat spatula, allowing surface to remain rough.

Bake in the oven for 40 minutes. Lower the temperature to 300° F. and bake an additional 35 minutes. Turn the oven off and leave cake in it, with the door slightly ajar, until cool.

Before serving sprinkle with some powdered sugar.

MIMMETTA
LO MONTE'S
CLASSIC
SICILIAN
COOKBOOK

•

306

BABÀ AL RUM

rum baba

serves 14 to 16

Babà al rum can be made in advance and stored in the refrigerator. Bring it to room temperature before serving—cold baba is hard.

I TABLESPOON YEAST	GRANULAR (I ENVELOPE)
¼ CUP WARM WATER	
2 CUPS FLOUR	UNBLEACHED, ALL-PURPOSE, UNSIFTED
2 TABLESPOONS SUGAR	
⅛ TEASPOON SALT	
IO TABLESPOONS (5 OUNCES) BUTTER	UNSALTED, AT ROOM TEMPERATURE
4 EGGS	EXTRA-LARGE, AT ROOM TEMPERATURE

Sauce

I CUP WHITE RUM	
I½ CUPS SUGAR	
I CUP WATER	
I PINT HEAVY CREAM	FOR TOPPING
MARASCHINO CHERRIES	FOR TOPPING

Preheat the oven to 450° F.

Coat a 10-inch ring pan with butter.

In a small bowl, dissolve the yeast in the warm water. Mix in ½ cup flour, lightly knead it, and roll it between the palm of your hands. It shouldn't stick. Cover and place it in a warm place to rise until doubled in size.

In the meantime, mix the rest of the flour with the sugar and the salt. If you have a countertop mixer, such as a Kitchen Aid, the task of mixing the dough is very easy. Put the dry ingredients in the mixer bowl, add the butter and one egg.

Beat with the flat beater, starting at lowest speed (speed 1), and increasing it to medium-low speed (speed 4) until well mixed. Add the risen yeast dough to it, and beat together until well blended. Add the rest of the eggs, one by one, beating at the lowest speed (speed 1) first, and then increasing to medium-low speed (speed 4). Beat well after each addition. After the last egg is added, beat for about 5 minutes. The dough should be stringing from the beater to the sides of the bowl, and will have a "slippery" consistency.

The dough may be beaten by hand, using exactly the same order to add and mix the ingredients. Beat the dough with both your hands wide open, up and down from the counter. Work the dough for about 10 minutes after the addition of each egg.

Place the dough in a heavy ceramic or similar bowl, cover, set aside in a warm place to rise until doubled in size. Beat it down with a heavy wooden spoon, and transfer it to the prepared pan. Cover and let rise again until triple the volume.

Bake in the oven for 15 minutes.

Let it cool. Unmold it on a dish with an edge top-side down. Pierce the cake with a thin skewer, repeatedly. Make the holes close together, all over the surface of the cake.

While cake is cooling, prepare the rum sauce. Bring the water and sugar to a boil in a saucepan, and gently boil until the consistency of a very thin syrup. Warm the rum in another small pan, over medium heat, and add it to the sugar syrup in a thin stream, stirring constantly.

Pour the rum sauce over the cake and let it soak for about 10 minutes while basting it with the syrup collected on the dish. Turn the cake top-side up and let it soak up the remaining syrup.

Serve the *Babà* with whipped cream,* and decorate it with maraschino cherries. Spoon some whipped cream in the center hole of the *Babà,* and if you wish, decorate the top with little mounds of cream and top with maraschino cherries. Spoon the remaining cream in a bowl, and add some to each slice of *Babà* as you cut it.

NOTE: THE DOUGH CAN BE BAKED IN SIXTEEN SMALL WELL-GREASED MUFFIN TINS. DISTRIBUTE IT AMONG THE TINS INSTEAD OF PUTTING IT IN A RING PAN. CUT THE BAKING TIME TO 10 MINUTES. MOISTEN THEM WELL WITH THE SAUCE, SLIT THEM ALONG ONE SIDE, AND FILL WITH CREAM. TOP WITH CHERRIES.

* HAVE 1 PINT CREAM WELL CHILLED IN THE MIXER BOWL. BEAT IT WELL PAST THE FLUFFY STAGE, UNTIL VERY STIFF.

PIZZA DOLCE DI PATATE

potato pizza, sweet

serves 6 to 8

The same old handwritten notebook that gave me the recipe for *Panini cresciuti* (see page 237) yielded another very interesting recipe, the *Pizza dolce di patate*. The taste and consistency of this dessert is unusual.

MIMMETTA
LO MONTE'S
CLASSIC
SICILIAN
COOKBOOK

•

308

BUTTER	FOR COATING
FLOUR	FOR DUSTING
1 TO 1½ POUNDS POTATOES	SMALL, BAKING (ALLOW EXTRA FOR WASTE)
1 CUP SUGAR	
9 EGG YOLKS	EXTRA-LARGE
1 TEASPOON GROUND CLOVES	
2 TEASPOONS LEMON PEEL	VERY FINELY CUT; LOOSELY PACKED

Preheat the oven to 350° F.

Coat an 8-inch or 10-inch springform baking dish with butter and dust with flour.

Place the potatoes in a large pot, cover with lots of water, bring to a boil, and boil about 20 minutes. Do not allow the peel to split or the potatoes will become water-logged. Do not pierce the potatoes to test for doneness. (If skins split while cooking, dry out the potatoes by tossing them around in a dry pot over low heat.) Peel the potatoes and while warm put them through a vegetable strainer, or a potato ricer. You want to end up with 1 pound net weight.

In a large bowl, beat together the potatoes, sugar, egg yolks, cloves, and lemon peel until very fluffy.

Pour the mixture into the prepared pan and bake in the oven for 40 minutes. Cool. Unmold.

This can be made 1 or 2 days in advance and kept unrefrigerated.

TORTA DI NOCCIOLE

hazelnut torte

serves 10 to 12

BUTTER	FOR COATING
FLOUR	FOR DUSTING
2½ CUPS HAZELNUTS	
6 EGGS	EXTRA-LARGE, SEPARATED
1⅔ CUPS POWDERED SUGAR	
¼ TEASPOON CREAM OF TARTAR	

Preheat the oven to 375° F.

Line the bottom of a 10-inch wide, 2-inch high round aluminum pan with parchment paper. Coat the parchment and the sides of the pan with butter and dust with flour.

Coarsely grind (like bulgur wheat) the hazelnuts. If a food processor or similar appliance is used for grinding, grind in small batches.

In a large bowl, beat the egg yolks and the sugar until very light, about 15 minutes. Beat in the hazelnuts. In another large bowl, beat the egg whites until foamy, add the cream of tartar, and continue beating until stiff.

Stir half of the whites into the egg yolk mixture, then fold in the rest. Pour the batter into the prepared pan and bake in the oven for 30 minutes. Lower the temperature to 300° F. and bake an additional 30 minutes. Turn off the oven and leave the cake in it for 1 hour, door closed. Cool on countertop.

Serve plain or topped with whipped cream. Or split the torte in two layers and fill with 4 ounces semisweet chocolate melted with 6 tablespoons cream, or with *Ripieno di cioccolata e pasta reale* (see page 301). Top the filled torte with whipped cream.

TORTA DI PATATE AMERICANE
american sweet potato cake

serves 10

BUTTER	FOR COATING
FLOUR	FOR DUSTING
2½ POUNDS SWEET POTATOES	ALLOW EXTRA FOR WASTE
⅔ CUP PLUS 2 TABLESPOONS COCOA	UNSWEETENED
1 CUP PLUS 2 TABLESPOONS ALMONDS	BLANCHED; FINELY GROUND (IF YOU BLANCH YOUR OWN ALMONDS MAKE SURE THEY ARE WELL DRY BEFORE GRINDING)
½ CUP CALVADOS	
2 EGGS	EXTRA-LARGE

Preheat the oven to 350° F.

Coat a 10- by 8-inch baking dish with butter and dust with flour. Line the bottom with wax paper and butter again.

Place the sweet potatoes in a large pot, cover with lots of water, and bring to a boil. From the boiling point cook about 35 minutes, until soft (if you have a count of four potatoes). Peel, rice, and set aside until lukewarm. You want to end up with 2 pounds net weight.

In a large bowl, mix the sugar and cocoa. Stir in the almonds and Calvados. Beat by hand or using the lowest speed of an electric mixer, until well blended. Add the eggs last and beat very briefly.

Pour the mixture into the prepared pan and bake in the oven for 50 minutes. Let it cool. Unmold.

CASTAGNACCIO

chestnut flour bread

serves 6

MIMMETTA
LO MONTE'S
CLASSIC
SICILIAN
COOKBOOK

•

310

Castagnaccio is a very wholesome, unfussy, quick recipe. Generally eaten at the end of a meal, as a dessert, it is not at all sweet. Very commonly eaten in northern Italian homes, it has many "supporters" in the rest of Italy, my brother one of them. My mother used to stir it up for him in just a few minutes. I like to eat it while still hot, with or without the addition of some sweetened whipped cream. Traditionally *Castagnaccio* is made with water, not milk, and is flavored with rosemary. My version is much more dessertlike, if not classical.

2¼ CUPS MILK
½ POUND CHESTNUT
   FLOUR
⅓ TO ½ CUP OLIVE OIL
½ CUP RAISINS
⅔ CUP PINE NUTS

Preheat the oven to 350° F.

Very generously coat an 8-inch round baking dish with oil (enough to see the oil floating on the bottom of the pan).

In a medium bowl, add the milk to the chestnut flour in a thin stream, while stirring. Beat by hand or with a hand beater, at medium speed, until fairly smooth. While beating, add 2 tablespoons oil. Stir in the raisins and the pine nuts.

Pour into the prepared dish and trickle 1 or 2 tablespoons of oil on top of it. Bake in the oven for 40 minutes.

TORTA DI SEMOLINO

cream of wheat cake

serves 6 to 8

BUTTER	FOR COATING
I SCANT CUP INSTANT CREAM OF WHEAT	PLUS SOME FOR COATING
2 CUPS MILK	
4 EGGS	EXTRA-LARGE, SEPARATED
⅓ TO ½ CUP SUGAR	
I TEASPOON VANILLA	
2 TABLESPOONS BRANDY	OR USE WHISKEY
⅛ TEASPOON SALT	
⅓ CUP HAZELNUTS	COARSELY GROUND
¾ TEASPOON LEMON ZEST	GRATED (OPTIONAL)
4 OUNCES CANDIED FRUIT	CUT INTO VERY SMALL PIECES (OPTIONAL)

Preheat the oven to 350° F.

Coat a 1-pound bread loaf pan with butter and dust with cream of wheat.

In a medium saucepan, bring the milk to a boil. Stir in cream of wheat, remove from the heat, and cool. Beat in egg yolks, sugar, vanilla, brandy, and salt. Stir in hazelnuts and, if using, the lemon rind.

In a large bowl, beat the egg whites until stiff peaks form. Gently fold in cream of wheat mixture by thirds.

If using the candied fruit, mix it with one quarter of the batter.

Spoon the batter into the prepared pan (using first batter mixed with the candied fruit, if desired). Bake in the oven for 55 minutes.

Eat warm or at room temperature. If eaten warm, serve in thick slices and top with whipped cream. If served cold, slice very thin and sprinkle lightly with cinnamon.

BUDINO DOLCE DI PANE

sweet bread pudding

serves 6 to 8

Butter	for coating
3 cups milk	
½ cup sugar	
1 lemon peel	grated
5 eggs	extra-large
1 loaf French bread	stale, cut into ½-inch rounds (about 10 ounces)
¾ cup currants	
½ cup pine nuts	

MIMMETTA
LO MONTE'S
CLASSIC
SICILIAN
COOKBOOK

•

312

Preheat the oven to 350° F.

Butter a baking dish large enough to accommodate the slices of bread in two layers.

In a bowl, beat the milk, sugar, lemon peel, and eggs until well mixed.

Dip the bread in the milk mixture and arrange a layer of the slices on the bottom of the baking dish. Sprinkle with half the currants and pine nuts. Cover with the remaining bread slices and top with the remaining currants and pine nuts. With the tips of your fingers, work the currants and the pine nuts into the layer of bread.

Bake in the oven for 50 minutes. Serve warm at room temperature.

A Word about my ricotta cakes

Do not expect these cakes to have the smooth texture of American cheesecakes. If after trying them you find that you like the flavor but cannot make up your mind about the texture, try the recipes again with a small change: Run the ricotta and the sugar in a food processor, using the steel blade, until very creamy, then transfer to a bowl and proceed as per instructions. The consistency of the cakes will be closer to that of American cheesecake.

TORTA DI RICOTTA

ricotta cheesecake

serves 8 to 10

BUTTER	FOR COATING
FLOUR	FOR DUSTING
2½ POUNDS RICOTTA	DRAINED; PAT SOME MOISTURE WITH PAPER TOWEL
1 CUP SUGAR	
¾ TEASPOON VANILLA	
1 TEASPOON ORANGE PEEL	(ZEST ONLY) CUT VERY FINELY
¼ CUP PISTACHIOS	RAW, UNSALTED, SHELLED; VERY COARSELY GROUND
3 EGGS	EXTRA-LARGE

Preheat the oven to 300° F.

Coat a 9-inch springform pan with butter and dust with flour.

In a large bowl, beat the ricotta with the sugar, vanilla, and orange peel. Beat well for a few minutes at medium-high speed (6 on a Kitchen Aid countertop mixer). Add the pistachios and the eggs, and beat at low speed, just enough to blend them in.

Pour the batter into the prepared pan. Bake in oven for 2 hours.

Cool before unmolding. (See note.) Refrigerate until thoroughly cold. Serve.

NOTE: IF THE PAN SIDES ARE LESS THAN 3 INCHES HIGH, MAKE A COLLAR WITH ALUMINUM FOIL TO EQUAL A 3-INCH HEIGHT. AS SOON AS CAKE IS OUT OF THE OVEN PIERCE THE TOP WITH A THIN SKEWER; THE HOLES SHOULD BE A COUPLE OF INCHES APART. GENTLY PRESS DOWN THE EDGE OF THE CAKE TO LOWER IT. THIS WILL GIVE THE CAKE AN EVEN TOP.

DOLCI

•

TORTA DI RICOTTA AL CAFFÈ

coffee-flavored ricotta cheesecake

serves 10

BUTTER	FOR COATING
FLOUR	FOR DUSTING
3 POUNDS RICOTTA	DRAINED; PAT DRY WITH PAPER TOWEL
1 CUP SUGAR	
⅓ CUP ESPRESSO COFFEE	VERY STRONG (SEE PAGE 273)
2½ TEASPOONS AMARETTO	
1 TEASPOON VANILLA	
5 EGGS	EXTRA-LARGE
½ CUP HAZELNUTS	FINELY GROUND

MIMMETTA
LO MONTE'S
CLASSIC
SICILIAN
COOKBOOK

•

314

Preheat the oven to 300° F.

Coat a 9-inch springform pan with butter and dust with flour.

In the large bowl of a Kitchen Aid countertop (or similar) mixer, beat the ricotta with the sugar for a few minutes at medium-high speed (6 for a Kitchen Aid).

Add the coffee, Amaretto, and the vanilla. Beat at medium-high speed until well blended. Add the eggs and beat at low speed, just until the eggs are mixed in.

Pour the batter into the prepared pan. Bake in the oven for 2 hours and 15 minutes.

Cool, then refrigerate it until thoroughly cold before unmolding it. (See note on page 313.) Sprinkle the hazelnuts on the top and on the sides.

TORTA DI RICOTTA E AMARENE

ricotta and sour cherries cheesecake

serves 8

BUTTER	FOR COATING
2 TABLESPOONS BREAD CRUMBS	UNFLAVORED
2 TABLESPOONS HAZELNUTS	FINELY GROUND
2 POUNDS RICOTTA	DRAIN EXCESS WATER FROM CONTAINER
¾ CUP SUGAR	
⅓ CUP FLOUR	UNBLEACHED, ALL-PURPOSE
3 EGGS	EXTRA-LARGE
¾ TEASPOON VANILLA	
1 POUND CAN SOUR CHERRIES	PITTED, DRAINED WELL

Preheat the oven to 300° F.

Coat an 8-inch springform pan with butter and dust with a mixture of the bread crumbs and hazelnuts.

In a large bowl, beat the ricotta and sugar until very smooth. Add and blend in the flour. Slowly blend in the eggs and vanilla. Do not overbeat. Stir in the cherries.

Pour the ricotta mixture into the prepared pan. Bake in the oven for 2 hours.

Cool, then refrigerate at least 2 hours on a dish to catch any liquid that may drain, before unmolding. (See note on page 313.)

TORTA NERA

black cake

serves 8

BUTTER	FOR COATING
FLOUR	FOR DUSTING
8 OUNCES SEMISWEET CHOCOLATE	
2 POUNDS RICOTTA	DO NOT DRAIN
¾ TEASPOON VANILLA	
⅔ CUP SUGAR	
⅓ CUP FLOUR	UNBLEACHED, ALL-PURPOSE
3 EGGS	EXTRA-LARGE

Preheat the oven to 300° F.

Generously coat an 8-inch springform pan with butter and dust with flour.

Melt the chocolate in the top of a double boiler over hot water and keep warm.

In a large bowl, beat the ricotta, vanilla, and sugar. Beat well for a few minutes at medium-high speed (6 on a Kitchen Aid countertop mixer). Blend in the flour. Add the melted warm chocolate and blend. Add the eggs and quickly beat them in. Do not overbeat.

Pour the mixture into the prepared pan. Bake in the oven for 2 hours.

Cool, then refrigerate until cold before unmolding. (See note on page 313.)

Can be made a few days in advance.

CROSTATE

pies

MIMMETTA
LO MONTE'S
CLASSIC
SICILIAN
COOKBOOK

•

316

PASTA FROLLA SENZA UOVA PER CROSTATE

eggless pie crust

yields 1 pie crust

This crust can be used for *Mortarette* (see page 325) and *Crostata di Valverde* (see page 322).

1 TEASPOON ORANGE PEEL	
1¾ CUPS FLOUR	BLEACHED, ALL-PURPOSE
½ TEASPOON BAKING POWDER	
¼ CUP SUGAR	
7 TABLESPOONS BUTTER	UNSALTED, COLD
¼ CUP MARSALA	OR MORE, DRY (OR USE MEDIUM-DRY SHERRY, OR BRANDY)

Use a sharp potato peeler to cut only the zest from the orange, avoiding the pith. Cut very finely.

In a large bowl, combine the flour, baking powder, and sugar. Cut in the butter, until it has the consistency of fine grains. Toss in the orange peel. Sprinkle the Marsala over the mixture and toss again quickly. Lightly knead just enough to keep the mixture together. If too dry, add small amounts of additional Marsala. Use the dough immediately, or wrap it in wax paper, refrigerate, and use it within a few days.

"CRUSTATA"

serves 10

BUTTER	UNSALTED, FOR COATING
FLOUR	UNBLEACHED, ALL-PURPOSE; FOR DUSTING

Crust

1 RECIPE *GENOVESI* CRUST (SEE PAGE 277), OR 1 RECIPE *PASTA SFOGLIA DEL DUCA* (SEE PAGE 318)

Filling

2 CUPS RICOTTA	WELL DRAINED
1 CUP ALMONDS	BLANCHED; VERY FINELY GROUND
¾ CUP APRICOT PRESERVES	
1 CUP APPLE BUTTER	
1 TABLESPOON GRATED PECORINO ROMANO	
1 TEASPOON ROSEWATER	
1 TO 4 OUNCES GRATED RICOTTA SALATA	IN ADDITION TO OTHER CHEESES (OPTIONAL)
3 EGGS	EXTRA-LARGE
1 EGG YOLK	EXTRA-LARGE
¼ TEASPOON GROUND CINNAMON	

Preheat the oven to 375° F.

Coat a baking pan approximately 7- by 11-inches with butter and dust with flour. (If using *Pasta sfoglia del duca* do not butter and flour the pan.)

In a food processor or mixer, blend the ricotta, almonds, preserves, apple butter, cheese, rosewater, and, if using, the ricotta salata. Blend in eggs and egg yolk briefly.

Line the pan with about two thirds of the dough. Pour in the ricotta mixture. (If using *Pasta sfoglia del duca,* brush the bottom with melted butter first.) Cover the ricotta filling with the remaining crust. (If using *pasta sfoglia del duca,* first moisten the edges of the dough lining the sides with water.) Press the edges well to seal. Cut off the excess dough (using a hot knife blade for *Pasta sfoglia del duca*) and flute.

Insert three small funnels made of foil into the top crust, at regular intervals, to let the steam escape. Bake in the oven for 1 hour. To remove funnels, press them down gently, while the pie is still hot, and then pull them out. Sprinkle the top with cinnamon and cool. Serve at room temperature.

PASTA SFOGLIA DEL DUCA

the duke's puff pastry

yields a 10- by 30-inch rectangle of unbaked dough

2 STICKS (½ POUND) BUTTER	UNSALTED, CHILLED
10 OUNCES FLOUR	(ABOUT 2 CUPS) UNBLEACHED, ALL-PURPOSE
1 EGG YOLK	LARGE
½ TABLESPOON LARD	

MIMMETTA
LO MONTE'S
CLASSIC
SICILIAN
COOKBOOK

•

318

Form the butter into an approximately 5½- by 6½-inch patty. Keep chilled.

Knead flour, egg yolk, lard, and ⅔ cup less 2 tablespoons water in a food processor, using the steel blade. If the dough is too stiff, it will not gather and you will have to add more water, tablespoon by tablespoon, until it will gather. To further facilitate the kneading process, you may want to divide the dough into two batches and push them against the processor blade. Knead for 3 to 4 minutes. The dough should be soft, elastic, and very smooth. If you knead by hand, it will take at least 10 minutes.

Let the dough rest, wrapped in foil, in the refrigerator for 30 minutes. Roll it out on a floured surface, preferably marble, into a rectangle over twice the length of the butter patty and 1½ inches wider, about 7 by 14 inches. Place the butter patty on the dough so that you can fold half of the dough over it. With moist fingers, tap the edges of the rectangle dough with water, fold it over, and tap edges of dough to seal together.

On a lightly floured surface, start rolling out the dough. Stretch the dough away from you with light pressing strokes, so that it measures about 10 inches in length (about 4 to 5 inches in width). Fold it over in thirds toward you. Turn it so that the short side of the rectangle is toward you and roll it out again. This time you should be able to roll the dough into a longer and wider rectangle, about 12 inches long and 6 inches wide. While rolling, lift the dough from the surface, and lightly dust it with flour. Repeat this procedure, from folding in thirds, seven more times, always rolling out the dough to about 12 by 6 inches. The butter will tend to ooze out as you approach the eighth fold. Keep dusting the dough and the surface with flour, and keep your rolling strokes very light.

After you have folded the dough the eighth time, roll it out to less than ¼ inch thick. It is best not to roll the puff pastry dough after it has been cut. Therefore, have your dough rolled out enough to be able to cut a large portion to line your baking dish and a small portion to top it.

To cut the dough, warm the blade of a long butcher knife on your burner until it is hot. Cut the dough, leaning the blade down and pressing. Do not drag the knife.

If you need to adjust the shape cut, moisten the edges of the scraps of dough and overlap them. Roll them out, moistening and attaching where needed, to obtain the desired shape.

The dough, at this stage, can be used in flat layers, to line molds, and, if cut into thin strips, can be arranged in different shapes, such as cornucopias (see below). The rolled-out dough (10- by 30-inch rectangle) will yield three 10-inch squares or three 10-inch rounds plus cuttings. To cut rounds, I use a lid with a sharp edge. The cuttings from the rounds will yield twelve 2½-inch cornucopias.

To make cornucopias: Moisten the edges and overlap the cuttings. Roll out the dough, fold it, and roll three to four times. Roll to about a ¼ inch thickness. Cut into ½-inch strips. Wrap the strips, overlapping the turns slightly, around aluminum cornucopia molds (about 3 to 4 inches long). Moisten the ends of the strips to attach each new strip to the preceding one. Wrap the mold until you have covered 2½ inches of it. (Number of strips needed will depend on the lengths of each strip.) Moisten the strip ends and press down to seal at the beginning and the ending of the cornucopias. Lay them on aluminum cookie sheets.

Bake the 10-inch squares or rounds in an oven preheated to 400° F. for 15 to 16 minutes; the cornucopias for 20 minutes.

In addition to the other recipes in this book which call for the above pastry, here is a simple dessert idea. Simply serve the three pastry layers with sweetened whipped cream and fresh berries (1 pint cream, whipped, and 1 pound of berries will be enough to stack the layers and to fill the cornucopias which can be used as decoration around the layers). Do not spread cream on the top layer. Instead, sprinkle it and the cornucopias with powdered sugar.

The layers can also be coated with an apricot or orange glaze in addition to being stacked with cream. Make the glaze by mixing ¾ cup apricot preserve or orange marmalade with ½ cup water. Cook it over medium-low heat until it is reduced to 1 cup, then puree it in a food processor. Brush the glaze on the two bottom layers.

The square layers or rounds plus cornucopias with cream and berries will serve 12.

Cut dough in ½-inch wide strips.

Wrap strips around aluminum molds, overlapping slightly on turns.

Moisten strip ends to attach each new strip to preceding one.

Wrap mold until 2½ inches of it is covered. Seal ends of cornucopia by moistening strip ends and pressing down.

TORTA RIPIENA DI MANDORLE

almond-filled torte

serves 8 to 10

Crust

¾ CUP FLOUR	UNBLEACHED, ALL-PURPOSE
½ CUP PLUS 2 TABLESPOONS SUGAR	
9 TABLESPOONS (4½ OUNCES) BUTTER	UNSALTED
2 EGG YOLKS	EXTRA-LARGE
PEEL OF ½ LEMON	FINELY GRATED
2 TABLESPOONS BRANDY OR BOURBON	OR AS MUCH AS NECESSARY TO GATHER THE DOUGH INTO A SOFT BALL

Filling

2 CUPS WHOLE ALMONDS	BLANCHED
⅔ CUP ORANGE MARMALADE	OR USE APRICOT PRESERVES
⅔ CUP SUGAR	
2 EGGS	EXTRA-LARGE
2 EGG YOLKS	EXTRA-LARGE

MIMMETTA
LO MONTE'S
CLASSIC
SICILIAN
COOKBOOK

•

320

Preheat the oven to 350° F.

To prepare the crust: In a medium bowl, combine the flour and sugar. Cut in the butter until mixture has the consistency of coarse crumbs. Cut in the egg yolks and the lemon peel and blend until well distributed.

Add 2 tablespoons brandy and mix it in, lightly handling the dough with your fingers. Add more brandy if the dough does not gather easily into a ball. Set aside in a cool place, wrapped in wax paper.

Line a 12- by 8- by 2-inch deep pan with about two thirds of the crust.

To prepare the filling: In a food processor fitted with the metal blade, finely grind the almonds. If you blanch your own, make sure they are very dry before grinding. Do not overgrind as this will draw out the oil; grinding in three different batches will help prevent overgrinding.

Add the marmalade and the sugar and process until mixed. Add the eggs, and process until blended. Do not over-process.

Spoon the filling into the pan lined with pastry. Cover the filling with a crust lattice. Trim the edges of the crust lining the pan so that the pastry is about ¾-inch above the filling. Fold it over the lattice ends.

Bake in the oven 45 to 50 minutes. Serve at room temperature. The torte can be kept unrefrigerated for a few days.

CROSTATA DI FRUTTA

fruit pie

serves 8 to 10

Crust

1 RECIPE *TORTA RIPIENA DI
MANDORLE* CRUST (SEE PAGE
320)

Filling

1 POUND MULBERRIES	FRESH OR FROZEN, DEFROSTED
1 POUND-CAN PITTED CHERRIES	(OR FRESH, ABOUT 1⅓ CUP) WELL DRAINED
1 POUND-CAN PITTED SOUR CHERRIES	(ABOUT 1⅔ CUP) WELL DRAINED
¾ CUP SUGAR	

Preheat the oven to 375° F.

Line two 8-inch pie pans with the crust. Press the sides with back of a fork. Make cuts at 1-inch intervals with a knife tip on the bottom and on the sides of the crust.

In a baking dish about 7 by 12 inches, combine the berries, cherries, and the sugar. Place the lined pans and the baking dish containing the fruit in the oven. Bake for 15 minutes. Check after 10 minutes. If the edges of the crust are getting too brown, reduce the heat to 350° F., or after 15 minutes, reduce the heat and bake at 350° F. for 5 minutes, or until crust is a light golden color.

While still hot, fill the pie crusts with the fruit. Let cool completely. Serve at room temperature.

CROSTATA DI FICHI

fig pie

serves 8

Crust
1 RECIPE *GENOVESI* CRUST   SEE PAGE 277

Filling
14 OUNCES TO 1 POUND FIGS   FRESH, RIPE

1 TABLESPOON SUGAR   OR 1 CUP PEACH PRESERVES

MIMMETTA
LO MONTE'S
CLASSIC
SICILIAN
COOKBOOK

•

322

Preheat the oven to 375° F.

Coat a low-sided 12- by 7-inch baking dish with butter and dust with flour (the size is approximate). Line the bottom and sides of the baking dish with about three quarters of the crust.

Figs must be extremely sweet, and tree ripened. A fresh, ripe fig should taste as if it were honey-dipped. If your figs do not taste like that, you will need to add the peach preserves—not the sugar—to fresh figs.

If the figs are the thick-skinned type, peel them. Cut them in half, lengthwise.

Arrange the figs on the bottom of the lined baking dish, cut-side up, and close together. Sprinkle the figs with sugar. (If the figs are not sweet and ripe, dab the cut side in the preserves before arranging them. Evenly distribute any leftover preserves on top.)

Make a lattice with the remaining crust. Fold the edge of the crust lining the sides over the ends of the lattice.

Bake in the oven for 45 minutes. Cool. Serve at room temperature.

CROSTATA DI VALVERDE

pie from valverde

makes one pie 7 by 12 inches

This recipe comes from the notebook of a nun who, luckily for us, left her convent to work as a cook for a Sicilian family. Had she not left the convent, we would never have been able to use her recipes.

Crust

I RECIPE *PASTA FROLLA SENZA UOVA PER CROSTATE* (SEE PAGE 316)	FOR A COVERED PIE, INCREASE THE INGREDIENTS BY HALF

Filling

2 MEDIUM HEADS ROMAINE LETTUCE	ABOUT 2 POUNDS
½ CUP PISTACHIOS	RAW, UNSALTED; SHELLED
I LEMON	PEELED; CUT INTO VERY THIN ROUNDS (USE ONLY IF MAKING AN OPEN PIE)
I CUP *CONSERVA DI ZUCCA*	SEE PAGE 275
I½ CUPS *CREMA DI LATTE*	SEE PAGE 324

Assembly

I EGG WHITE	EXTRA-LARGE
FLOUR	UNBLEACHED, ALL-PURPOSE; FOR DUSTING
BUTTER	UNSALTED; FOR COATING

Preheat the oven to 375° F.

Coat a baking dish that measures approximately 7 by 12 inches with butter and dust with flour.

Discard the outer leaves of the lettuce; steam the other leaves until tender. Squeeze out the liquid until you can pack the leaves into ⅔ cup.

In a food processor fitted with the metal blade, puree the lettuce and grind the pistachios. Mix together by hand the *Conserva di zucca* and the *Crema di latte*.

Roll the dough (see page 325).

For an open pie, line the pan with the sides at least 1½ inches high. Brush the bottom with egg white, evenly spread the filling, and cover it with the lemon rounds. Tuck the crust edges over the filling.

For a covered pie, line the pan as above and fill it, omitting the lemon rounds. Cover with a crust layer 2 inches wider and longer than the top of the dish, centering it on the filling. Pat down the crust, pressing out any air bubbles. Seal together the edges of the bottom layer and the top layer. Cut the excess with a zigzag edge pastry wheel, making sure you leave a dough border of at least ½ inch. Flute the edge. Pierce the top crust with several rows of holes. Insert three small funnels made of foil at regular intervals into the crust top to allow steam to escape.

Bake in the oven 35 to 40 minutes for the open pie and 45 to 50 minutes for the covered pie.

To remove the funnels, press them down gently, while the pie is still hot, and then pull them out. Let the pie cool. To unmold, see page 325.

CREMA DI LATTE

milk pudding

2¼ TABLESPOONS CORNSTARCH
2 TABLESPOONS SUGAR
1½ CUPS MILK

In a small saucepan, combine the cornstarch and sugar. Blend in a tablespoon of milk, then keep adding milk in small quantities until you have a thin, smooth paste. Stir in the remaining milk.

Place over medium-low heat, and stir constantly, evenly, and quickly, well down to the bottom of the pan, from the center to the sides, and back to the center. The pudding will thicken near the boiling point. After the pudding reaches the boiling point, cook 1 more minute, and remove from the heat.

MIMMETTA
LO MONTE'S
CLASSIC
SICILIAN
COOKBOOK

•

324

CONSERVA DI POMODORO

tomato preserves

yields about 2 cups

1½ POUNDS FRESH TOMATOES NET WEIGHT (AFTER THE PEEL AND SEEDS HAVE
                          BEEN REMOVED)

14 OUNCES SUGAR

Use firm, not-quite-ripe tomatoes. Those green and pale red, stone-like tomatoes, offered by most supermarkets, and so unfit for a good salad, are very desirable to make these preserves. Remove the peel and seeds from the tomatoes. Cut them into ¼-inch cubes.

In a heavy nonreactive saucepan, stir together the tomatoes and sugar. Cover, and cook over low heat 20 minutes. Uncover, and let the tomatoes simmer slowly until the liquid gets to the consistency of a heavy syrup, about 1½ to 2 hours.

Cool, place in a jar and refrigerate, or use immediately.

MORTARETTE

makes 6 small tarts or one 7- by 12-inch tart

This is a tart recipe from the town of Sciacca as described to me by the father-in-law of one of my cousins. He remembered his mother making it for him as a child.

2 ORANGES	
2 CUPS *CONSERVA DI POMODORO*	SEE PAGE 324
BUTTER	UNSALTED; FOR COATING
FLOUR	UNBLEACHED, ALL-PURPOSE; FOR DUSTING
I RECIPE *PASTA FROLLA SENZA*	
UOVA PER CROSTATE	SEE PAGE 316
½ CUP RAW PISTACHIOS	UNSALTED; SHELLED AND GROUND

Preheat the oven to 375° F.

Shave the top layer of the orange peel, zest only. Very finely cut (makes about 1 tablespoon). Mix with the *Conserva di pomodoro*.

Remove the rest of the peel from the oranges, being careful not to cut into the flesh. Cut the oranges in half, lengthwise, and thinly slice them crosswise. Remove the seeds.

Coat your baking pan or your individual tart molds with butter and dust with flour. Divide the dough into six parts if you are making individual tarts.

Roll out the crust between two sheets of wax paper. Roll it some, peel off the paper from the top, invert it, and peel the second sheet. Roll some more, and repeat until the crust is the desired size. If the dough is sticking, dust it with more flour.

The crust shouldn't be too thin, and, laid in the pan or the individual molds, the sides should be about 1½ inches high, so that once folded over the filling, they will give the pie a good edge. Cover the bottom with a layer of the *Conserva di pomodoro* mixture, and evenly sprinkle the pistachios over it.

If you are baking a large pie, arrange the orange slices on the pistachios in even rows, or in a pinwheel for the individual tarts. Fold the edges of the crust over the filling. Bake in the oven for 45 minutes.

Let the tart(s) cool. Run a narrow, pointed knife between the edge of the crust and the baking dish(es) edge. Unmold. To prevent the single tart from breaking while unmolding it, fit a fairly stiff and flat object right on top of it (such as a disposable heavy foil baking dish, that can be cut, if too large). Then, holding the dish firmly with your hand spread out against the top of the tart, quickly turn it upside down, and immediately invert it on your serving dish.

PASTICCIO DI MAIALE

pork "pasticcio"

serves 10 to 12

Crust

¾ CUP SUGAR	
⅛ TEASPOON SALT	
2¾ CUPS FLOUR	UNBLEACHED, ALL-PURPOSE
8 TABLESPOONS (4 OUNCES) BUTTER	UNSALTED, CHILLED
3 EGGS	EXTRA-LARGE

Filling

1¾ POUNDS PORK LOIN	VERY LEAN; GROUND
4 EGGS	EXTRA-LARGE; SEPARATED (PLUS SOME EGG WHITE FOR BRUSHING AND SEALING)
2 CUPS SUGAR	
2 CUPS COCOA	
1½ CUPS ALMONDS	SKINS ON, TOASTED (SEE PAGE 49); GROUND COARSELY
1 CUP CONSERVA DI ZUCCA	SEE PAGE 275 (MAY USE GROUND CITRON INSTEAD)
1 TEASPOON GROUND CINNAMON	
1 ORANGE PEEL	GRATED
½ LEMON PEEL	GRATED
BUTTER	FOR COATING
FLOUR	FOR DUSTING

MIMMETTA
LO MONTE'S
CLASSIC
SICILIAN
COOKBOOK

•

326

To prepare the crust: Mix the sugar and salt with the flour. Cut in the butter until the mixture has the consistency of coarse crumbs. Cut in the eggs and mix just enough for the dough to hold together. Set in a cool place, wrapped in wax paper.

Preheat the oven to 350° F.

To prepare the filling: In a medium-sized noncast-iron skillet, mix the pork with ⅓ cup water and cook, covered, for 30 minutes. Let it cool. The pork should be in fine crumbs, not clumps. Mix in the egg yolks, sugar, cocoa, almonds, *Conserva di zucca,* cinnamon, and orange and lemon peel until very well blended.

Coat with butter and dust with flour a baking dish about 12 by 7 inches. Line with two thirds of the dough, letting it come up well to the pan edge.

Brush the bottom of the crust with some egg white. Have the remaining third of the crust rolled out to fit the top of the pan.

Whip the 4 egg whites until stiff. Gently mix them into the pork mixture. Then, place the filling onto the crust, moisten the edges of the crust with egg white, and cover with the top crust. Seal the edges and remove any edge in excess with ravioli wheel. With a knife blade, make three rows of incisions on the top crust.

Bake for 40 minutes in the oven. Increase the heat to 375° F. and bake 15 minutes more. Let it cool before serving.

TORTA MADONITA

cheesecake from the madonie mountains

serves 12

Traditionally, this cake is made with fresh, unsalted sheep-milk cheese, tuma, and sheep-milk ricotta.

Crust

2¾ CUPS FLOUR	UNBLEACHED, ALL-PURPOSE
¾ CUP SUGAR	
⅛ TEASPOON SALT	
8 TABLESPOONS (4 OUNCES) BUTTER	UNSALTED; CHILLED
3 EGGS	EXTRA-LARGE

Filling

2 POUNDS TUMA CHEESE	OR USE ½ POUND LOW-SALT FETA AND 1½ POUNDS VERY MILD FIRM CHEESE, SUCH AS A SCANDIC SWEDISH MINI-CHOL
1 POUND RICOTTA	DRAINED WELL
1 TEASPOON VANILLA	
1 CUP SUGAR	
4 EGGS	EXTRA-LARGE (PLUS 1 EGG YOLK AND EGG WHITE FOR BRUSHING AND SEALING)
1 CUP *CONSERVA DI ZUCCA*	SEE PAGE 275 OR USE CANDIED CITRON, COARSELY GROUND
4 OUNCES SEMISWEET CHOCOLATE	CUT INTO SMALL PIECES
BUTTER	UNSALTED FOR COATING
FLOUR	UNBLEACHED, ALL-PURPOSE; FOR DUSTING

To prepare the crust: Mix the flour with the sugar and salt. Cut in the butter until the mixture has the consistency of coarse crumbs. Stir in the eggs with a fork, then mix, using your fingers, just enough for the dough to hold together. Wrap with wax paper and put in refrigerator until cool.

To prepare the filling: Shred the cheese in large flakes, keeping Scandic and feta separate, if that is what you are using.

In a food processor fitted with the steel blade, combine the ricotta, vanilla, and sugar. (If using feta-Scandic combination, add feta at this point.) Process until very creamy. Add 4 eggs and the egg yolk and process briefly to blend. Fold in tuma (or Scandic), *Conserva di zucca,* and chocolate.

Preheat the oven to 350° F.

To assemble the cake: Coat with butter and dust with flour a baking dish about 12 by 7 by 2 inches. Line the bottom and the sides with about two thirds of the crust. Brush the bottom with some of the egg white. Spoon in the filling. Moisten the inside of the edge of the crust with the egg white. Cover with the remaining crust, seal the edges, and flute. Insert 3 small funnels made of foil into the top of the crust at regular intervals to allow steam to escape. Make three rows of slits, 1 inch apart.

Bake 1 hour in the oven. While baking, gently press down the crust a couple of times during the second half hour, to allow steam to escape. If necessary clear the slits by re-opening them with the blade of a knife. Remove funnels while warm.

Unmold when thoroughly cool.

MIMMETTA
LO MONTE'S
CLASSIC
SICILIAN
COOKBOOK

•

328

Some Reflections on Cheese

While related only in memories, these recollections of visiting the Springs of Cefalà Diana bring to mind the importance of cheese to Sicilians and something about its origins:

I had heard about the springs called "*I bagni di Cefalà Diana*" from Father long before I visited them. He had taken the trip there many times at a very young age, in a horse-drawn coach, with his grandmother. It was on one of those trips that "Cicciuzzu," my father, was given a cinnamon stick to suck on, to distract him from the tedious length and discomfort of the journey.

Hoofs and wheels stirred up the fine dust that covered the countryside during the dry season and blew it inside the coach through the windows left open for air to come in. Nonna Rosalia had a light black veil draped around her hair and her face to try to keep the dust off her braid and out of her lungs. Her braid was her pride. I knew Nonna Rosalia when she was very old and hunched over, but her braid was still neatly arranged in coils, rather elaborately, and pinned to the nape of her neck. Age had barely streaked her hair with white and had not clouded the clear blue of her eyes.

She was a firm believer in the therapeutic qualities of those springs, and was willing to go through hours of rough travel in the hot Sicilian summer for the pleasure of soaking in the tepid water which, bubbling up from the underground spring, kept filling the pool built by the Arabs, then overflowed into the creek outside the building that encloses the pool.

The building is the only Arab dwelling that still stands intact in all of Sicily. In the distance, built on an escarpment, stands what is left of the "Castello Diana," another reminder of the Saracens' presence on the island.

The building enclosing the baths is small and bare, but its unadorned architecture achieves a perfect balance of lines and spaces. Water has gently bubbled in and out of its walls, century after century, in a flow as uninterrupted as the flow of people who have enjoyed its soothing touch in a continuity of time that links today's people and their pleasures to those of the past.

Nonna Rosalia would get out of the coach, shake the dust from her black clothing —she had never stopped wearing black after her daughter Domenica died—and with one hand firmly holding one of Cicciuzzu's (to keep him from running off), she would enter the building, followed by other women of the family.

They waded into the pool, the women wearing long white chemises, the little boy in his white linen drawstring trunks. The coachman splashed into the stream outside, benefiting from the warm water that flowed there from the pool, letting it rid him of the dust, the heat, and his fatigue without disturbing the ladies.

My father would then be rubbed dry and dressed despite his protests. The women would change into dry clothes, taking turns to shelter themselves from strangers' eyes, though the light let in by the slotlike windows revealed only silhouettes. The journey back would start, following a very simple lunch consumed quickly in the thin blade of shade projected by the building.

The only other shade available was under the trees that grew along the creek— solitary traces of green in the harsh countryside. The thistles covering the ground forbade that shade to the ladies because of their long dresses.

Sitting on blocks of stone that still bore the heat of the sun, they would pass around slices of dark bread, lightly salted cheese, olives, and fresh fruit. Everybody welcomed a drink of water, kept perennially cool by the *"bummulu,"* the unglazed earthenware container in which it was stored. The meal was one that could endure heat without spoiling. Such a meal is still typical of the people who work in the fields, and very likely it was the meal of the people who worked at building the bathhouse. Like the flow of the spring, the type of food eaten has been unchanged by the passage of centuries.

Visiting the site only a few years ago I found that it matched my father's description: still very hard to reach, away from beaten paths, and used mostly by the local people. I could see people bathing in the creek below the bathhouse. Inside the building, once my eyes got used to the dim light, I saw an empty bottle of Johnson's baby shampoo left on the pool wall.

Outside was a very large sign by the *Sovrintendenza alle Belle Arti* announcing that restoration work was to start soon. One of the friends I was with happened to be the curator of the restoration project. Through him I learned that the small cluster of low one-room structures which people from the area had slowly built for their own needs was going to be torn down in order to return the site to its original appearance. It seemed unnecessary and wrong to me—the buildings provided the much needed daytime shelter for the workers and their animals and were not meant to be permanent housing.

The structures had been built with the same sandstone out of which the Greeks and the Romans had built their temples and their theaters, of which the Arabs had built their castles and fountains, the Normans their churches and palaces, and which is still used in many contemporary structures. The pale yellow of the stone made the cluster hardly noticeable on ground covered by thistles of the same color. To me the structures seemed totally timeless and harmless, not at all disturbing the identity of the bath- house.

The people I had seen in the stream, a couple of men, came out and were quickly hidden by the trees. After a few minutes they reappeared, and only then, from the clothes that they had put on, could I tell that they were farmhands. They sat under the trees. One got up and took a satchel and a *"bummulu"* from the saddle of the mule that had been grazing lazily.

The man pulled a large loaf of bread out of the bag: I watched both men as they ate it along with something I could not see. Swinging the *"bummulu"* up and propping it over his arm, each man drank from it. I was sure they were drinking water, not wine; no worker drinks wine in the heat of the day. If I could not tell what they were eating with the bread, I could logically deduce what they were *not* eating. No pork, as it is thought to poison the system if eaten from late spring to early fall; no dried nuts or figs, since they "overheat" the body; no meat of any kind, which is eaten only on Sundays (plus it spoils in the heat).

I continued to watch: the one hand holding the bread was brought to the mouth in succession to the other hand. The bread was replenished regularly, but whatever was in the other hand was never replenished, so it must have been something very small that could go a long way. Then I knew it was cheese, certainly made by them. When I was little I partook in a game during which, the phrase *poco poco cacio, molto molto pane* was repeated over and over again. That saying really sums up the philosophy of restraint and thrift of one side of the Sicilian character. Apparently I needed to have that principle reinforced because I tended toward the opposite: *molto molto cacio, poco poco pane*. I suspect the genes of the Spaniards must have prevailed in me.

I like the story I have heard of how cheese came about. In very ancient times an Arab who had to go on a trip through the desert stored some milk in the only pouch available to him: a lamb's stomach. The milk combined with the rennet still contained in the stomach, so by the time the traveler paused and started to drink his milk, he found that it had solidified into what we know as cheese.

MIMMETTA
LO MONTE'S
CLASSIC
SICILIAN
COOKBOOK

•

330

STRUDEL DI MELE

apple strudel

serves 6 to 8

Strudel dough

1⅓ CUPS FLOUR	UNBLEACHED, ALL-PURPOSE
3 TABLESPOONS OLIVE OIL	
½ CUP WARM WATER	ABOUT 115 TO 120° F.

Filling and assembly ingredients

½ CUP BREAD CRUMBS	UNFLAVORED
6 TABLESPOONS (3 OUNCES) BUTTER	UNSALTED; MELTED
5 MEDIUM APPLES	VERY FIRM, TART ONES; PEELED AND
	CORED, CUT INTO ¼-INCH CUBES
½ CUP RAISINS	
½ CUP WALNUTS	IN SMALL PIECES
½ CUP SUGAR	
1 EGG YOLK	EXTRA-LARGE (OPTIONAL)

To prepare the pastry: On a counter, stir the oil into the flour. Stir in ½ cup of warm water. The dough will be very sticky. Beat the dough up and down from the counter with your open hands. Keep on beating it energetically until the dough is very smooth and elastic. When ready, the dough will not stick anymore.

Place the dough on a lightly floured wooden counter and cover with a hot ceramic bowl and several layers of cloth. Let it rest 30 minutes.

To prepare the filling: In a heavy skillet, stir the bread crumbs and 2 tablespoons of the butter over medium heat until toasted (not burned!). In a bowl, mix the apples, raisins, and walnuts along with the buttered crumbs.

To assemble the strudel: Preheat the oven to 350° F. Stretch the dough into a 16-inch round on a lightly floured cloth. To stretch the dough start by forming first an 8-inch round, from the ball of dough. Work in quadrants, from the center out, gently pulling the dough with your fingers, while supporting it and stretching it with the back of your hands. Stop when the dough is transparent, almost skinlike thin. The edge of the round will be thicker; thin it out some by pinching and stretching it with your fingers.

Sprinkle the round with 3 tablespoons of the melted butter and pat gently down with your open hands to evenly distribute. Distribute the filling on the round, keeping it ½ inch away from the edge and leaving the top fourth of the round—the part away from you—without filling.

Roll the strudel by lifting the edge of the cloth that is nearest to you, hold it up, and move it away from you so that it will form a roll.

Coat a cookie sheet with some of the remaining butter, flip the strudel from the cloth onto the cookie sheet, sprinkle the top and side with the rest of the melted butter, pat gently to spread it. Bake 55 minutes in the oven.

In the last 5 minutes, brush top and sides with the egg yolk, if desired.

Strudel can be eaten warm or at room temperature.

MIMMETTA
LO MONTE'S
CLASSIC
SICILIAN
COOKBOOK

•

332

INDEX

INDEX

•